THE CAMBRIDGE COMPANION TO
APOCALYPTIC LITERATURE

Jewish and Christian apocalypses have captivated theologians, writers, artists, and the general public for centuries, and have had a profound influence on world history from their initial production by persecuted Jews during the second century BCE to the birth of Christianity—through the demise of the Western Roman Empire and the medieval period, and continuing into modernity. Far from being an outlier concern, or an academic one that may be relegated to the dustbin of history, apocalyptic thinking is ubiquitous and continues to inform nearly all aspects of modern-day life. It addresses universal human concerns: the search for identity and belonging, speculation about the future, and (for some) a blueprint that provides meaning and structure to a seemingly chaotic world. The *Cambridge Companion to Apocalyptic Literature* brings together a field of leading experts to provide a comprehensive overview of the subject.

COLIN MCALLISTER is Assistant Professor of Music at the University of Colorado, Colorado Springs. His publications include *The Vanguard Guitar* (2004) and *Fourteenth Century Counterpoint: Music of the Chantilly Codex* (2005) as well as a translation of the *Cambridge Glossa in Apocalypsin* (forthcoming). He directs the annual *Through a Glass Darkly: Symposium on Apocalyptica.*

CAMBRIDGE COMPANIONS TO RELIGION

This is a series of companions to major topics and key figures in theology and religious studies. Each volume contains specially commissioned chapters by international scholars, which provide an accessible and stimulating introduction to the subject for new readers and nonspecialists.

Other Titles in the Series

AMERICAN ISLAM Edited by *Juliane Hammer and Omid Safi*

AMERICAN JUDAISM Edited by *Dana Evan Kaplan*

AMERICAN METHODISM Edited by *Jason E. Vickers*

ANCIENT MEDITERRANEAN RELIGIONS Edited by *Barbette Stanley Spaeth*

AUGUSTINE'S "CONFESSIONS" Edited by *Tarmo Toom*

KARL BARTH Edited by *John Webster*

THE BIBLE, 2nd edition Edited by Bruce Chilton

BIBLE AND LITERATURE Edited by *Calum Carmichael*

BIBLICAL INTERPRETATION Edited by *John Barton*

DIETRICH BONHOEFFER Edited by *John de Gruchy*

JOHN CALVIN Edited by *Donald K. McKim*

CHRISTIAN DOCTRINE Edited by *Colin Gunton*

CHRISTIAN ETHICS Edited by *Robin Gill*

CHRISTIAN MYSTICISM Edited by *Amy Hollywood and Patricia Z. Beckman*

CHRISTIAN PHILOSOPHICAL THEOLOGY Edited by *Charles Taliaferro and Chad V. Meister*

CLASSICAL ISLAMIC THEOLOGY Edited by *Tim Winter*

HEBREW BIBLE/OLD TESTAMENT Edited by *Stephen B. Chapman and Marvin A. Sweeney*

JONATHAN EDWARDS Edited by *Stephen J. Stein*

FEMINIST THEOLOGY Edited by *Susan Frank Parsons*

THE JESUITS Edited by *Thomas Worcester*

JESUS Edited by *Markus Bockmuehl*

JUDAISM AND LAW Edited by *Christopher Hayes*

C. S. LEWIS Edited by *Robert MacSwain and Michael Ward*

LIBERATION THEOLOGY Edited by *Chris Rowland*

MARTIN LUTHER Edited by *Donald K. McKim*

MEDIEVAL JEWISH PHILOSOPHY Edited by *Daniel H. Frank and Oliver Leaman*

MODERN JEWISH PHILOSOPHY Edited by *Michael L. Morgan and Peter Eli Gordon*

MOHAMMED Edited by *Jonathan E. Brockup*

PENTECOSTALISM Edited by *Cecil M. Robeck, Jr and Amos Yong*

POLITICAL THEOLOGY Edited by *Craig Hovey and Elizabeth Phillips*

(continued after index)

THE CAMBRIDGE COMPANION TO

APOCALYPTIC LITERATURE

Edited by

Colin McAllister
University of Colorado, Colorado Springs

CAMBRIDGE
UNIVERSITY PRESS

CAMBRIDGE
UNIVERSITY PRESS

University Printing House, Cambridge CB2 8BS, United Kingdom

One Liberty Plaza, 20th Floor, New York, NY 10006, USA

477 Williamstown Road, Port Melbourne, VIC 3207, Australia

314–321, 3rd Floor, Plot 3, Splendor Forum, Jasola District Centre,
New Delhi – 110025, India

79 Anson Road, #06–04/06, Singapore 079906

Cambridge University Press is part of the University of Cambridge.

It furthers the University's mission by disseminating knowledge in the pursuit of education, learning, and research at the highest international levels of excellence.

www.cambridge.org
Information on this title: www.cambridge.org/9781108422703
DOI: 10.1017/9781108394994

First published 2020

Printed in the United Kingdom by TJ International Ltd, Padstow Cornwall

A catalogue record for this publication is available from the British Library.

Library of Congress Cataloging-in-Publication Data
NAMES: McAllister, Colin, 1970– editor.
TITLE: The Cambridge companion to apocalyptic literature / edited by Colin McAllister, University of Colorado, Colorado Springs.
DESCRIPTION: Cambridge, United Kingdom ; New York, NY, USA : Cambridge University Press, 2020. | Series: Cambridge companions to religion | Includes bibliographical references and index.
IDENTIFIERS: LCCN 2019042576 (print) | LCCN 2019042577 (ebook) | ISBN 9781108422703 (hardback) | ISBN 9781108436892 (paperback) | ISBN 9781108394994 (epub)
SUBJECTS: LCSH: Apocalyptic literature–History and criticism.
CLASSIFICATION: LCC BS646 .C36 2020 (print) | LCC BS646 (ebook) | DDC 220/.046–dc23
LC record available at https://lccn.loc.gov/2019042576
LC ebook record available at https://lccn.loc.gov/2019042577

ISBN 978-1-108-42270-3 Hardback
ISBN 978-1-108-43689-2 Paperback

To Barbara—tan cerca que se cierran tus ojos con mi sueño.

Contents

Figures

Contributors

Ian Boxall is Associate Professor of New Testament at the Catholic University of America.

Dylan M. Burns is a research associate at the Egyptological Seminar, Freie Universität Berlin.

John Carey is Professor of Early and Medieval Irish at University College Cork.

John J. Collins is Holmes Professor of Old Testament Criticism and Interpretation at Yale University.

David Cook is Professor of Religious Studies at Rice University.

Lorenzo DiTommaso is Professor of Religions & Cultures at Concordia University, Montréal.

Brian Duvick is Associate Professor of History at the University of Colorado, Colorado Springs.

Francis X. Gumerlock teaches Latin in the Archdiocese of Denver and is Visiting Professor of Latin at Colorado College.

Jesse A. Hoover received his PhD in historical theology in 2014 from Baylor University, where he currently teaches.

Kevin L. Hughes is Professor of Historical Theology in the Departments of Humanities and Theology & Religious Studies at Villanova University.

Daniel G. Hummel is a member of the staff of Upper House, a Christian study center located on the campus of the University of Wisconsin-Madison. He is also a fellow at the University of Wisconsin-Madison's Department of History.

András Kraft is a postdoctoral fellow at the Seeger Center for Hellenic Studies, Princeton University.

E. Ann Matter, William R. Kenan, Jr. Professor Emerita at the University of Pennsylvania, specializes in the history of Christian spirituality and biblical study.

Colin McAllister is Assistant Professor of Music at the University of Colorado, Colorado Springs.

Ian Paul is Adjunct Professor at Fuller Theological Seminary, Associate Minister at St. Nicholas' Church, Nottingham, and Managing Editor at Grove Books Ltd., Cambridge.

Christopher Rowland is Dean Ireland's Professor Emeritus of the Exegesis of Holy Scripture at the University of Oxford.

Brett Edward Whalen is Associate Professor of European History at the University of North Carolina, Chapel Hill.

Acknowledgements

One of the main functions of apocalyptic literature is to maintain and validate group identity. At one such group gathering, the North American Patristics Society annual meeting in Chicago in May 2016, I met Beatrice Rehl of Cambridge University Press, and our ensuing discussions resulted in the volume you now hold in your hands. I thank Beatrice for her wisdom, guidance, and patience these past three years.

It is my privilege to offer my profound gratitude to those who have helped this project come to fruition: To my contributing authors—thank you for entrusting me with your words and ideas. The support and collegiality I have experienced with all of you means more to me than I can say. John J. Collins, Brian Duvick, Lorenzo DiTommaso, and Frank Gumerlock have not only been collaborators, but also mentors, and I thank them for their time and passion for our discipline.

I first met many of these authors—and preliminary versions of some of these chapters were first aired—at the "Through a Glass Darkly" symposium, which I have organized yearly at the Heller Center for Arts & Humanities on the campus of the University of Colorado, Colorado Springs (UCCS), since 2015. This symposium would not be possible without the generous support of numerous entities and individuals at UCCS: the Humanities Program (Teresa Meadows and Dorothea Olkowski, former and current chairs), the Department of Visual and Performing Arts (Suzanne MacAulay, Chair), the Department of History (Christina Jiménez, Chair), the Heller Center for Arts & Humanities (Rhonda Goodman-Gaghan, Curator), and the Center for Religious Diversity and Public Life (Jeffrey Scholes, Director). I also want to thank Bernard McGinn, who was a gracious guest at the first edition of the symposium. Although I never had the privilege of studying under him, he continues to be a wonderful mentor from a distance.

To my additional colleagues at UCCS—thank you for making our campus a *locus amoenus* to pursue interdisciplinary research, teaching, and collaboration. Many of you have offered support and encouragement along the way, especially Peter Braza, Mary France, Katherine Guinness, Kevin Landis, Roger Martínez-Dávila, Jane Rigler, Rob Sackett, Michaela Steen, Rex Welshon, and Glen Whitehead.

To all of my students who have enrolled in my Humanities 3990 course on apocalypticism, and especially to Don Unger, my fabulous teaching and research assistant—thank you for reading draft versions of several of these papers, and for your open-mindedness, honesty, and collaborative elan.

A special thanks to my friend James Romano, fellow Manitou Springs resident and Affiliate Assistant Professor of New Testament at Fuller Theological Seminary, who provided invaluable assistance and insights during the final editing process. His keen eye and expertise rescued me from many lapses.

Most importantly, I wish to thank my family: my parents Newman and Bonny McAllister, and my brother David (who first encouraged me to take up the study of Latin, and whose love of learning continues to inspire me). To my children—Cameron, Cayla, Dana, and Lisa—thank you for putting up with the constant stacks of books on the dining room table, and my frequent weekend and evening mental absences as I pondered the end of the world. Finally, to my darling wife Barbara, I owe everything … te amaré hasta el fin de los tiempos querida!

Abbreviations

ACT	Ancient Christian Texts
CCCM	Corpus Christianorum: Continuatio Mediaevalis
CCS	Consolamini Commentary Series
CCSA	Corpus Christianorum Series Apocryphorum
CCSL	Corpus Christianorum: Series Latina
CCT	Corpus Christianorum in Translation
CSEL	Corpus Scriptorum Ecclesiasticorum Latinorum
FC	Fathers of the Church
JECS	*Journal of Early Christian Studies*
JSJSup	Supplements to the Journal for the Study of Judaism
JTS	*Journal of Theological Studies*
LLT	Library of Latin Texts
MGH	Monumenta Germaniae Historica
MIP	Medieval Institute Publications (Kalamazoo)
NHC	Nag Hammadi Codices
OSA	*Oeuvres de St Augustin*
PG	Patrologia Graeca
PL	Patrologiae cursus completus, series latina
PLS	Patrologiae Latinae Supplementum
SC	Sources Chrétiennes
TTH	Translated Texts for Historians
WSA	*The Works of Saint Augustine*
WUNT	Wissenschaftliche Untersuchungen zum Neuen Testament

1 Through a Glass Darkly: Time, the End, and the Essence of *Apocalyptica*

COLIN MCALLISTER

I have been a die-hard fan of the band Blue Öyster Cult since a friend loaned me a copy of *The Revolution by Night* in the seventh grade. Donald Roeser (a.k.a. Buck Dharma) is, in my opinion, one of the most underrated guitarists in rock-and-roll history. Although many people might not recognize the name, they probably know his best-known song, "(Don't Fear) the Reaper." It was used in the original *Halloween* movie, and later—more prominently—during the opening credits of the television adaptation of Stephen King's *The Stand*. It continues to enjoy steady rotation on classic rock radio, and experienced something of a renaissance at the turn of the millennium after being featured in the classic *Saturday Night Live* sketch "More Cowbell" starring Will Ferrell and Christopher Walken.

But hardly anyone still listens to the first track on that same 1976 album, *Agents of Fortune*. After an opening salvo of pick slides and ominous minor third alternations of A and C power chords, the lead singer Eric Bloom snarls:

> This ain't the garden of Eden
> There ain't no angels above
> And things ain't what they're supposed to be
> And this ain't the summer of love

And so perhaps I was destined to take an interest in apocalyptic literature.[1] Apocalyptic speculation is largely a response to scenarios—

[1] I use the term *apocalyptica* to refer to all phenomena—e.g., literature, visual art, music, film, philosophy—that are integrally informed by an apocalyptic worldview, defined by Lorenzo DiTommaso as "a fundamental cognitive orientation that makes axiomatic claims about space, time and human existence." See Lorenzo DiTommaso, "Apocalypticism in Popular Culture," in *The Oxford Handbook of Apocalyptic Literature*, ed. John J. Collins (New York: Oxford University Press, 2014), 474; and Lorenzo DiTommaso, "The Apocalyptic Other," in *The "Other" in Second Temple Judaism: Essays in Honor of John J. Collins*, ed. Daniel C. Harlow, Karina Martin

societal, cultural, political, environmental—that seem untenable and insurmountable, beyond human cognition and agency: the order of the world is not how it is supposed to be. Jewish and Christian apocalypses—the best-known example of which is the New Testament Book of Revelation—have captivated theologians, writers, artists of all types, and the general public for centuries. This corpus of literature has had a profound influence on world history from its initial production by persecuted Jews during the second century BCE to the birth of Christianity—Ernst Käsemann famously (and provocatively) declaimed that "apocalyptic was the mother of all Christian theology"[2]—through the demise of the Western Roman Empire and the medieval period, and continuing into modernity.[3] Far from being an outlier concern, or an academic one that may be relegated to the dustbin of history, apocalyptic thinking is ubiquitous and continues to inform nearly all aspects of modern-day life. It addresses universal human concerns: the search for identity and belonging, speculation about the future, and (for some) a blueprint that provides meaning and structure to a seemingly chaotic world.

Joachim of Fiore—the Calabrian abbot, the *sine qua non* for the revival of apocalyptic thinking in the twelfth century—was inspired to take up a career as a writer and prophet by two visionary experiences he had when he was in his late forties.[4] Like Joachim, I also came to the study of apocalyptic literature later in life, having spent most of my career as a classical guitarist and conductor, focused especially on the premiering of new works. Although I cannot claim to have labored "twelve years day and night," as Thomas Malvenda did in composing his leviathan *Eleven Books on Antichrist*, published in 1604,[5] this volume has been a few years in gestation, and so I have often mentioned

Hogan, Matthew Goff, and Joel S. Kaminsky (Grand Rapids, MI: Eerdmans, 2011), 221–22.

[2] Ernst Käsemann, "The Beginnings of Christian Theology," *Journal for Theology and the Church* 6 (1969): 40.

[3] For a magisterial overview of what properly constitutes the apocalypse genre, and the societal and cultural matrix of its genesis, see John J. Collins, *The Apocalyptic Imagination: An Introduction to Jewish Apocalyptic Literature*, 3rd ed. (Grand Rapids, MI: Eerdmans, 2016), 1–52.

[4] Bernard McGinn, *The Calabrian Abbot: Joachim of Fiore in the History of Western Thought* (New York: Macmillan, 1985), 22.

[5] Thomas Malvenda, *De Antichristo: libri undecim* (Rome: C. Vullietus, 1604), author's note to the reader. Quoted in Bernard McGinn, *Antichrist: Two Thousand Years of the Human Fascination with Evil* (New York: HarperSanFrancisco, 1994), 229.

to musical colleagues that I'm working on a book. Subsequent inquiry frequently leads to a nonplussed look and the question, "but why are you editing a volume on apocalyptic literature?" Why indeed. Well, studying apocalyptic literature and being a performing musician are both intimately concerned with time and the End.

I have always been fascinated with conceptions of the "end" in music, particularly the demise of tonality and metrical time in the Western classical tradition.[6] Tonal music, after all, is teleological, that is, its *raison d'être* is dictated by its end result, in this case, the impetus to resolve the inherent dissonance in the binary construction of tonic and dominant.[7] The eventual "ending" of tonality was largely set in motion by the composer Richard Wagner in the mid-nineteenth-century. In the opera *Tristan und Isolde*, based on the famous medieval story of forbidden love, longing, desire, and death, everything that unfolds is prescribed from the very beginning. Via the opening famous "Tristan chord," and the successive dominant seventh, a musical tension is immediately introduced, to which Wagner then maps the psychological, emotional, and sexual tension of the storyline. Through a variety of compositional techniques, Wagner prolongs this tension to the breaking point. Three acts and an astonishing four hours later, the music at last reaches a cataclysmic authentic cadence and resolution when Isolde—after singing out her broken heart in the final aria, the *Liebestod* (love/death)—collapses lifeless on the body of Tristan. The developments and implications that Wagner introduced could not be ignored by future generations of composers, especially Arnold Schoenberg.

Through the composition of his String Quartet no. 2, op. 10 (1907–08), Schoenberg posited that tonality might be no more. The turning point of the work occurs in the second movement, when the

[6] Tonality is a system of musical organization wherein melody and harmony are derived from a central *tonic* pitch and scale. Gradually developed by practice over hundreds of years, it was fully realized during the seventeenth century and governed the composition of music in the Western classical tradition until the early twentieth century (and continues to do so for most popular genres today). "Metrical time" refers to recurring patterns of stresses or accents that provide a pulse or beat (usually in groups of two, three, or four).

[7] Jeremy S. Begbie notes that many twentieth-century compositional techniques—especially the advent of non-tonal (or atonal) music—aimed towards a reversal of the dominant relationship between time and space, and that such works achieve a timelessness in music, thus moving beyond a purpose related to "the end." See *Theology, Music and Time* (Cambridge: Cambridge University Press, 2000), esp. 34, 141.

thematic development abruptly ceases and gives way to a quotation of the popular Viennese folk tune "O du lieber Augustin." According to the apocryphal tale, Augustin was an alcoholic musician who became so stupefied while making his rounds of the inns during the 1679 plague in Vienna that he was taken for dead and thrown into a mass grave for victims of the epidemic. Upon awakening the following morning, he climbed out of the pit and composed this tune with the refrain "O du lieber Augustin, Alles ist hin"—an ironic ode to life. Commentators have puzzled over this juxtaposition of a popular melody within a highly chromatic, contrapuntal texture. Is it a musical metaphor pointing to Schoenberg's awareness that he had pushed tonality beyond the breaking point?

The appearance of Augustin represents a dramatic turning point that prepares for the expression, in the following two movements, of an epitaph for the world that has been lost, and the ecstatic expectancy of new worlds to come. In these final two movements, we bid adieu to any true functional tonality. Schoenberg adds a soprano voice, setting two poems from *Der siebente Ring* of Stefan George, whose remote and aristocratic ethos resulted in works that "created a mythic world of the imagination in which the poet often assumes the persona of a solitary pilgrim estranged from his true homeland of the spirit."[8] At the conclusion of the fourth movement, "Entrückung" ("Rapture"), which begins "Ich fühle Luft von anderem Planeten" ("I feel the air from another planet"), we do at last reach a final, eminently satisfying cadence. And yet, after this long traverse, the sense of homecoming is replaced by one of wistful, bittersweet nostalgia. We look back through a long, dark corridor to a dimly lighted room that is becoming enshrouded in mist, already fading from our perception.

The end of metrical time is addressed in Olivier Messiaen's *Quartet for the End of Time*, an important and far-reaching work within the musical, political, and cultural history of the twentieth century. Written and premiered in a Nazi prison camp in 1941, it was directly inspired by Revelation 10, where the descending angel wrapped in a cloud and with a rainbow over his head announces that there will be "time no longer."[9] Messiaen stated that the lack of nourishment as a prisoner of war led him to dream in color and to see images of the

[8] Bryan R. Simms, *The Atonal Music of Arnold Schoenberg, 1908–1923* (New York: Oxford University Press, 2000), 29.

[9] King James Version, although most English translations say there should be "no more delay." The Greek word is χρόνος.

rainbow of the angel, an experience perhaps not unlike that of the visionaries who composed the ancient apocalyptic literature. The title *Quartet for the End of Time* primarily refers to the composer's engagement throughout his career with the aspect of rhythm in music. Messiaen explained that the "dual meaning of the title rests not with the notion of the interminability of captivity, but with the ... desire to eliminate conventional notions of musical time and of past and future."[10] By using birdsong, Hindu rhythms, augmentation and diminution of note values, rhythmic palindromes, and often very slow tempi, Messiaen thwarted any sense of metrical regularity within the music, and declared that "time is no longer," inviting the listener to contemplate eternity.

I have also pondered the concept of time, particularly how it is perceived by a performer.[11] When I am on stage, I know that my experience of time is very different from that of the audience. There is nothing "normal" about performing music—a heightened mental awareness, the exacting kinesthetic demands on the motor apparatus, and a desire to elicit an emotional response quickening the entire setting. In addition, I often perform contemporary works that demand a finely articulated sense of temporality: my internal time-keeper is on overdrive, calibrating and executing more than one stream of rhythmic activity simultaneously. There is also a marked phenomenon of time compression, as what took dozens, or even hundreds, of hours in the rehearsal atelier burns "like a kind of musical lignite" in just a few minutes on the concert stage.[12]

This is my experience of living in what Gabriel Motzkin calls "abnormal time," a transcendent state that "can be experienced only at those rare moments when the normal, everyday world loses its meaning," thus making this kind of time more "authentic."[13] Motzkin contends that a "change in the underlying temporal structure is presupposed in different conceptions of the apocalypse," that is, an

[10] Rebecca Rischin, *For the End of Time: The Story of the Messiaen Quartet* (Ithaca, NY: Cornell University Press, 2003), 52.

[11] Not much has been written about this, although there certainly has been significant research on the temporal perception of the *listener*. For a recent contribution see Richard Glover, Jennie Gottschalk, and Bryn Harrison, *Being Time: Case Studies in Musical Temporality* (New York: Bloomsbury, 2019).

[12] Steven Schick, "Developing an Interpretive Context: Learning Brian Ferneyhough's 'Bone Alphabet,'" *Perspectives of New Music* 32, no. 1 (1994), 133.

[13] Gabriel Motzkin, "Abnormal and Normal Time," in *Apocalyptic Time*, ed. Albert I. Baumgarten (Leiden: Brill, 2000), 203.

"apocalyptic time."[14] This is an analogue to my performative time. I'm experiencing, as Augustine called it, the *distentio animi*, the distension of the mind that refers to its stretching out in relation to past and future, a "three-fold present known in memory, attention, and expectation."[15] I know where I am within the architecture of the piece, am calibrating what I am doing on the basis of what came before, and am always anticipating the end, regardless of how far off it is. This is the same for apocalyptic expectation: not only are we headed towards the future, but the future is also "reaching out to us in our anticipation of it."[16] Apocalyptic literature is not just about what will happen in the future; it is also about the past, and—most importantly—about the here and now. Apocalyptic literature, like music, asks us to reflect not only on where we are going, but on where we currently are, as well as from where we have come.

In the concluding chapter of this volume, Lorenzo DiTommaso observes that the immediacy of apocalypticism has and is becoming more pervasive. Apocalyptic predictions, he writes," have become more public, pervasive and participatory. The passport is Internet access. Where once apocalyptic revelation was transmitted from prophet or seer to prophetic community along restricted channels, now it can be broadcast across the entire social bandwidth. The prophet today has six billion faces, *and that prophet is us*." The apocalyptic mindset paints a picture of the world in sharp, binary contrasts: light against darkness, good vs. evil, God against Satan, "Us" vs. "Them"—themes that seem to resonate more loudly in the tenor of our time.

And yet apocalyptic literature is also about hope. As John Collins notes:

> To be sure, the hope of salvation in another world, whether conceived as a new creation in the future or as a heavenly world of eternal life, is not without its problems, as it lends itself to displacement of human endeavor. But at the least we should give it credit for its indomitable hope, which is not always supported by rational analysis of human affairs, but may well be indispensable to human flourishing.

* * * * * * *

[14] Ibid., 209. See also Charles B. Strozier and Katharine Boyd, "The Psychology of Apocalypticism," in *The Apocalyptic Complex: Perspectives, Histories, Persistence*, ed. Nadia Al-Bagdadi, David Marno, and Matthias Riedl (Budapest: Central European University Press, 2018), 54–55.

[15] Begbie, *Theology, Music and Time*, 78.

[16] Motzkin, "Abnormal and Normal Time," 209.

John J. Collins is the preeminent authority on ancient apocalyptic literature. His overview "Apocalypticism as a Worldview in Ancient Judaism and Christianity" follows this chapter. The genre takes its name from the Apocalypse of John (or Book of Revelation), the last book of the New Testament. But it is important to understand that Revelation stands within a tradition of Jewish literature that includes the Book of Daniel in the Hebrew Bible or Old Testament, but also noncanonical works such as Fourth Ezra, Second Baruch, and various works attributed to the antediluvian sage Enoch. Although akin to prophecy, these texts differ from earlier prophetic works like Isaiah or Jeremiah in significant respects: they contain elaborate visual imagery, the revelation is mediated by a heavenly figure, and the visionaries themselves—with the exception of the author of Revelation—are typically pseudonymous, legendary figures from the past.

This phenomenon of apocalyptic literature did not arise in a cultural vacuum. Collins reminds us—as Hermann Gunkel affirmed at the end of the nineteenth century—that there is a great affinity between apocalyptic literature and Near Eastern combat and creation myths, notably the Babylonian *Enuma Elish* and the Canaanite Baal cycle. These affinities are useful when we seek to understand much of the symbolism found in Daniel and Revelation. The apocalyptic texts also reflect a worldview—apocalypticism—that concerns itself with an attempt to comprehend the totality of history (from creation to the coming eschaton), the role of supernatural beings in human affairs, and the nature of the heavenly and, sometimes, infernal realms. Apocalypticism is also deterministic; in other words, the course of events cannot be altered by human intervention: history has its own momentum. And it is dualistic: the grand scheme of history may be reduced to a conflict between two opposing principles, often characterized by "good" vs. "evil."

Modern-day forms of apocalypticism may seem to promote polarization, intolerance, and extremism. Classical apocalypticism assumes "a situation characterized by anomie, a loss of 'world,' or erosion of structures, psychic and cultural." And yet, as Collins contends, the classical apocalypses also contain a core of hope: hope that we live on in an immortal soul, or through resurrection, hope for the ultimate triumph of the good, and hope for a reunion with the divine at the end of history.

Next, Ian Paul lays out a thorough "Introduction to the Book of Revelation." Revelation is a rich and complex work that constructs its theology "not only through its semantic content and metaphorical signification, but also though its structure and fabric." Its language and imagery draw extensively on both the Old Testament and contemporaneous Roman imperial cult practice, mythology, and propaganda. After noting the unique characteristics of Revelation in comparison with the general corpus of the genre, Paul discusses the composition, date, and authorship of the book, arguing that the text was written by a single author (as opposed to a composite work), who may or may not have been the apostle John. It was likely written during the reign of Domitian (ca. 95–96 CE), a dating based primarily on evidence *external* to the text. Paul then moves on to summarize the temporal and spatial aspects, noting that the narrative is disrupted by frequent use of anticipation and recapitulation. As he puts it, "the eschatological finale casts its shadow (or, perhaps better, casts its light) ahead of itself into the early narrative sections." Revelation is striking in its pervasive use of numerology, not only as an explicit structuring device—seven lampstands, seven assemblies, seven seals, seven trumpets, seven bowls—but also as words that occur with particular frequency, evidence that Revelation is a very carefully composed text. The author also makes use of the properties of "square" (144; 1,000), "triangular" (666), and "rectangular" (42, 1,260) numbers, and employs the technique of *gematria*—assigning a specific numerical value to each letter of the alphabet—to calculate the "number of the beast" in Rev 13:18.

Paul then explains the four historical stances of interpretation (idealist, futurist, church historical, and contemporary historical, or preterist) as well as dominant understandings of the controversial millennium of Rev 20: premillennial, amillennial, postmillennial, dispensational premillennial. He ends the chapter with a discussion of the salient theological themes in the book, concluding that "in the narrative world of Revelation, to become a follower of the Lamb is to enter into a sense of history as the story of God's faithful dealings with his people in the past, and the eschatological story of God's redemption and renewal of the whole of creation."

One common thread that weaves throughout this volume is the difficulty of defining and delimiting what properly constitutes "apocalyptic" literature within various geographical regions, language groups, and temporal epochs—a concern that continues to be addressed forty years after the publication of the seminal *Semeia* 14, the fruit of the Society of Biblical Literature group headed by John J. Collins. Addressing another notoriously difficult topic, "Gnostic literature," what he calls apocalyptic literature's "unruly cousin," Dylan M. Burns contributes a chapter entitled "The Gnostic Apocalypses." If we include texts commonly called "revelation discourses" as "apocalypses without a heavenly journey," we may count about twenty-five apocalypses with Gnostic features—nearly all of which are preserved in the collection found at Nag Hammadi in 1945—and these are some of the most fascinating examples in the corpus. Using two examples as case studies, the *Apocryphon* (*Secret Book*) *of John*—perhaps the best-known extant Gnostic work—and the *Apocalypse of Paul*, Burns investigates the questions of who wrote these apocalyptic texts, and the social dynamics behind them. The *Apocalypse of Paul* features a heavenly journey that highlights the fate of souls after death, whereas in the *Apocryphon of John*—exemplifying the complexity of the genre discussion—the "cosmic trip" is actually one into the human mind, the true heaven. These Gnostic apocalypses are also of great importance for our understanding of late antique philosophy and religion in their reception history, especially in the arenas of later Greek philosophy, Jewish mysticism, Coptic literature, and the formation of two new religions that emerged in late antiquity: Manichaeism and Islam.

In "Exegeting the Apocalypse with the Donatist Communion," Jesse Hoover takes us to the "Bible Belt" of late antiquity to investigate the apocalyptic claims of the Donatists, an ecclesiastical community that, for a brief period of time, constituted the majority church in Roman North Africa—modern-day Tunisia, Algeria, and Libya. The Donatist position was defined by a question of ecclesiastical purity. During the Great Persecution of Diocletian (303–13 CE), many bishops and priests relinquished the Scriptures to be burned in order to appease the authorities. According to the Donatists, the prayers and sacraments administered by these *traditores* were no longer valid. Contrary to the views of many twentieth-century historians (following in the footsteps of Augustine), Hoover argues that the Donatists were not apocalyptic fanatics, and that their eschatology was more complex and nuanced than has been supposed. Although their position may be firmly situated within a fifth-century context—which, *contra* Augustine was replete with speculation about the imminent End of Days (see the chapter in this volume by Brian Duvick)—there are key divergences with other contemporary exegetes. Hoover discusses these differences, which include the number of the beast as 616 (a marker for Donatist exegetical texts and later authors dependent on them) and aspects of a "remnant ecclesiology ... which posited that the hostility of the wider ecclesiastical world towards the Donatist cause constituted a fulfillment of prophecy." Hoover concludes with a discussion of the "rogue" Donatist Tyconius, whose *Exposition of the Apocalypse* was a reaction against the rising popularity of this remnant ecclesiology, and which significantly influenced the early medieval commentary tradition in the West (for more on this, see Ann Matter's chapter).

Brian Duvick's "Tests of Faith, Rebirth out of Corruption, or Endless Cycles of Regeneration: Experiments in the Restoration of the Late Roman Empire" takes an historical approach, addressing societal and ecclesiastical concerns at the twilight of the Western Roman Empire, with particular examples of collapse in North Africa and southern Gaul. The barbarian incursions and critical military losses that Rome experienced in the late fourth and early fifth-centuries—including the devastating defeat at the Battle of Adrianople in 378 CE and the sack of Rome by the Visigoths under Alaric in 410—significantly destabilized Roman institutions and belief systems. The ensuing political, economic and religious crises began a "long process of socio-political transformation ... whose identity contemporary witnesses contested with a rich variety of traditional and innovative ideology and with a literary verve equal to the intensity of the times." Duvick discusses a variety of apocalyptic literature from the early fifth century—sermons, imperial biographies, and theological tracts, both Christian and pagan—including Augustine's *City of God*, his pupil Quodvultdeus's *Book of the Promises and Predictions of God*, Salvian of Marseilles's *On the Governance of God*, and other works by Paulus Orosius, Rutilius Namantianus, Peter Chrysologus, and the biographer of the *Historia Augusta*. Reacting to contemporary affairs, common threads in these works demonstrate a renewed imminence of catastrophe and divine judgment and a concern for moral reform as well as political and cosmic transformation and restoration, themes advanced in the papers collected in Matthew Gabriele and James T. Palmer's recent *Apocalypse and Reform from Late Antiquity to the Middle Ages*.

When contemplating this volume, one of my first ideas for an essay was to approach E. Ann Matter (whom I had met at the "Through a Glass Darkly" symposium in 2016) with the idea of revisiting her seminal 1992 article on the early medieval commentary tradition in the Latin West, which to this day is the standard introduction to the topic.[17] I believed that a revised and augmented version would be an invaluable contribution in light of the many new critical editions and

[17] E. Ann Matter, "The Apocalypse in Early Medieval Exegesis," in *The Apocalypse in the Middle Ages*, ed. Richard K. Emmerson and Bernard McGinn (Ithaca, NY: Cornell University Press, 1992), 38–50.

translations that have appeared in the last quarter-century.[18] Ann graciously agreed, and I am very pleased to present this updated version, "Latin Reception of the Apocalypse in the Early Middle Ages." This is an overview of the development of the Latin Apocalypse commentary tradition to the ninth century, with especial attention to how "each author adapted received material into new forms in response to the particular concerns of the church of his age." Although spiritual and anagogic interpretations of the Apocalypse prevailed until the twelfth century, this tradition interestingly coexisted with widespread speculation about the figure of Antichrist, as exemplified by Adso's *De ortu et tempore Antichristi* ("On the Origin and Time of Antichrist"). This closely intersects with much of my own work, and I have appended a summary chart on early medieval commentaries to the end of this volume as the Appendix.

In "Exegesis of the Apocalypse in the Tenth Century," Francis X. Gumerlock extends the time period discussed by Matter, focusing on three commentaries from the 900s CE, two in Latin and one in Greek, none of which has been completely translated into English: the *Catechesis Celtica*, an anonymous *Gloss on the Apocalypse of John*, and the *Commentary on the Apocalypse* by Arethas of Caesarea. This was an epoch marked by the relative sparseness of commentaries in comparison with the effusive period of the Carolingian *renovatio* in the eighth and ninth centuries. After noting some general features of the texts—especially their marked dependence on earlier authors and their lack of a millennial interpretation—Gumerlock proceeds to discuss each one, including details about the manuscripts and printed editions, underlying sources and exegetical purpose, and an elucidation of select passages. He concludes with a valuable service to readers: a complete English translation of the brief *Gloss on the Apocalypse of John*, which draws heavily on the eighth-century commentary of Bede the Venerable and is primarily concerned with clarifying the meanings of certain words from the Latin text of Revelation, especially the stones adorning the New Jerusalem of Rev 21. I hope this short text might prove a

[18] Especially Roger Gryson's 2011 reconstruction of Tyconius, but also new editions of Victorinus, Oecumenius, the *Scholia in Apocalypsin*, Apringius, Cassiodorus, *De Monogramma*, the Ps.-Jerome *Commemoratorium*, Bede, *De Enigmatibus*, Beatus of Liébana, Theodulf and the *Cambridge Gloss*; and English translations of Victorinus, Tyconius, Oecumenius, Caesarius, Apringius, Andrew of Caesarea, the *Commemoratorium*, Bede, *De Enigmatibus*, Beatus of Liébana, Ps.-Alcuin, Theodulf, the *Cambridge Gloss* and Smaragdus of St. Mihiel (see Appendix).

manageable example from the Western commentary tradition for study by our readers.

We next voyage to "The End of the World at the Ends of the Earth" for John Carey's masterful survey of apocalyptic thought in medieval Ireland, a place that looms large in the history of apocalyptic literature: Saint Patrick himself was said to recite the Apocalypse of John daily, and thought of himself as living in the last days before the Second Coming. Carey weaves together a survey of essential Irish eschatological texts, including the Fifteen Signs of Doomsday, *The Vision of Adomnán* (*Fis Adomnáin*), the *Transitus beati Fursei*, *The Vision of Laisrén*, the *Voyage of St. Brendan* (*Navigatio Sancti Brendani*), and *The Ever New Tongue* (*In Tenga Bithnúa*), demonstrating their frequent dependence on earlier sources, including the *Visio Sancti Pauli* and the *Apocalypse of Thomas*. More specifically, he discusses two aspects in detail: the nature of embodiment or disembodiment of the visionary, and the extent to which the regions of the afterlife are imagined as belonging to earthly geography. In Carey's words, when the world meets its end, it will happen "in Ireland in a specifically Irish fashion; and the Irish set the joys of paradise, and the horrors of the hells, in the depths of the Ocean that washed their western shores … This is the place of apocalypse."

In "Byzantine Apocalyptic Literature," András Kraft provides what is, to my knowledge, the first handbook overview of Byzantine apocalypses—that is, Greek medieval apocalyptic literature written for Christian audiences—since David Olster's essay appeared in the *Encyclopedia of Apocalypticism* nearly twenty years ago.[19] The production and distribution of this material reached its zenith during times of distress in Byzantium—including the rise and incursion of nascent Islam in the seventh century, and the two catastrophic defeats of Constantinople, the first in 1204 by the Latins during the Fourth Crusade, and the second, finally, by the Ottomans in 1453, which marked the end of the Byzantine Empire. This apocalyptic imagination was portrayed through a variety of visual, oral, and literary genres (including histories and hagiographies). Kraft notes that the Byzantine apocalyptic texts lent themselves well to insertions and additions, updating the prophetic material to render it meaningful in light of changing historical circumstances.

[19] David Olster, "Byzantine Apocalypses," in *The Encyclopedia of Apocalypticism*, vol. 2, *Apocalypticism in Western History and Culture*, ed. Bernard McGinn (New York: Continuum, 2000), 48–73.

He begins by tackling the difficult problem of definitions and genre: What is a Byzantine apocalypse? Conceding that the "fuzzy boundaries of the genre" complicate any definitive approach in regard to the medieval Greek apocalypses, Kraft begins with the well-known definition of an apocalypse as formulated by John J. Collins and the Society of Biblical Literature group in 1979, while also advancing a prototypical approach proposed by Carol A. Newsom, whereby "membership in the genre is not merely dependent on containing particular elements or features; it rather depends on how elements relate to one another in the *gestalt* structure of a given text." He then goes on to discuss typical literary motifs and devices, especially the use of typology, whereby earlier characters or events are mapped onto more recent ones.

Byzantine apocalypses were composed in both verse and prose (with a majority of the latter) and appear in both the historical and moral varieties. Kraft focuses his analysis on five historical apocalypses: the *Oracles of Leo the Wise*, the *Apocalypse of Pseudo-Methodios*, the *Apocalypse of St. Andrew the Fool*, *The Last Vision of the Prophet Daniel*, and the *Apocalypse of Leo of Constantinople*. He summarizes each, including a discussion of an underlying standard narrative structure. He concludes with an overview of the manuscript tradition and a call for apocalyptic literature to be seen as a continuous project in textual interpretation by the scholarly community.

In several of the chapters found in this volume, we encounter one especially important figure in the history of apocalyptic thought, whose writings cast a long shadow, profoundly influencing later generations of exegetes. In "Joachim of Fiore and the Apocalyptic Revival of the Twelfth Century," Brett Whalen examines some of Joachim's essential works (especially the *Genealogy*, *On the Seven Seals*, and the *Letter to All the Faithful*), highlighting the abbot's "apocalyptic memory: his remembrance of the past and anticipation of the future, framed by his presentist reading of Scripture." Joachim is best known for his idea that the arc of history reflects the nature of the Trinity and can be divided into three temporal eras (*status*), those of the Father, the Son, and the Holy Spirit (which would come to pass very soon: Joachim predicted that only two generations remained until the End). By understanding patterns of history in their totality, it becomes possible to see the apocalyptic significance of the present. Joachim took great pains to explain this by creating detailed concordances of meaning between aspects of the Old and New Testaments, as well as highlighting the importance of the contemporary Roman church as a key player at the close of the long span of history. Despite certain aspects of Joachim's theology being condemned by the Fourth Lateran Council shortly after his death, his acolytes—including Gerard of Borgo San Donnino, Peter John Olivi, John of Rupescissa, and Christopher Columbus—carried the torch of his millennial ideas into the thirteenth century and beyond, leaving a far-reaching and lost-lasting legacy.

At first glance, Renaissance Europe may seem an unlikely time and place for apocalyptic enthusiasm. After all, key tenets that we associate with this period—the revival of classical learning, a blossoming of art and scholarship, a move from a theocentric to an anthropocentric world-view—seem incompatible with speculation about the end-time. And yet, as Ian Boxall reminds us in "Apocalyptic Sensibility in Renaissance Europe," "'apocalyptic sensibilities'—outlooks shaped by apocalyptic traditions and texts, not least the Book of Revelation—were a significant dimension of this cultural, political, and artistic 'rebirth.'" Using Alessandro Botticelli's *Mystic Nativity* as an entrée, Boxall proceeds to discuss two aspects of the period that especially pertained to the interpretation of apocalyptic texts: the revival of the Greek language and developments in visual art. Despite the new perspectives and inclinations of Renaissance scholars, their worldview was still conditioned by medieval conceptions of the end-time.

Changes in the social and political sphere—not least the Protestant Reformation and ensuing Catholic response—contributed to a sense of apocalyptic anxiety, and led to questions about the Book of Revelation itself. Both Desiderius Erasmus and Martin Luther queried the canonicity and validity of the book, and numerous new commentaries on Revelation were produced by exegetes on both sides of the Protestant–Catholic divide during the sixteenth century. The millennial promise of Joachim of Fiore could still be perceived in various religious movements—Fraticelli, Lollards, Hussites, Taborites, Jesuits—and was manifested in the "Age of Exploration." Both Christopher Columbus and Amerigo Vespucci heralded the encountering of hitherto unknown islands and peoples in the New World as "a new heaven and a new earth" (Rev 21:1).

Apocalyptic thought is not just about contemplating the eschaton; it is also about the unveiling of heavenly mysteries. John Dee—mathematician, astronomer, Fellow of Trinity College, Cambridge, and advisor to Queen Elizabeth I—was keenly involved in magical pursuits, in particular, communication with the higher world. Through the practice of "scrying," Dee believed he communicated with angels, and that the revelation of these mysteries "brought him close to the goal of his scientific quest for 'the ultimate truths of nature.'" The moniker of the "Age of Reason" or "Age of Enlightenment" leads us to assume that thinkers of this period prioritized science, rational enquiry, and a firm reliance on established tradition. But in his chapter "'Pride & Vanity of the Imagination, That Disdains to Follow This World's Fashion': Apocalypticism in the Age of Reason," Christopher Rowland demonstrates that apocalyptic ideas and a claim to knowledge based on divine revelation formed a significant part of theology during the seventeenth and eighteenth centuries, just as they did during the Renaissance.[20]

Two patterns of biblical interpretation emerged during this period. The first deferred the visionary experience to the power of the written word, as advocated by Reformers John Calvin and Martin Luther, whose main criticism of Revelation was that its visionary character did not "prophesy in plain, clear words" as contrasted with the Gospels.[21] As such, it remained without interpretation and was of little use to the Christian. A second stance prioritized the subjective experience of revelation over authoritative texts and tradition, as exegetes sought to juxtapose the biblical text with their own experiences to inform understanding. This idea had its roots in the Bible, particularly in the Gospel of John, where Jesus privileges "divine impulse" rather than the Law as a basis for his actions and teachings. This was exemplified in figures such as Anne Hutchinson, Gerrard Winstanley, Joanna Southcott, and especially William Blake, who championed the multivalent, unexplicit apocalyptic texts as "the fittest for instruction." Inspired by Jesus as the supreme prophetic figure, who "acted from impulse, not from rules," Blake saw his own vocation as one that would "cleanse the doors of perception to lift the veil on the everyday world and see it in the light of eternity."

The trio of contemporary European philosophers René Girard, Ivan Illich, and Giorgio Agamben represent figures "calling from the margins of the Christian tradition for the renewal and recovery of the symbol of Antichrist, in all its rich complexity." Kevin L. Hughes echoes this

[20] Sir Isaac Newton, for example, produced an astonishing output of some one million words on alchemy, and four million words on religious topics, including biblical prophecy and the dimensions of Solomon's Temple. Writing a decade after the auctioning of Newton's alchemical and religious papers at Sotheby's in 1936, John Maynard Keynes called Newton "... not the first of the age of reason ... he was the last of the magicians." See www.newtonproject.ox.ac.uk/texts/newtons-works/religious (accessed June 10, 2019), and also the illuminating new study by William R. Newman, *Newton the Alchemist: Science, Enigma, and the Quest for Nature's "Secret Fire"* (Princeton: Princeton University Press, 2019).

[21] "Preface to the Revelation of St. John," September Testament of 1522, in *Luther's Works*, vol. 35, *Word and Sacrament 1*, ed. Theodore Bachmann (Philadelphia: Fortress, 1960), 398–99.

sentiment in "The Formation of Antichrist in Medieval Western Christian Thought," noting that, despite the decline of the Antichrist figure since the Reformation, this "... sophisticated tradition of symbolic theology ..." can be a "powerful tool for reflection on the 'signs of the times,' where faith meets history." The Antichrist tradition has its origin in key biblical texts: the First Letter of John, Revelation, Daniel, the "Olivet Discourse" of the Synoptic Gospels, and especially Paul's captivating and enigmatic Second Letter to the Thessalonians, the vagueness of which became an open framework around which later exegetes expounded their interpretations regarding the final Adversary. Hughes discusses three axes, or polarities, of interpretation—internal/external, dread/deception, and imminent/immanent—and two broad traditions that emerged from this. The first Hughes calls "apocalyptic realism": the idea that Antichrist is one who is coming, an individual who will persecute the church in the future. The second, the "Latin spiritual interpretation," had its roots in the fourth-century Donatist Tyconius, and was later expanded by Augustine and Gregory the Great. It correlates the Body of Antichrist to iniquity within the midst of the church, as well as within the hearts of individual believers. Hughes then charts the evolution and synthesis of these interpretations as expounded through various exegetes of the Middle Ages, including Alcuin of York, Rabanus Maurus, Haimo of Auxerre, Adso of Montier-en-Der, Joachim of Fiore, and Bonaventure of Bagnoregio, before concluding with some reflections on Antichrist today.

In the initial planning stages of this volume, I felt it very important to include a chapter on Islamic apocalypticism. In "From Dabiq to Jerusalem: Trajectories of Contemporary Salafi-jihadi Apocalypticism," David Cook explains that Salafi-jihadism has not always been known for apocalyptic tendencies, but that "with the rise of the Islamic State (2013–14), this trend changed quite radically, as this latter group embraced apocalyptic fighting traditions—usually those centered geographically in Syria and Iraq—and adopted the mythology of an end-times battle, similar to Armageddon, to occur in the valleys of northern Syria." Cook explores this change, beginning with *The Book of Tribulations*—the earliest extant Islamic apocalyptic text—and then traces the development of a large body of tradition about the end-times, particularly in Syria, the location of many battles between the Muslims and the Byzantines during the seventh and eighth centuries. Because of its geographical location as a center of Christianity and its perceived decadence, the Byzantine Empire was a primary foe, and conquering Constantinople was an urgent objective for the Muslims—an important event that needed to occur before the end of the world. Cook finishes with a fascinating analysis of the Islamic State (IS) in light of the application of this earlier tradition to contemporary events, concluding that IS is an "opportunistic apocalyptic Salafi-jihadi movement" that does indeed see itself as a continuation of this classical Syrian-Muslim tradition which hopes for a conquest of the Byzantine state (perhaps represented in the contemporary world by the United States or "world Christians" generally).

Daniel G. Hummel's "American Evangelicals and the Apocalypse" focuses our lens on the apocalyptic outlook in contemporary American society, particularly as reflected in Christian evangelicalism. Using the themes of theology, culture, and politics, Hummel charts the development of dispensationalism (the division of history into "dispensations," each marking a period of God's relationship to humanity) especially in its premillennial variety (a violent irruption of Christ into history in order to establish the kingdom on earth). In the decades following the Civil War, and coming out of American fascination with technology and an attempt to apply "scientific" methods to biblical interpretation, dispensational premillenialism grew as a theology—largely through the writings of John Nelson Darby—and popularized concepts such as the rapture and a seven-year tribulation. Dispensationalism became tied to the evangelical movement, and was systematized and spread via institutional support and theological production to reach a "scholastic golden age," as Hummel calls it, from 1940 to 1965. Although dispensationalism then began to decline in academic circles, it experienced a rise in popular culture—think of Hal Lindsey's *The Late Great Planet Earth*, the *Left Behind* franchise, or the 1999 movie *The Omega Code*—through the genre of biblical prophecy interpretation that continues to thrive and adapt itself to new geopolitical situations from the Cold War to support for Israel, as it "operates on a perpetual imminency paradigm that fits the apocalyptic message to each new historical moment."

In his powerful concluding chapter "Apocalypticism in the Contemporary World," Lorenzo DiTommaso looks to unpack the "DNA" of apocalyptic. Drawing on his previous work, he posits the "apocalyptic worldview," "axiomatic propositions about the nature of space, time, and human existence." What we define as apocalyptic—texts, music, artwork, rhetoric, social communities—are given their valence only through "a notional framework that features claims regarding the nature of being, knowing, salvation, and justice," an *architecture of apocalypticism*. DiTommaso describes two functions of apocalyptic speculation: operational (serving to reveal the true nature of things to the elect members of a group) and social (maintaining and validating group identity in the face of perceived threat). And we humans—by nature social animals—look to the "apocalyptic" to provide answers to situations that seem beyond our control and understanding. The apocalyptic worldview is, at its core, simple: its dualistic and reductive nature functions "like a polarizing filter by which certain details are brought into sharper focus, throwing the rest out of focus. In doing so, it streamlines a complex problem into one that (1) can be grasped in basic terms and (2) indicates a clear and unambiguous course of action." Climate change is a prime example of this.

DiTommaso argues for the recent emergence of an "apocalyptic shift"—especially pronounced since the turn of the millennium—whereby individuals across the globe have increasingly seen themselves and their situation through the lens of the apocalyptic worldview. This is evident in the recent proliferation of apocalyptic fiction of all sorts (novels, films, television, anime, manga, video games); the nature of the "superflat" Digital Age, whereby apocalyptic predictions have become "public, pervasive, and participatory"; the resurgence of apocalyptic thinking in both new and traditional religious movements; and the rise of international illiberalist politics. In 1919, one century ago, William Butler Yeats wrote, "Things fall apart; the centre cannot hold." The fact that the apocalyptic mindset readily indicates a solution to the anxieties of our age is a true sign of the times.

* * * * * * *

Over fifty years ago, Frank Kermode eloquently stated that we as humans rush "into the middest"—*in medias res*—when we are born and that we also die *in mediis rebus*, in the middle of things. To make sense of and give meaning to this arbitrary span of life we construct fictive concords with beginnings and ends. We imagine arbitrary chronological divisions—*saecula*—to bear the weight of our anxieties and hopes. We project them onto history to create a "perpetual calendar of human anxiety." We claim to live in perpetual transition, and "perpetual transition in technological and artistic matters is understandably an age of perpetual crisis in morals and politics." Thus, apocalyptic speculation continues to undergird our ways of making sense of the world.[22] For the producers (and consumers) of apocalyptic literature—now as then—"things ain't what they're supposed to be | And this ain't the summer of love."

[22] Frank Kermode, *The Sense of an Ending: Studies in the Theory of Fiction* (London: Oxford University Press, 1967), esp. chapter 1, "The End."

2 Apocalypticism as a Worldview in Ancient Judaism and Christianity

JOHN J. COLLINS

The phenomenon of apocalypticism takes its name from the literary genre "apocalypse," and ultimately from the Apocalypse of John, the last book of the New Testament, usually dated to the last decade of the first century CE.[1] This is not to say that the canonical apocalypse should be considered normative for the genre, but is simply an historical fact; this is in fact the way the genre came to be identified. Revelation itself stood in a literary tradition that had developed in Judaism in the centuries before the turn of the era. The most obvious precedent is found in the visions of the Book of Daniel, which dates from the Maccabean era (ca. 164 BCE). A few other apocalypses in the Danielic tradition, attributed to Ezra and Baruch, are roughly contemporary with Revelation. A different, but related, strand of apocalyptic tradition is found in books attributed to Enoch, a patriarch who supposedly lived before the Noachian flood, but started to publish only in the Hellenistic period.

A DISTINCTIVE PHENOMENON

The writings that we call apocalyptic literature represented a new phenomenon in Judaism in the Hellenistic period (323–31 BCE). They were revelations, and as such might reasonably be regarded as a development of biblical prophecy. All of these books are in fact classified as prophecy in Christian tradition.[2] They differed, however, from the

[1] John J. Collins, *The Apocalyptic Imagination: An Introduction to Jewish Apocalyptic Literature*, 3rd ed. (Grand Rapids, MI: Eerdmans, 2016), 3–5.

[2] Hindy Najman, "The Inheritance of Prophecy in Apocalypse," in *The Oxford Handbook of Apocalyptic Literature*, ed. John J. Collins (New York: Oxford University Press, 2014), 36–51.

prophecies of Isaiah or Jeremiah in significant respects.[3] The older prophets typically pronounced oracles in the name of the Lord. Such prophetic speech is rare in the apocalypses, which present their revelations in visual form. Of course, the prophets also had visions, and there are clear lines of continuity between prophecy and apocalypses in this respect. But the apocalyptic visions are more elaborate, or, as Susan Niditch has dubbed them, "baroque."[4] They are always mediated to the human visionary by an angel or other heavenly figure, who explains the mysterious symbols of the vision, or takes the visionary on a tour of places beyond the range of normal human experience. The visionaries are typically pseudonymous, famous worthies such as Enoch, who were supposed to have lived centuries before these books were actually written, although the Apocalypse of John is an exception in this regard.

But the novelty of the apocalypses was not just a matter of literary form. In this case, at least, the genre bespoke a worldview, which I shall call apocalypticism. By "worldview" I mean a distinctive set of assumptions about the way the world works and the destiny of human beings within it. In the case of apocalypticism, the novel aspects of this worldview concerned the way history was conceived, the role of superhuman agents, angels and demons in human affairs, and expectations relating to the end of history and a life beyond this one.

HISTORY

Two subgenres may be distinguished in the corpus of ancient apocalypses that has come down to us.[5] One focuses on the course of history, the other on the order of the heavens, or in some cases the nether regions. Many of the better-known apocalypses, such as Daniel and Revelation, are of the historical type. There is some overlap between the two subgenres. In Revelation, for example, the visionary ascends to heaven, although he is not given a tour (Rev 4:1–2).

The more elaborate historical apocalypses include a review of the whole course of history, or of a large portion of it, in the guise of prophecy by an ancient figure. In Dan 2, the Babylonian king

[3] John J. Collins, "Apocalypticism and the Transformation of Prophecy in the Second Temple Period," in *Apocalypse, Prophecy, and Pseudepigraphy: On Jewish Apocalyptic Literature*, ed. John J. Collins (Grand Rapids, MI: Eerdmans, 2015), 54–69.

[4] Susan Niditch, *The Symbolic Vision in Biblical Tradition*, Harvard Semitic Monographs 30 (Chico, CA: Scholars Press, 1983), 177.

[5] John J. Collins, ed., "Apocalypse: The Morphology of a Genre," special issue, *Semeia* 14 (1979).

Nebuchadnezzar sees a statue composed of four metals: the head of fine gold, the chest and arms of silver, the middle and thighs of bronze, and the legs part of iron and partly clay.[6] Daniel interprets these so that the head of gold is Nebuchadnezzar, and the other metals represent other kingdoms inferior to him. In the context of Daniel, it is clear that these are the kingdoms of the Medes, the Persians, and the Greeks. (The division of the Greek kingdom admits of various explanations: Alexander's kingdom was divided among his successors, and two of the resulting dynasties intermarried.) In the end, the whole statue is destroyed by a stone that becomes a mountain. This represents the kingdom of God. For a Jewish reader, the mountain clearly signifies Mount Zion, although this point is not elaborated for Nebuchadnezzar. Other overviews of history from the Babylonian era forward are found in Dan 7, again in the form of four kingdoms, and Dan 9, where Jeremiah's prophecy that Jerusalem would be desolate for seventy years is reinterpreted as seventy weeks of years. Other apocalyptic visions offer even more elaborate overviews of history. Enoch, who supposedly lived before the Noachian flood, sees the whole history of humanity inscribed on heavenly tablets and divided into "weeks" (*The Apocalypse of Weeks*; 1 En. 93; 91:11–17). Another section of 1 Enoch, known as the *Animal Apocalypse* (1 En. 85–90), describes a vision of Enoch in which all biblical history, beginning with Adam, is told allegorically, with all the characters depicted as animals.

Paul Kosmin has recently suggested that the long view of history in the apocalyptic literature was a reaction to the ideology of the Seleucid kings.[7] Traditionally in the ancient Near East, dates were calculated by reference to the reigns of individual kings. The Seleucids, however, introduced the dynastic era, by dating everything from Seleucus I. The Seleucid system of dating was certainly remarkable in the context of the ancient Near East, and was a striking affirmation of imperial power. It set the scene for other later totalizing claims of historical significance. Whether it can be used to explain the apocalyptic idea of "total history," however, seems to me doubtful. There were at least some earlier precedents, most notably Hesiod's *Works and Days*, that encompassed all of history in a grand scheme of ages, symbolized by

[6] For commentary, see John J. Collins, *Daniel:A Commentary on the Book of Daniel*, Hermeneia (Minneapolis, MN: Fortress, 1993), 162–71.

[7] Paul Kosmin, *Time and Its Adversaries in the Seleucid Empire* (Cambridge, MA: Harvard University Press, 2018).

metals. The apocalyptic view of history is also attested in Persia.[8] The relevance of the Persian material is perennially disputed. The main Persian sources, such as the *Bundahishn* and the *Zand-I Vohuman Yasn*, date from the early Middle Ages. They very probably preserve much older material, but the dating of that material is difficult. Even the biblical tradition, however, preserves grand sweeps of history, even if it is not organized as neatly as it is in the apocalypses. I would argue that the attempt to comprehend the totality of history was not only, or primarily, an act of political resistance, although it was sometimes used for that purpose. It was primarily an intellectual exercise. It occurs more frequently in the Hellenistic period than at any earlier time, and one may suspect that it was related to the increasing unification of the world, from Greece to India, that followed the conquests of Alexander.

DETERMINISM

These overviews of history are significant in several respects. Since the course of history was already known, before the Noachian flood in the case of Enoch, or in the Babylonian exile in the case of Daniel, it would have seemed to be fixed in advance. In most of the Hebrew Bible, the course of events is determined by human actions. This is the logic of the covenant in Deuteronomy: if Israel kept the covenantal laws it would prosper, but if not it would be punished. In the apocalypses, however, the course of events cannot be altered. Dan 9 contains a prayer by Daniel in which he confesses Israel's sin and implores God to have mercy and restore her. The revelation he receives at the end of his prayer, however, explains that the duration of Israel's punishment and its eventual restoration are already decreed. Seventy weeks of years, or 490 years, must pass before the deliverance: "Seventy weeks are decreed for your people and your holy city, to finish the transgression, to put an end to sin, and to atone for iniquity" (Dan 9:24). History has its own momentum, and is not subject to random intervention, even on the part of the deity.

While the course of history may be determined, however, this does not mean that the destiny of individual human beings is determined in

8 Anders Hultgård, "Persian Apocalypticism," in John J. Collins, ed., *The Encyclopedia of Apocalypticism*, vol. 1, *The Origins of Apocalypticism in Judaism and Christianity* (New York: Continuum, 1998), 39–83; Domenico Agostini, "On Iranian and Jewish Apocalyptics, Again," *Journal of the American Oriental Society* 136, no. 3 (2016): 495–505.

advance. On the contrary, the inevitability of certain events sharpens the decisions that individuals must make. Typically, the extended reviews of history are presented as prophecies, uttered long ago. Most of the duration of history is already past by the time the reviews are actually written. The actual time of the author can be recognized because at some point the predicted history no longer corresponds with recorded events. So, for example, Dan 11 provides an accurate "prediction" of history for most of the Hellenistic age, down to, and including, the suppression of the Jewish cult by Antiochus Epiphanes in the Maccabean era.[9] It goes on, however, to predict that the king would die "between the sea and the holy mountain," that is, in the land of Israel (Dan 11:45). This did not happen. (The king died in Persia, after a failed raid on the temple of Artemis in Elymais in December 164 BCE.)[10] On the basis of this observation, the pagan philosopher Porphyry was able to infer that the predictions had not been composed in the Babylonian era but rather shortly before the death of Antiochus.[11] We can appreciate, however, the purpose of the fiction. The fact that so much of history had ostensibly been predicted accurately inspired confidence in the actual prediction of the death of the king and the vindication of the righteous. The apocalyptic vision could thus encourage the persecuted Jews to endure, in the conviction that the remaining time was short.

COSMOGONIC MYTH

The vision of Daniel, however, was not only concerned with the events of the Maccabean era. It professed to disclose the meaning of history, from creation to the Final Judgment. One of the most effective ways of unifying history was by taking ancient myths that were originally designed to describe the creation of the world and projecting them into the eschatological future. In Dan 7, the visionary sees four winds of heaven stirring up the great sea, and four great beasts coming up out of it.[12] These are eventually explained as four kings or kingdoms. In the

[9] Collins, *Daniel*, 377–90.

[10] Polybius, *Histories* 31.9.

[11] As reported in St. Jerome's preface to his commentary on Daniel. See P. M. Casey, "Porphyry and the Book of Daniel," *JTS* 27 (1976): 15–18.

[12] John J. Collins, "Stirring up the Great Sea: The Religio-Historical Background of Daniel 7," in *Seers, Sibyls, and Sages in Hellenistic-Roman Judaism*, JSJSup 54 (Leiden: Brill, 1997), 139–56. I find singularly unpersuasive the suggestion of Carol A. Newsom, "The Reuse of Ugaritic Myhology in Daniel 7: An Optical Illusion," in *Biblical Essays in Honor of Daniel J. Harrington, S.J., and Richard J. Clifford, S.J:*

context of Daniel, they correspond to the four kingdoms of Nebuchadnezzar's statue in Dan 2: Babylon, Media, Persia, and Greece. The fourth beast here is the most terrible. The description of the beasts is followed by a heavenly vision of an ancient figure seated on a throne, surrounded by thousands of attendants. He is approached by another figure riding on the clouds. Then there is a judgment, and the fourth beast is consigned to the fire, while the figure on the clouds receives an everlasting kingdom. Similarly, in Revelation, John of Patmos sees a beast rising from the sea, and another rising from the earth.[13] Eventually the beasts are thrown alive into a lake of fire in Rev 19:20. Similar visions, directly influenced by Daniel, can be found in the apocalypse of 4 Ezra at the end of the first century BCE.

At the end of the nineteenth century, a great German biblical scholar named Hermann Gunkel perceived the affinity between these apocalyptic visions and old Near Eastern myths that had recently come to light.[14] The main exemplar of this kind of myth, often called the combat myth, that was available to Gunkel was the Babylonian creation myth, the *Enuma Elish*. That myth described a dramatic battle between the young hero-god Marduk and Tiamat, who was at once the mother goddess and source of life and a monster threatening to devour her offspring. Marduk prevails in the battle, and constructs the universe from Tiamat's carcass. Gunkel recognized that the name Tiamat was cognate to the Hebrew *tehom*, the word for the primeval deep waters in the opening chapter of Genesis. He also recognized the affinity between Tiamat and the stormy sea from which the beasts emerge in Daniel. This led him to perceive a fundamental axiom of apocalyptic thought: *Urzeit gleicht Endzeit:* the primeval time of beginning is like the eschatological end-time.

Closer parallels to the biblical apocalypses came to light at Ugarit in northern Syria a few years before Gunkel's death.[15] These were

Opportunity for No Little Instruction, ed. Christopher G. Frechette, Christopher R. Matthews, and Thomas D. Stegman, SJ (Mahwah, NJ: Paulist, 2014), 85–100, that the perception of mythic allusions is an optical illusion.

[13] Adela Yarbro Collins, *The Combat Myth in the Book of Revelation* (Missoula, MT: Scholars Press, 1976), 157–206.

[14] Hermann Gunkel, *Schöpfung und Chaos in Urzeit und Endzeit* (Göttingen: Vandenhoeck & Ruprecht, 1895), 189; trans. William Whitney as *Creation and Chaos in the Primeval Era and the Eschaton: A Religio-Historical Study of Genesis 1 and Revelation 12* (Grand Rapids, MI: Eerdmans, 2006).

[15] Frank Moore Cross, *Canaanite Myth and Hebrew Epic: Essays in the History of the Religion of Israel* (Cambridge, MA: Harvard University Press, 1973), 112–20; John Day, *God's Conflict with the Dragon and the Sea: Echoes of a Canaanite Myth in the*

Canaanite myths about struggles for the kingship of the gods. In Canaanite tradition, the high god was El, father of the gods, who also appears in the Bible and is identified with the God of Israel. In the Canaanite stories, however, El is a venerable, aged figure, who retains symbolic authority but cedes the exercise of kingship to a younger generation. The prime contender is the god Baal, a storm-god, who is called "rider of the clouds" and is well known from the Bible. He is opposed by turbulent rivals. One is the Sea, *Yamm*, which is associated with sea-monsters, notably *Lotan* or Leviathan. The other is *Mot* or Death. Baal defeats *Yamm* in battle, and splits him with a club. *Mot* is a more formidable enemy. At one point, he swallows Baal: he opens his mouth, "one lip to earth, one lip to heaven," and Baal goes down into him like an olive cake.[16] Then the rains fail, wadis dry up, and everything withers. Fortunately for Baal, he has a redoubtable sister named Anath, who rescues him from the maw of Death and restores his vitality by copulating with him. Then the rains return, the wadis run, and fertility is restored.

The Canaanite myths are especially helpful for understanding the symbolism of Daniel, and later of Revelation. One of the puzzles of Daniel's vision is the juxtaposition of two divine figures, one an "ancient of days" and the other, one "like a human being," riding on the clouds. Jewish tradition was monotheistic, at least from early times. Yet the imagery of riding on the clouds is most often associated with YHWH, the God of Israel, and here there is another god above him.[17] The imagery makes perfect sense in the Canaanite tradition, where El is the supreme deity but Baal is the dynamic ruler who brings fertility. (In the Jewish context, the rider on the clouds is reinterpreted as Michael, the patron angel of Israel.)[18] The Baal myth was well known in Israel, and to a great degree it was adapted in the Israelite cult so that YHWH rather than Baal was the hero. Already in the later prophetic books, the battle with the chaos monster was projected into the future. Isaiah 24–27, a late insertion in the Book of Isaiah, were written at some

Old Testament (Cambridge: Cambridge University Press, 1985). For the texts see M. D. Coogan and M. S. Smith, *Stories from Ancient Canaan*, 2nd ed. (Louisville, KY: Westminster John Knox, 2012).

16 H. L. Ginsberg, trans., "Ugaritic Myths, Epics, and Legends," in *Ancient Near Eastern Texts: Relating to the Old Testament*, ed. James B. Pritchard (Princeton, NJ: Princeton University Press, 1969), 129–55, at 132, 138.

17 John A. Emerton, "The Origin of the Son of Man Imagery," *JTS* 9 (1958): 225–42.

18 Collins, *Daniel*, 304–10.

time after the Babylonian exile, at a low point in Israelite or Judean history.[19] Like many of the prophecies of this period, they seek consolation in the future. So, we are told, the Lord, at some undetermined time, will make a feast on Mount Zion, and "he will swallow up death forever," in effect, doing to Death or *Mot* what *Mot* did to Baal in the Canaanite myth. By swallowing death, the Lord "will wipe away the tears from all faces, and the disgrace of his people he will take away from all the earth" (Isa 25:8). In effect, he will set right everything that is wrong with this world. Again, "On that day, the Lord with his cruel and great and strong sword will punish Leviathan the fleeing serpent, Leviathan the twisting serpent, and he will kill the dragon that is in the sea" (Isa 27:1). This imagery is continued in Daniel and Revelation. In the beginning, the creator God brought order to the world by defeating a monster that signified chaos, everything that threatens human life and flourishing. In the course of history, it often seems as if chaos has gained the upper hand. The apocalyptic vision affirms that in the end the good God will prevail. In Rev 21, the visionary sees that "the sea was no more," and hears a voice proclaim that death will be no more, eliminating the enemies of Baal in the old Canaanite myths.

DUALISM

The evocation of the old combat/creation myths unifies, and simplifies history by suggesting that it is essentially reducible to a conflict of opposing principles. The negative, chaos principle can be specified in many ways. It may refer to the untamed forces of nature, or to moral evil, or just to political opposition. But the myth asserts that life is an arena of conflict, and that the good will prevail. In the Dead Sea Scrolls, the conflict is between forces of light and darkness, in terms drawn from Zoroastrian dualism.[20] This is a more balanced conflict than we usually find in the apocalypses. But dualism of some sort is intrinsic to the apocalyptic worldview. This is not a worldview that encourages moderation. Rather, in the words of Revelation, "I wish that you were either cold or hot. So, because you are lukewarm, and neither cold nor hot, I am about to spit you out of my mouth" (Rev 3:15–16). Dualism

[19] John J. Collins, "The Beginning of the End of the World in the Hebrew Bible," in *Apocalypse, Prophecy, and Pseudepigraphy*, 34–53.

[20] John J. Collins, *Apocalypticism in the Dead Sea Scrolls* (London: Routledge, 1997), 41–51, 93–109.

encourages intransigence and extremism. One can understand the attraction of dualistic worldviews, but they are often problematic.

Besides the implicit dualism, the evocation of ancient myths expresses a sense that human affairs are beyond human control. Daniel's visions deal with political struggles of the Hellenistic age, especially the conflicts between Seleucids and Jews in the Maccabean period. But this is only surface appearance. The angel Gabriel explains to Daniel that the real conflict is between angelic "princes," the "prince" or patron angel of Greece and the archangel Michael, "prince of Israel" (Dan 10:13, 20). The conflict is resolved, not by the arms of the Maccabees but by Michael, who arises in victory in Dan 12:1. Similarly the kings of the various kingdoms are beasts that rise from the sea, embodiments of primordial chaos. On the one hand, this suggests a sense of powerlessness: the course of events is beyond human control. On the other, it actually suggests a sense of security, since the victory is assured.

HEAVENLY BEINGS

The sense that life on earth is subject to higher powers is also reflected in the increased prominence of angels and demons in apocalyptic texts. The idea of a heavenly council, where the supreme god was surrounded and supported by other divine beings, was prevalent in the ancient Near East, and is often attested in the Hebrew Bible.[21] The heavenly world was understood by analogy with the earthly. Divine councils in heaven reflected royal councils on earth. This is as true of the early apocalyptic literature as it had been for the older myths.[22]

The role of these heavenly beings in apocalyptic literature differs from that of the older divine council in the degree of their activity in human affairs. It is in the apocalyptic literature that angels are first given names: Michael and Gabriel in Daniel, several others in the Enoch literature (Raphael, Reuel, Sariel, Remiel, Uriel).[23] The Watchers, or fallen angels, are also given names in First Enoch, most notably their leaders Asael and Shemihazah. In earlier times, God fought directly on

[21] E. T. Mullen, *The Divine Council in Canaanite and Early Hebrew Literature* (Missoula, MT: Scholars Press, 1980).

[22] Philip F. Esler, *God's Court and Courtiers in the* Book of the Watchers*: Re-interpreting Heaven in 1 Enoch 1–36* (Eugene, OR: Cascade Books, 2017).

[23] On the names of the angels, see Saul M. Olyan, *A Thousand Thousands Served Him: Exegesis and the Naming of Angels in Ancient Judaism* (Tübingen: Mohr Siebeck, 1980).

behalf of Israel. In Daniel, this role is delegated to Michael. This phenomenon is part of what James Kugel has called "the great shift" in the way God is encountered in biblical times.[24] In the early books of the Bible, God converses in familiar ways with Adam, Abraham, and Moses. In the later, postexilic books, divine communication is mediated through human-sized angels who could communicate with prophets and sages by addressing them face to face.[25] This phenomenon first appears in late prophecy, in the Book of Zechariah and the later part of Ezekiel. In Daniel and Enoch, it is standard. It undoubtedly reflects the changing political circumstances of the Persian and Hellenistic ages, where rulers were increasingly distant, and administration was increasingly delegated to the imperial bureaucracy.

ACCESS TO THE HEAVENS

But if heavenly beings under God were assigned a greater role in human affairs in apocalyptic literature than they had enjoyed in earlier times, human beings were also granted an unprecedented level of access to the heavenly regions.[26] There were, of course, precedents. Gilgamesh had journeyed to the world beyond. Enoch and Elijah had been taken up to heaven. In the development of Jewish apocalypticism, the figure of Enoch was pivotal. He had "walked with *elohim*," and had been taken up to heaven at the end of his life. In the writings attributed to Enoch in the Hellenistic period, *elohim* was understood as angels rather than God: "his works were with the Watchers, and with the holy ones were his days" (1 En. 12:2).[27] The *Book of the Watchers* (1 En. 1–36) describes Enoch's transportation to heaven and a tour of places beyond the normal range of human experience.[28] These include the foundations of the earth, the prison of the fallen angels, the chambers where the dead are kept for judgment, the place prepared for the Final Judgment, and paradise. In later apocalypses, this heavenly tour is stylized, so that the visionary ascends through a set number of heavens—three in

[24] James L. Kugel, *The Great Shift: Encountering God in Biblical Times* (New York: Houghton Mifflin Harcourt, 2017).

[25] Ibid., 235–40.

[26] John J. Collins, "Journeys to the World beyond in Ancient Judaism," in *Apocalypse, Prophecy, and Pseudepigraphy*, 178–97.

[27] Trans. George W. E. Nickelsburg and James C. VanderKam in *1 Enoch: The Hermeneia Translation* (Minneapolis, MN: Fortress, 2012), 31.

[28] Kelley Coblentz Bautch, *A Study of the Geography of 1 Enoch 17–19: "No One Has Seen What I Have Seen,"* JSJSup 81 (Leiden: Brill, 2003).

older works such as the Aramaic Levi Apocryphon, and later seven, or even ten.[29]

All the heavenly tours in Jewish apocalypses are ascribed to legendary figures from the distant past: Enoch, Levi, Abraham, etc. It is unclear whether they at all reflect a mystical practice in Second Temple Judaism. At the least, it is apparent that some Jewish authors imagined ascent through the heavens, and did so in great detail. Whether there was any tradition of mystical practice or not, the idea that such ascents were possible evidently gained currency.

But another aspect of the permeability of the heavens was even more important. This was the ascent of the soul, or spirit, of the righteous dead, and conversely, the idea that the souls or spirits of the wicked would be condemned to punishment in the hereafter. The Hebrew Bible offers little hope to mortals in the face of death:

> Like sheep they are appointed for Sheol;
> Death will be their shepherd
> Straight to the grave they descend
> And their form shall waste away;
> Sheol will be their home.
>
> (Ps 49:14)[30]

Occasional exceptions might be made, but for the common lot of humanity there would be no inquiry about life in Sheol. Daniel, the latest book of the Hebrew Bible, is the only one to hold out hope of a resurrection of the dead:

> At that time, your people shall be delivered, everyone who is found written in the book. Many of those who sleep in the land of dust shall awake, some to everlasting life and some to shame and everlasting contempt. Those who are wise shall shine like the brightness of the sky, and those who lead many to righteousness, like the stars forever. (Dan 12:1–3)[31]

This early formulation does not envision universal resurrection, only the very good and the very bad. The scope would be extended in later apocalypses. It does not suppose that the dead will return to earth. The

[29] Adela Yarbro Collins, "The Seven Heavens in Jewish and Christian Apocalypses," in *Cosmology and Eschatology in Jewish and Christian Apocalypticism*, JSJSup 50 (Leiden: Brill, 1996), 21–54.

[30] John J. Collins, "Death and Afterlife," in *The Biblical World*, ed. John Barton (London: Routledge, 2002), 357–77.

[31] Collins, *Daniel*, 391–94.

location of the resurrected life is specified only in the case of the "wise," many of whom are said to lose their lives in the time of persecution. They will shine like the stars, which, in apocalyptic idiom, means that they will become companions of the angelic host. The point is clarified in the *Epistle of Enoch* (the last section of 1 Enoch), where the righteous are told:

> You will shine like the luminaries of heaven;
> You will shine and appear,
> And the portals of heaven will be opened for you . . .
> For you will be companions of the host of heaven.
> (1 En. 104: 2, 6)[32]

What is involved here is not the restoration of life on earth but the transformation of human life to a higher level.[33] Similarly, according to the Community Rule from Qumran, the destiny of the children of light is "everlasting blessing and eternal joy in life without end, a crown of glory and a garment of majesty in unending light."[34] These formulations assume that the resurrected dead will have some kind of body,[35] but not a body of flesh and blood, although the idea of a physical resurrection would eventually take hold in both Judaism and Christianity. One of the most detailed discussions of the resurrected body is provided by Paul in 1 Cor 15:

> What you sow does not come to life unless it dies. And as for what you sow, you do not sow the body that is to be, but a bare seed, perhaps of wheat or of some other grain . . . So it is with the resurrection of the dead. What is sown is perishable, what is raised is imperishable . . . It is sown a physical body, it is raised a spiritual body. If there is a physical body, there is also a spiritual body. (1 Cor 15:36–44)

[32] George W. E. Nickelsburg, *Resurrection, Immortality, and Eternal Life in Intertestamental Judaism*, 2nd ed. (Cambridge, MA: Harvard University Press, 2006), 141–62.

[33] C. D. Elledge, *Resurrection of the Dead in Early Judaism, 200 BCE – CE 200* (Oxford: Oxford University Press, 2017), 130–49, argues that the *Book of the Watchers* envisions an earthly resurrection. If this is so, it is exceptional in the early apocalyptic literature.

[34] 1QS 4:7, trans. Geza Vermes in *The Complete Dead Sea Scrolls in English*, rev. ed. (London: Penguin Books, 2004), 102; John J. Collins, "The Essenes and the Afterlife," in *Scriptures and Sectarianism*, WUNT 332 (Tübingen: Mohr Siebeck, 2014), 212–26, esp. 220–22.

[35] Dale B. Martin, *The Corinthian Body* (New Haven, CT: Yale University Press, 1995), 104–36, esp. 115.

The apocalyptic hope for resurrection pertains to what has been called "the discovery of transcendence" in the so-called axial cultures of the second half of the last millennium before the turn of the era. The idea of an axial age is, to my mind, problematic, but it is undeniable that profound cultural and intellectual shifts took place in the eastern Mediterranean world and the Middle East, and that these entailed "a sharp distinction between this world and the transcendent realm of truth and normativity."[36] I am inclined to attribute these shifts to cultural factors in the Hellenistic age, rather than to evolutionary biology. The idea of an immortal soul had been developed in Greece around the middle of the first millennium BCE, by the Pythagoreans and Orphics, and spread especially by Plato.[37] The conception of the immortal spirit or soul in Jewish apocalypticism is unlikely to be derived directly from Platonic philosophy, but it represents a kindred development in a neighboring culture, in the great melting-pot of cultures in the Hellenistic age.

THE CHRISTIAN APPROPRIATION OF APOCALYTICISM

It was through the rise of Christianity, however, that the apocalyptic worldview would have its greatest impact.[38] Paul promised the Corinthians:

> We will not all die, but we will all be changed, in a moment, in the twinkling of an eye, at the last trumpet. For the trumpet will sound, and the dead will be raised imperishable, and we will be changed. (1 Cor 15:51–52)

The belief that the end of history and the resurrection of the dead were at hand is what enabled the belief that Christ had been raised, "the first fruits of those who have died" (1 Cor 15:20).[39]

[36] Matthias Jung, "Embodiment, Transcendence, and Contingency: Anthropological Features of the Axial Age," in *The Axial Age and Its Consequences*, ed. Robert N. Bellah and Hans Joas (Cambridge, MA: Harvard University Press, 2012), 77.

[37] Jan N. Bremmer, *The Rise and Fall of the Afterlife* (London: Routledge, 2002), 11–26.

[38] On the influence of Jewish apocalypticism on the New Testament see Benjamin E. Reynolds and Loren T. Stuckenbruck, eds., *The Jewish Apocalyptic Tradition and the Shaping of New Testament Thought* (Minneapolis, MN: Fortress, 2017).

[39] See further Ben C. Blackwell, John K. Goodrich, and Jason Maston, eds., *Paul and the Apocalyptic Imagination* (Minneapolis, MN: Fortress, 2016).

The main difference between Jewish and early Christian apocalypticism lay in the foreshortening of history in the New Testament.[40] Rather than looking back to the time of Enoch or Daniel, the New Testament writers focus on the period inaugurated by Jesus. This intensifies the sense of imminent expectation. Revelation is concerned with "what must soon take place" (Rev 1:1). This sense of imminent expectation is, of course, difficult to maintain over the long run, but it has recurred periodically throughout Christian history.

The early Christian appropriation of apocalypticism is also colored by the paradigmatic importance assigned to the death and resurrection of Jesus. In Revelation, Jesus is the Lamb that was slaughtered, and redeemed the saints by his blood (Rev 5:9). Satan is conquered by the blood of the Lamb and the testimony of the martyrs (Rev 12:11). Those who died in time of persecution already had a prominent role in Daniel. Their role is intensified in Revelation. Revelation promises the transformation of this world in a new creation, but a central emphasis of the work is on the transcendence of death. Indeed, in the new creation, as in the so-called Apocalypse of Isaiah, "death will be no more ... for the first things have passed away" (Rev 21:4).

Even in Revelation, however, the emphasis on individual salvation is integrated in a comprehensive vision of the world, which is profoundly indebted to the ancient myths. Michael fights with the dragon in heaven, beasts rise from sea and land, and there is a great climactic battle followed by a new creation. The vision of the world is one of a fragile place, constantly beset with crises that seem beyond human control. Anarchy is repeatedly loosed on the world. This vision acquires much of its power from the symbolism through which it is expressed. The fact that Revelation speaks of beasts and dragons, even if John of Patmos had specific referents in mind, means that these symbols can be reapplied, and the referents updated, to interpret new crises throughout history. The appeal of apocalypticism arises from the fact that such crises are always with us. The surplus of meaning in the ancient texts is in no danger of being exhausted.

MODERN APOCALYPTICISM

Apocalypticism, in one form or other, is still very much with us in the modern world. In the English-speaking world, it was given a distinctive

[40] John J. Collins, "The Christian Adaptation of the Apocalyptic Genre," in *Seers, Sibyls, and Sages*, 115–27.

cast by the dispensationalist movement led by John Nelson Darby in the nineteenth century.[41] This way of reading the apocalyptic tradition is narrowly focused on identifying modern referents for the symbols and using them to predict political events in the contemporary world. The classic apocalyptic work of this kind is Hal Lindsey's *The Late Great Planet Earth*, originally published in 1970, which became the best-selling non-fiction book of the decade, eventually sold more than 28 million copies, and identified signs of the end-times in the founding of the state of Israel and the development of the European Union.[42] A similar worldview was more recently popularized by the *Left Behind* series, authored by Tim LaHaye and Jerry B. Jenkins.[43] These books have promoted a conservative social agenda and unquestioning support for the state of Israel. Despite their popularity, they have been singularly lacking in literary merit, and have led to the widespread assumption that apocalypticism entails a doctrinaire, fundamentalistic view of the world. The fact that Islamic extremism is also fueled by beliefs about imminent divine intervention and a dualistic view of the world has added to the disrepute of apocalypticism, at least in academic circles and among people who are politically progressive. In its modern form, apocalypticism often seems to promote extremism and intolerance. Can the same charges be legitimately brought against the classic apocalyptic worldview?

Lorenzo DiTommaso, one of the leading authorities on Jewish and Christian apocalypticism at the present time, thinks they can.[44] Amos Wilder, long-time professor of New Testament at Harvard and brother of the playwright Thornton Wilder, argued that the ancient texts, in contrast to their modern appropriations, testify to "genuine transcendental apocalyptic."[45] DiTommaso denies that there is any such thing. He argues that "apocalypticism is an unhealthy worldview, particularly in its biblical form. It is inimical to a mature vision of human destiny, or

41 Paul Boyer, *When Time Shall Be No More: Prophecy Belief in Modern American Culture* (Cambridge, MA: Belknap, 1992), 86–90.

42 Hal Lindsey with C. C. Carlson, *The Late Great Planet Earth* (Grand Rapids, MI: Zondervan, 1970).

43 A sixteen-volume set of novels, beginning with Tim LaHaye and Jerry B. Jenkins, *Left Behind: A Novel of the Earth's Last Days* (Wheaton, IL: Tyndale, 1995).

44 Lorenzo DiTommaso, "The Apocalyptic Other," in *The "Other" in Second Temple Judaism: Essays in Honor of John J. Collins*, ed. Daniel C. Harlow, Karina Martin Hogan, Matthew Goff, and Joel S. Kaminsky (Grand Rapids, MI: Eerdmans, 2011), 221–46.

45 Amos N. Wilder, "The Rhetoric of Ancient and Modern Apocalyptic," *Interpretation* 25, no. 4 (1971): 440.

any social order founded on humanistic ideals."[46] The negative judgment extends to the apocalyptic simplification of history. DiTommaso sees it as a totalizing worldview, akin to Marxism, unable to accept historical causality based on the interaction of circumstance, happenstance, and human decision. It relies on "the revelation of unimpeachable knowledge, imparted by a transcendent reality."[47] As such, it is incompatible with a pluralistic approach to reality and the compromises that pluralism requires.

Apocalypticism is surely not a worldview for all seasons.[48] As Wilder already noted, classical apocalypticism presupposes a "situation characterized by anomie, a loss of 'world,' or erosion of structures, psychic and cultural."[49] It works best when the world is truly out of joint, and not amenable to reasoned dialogue. Even in such situations, it is likely to exacerbate rather than to ameliorate conflict. Even though apocalyptic texts seldom exhort their readers to violence explicitly, they are often complicit in violence because of their polarized and uncompromising view of the world.

Nonetheless, it seems to me that the classical apocalypticism of ancient Judaism and Christianity is far more nuanced than its latter-day dispensationalist progeny. The writings of Hal Lindsey and Tim LaHaye are virtually devoid of symbolism. The mythic images of Daniel and Revelation, in contrast, are inherently multivalent, and can never be adequately decoded into prosaic language. They are essentially poetic visions of a world in disarray. In this sense, the poems of Yeats or T. S. Eliot are more faithful to the classic apocalypses than the *Left Behind* series.

When Wilder contrasted ancient and modern apocalypticism, however, it was not the dispensationalists that he had in mind, but the secular appropriation of apocalypticism in some strands of modern literature.[50] It was well represented in Eliot's poem *The Waste Land*, and even more vividly, long after Wilder wrote, in the writings of Cormac McCarthy, such as *The Road*, which are sometimes described as "post-apocalyptic."[51] What Wilder missed in this kind of literature is

46 DiTommaso, "The Apocalyptic Other," 236.

47 Ibid., 237.

48 John J. Collins, "The Legacy of Apocalypticism," in *Encounters with Biblical Theology* (Minneapolis, MN: Fortress, 2005), 155–66.

49 Wilder, "The Rhetoric of Ancient and Modern Apocalyptic," 440.

50 See Frank Kermode, "The Modern Apocalypse," in *The Sense of an Ending: Studies in the Theory of Fiction* (New York: Oxford University Press, 1967), 93–124.

51 Cormac McCarthy, *The Road* (New York: Knopf, 2006).

"the phase of miraculous renovation and that world affirmation which has gone through the experience of world negation."[52] A catastrophic imagination alone is not genuinely apocalyptic. McCarthy, certainly, provides a glimmer of hope in a single flower that blossoms in his post-apocalyptic landscape. Classical apocalypticism was more robust in its hope. To be sure, the hope of salvation in another world, whether conceived as a new creation in the future or as a heavenly world of eternal life, is not without its problems, as it lends itself to displacement of human endeavor. But at the least we should give it credit for its indomitable hope, which is not always supported by rational analysis of human affairs, but may well be indispensable to human flourishing.

Selected Further Reading

Collins, Adela Yarbro. *The Combat Myth in the Book of Revelation*. Missoula, MT: Scholars Press, 1976.

Collins, Adela Yarbro. "The Seven Heavens in Jewish and Christian Apocalypses." In *Cosmology and Eschatology in Jewish and Christian Apocalypticism*, 21–54. Supplements to the Journal for the Study of Judaism 50. Leiden: Brill, 1996.

Collins, John J. *The Apocalyptic Imagination: An Introduction to Jewish Apocalyptic Literature*. 3rd ed. Grand Rapids, MI: Eerdmans, 2016.

Collins, John J. *Apocalypticism in the Dead Sea Scrolls*. London: Routledge, 1997.

Collins, John J. *Daniel: A Commentary on the Book of Daniel*. Hermeneia. Minneapolis, MN: Fortress, 1993.

Collins, John J. ed. "Apocalypse: The Morphology of a Genre." Special issue, *Semeia* 14 (1979).

Collins, John J. ed. *The Encyclopedia of Apocalypticism*. Vol. 1, *The Origins of Apocalypticism in Judaism and Christianity*. New York: Continuum, 1998.

DiTommaso, Lorenzo. "The Apocalyptic Other." In *The "Other" in Second Temple Judaism: Essays in Honor of John J. Collins*, 221–46. Edited by Daniel C. Harlow, Karina Martin Hogan, Matthew Goff, and Joel S. Kaminsky. Grand Rapids, MI: Eerdmans, 2011.

Reynolds, Benjamin E., and Loren T. Stuckenbruck, eds. *The Jewish Apocalyptic Tradition and the Shaping of New Testament Thought*. Minneapolis, MN: Fortress, 2017.

Wilder, Amos N. "The Rhetoric of Ancient and Modern Apocalyptic." *Interpretation* 25, no. 4 (1971): 436–53.

[52] Wilder, "The Rhetoric of Ancient and Modern Apocalyptic," 451.

3 Introduction to the Book of Revelation

IAN PAUL

The Book of Revelation sits in an odd place in relation to the collection of other apocalyptic literature. It draws extensively on the Book of Daniel (according to Charlesworth the only apocalypse in the Old Testament canon)[1] as well as the visionary books of Ezekiel and Zechariah—but it does so by transforming and reinterpreting much of their imagery. There are some very clear connections in the imagery and language of Revelation and Second Temple apocalyptic works, especially First Enoch and Fourth Ezra,[2] and Revelation shares the episodic nature of many of these books.

But there are also some very significant differences, the most striking being that it is Revelation alone which explicitly calls itself an "apocalypse" ("The revelation [*apocalypsis*] of Jesus Christ ...": Rev 1:1), thus lending its name to a whole collection of literature, in which no other work makes that explicit self-designation. Rather than present itself as a *vaticinium ex eventu*, a prophetic word retrojected to an earlier time and written in the name of an earlier prophetic figure, "John" is content to speak to his contemporaries, claiming no other authority than the power of the prophetic, visionary revelation that he circulates in letter form to assemblies of followers of Jesus in seven selected cities in the Roman province of Asia,[3] the western end of

[1] James H. Charlesworth, *The Old Testament Pseudepigrapha*, 2 vols. (Peabody, MA: Hendrickson, 2010), 1:3.

[2] For example, mountains being leveled or removed (1 En. 1:6; Rev 6:14); an interest in angels, though all but Michael are unnamed in Revelation; plagues and fire of judgment (1 En. 10:6; Rev 15:1, 19:20); God enthroned and surrounded by ten thousand times ten thousand (1 En. 14:18–23; Rev 4:2, 5:11); the use of numbers, including seven mountains in 1 En. 77 (Rev 17:9); and Jerusalem as a woman (4 Ezra 10:25–28; Rev 21:2).

[3] "Assemblies" is a better translation of *ekklesiae* than "churches." Craig R. Koester, *Revelation: A New Translation with Introduction and Commentary* (New Haven, CT: Yale University Press, 2014), 215;. Ralph J. Korner, *The Origin and Meaning of Ekklesia in the Early Jesus Movement* (Leiden and Boston: Brill, 2017).

modern-day Turkey. Revelation is much more carefully structured than any other work in the apocalyptic canon, makes greater use of Old Testament ideas, has a more diverse and developed use of numerology, and incorporates symbols and myths from Roman imperial propaganda and cult practice, as well as ideas from magical cults. It is an altogether fascinating text that has had unparalleled influence on the history of Christian art, culture, and worship.[4]

COMPOSITION, DATE, AND AUTHOR

Some scholars have argued that Revelation is a composite work, though in quite a different way from the composite nature of other apocalyptic texts. R. H. Charles proposed that the final text we have has four distinct layers of writing and redaction, and that successive redactors did not understand the prior texts that they were working with, to the extent that the text we now have makes no actual sense in its final literary form.[5] J. M. Ford argued that Revelation contained an underlying pre-Christian text written by a follower of John the Baptist, which has been thinly Christianized.[6] More recently, David Aune revived the idea of a composite text subject to later redaction to integrate the different visions together, on the basis of the discontinuity of *dramatis personae* in each of the distinct episodes.[7] Aune is right to observe character discontinuity from one episode to another, but his attribution of this to distinct underlying sources rather than as a function of John's literary style runs into serious problems. There is more linguistic and theological coherence to the text than Aune allows—and a good test of this is the distribution of significant words that appear with special

[4] On Revelation's influence on Western art, see Natasha O'Hear and Anthony O'Hear, *Picturing the Apocalypse: The Book of Revelation in the Arts over Two Millennia* (New York: Oxford University Press, 2015). For an historical perspective, see James T. Palmer, *The Apocalypse in the Early Middle Ages* (New York: Cambridge University Press, 2014).

[5] R. H. Charles, *A Critical and Exegetical Commentary on the Revelation of St. John*, 2 vols., International Critical Commentary on the Holy Scriptures of the Old and New Testaments (Edinburgh: T&T Clark, 1920).

[6] J. Massyngberde Ford, *Revelation*, Anchor Bible 38 (Garden City, NY: Doubleday, 1975).

[7] David E. Aune, *Revelation 1–5*, Word Biblical Commentary 52 (Dallas, TX: Word, 1997). See esp. pp. cxvii–cxxxiv. One difficulty with Aune's theory is that he does not identify the compositional units and their redaction consistently across the three volumes of his commentary.

frequencies (7, 10, 12, 14, and 28) and are distributed throughout the different episodes of the text, strongly suggesting authorial coherence.[8]

Most commentators now treat Revelation as a single text, and there are no serious arguments to suggest that it was written later than the first century. The "internal" evidence—that is, arguments which interpret the details of the text in particular ways—is ambiguous, some arguments pointing to an earlier date (perhaps under Nero in the late 60s CE) and others to a later date (perhaps under Domitian in the early 90s). The comment about "not damaging the olive oil and the wine" in Rev 6:6 would fit well with the context of Domitian's edict of 92 to uproot vines, and the "blazing mountain" of Rev 8:8 would evoke in readers the eruption of Vesuvius in 79. But in both cases the language is symbolic, and both food shortages and natural disasters (including serious earthquakes) were not uncommon in the Roman period, so such identifications can never be determinative.

Three other major pieces of textual data are the measuring of the Temple in Rev 11:1–2, the discussion of "seven" and then "ten" kings in Rev 17:9–14, and the identification of the beast in Rev 13:18. Commentators are divided as to whether the Temple-measuring indicates that the Temple is still standing (indicating a date before 70) or has fallen (indicating a date after 70 for the text)—or even was originally written *during* the First Jewish–Roman War of 67–70 when the Temple was in the process of being destroyed. But all these arguments fail to take seriously the *symbolic* significance of the Temple, as standing for the people of God (e.g., 1 Cor 3:16), and impose on the text an assumption of whether or not John could make use of temple imagery either before or after its destruction.[9] The enumeration of kings in Rev 17 might be thought to offer us a decisive clue to dating, but John's purpose here is *not* to tell his readers the date at which he is writing and they are reading, as presumably they are aware of that already. Rather, he is helping them to understand the significance of the time in which they are living. The symbolism of the kings is also a symbolism of the "seven hills" of the great city (Rev 17:9), which complicates the interpretation—and any allocation of the seven kings together with the "eighth who belongs to the seven" to historical figures faces insuperable

[8] See my "Source, Structure and Composition in the Book of Revelation," in *The Book of Revelation: Currents in British Research on the Apocalypse*, ed. Garrick Allen, Ian Paul, and Simon Woodman, WUNT 2.411 (Tübingen: Mohr Siebeck, 2015), 41–54.

[9] See Stephen Smalley, *The Revelation to John: A Commentary on the Greek Text of the Apocalypse* (London: SPCK, 2005), 269–74.

obstacles.[10] There is now a strong consensus that the *gematria* clue of 666 as the number of the beast and the number of a man in Rev 13:18 points to Nero (see below on numerology). But John is, in effect, saying, "If you want to remember the real nature of Roman imperial power, think of Nero." This gives us a *terminus a quo* for dating, but no more.

So our primary evidence is that *external* to the text. Irenaeus, the second-century bishop of Lugdunum in Gaul, comments:

> We will not, however, incur the risk of pronouncing positively as to the name of Antichrist; for if it were necessary that his name should be distinctly revealed in this present time, it would have been announced by him who beheld the apocalyptic vision. *For that was seen no very long time since, but almost in our day, towards the end of Domitian's reign.* (*Against Heresies* 5.30.3, emphasis added)[11]

Irenaeus was probably born and raised in Smyrna and was a student of Polycarp, the bishop of Smyrna who was martyred at the age of eighty-six and claimed to have known John. He does not deduce the timing from the idea of Domitian as a "great persecutor" but simply records it as a chronological fact, and this concurs with other external evidence. Laodicea was destroyed by an earthquake in 60, and the message to the assembly there seems to assume that it is now prosperous and well established, which must be some time later. Polycarp himself says (*Philippians* 11) that the church in Smyrna did not exist in the time of Paul, also implying a later date. Epiphanius, writing much later (in his *Panarion*), notes that it was believed there was no Christian community in Thyatira until late in the first century.

The author of Revelation names himself as "John" four times in the text, three at the beginning (1:1, 4, 9) and once near the end (22:8). He makes a strong claim to identify with his audience, addressing them directly in the epistolary opening (1:4) and describing himself as "brother and companion" (1:9). This claim seems very well supported by the local detail that is found in Rev 2–3, where there are numerous aspects of the messages that appear to make particular sense regarding

[10] Albert A. Bell, "The Date of John's Apocalypse: The Evidence of Some Roman Historians Reconsidered," *New Testament Studies* 25, no. 1 (1978): 93–102.

[11] Trans. Alexander Roberts and William Rambaut in Alexander Roberts, James Donaldson, and A. Cleveland Coxe, eds., *Ante-Nicene Fathers*, vol. 1 (Buffalo, NY: Christian Literature Publishing Co., 1885), rev. and ed. for New Advent by Kevin Knight, www.newadvent.org/fathers/0103530.htm (accessed 16 October 2019).

local features and culture of the cities that are addressed here.[12] It is also evident in several parts of the text that John had a well-developed knowledge of the workings of the Roman Empire, particularly expressed in the details of the twenty-eight cargoes that the merchants of the earth mourn they will never be able to trade again in 18:11–13.[13]

It is striking that John does not describe himself as an "apostle"—though of course Paul does not do so in all his letters either.[14] However, John does describe himself as part of a chain of transmission in which each person is "sent" (*apostello*) by God (1:1; 22:6); he claims that what he passes on is no less than the "revelation of Jesus Christ." And, quite remarkably, in the closing of his letter, he appears to claim to be the amanuensis for a letter which is really by Jesus himself and—in line with conventional understandings of the significance of letters in the ancient world—that what he writes to the assemblies in the seven cities represents the presence and words of Jesus to them.

Despite the lack of the title, this John was believed to be the apostle John by Justin Martyr (*Dialogue with Trypho* 81.4) and Irenaeus (*Against Heresies* 5.30.3), but the apostolic authorship was then questioned because of Revelation's importance to chiliasm, an early millennial movement that believed in a future literal reign of Christ for 1,000 years on the basis of Rev 20. Eusebius of Caesarea (ca. 260–340 CE) was a vocal opponent of chiliasm, and he cites Papias (ca. 60–130 CE), bishop of Hierapolis, whose work we have only in citations by others, to suggest that there were *two* Johns in Ephesus, John the apostle and another otherwise unknown figure, John the Elder.[15] Eusebius is probably misreading Papias here, since Papias refers to the Twelve as both "elders" and "apostles" as well as "disciples of the Lord," but it could have suited Eusebius to distance Revelation from apostolic authorship.

[12] See Colin Hemer, *Letters to the Seven Churches of Asia in Their Local Setting*, Journal for the Study of the New Testament Supplement Series 11 (Sheffield: Sheffield Academic Press, 1989), building on the earlier Sir William Mitchell Ramsay, *The Letters to the Seven Churches*, ed. Mark W. Wilson, rev. ed. (Peabody, MA: Hendrickson, 1994), though qualified by my "Cities in the Book of Revelation," in *The Urban World and the First Christians*, ed. Steve Walton, Paul Trebilco, and David Gill (Grand Rapids, MI: Eerdmans, 2017), 304–19.

[13] Richard Bauckham, "The Economic Critique of Rome in Revelation 18," in *The Climax of Prophecy: Studies on the Book of Revelation* (Edinburgh: T&T Clark, 1993), 338–83. See also Koester, *Revelation*, 702–07.

[14] Paul is identified as "apostle" in the opening greetings of Romans, First and Second Corinthians, and Galatians, as well as in Ephesians, Colossians, First and Second Timothy, and Titus, but not in Philemon, Philippians or First and Second Thessalonians.

[15] Eusebius, *History of the Church* III, chap. 39.

The relationship between Revelation and the Fourth Gospel is complex. Both make extensive use of metaphorical language, often drawing on archetypal binary imagery of light and dark, good and evil. But they are also significantly different, not only in their language but in their theological expressions. John 1:29 uses *amnos*, but throughout Revelation uses *arnion*, which the Gospel uses only once (John 21:15) and then to refer to believers, not Jesus. In the Gospel, light imagery focuses on Jesus in his ministry and relationships, and the metaphor appears to derive from texts in Gen 1, Isa 42:6 and 49:6, and Pss 27:1 and 36:9. In Revelation, light is mentioned in relation to God and the Lamb in the New Jerusalem, and imagery derives from Isa 60:3, 19 and Zech 14:7. There is phraseology in common, such as "preparing a place" (John 14:2–3; Rev 12:6), "practicing truth" (John 3:21) and "practicing falsehood" (Rev 22:15), and "having a share" (John 13:8; Rev 20:6), but there are also numerous words and constructions, some of them quite common, which occur in the Gospel but are absent from Revelation.[16] Perhaps the most significant difference in theology is what appears to be a highly "realized" eschatology in the Gospel, expressed in the phrase "eternal life" (more or less equivalent to the "kingdom of God" in the Synoptic Gospels), which is contrasted with the very much future eschatology of Revelation. The most significant linguistic difference is that the entire register of the Greek used in Revelation is different; the Gospel is written in a grammatical Greek style, while the peculiarities and grammatical anomalies of Revelation continue to be the subject of much debate.

So there is no definitive case for a common author of the Gospel and the Apocalypse. Likewise, the author of Revelation may not be John the apostle.

TIME AND SPACE

As part of the extended epistolary opening (which runs from Rev 1:4 to 1:11), John locates himself temporally, spatially, relationally, and spiritually in a series of "in" statements:

> I, John, your brother and companion
> *in* the tribulation and kingdom and patient-endurance that are ours
> *in* Jesus was

[16] For a full list, see Koester, *Revelation*, 80–83.

in the island called Patmos . . . I was
in the Spirit
in the Lord's day . . .

This striking succession of "in" phrases (Greek *en*, idiomatically translated by a variety of words) locates John temporally—explicitly "on the Lord's day," implicitly in the recent past, more or less contemporaneous with his readers—and spatially "on the island called Patmos." Relationally, John is "brother" to those to whom he writes, using the most common term in the early Jesus movement that redrew the boundaries of familial loyalty (Matt 12:46–50). But his spatial location also has implicit relational overtones, since from Patmos, John is just able to see the hills on the coast of the Roman province of Asia surrounding Ephesus, the nearest of the seven cities addressed. He is at some distance, but as a pastor-in-exile he is not remote.

Spiritually, he and his readers are "in Jesus," a phrase echoing the central theological term of incorporation within the Pauline corpus, "in Christ." But John understands this incorporation to include "tribulation" as well as "kingdom," and in doing so is following both the temporal claim of Peter that Pentecost signifies the beginning of the "last days" (Acts 2:16–17) and Paul's teaching that entry into the kingdom of God will entail "tribulation" (*thlipsis*) or suffering (Acts 14:22). John's spatial location on Patmos also has an implicit theological, or perhaps mythological, significance, being seventy miles due west from Delos, the arena where the central action of the Apollo–Leto–Python myth was played out, which John draws on extensively in the central narrative of Rev 12.

The classic definition of the apocalyptic genre, developed by John J. Collins and others, highlights both the temporal and spatial aspects of apocalyptic literature, reflecting the fact that, in other apocalypses, the "seer" is taken on an otherworldly journey.[17] The Book of Revelation appears at first to conform to this, with John being invited to "come up here" to see "what must take place after this," and apparently going through a door into a heavenly throne room (Rev 4:1). But this sense of "otherworldly journey" is disrupted as the text develops. Although John

[17] "An apocalypse is a genre of revelatory literature with a narrative framework, in which a revelation is mediated by an otherworldly being to a human recipient, disclosing a transcendent reality which is both temporal, insofar as it envisages eschatological salvation, and spatial, insofar as it involves another, supernatural world." John J. Collins, *The Apocalyptic Imagination: An Introduction to Jewish Apocalyptic Literature*, 3rd ed. (Grand Rapids, MI: Eerdmans, 2016), 5.

enters this heavenly throne room, he never appears to leave it, even at the very end of his vision report, and what he sees appears to alternate between the heavenly and the earthly with no clear distinction. The audition of the 144,000 that becomes a vision of an uncountable people in chapter 7 is located explicitly on earth, but the next vision of the 144,000 is quite clearly heavenly, being located on a spiritual "Mount Zion" where they sing "before the throne" (Rev 14:3). In Rev 13:6–7, the first beast "from the sea" (later simply called "the beast") blasphemes and makes war against God's people, described as "those who dwell in heaven." They are contrasted with "the inhabitants of the earth" (a phrase repeated ten times: in 3:10; 6:10; 8:13; 11:10 [twice]; 13:8; 13:14 [twice]; 17:2; 17:8) who follow the beast, and this partition of humanity corresponds to the partition between those who receive the seal of the living God in Rev 7:2 (which appears to be identified as the "name of the Lamb and his Father" in 14:1) and those who receive the mark of the beast (mentioned twice in Rev 13:16–18 and in 14:9, 11; 16:2; 19:20; and 20:4, making seven occurrences in all). These spatial references function as an extended metaphor for humanity's spiritual state, and the descriptions of the heavenly realm suggest a spiritual, prophetic perspective on the mundane realities of the earthly realm. The consummation of John's vision report is the coming of the New Jerusalem down from heaven to earth, where the two realities finally converge.

Any simple configuration of Revelation's temporal dynamics is immediately challenged by the large-scale structure of the text. Though the closing chapters have an eschatological finality about them, almost every major earlier section also includes eschatological motifs in anticipation. So, for example, each of the series of seven seals, trumpets, and bowls ends with an eschatological idea, following some sort of interlude, the one associated with the final trumpet being particularly developed:

> The kingdom of the world has become
> the kingdom of our Lord and of his Messiah,
> and he will reign for ever and ever.
>
> (Rev 11:15)

There are also eschatological anticipations at the end of the vision-interval between the sixth and seventh seals, in Rev 7:15–17 ("They will hunger no more, and thirst no more ...") and in the central, pivotal narrative in Rev 12:10–12 ("Now have come the salvation and the power and the kingdom of our God, and the authority of his

Messiah ..."). In this way, throughout the text, the eschatological finale casts its shadow (or, perhaps better, casts its light) ahead of itself into the early narrative sections. This sense of recapitulation and anticipation reminds us that John's repeated use of "And I saw ..." in the past tense indicates the temporality of his vision experience, and not the temporal significance of the events that the visions symbolize.

This pattern is evident in the use of two key eschatological terms: "woe" and "tribulation." The association of "woe" with eschatological judgment is made clear in chapter 18, where the fall of the great city Babylon (symbolically representing Rome as an archetypal human empire) is mourned with double woes by three groups—the client "kings of the earth," merchants, and sea captains—who have until then profited from the city's power and trade (18:10, 16, and 19). But proclamations of "woe" are also brought forward as a disruptive overlay on the sequence of seven trumpets. In Rev 8:13, a flying eagle (a pagan symbol of divine guidance) declares the final three trumpet blasts to be a threefold "woe," and this is confirmed for the fifth and sixth trumpet blasts by a repeated formula in 9:12 and 11:14:

> The first woe has passed; there are still two woes to come.
> The second woe has passed; the third woe is coming very soon.

But the strong anticipation (that the final trumpet is the third woe) is disrupted, with no mention of "woe" in relation to the final blast, which instead leads to a declaration of eschatological triumph. So where is the third "woe?" It actually comes in the following chapter and is connected with the victory of God's anointed one ("Messiah") achieved through his death on the cross:

> Rejoice then, you heavens
> and those who dwell in them!
> But *woe* to the earth and the sea ...
> (Rev 12:12)[18]

This statement connects the preceding narrative, and the identity of the "male son who is to rule the nations with a rod of iron" (12:5; compare 2:27 and 19:15), with the "Lamb standing as if it had been slaughtered" in 5:6 and further back to the atoning, kingdom-forming

[18] *Contra* Koester, *Revelation*, 504, but agreeing with James L. Resseguie, *The Revelation of John: A Narrative Commentary* (Grand Rapids, MI: Baker Academic, 2009), 175. The connection with the other "woes" is confirmed by the occurrence of the word fourteen times in total.

death ("blood") of Jesus in 1:5–6. The time of the third woe is, therefore, the time in which John is writing and in which his readers are living—a time of "persecution, and the kingdom and the patient endurance" (1:9) as John set out from the very beginning.

The dual nature of the present time is expressed numerologically by John in the three equivalent phrases "forty-two months," "one thousand two hundred and sixty days," and "a time, and times, and half a time" that link together the otherwise highly differentiated chapters 11 and 12 (occurring in 11:2 and 3; 12:6 and 14). The third phrase derives from Daniel's half-week of tribulation in Dan 7:25 and 12:7, calculated there as being equal to either 1,290 or 1,335 days. John changes this calculation by eliminating any intercalated months, so it equals $30 \times 12 \times 3.5 = 1{,}260$ days or forty-two months.[19] This then corresponds with the forty-two years and forty-two stations of the wilderness wanderings listed in Num 33. For John and his readers, the present time of tribulation is also the time of Exodus wanderings; they have been "freed from [the slavery] of our sins" (Rev 1:5) but have not yet entered the Promised Land.[20]

So the present age is a time of victory, since the death of Jesus has brought the final, eschatological victory of God into the present. But that victory is not yet completely realized, and the Enemy and the enemies of God are still at large, causing the people of God to suffer and even die. This ambiguity forms the very basis of the appeal of the risen Jesus to "conquer" (2:7, 11, 17, 26; 3:5, 12, 21): to live out the as yet not fully realized victory of the Lamb, rather than succumbing to the apparent but passing power of their opponents.

NUMEROLOGY

One of the most striking features of Revelation is its use of numerology in much more all-pervasive and developed ways than other apocalyptic texts. The first and most obvious use of numbers is when they occur as explicit structuring devices within the text. Thus we are told that there are seven assemblies (1:4) represented by seven lampstands in 1:20, and

[19] See Richard Bauckham, "Nero and the Beast," in *The Climax of Prophecy*, 384–452, esp. 401–04.

[20] Exodus is alluded to fifty-three times in Revelation. Ian Paul, *Revelation: An Introduction and Commentary*, Tyndale New Testament Commentaries 20 (London: InterVarsity Press, 2018), 39; see also Judith Kovacs and Christopher Rowland, *Revelation: The Apocalypse of Jesus Christ*, Blackwell Bible Commentaries (Oxford: Blackwell, 2004), 284–95.

the messages that follow naturally fit this sevenfold pattern. But we are immediately confronted with the symbolic (or, rather, metaphorical) meaning of this number "seven" since we know that there were Christians living in other nearby cities in the region (most notably Miletus, Colossae, Hierapolis, and Troas, also probably Tralles and Magnesia) who are not included in this list.[21] In the ancient world, seven suggested completeness, since there were seven days in the week, seven seas, and seven known planets. We can see that the messages were clearly intended to be read by those in other cities as well as the one to which it was addressed, and John assumes a wider audience for his work, so we might confidently infer that these particular seven symbolized the whole of the early Christian movement, and were relevant to them all.[22] Similarly, we notice that there are seven seals on the scroll that are opened (6:1–8:1), seven trumpets that are sounded (8:2–11:19), and seven bowls that are poured out (16:1–21), and each of these shapes the structure of what follows. What we might not notice, though, is that John uses a sevenfold structure elsewhere, so there are seven characteristics of the 144,000 in 14:4–5, and seven unnumbered visions in 19:11 through to 21:1.[23]

This leads on to the second use of numbers by John: words occurring with particular frequencies in the text. There are seven blessings, seven "sickles" in Rev 14, seven times God is titled "Lord God Almighty," seven occurrences of "Christ," "testimony of Jesus," "prophecy," "I am coming," "sign," "endurance," "cloud," and seven mentions of the elders and living creatures together. Jesus, the Spirit, and the saints are each mentioned fourteen times, significant as 2×7, where two is the number of reliable witnesses according to Deut 17:6, so all three are connected with "faithful witness."[24] There continues to be debate about the meaning and importance of these word frequencies. But they

[21] Ramsay suggested that these seven were natural centers of communication. Ramsay, *The Letters to the Seven Churches*, 128–32, summarized in Hemer, *Letters*, 15. G. K. Beale, *Revelation: A Commentary on the Greek Text*, New International Greek Testament Commentary (Grand Rapids, MI: Eerdmans, 1999), 204, shows that this, like all other explanations, is "conjecture."

[22] On the communication between Christian communities in the ancient world, see Richard Bauckham, *The Gospel for All Christians: Rethinking the Gospel Audiences* (Edinburgh: T&T Clark, 1997).

[23] For a partial comparison with other apocalypses (especially Fourth Ezra) see Christopher R. Smith, "The Structure of the Book of Revelation in Light of Apocalyptic Literary Conventions," *Novum Testamentum* 36, no. 4 (1994): 373–93.

[24] See Richard Bauckham, "Structure and Composition," in *The Climax of Prophecy*, 1–37.

offer strong evidence that Revelation is a very carefully composed text which uses more (but not less) than the meaning of its words to communicate its messages.

The third way in which Revelation uses numbers is in drawing on the mathematical significance of square, triangular, and rectangular numbers. Though we continue to use the language of "square" numbers, the reason for the term is obscured in positional decimal systems, like our widely used Arabic number system, where digits symbolize numbers of different value. But the "shape" of numbers is more evident in a cultural context that makes greater use of physical counters in calculation and enumeration. "Square" numbers are the products of a number multiplied by itself, such as 16 = 4 × 4, which means that this number of counters can be arranged in a square array, and are also the sum of successive odd numbers (in this case 1 + 3 + 5 + 7 = 16). In an analogous way, a number is triangular if that number of items could be arranged in an equilateral triangle and is the sum of successive integers (so the triangle 10 = 1 + 2 + 3 + 4). A number that is the product of successive integers, such as 4 × 5 = 20, is the sum of successive even numbers (2 + 4 + 6 + 8) and can be arranged as a rectangle. Such numbers share some properties with square numbers (the fourth rectangle 20 is the fourth square number plus 4) and with triangular numbers (20 is twice the fourth triangle, 10).

But our interest lies in the way Revelation makes use of these properties.[25] Because of the distinctive square shape of Hebrew altars in the Old Testament (in contrast with pagan altars, which were rectangular or round) and the shape of the holy of holies as a cube (1 Kgs 6:20), John consistently uses the square and cubic numbers 144 and 1,000 to designate the things of God, in particular the people of God. By contrast, he uses the triangular 666 to designate the opponent of God, and in a fascinating conjunction of maths and theology, he uses rectangular numbers (which have something in common with both squares and triangles) to designate that period of time when God's people are oppressed by their opponents and yet enjoy the protection of God: the forty-two months (6 × 7) equal the 1,260 days (35 × 36) of Rev 11:2–3 and 12:6.

The fourth way in which Revelation uses numbers is perhaps the most notorious: the *isopsephism* (the Greek meaning "same calculation") or *gematria* (the Hebrew adaptation of the Greek word for

[25] See Bauckham, "Nero and the Beast," 384–452.

"geometry") involved in calculating the number of the beast, 666, in 13:18. The possibility of *gematria* arises from the use of letters of the alphabet as a number system by allocating a numerical value to each letter, and the calculation of the values of words in this way occurred in a wide range of contexts. In the ruins of Pompeii, it is possible to make out a graffito: "I love her whose number is 545."[26] Presumably the person who was the object of affection here knew her own number, and so would understand the message. But while it is easy to move from name to number, it is difficult to move in the other direction, which means that the lover's secret was safe. In the Christianized apocalyptic work the *Sibylline Oracles* 1:324–29, it is "predicted" that the name of the Messiah would add up to 888, which the name "Jesus" does in Greek. The number 8 was associated with the overflow of blessing that would be the hallmark of the age to come. The Roman historian Suetonius (*Nero* 39) refers to a ditty circulating in Rome in his chapter on Nero: "A calculation new. Nero his mother slew,"[27] which relies on the fact that the numerical value of the name "Nero" in this scheme is 1005, the same as the numerical value of the phrase "killed his own mother," suggesting that the statement was true. The numerical value of the Hebrew term for "branch" in the messianic title "branch of David" (Jer 23:5) is 138, the same as the name "Menachem" meaning "comforter," so there was an expectation that the Messiah would bring comfort to his people (cf. from Talmudic literature: j. Berakot 5a; Lamentations Rabbah 1.16).

In Rev 13:18, the identification of the "beast from the sea" with Roman Imperial power is confirmed by the *gematria* that identifies "beast'" with "Nero(n) Caesar" by transliterating the Greek terms into Hebrew letters:

Term	Greek	Hebrew transliteration	Sum	Value
beast	*thērion*	TRYWN	400 + 200 + 10 + 6 + 50	666
Nero Caesar	*Nerōn Kaisar*	NRWN QSR	50 + 200 + 6 + 50 + 100 + 60 + 200	666

[26] Adolf Deissmann, *Light from the Ancient East: The New Testament Illustrated by Recently Discovered Texts of the Graeco-Roman World* (London: Hodder & Stoughton, 1910), 276.

[27] *Suetonius, with an English Translation*, trans. J. C. Rolfe, vol. 2, Loeb Classical Library 38 (Cambridge, MA: Harvard University Press, 1979), 159.

This interpretation is confirmed internally by noting a similar identification of the angel in chapter 21 with the number associated with the holy city:

angel	*angelos*	ANGLS	1 + 50 + 3 + 30 + 60	144

And it is confirmed externally by the textual variant found in the Oxyrhynchus papyrus P115, where the number has been changed to 616—which corresponds to correlating "beast" in the genitive (*thēriou*) with Nero spelled without the final "n," in both cases losing 50 from the value. In all these uses of numerology, the text of Revelation communicates its theological vision not only through its semantic content and metaphorical signification, but also through its structure and fabric.

USE OF THE OLD TESTAMENT AND IMPERIAL IMAGERY

Even if the text of Revelation as we have it is not a composite of earlier documents, it is still clear that John draws extensively on two major sources for his language and imagery: the written text of the Old Testament and the symbolic world of Roman imperial practice, mythology, and propaganda.

There is wide agreement that Revelation includes extensive allusion to the Old Testament, whether this was done "consciously" by John as author or simply the natural result of someone speaking in a "biblical" register,[28] and whether the meanings of Old Testament texts carry unchanged into the text of Revelation or change.[29] In relation to specific texts, there is also the central question of method in identifying allusions to the Old Testament, since formal citations are almost entirely absent.[30]

It has also been noted that Revelation makes significant symbolic allusion to aspects of imperial mythology and propaganda, both on a

[28] The first view is found throughout Bauckham, *The Climax of Prophecy*. The second view shapes Kovacs and Rowland's approach, despite the very full table of allusions in Kovacs and Rowland, *Revelation*, 284–95.

[29] G. K. Beale, who argues for stability of meaning across texts, contrasted with Steve Moyise, who argues for Revelation's creative reuse of Old Testament language. Beale, *Revelation*, 97–99; Steve Moyise, "Does the Author of Revelation Misappropriate the Scriptures?," *Andrews University Seminary Studies* 40, no. 1 (2002): 3–21.

[30] On the question of method, see Ian Paul, "The Use of the Old Testament in Rev 12," in *Old Testament in the New Testament: Essays in Honour of J. L. North*, ed. Steve Moyise (Sheffield: Continnuum, 2000), 256–77.

broad scale throughout the text,[31] and also in specific textual details.[32] What is striking in these examples, alongside the vivid and dynamic nature of the metaphorical language,[33] is the way in which the allusions to these quite contrasting symbolic worlds (the Old Testament and imperial ideology) are intertwined within the text, particularly in chapters 4 and 12.

Chapter 4 of Revelation is often considered to be the beginning of the "apocalyptic" section of the text proper, in part because of the contrast with the more mundane nature of the seven royal announcement messages in the previous two chapters, but also because of the language of ascent into the heavenly realm by being "in the Spirit," providing a double allusion to Ezekiel's vision (Ezek 3:12, 14; 8:3; 11:1, 24; 43:5). The heavenly vision is furnished with numerous biblical images: the voice "like a trumpet" (in the Old Testament a call to worship or summons to battle); God as one enthroned (as king over creation and his people); the gems carnelian and jasper (the first and last stones on the high priest's breastplate in Exod 28:17–20); the rainbow encircling the throne (the promise to Noah in Gen 9:13); and thunder and lightning (as occurred at Sinai in Exod 19:16). The "sea of glass" alludes to the bronze "sea" in front of Solomon's temple (1 Kgs 7:23–26; 2 Chr 4:2–5); the living creatures incorporate details from Ezekiel's vision (Ezek 1:4–14) and the wings of Isaiah's seraphim, and repeat the *trisagion* from Isa 6:3.

Yet at the same time, key elements of the action seem quite distinct from Old Testament imagery. God's throne is in a heavenly room with a door; those around the throne are elders, not priests as we would expect; there are twenty-four of them, rather than the twelve we might expect to represent the tribes of Israel (compare the enumeration of the tribes

[31] See particularly Leonard L. Thompson, *The Book of Revelation: Apocalypse & Empire* (New York: Oxford University Press, 1990), interacting with historical evidence; Steven J. Friesen, *Imperial Cults and the Apocalypse of John: Reading Revelation in the Ruins* (New York: Oxford University Press, 2001), interacting with archeological evidence; and Wes Howard-Brook and Anthony Gwyther, *Unveiling Empire: Reading Revelation Then and Now* (Maryknoll, NY: Orbis Books, 1999), offering a taxonomy of imperial ideology as part of a contemporary reading strategy.

[32] The role of imperial court ceremonial in influencing the visions of Rev 4 and 5 is explored in David E. Aune, *Apocalypticism, Prophecy, and Magic in Early Christianity: Collected Essays* (Grand Rapids, MI: Baker Academic, 2008), 99–119. Connections with cultic practice and Rev 13 are explored in Allen Kerkeslager, "Apollo, Greco-Roman Prophecy, and the Rider on the White Horse in Rev 6.2," *Journal of Biblical Literature* 112, no. 1 (1993): 116–21.

[33] I explore the specific dynamics of the metaphorical language of Revelation in "Cities in the Book of Revelation."

in Rev 7:5–8); they are dressed in white, the common pagan color of worship, and cast down golden crowns while singing repetitive choruses of exaltation, rather than using the language of the psalms that we might expect to hear. As David Aune demonstrates, all these elements can be traced, more or less clearly, to the practices of imperial court ceremonial, and would be clearly resonant to anyone in the first century familiar with the imperial cult. Among the attributes ascribed to God, we even see traces of imperial language: "worthy" (*axios*) is not a characteristic term of praise in the Old Testament, but relates to the notion of the *consensus omnium*, according to which, despite appearances of despotism, the emperor actually rules by the will of all and for the good of all. In this way, Revelation is quite polemical, displacing the emperor from all merit of praise, which belongs to God alone. Aune concludes: "The result is that the sovereignty of God and the lamb have been elevated so far above all pretentions and claims of earthly rulers that the latter, upon comparison, become only pale, even diabolical imitations of the transcendent majesty of the King of kings and Lord of lords."[34] This "elevation" is precisely achieved by the interplay of Old Testament and imperial imagery in the text.

In Rev 12, the interaction between Old Testament images and imperial narrative is more structured. All the *dramatis personae* derive (implicitly or explicitly) from the Old Testament.

a. The four terms used to describe the "woman clothed with the sun" in 12:2—she is *pregnant* (using the Greek idiom "having in the belly") and *cries out* in *birth pains*, in the *agonies* of *giving birth*—exactly match those in Isa 26:17 where God's people in distress are likened to a woman giving birth. Similar language is used in Isa 66:7–9 where Jerusalem is the woman as a metonym for God's people, and it recurs in Mic 4:8–10 and 5:3.
b. The "dragon" alludes to the "monsters of the waters" in Ps 74:13–14 (LXX), the one whom God tramples in Ps 91:13, but also imperial power in Jer 51:34 and Ezek 29:3. The "seven heads and ten horns" combine the heads and horns of the four beasts of Dan 7:2–7 that signify four successive empires. And there is further combination of the whole range of images opposed to God in Rev 12:9: the "ancient serpent" in the Garden of Eden was by the first century identified with "Satan," the accuser, called in Greek "the devil" (*diabolos*).

[34] Aune, *Apocalypticism, Prophecy, and Magic in Early Christianity*, 119.

c. The child who is born is described redundantly as a "male son" (a Hebrew idiom found in Jer 20:15) and is the one to "rule the nations with a rod of iron" in fulfillment of the messianic promise of Ps 2:9, also used to describe the "Word of God" riding a white horse in Rev 19:15.
d. Michael is the "chief of princes" in Dan 10:13, 10:21, and 12:1 who has a particular role in protecting God's people.

But the shape of the narrative action does not look like anything in the Old Testament, and is in fact drawn from the Apollo–Leto–Python myth, which was well known in various forms in the region at the time.[35] It tells of Leto, who became pregnant by Zeus, being pursued by the dragon Python, who knew by an oracle that Leto's son would threaten him. But Leto is carried away by the north wind to a safe place, the island of Delos (near to Patmos), and she gives birth to Artemis's brother Apollo, who quickly kills Python by shooting him with arrows. The myth was important as part of imperial propaganda, in which the emperor played the role of Apollo, "slaying" the forces of chaos and evil by means of imperial rule and prosperity. Its use in Revelation functions in the same way as many political cartoons of our day, by locating characters from one context (the Old Testament narrative) into another (the Apollo–Leto–Python myth), and in doing so inverts the meaning of the myth. It is the Jewish Messiah who plays the role of chaos-slaying Apollo, and imperial power is either allied to or identified with the chaos monster opposed to God and to peace.[36]

APPROACHES TO INTERPRETATION

Within the history of interpretation of Revelation, there have been four major distinctive approaches.[37]

Idealist. This sees the text as describing timeless spiritual truths about the nature and purposes of God, and the relationship between the

[35] Hyginus (ca. 64 BCE – 17 CE), *Fabulae* no. 140.

[36] Note the similar criticism in how Tacitus records the words of the Caledonian chieftain Calgacus: "To plunder, butcher, steal, these things they misname of empire: they make a desolation and they call it peace." *Agricola* 30; *Tacitus: Agricola, Germania, Dialogus*, trans. M. Hutton, rev. R. M. Ogilvie, Loeb Classical Library 35 (Cambridge, MA: Harvard University Press, 1970), 81.

[37] For a full exploration of these four approaches, see Kenneth L. Gentry et al., *Four Views on the Book of Revelation* (Grand Rapids, MI: Zondervan, 1998).

church and the world. Some of the earliest allegorical interpretations of Revelation took this approach.[38]

Futurist. A rival school of early interpreters saw in Revelation the prediction of an imminent end and the advent of the millennial age. Joachim of Fiore (ca. 1135–1202) understood it as predicting the end in his time,[39] and there has been a strong revival of this approach in the twentieth century.

Church historical. Berengaudus (840–92) was the first to suggest that Revelation described events through history to the writer's day in his Latin *Exposition of the Seven Visions of the Book of Revelation.*

Contemporary historical (or *preterist*). This approach reads Revelation as primarily speaking to its own day, and only secondarily (and derivatively) to later readers. A particular variant of this approach sees the whole of the text as referring to events prior to the destruction of Jerusalem (which is interpreted as "the great city" and "Babylon") and that the End is fulfilled in Jerusalem's destruction.[40]

In contemporary interpretation, each of these approaches has something to contribute. Revelation is clearly written to first-century Christians (contemporary historical) but makes sense of their situation in the light of the ultimate destiny of the world (futurist). Subsequent commentators have reapplied Revelation's imagery in their own, successive contexts (church historical), which in turn has led to considerations about the nature of God and his relation to the world (idealist).

These four approaches are often closely related to different interpretations of the millennium of Rev 20. The four dominant understandings of the millennium (which do not correspond directly to the four strategies above) are the following.

Premillennialism. This approach understands the thousand years as a literal period which follows the return of Jesus to earth (the "pre-" relates to when Jesus's return takes place, i.e., it is before, "pre-" the millennium). This was the most common reading of Rev 20 in the early church, and can be dated back as far as Papias of Hierapolis, who died in 130. It was followed by Justin Martyr and Irenaeus, but began to be opposed in the early third century. The difficulty with this reading is

[38] Most notably Methodius of Olympus (d. 311), in his treatise *Symposium, or On Virginity*, in which he comments on the meaning of Rev 12; cited in William C. Weinrich, *Revelation*, Ancient Christian Commentary on Scripture 12 (Downers Grove, IL: InterVarsity Press, 2006), 178–92.

[39] Joachim of Fiore, *Expositio in Apocalypsim.*

[40] A recent exponent of this view is Peter J. Leithart, *Revelation 1–11*, International Theological Commentary (New York: Bloomsbury, 2018).

that it takes the number 1,000 as literal alone among all the numbers in Revelation, and it is hard to make sense of the release of Satan within a chronological schema.

Amillennialism. In the third century there was a move to understand the millennium "spiritually" rather than literally, and Tyconius (late fourth century) was the first to propose that the millennium was another way of describing the period between Jesus's exaltation and his return, a view that was followed by Augustine and remained influential for centuries.[41] The difficulty with this reading is that John already has numbers to describe this period—three-and-a-half years, forty-two months, and 1,260 days—and it seems impossible to reconcile the *binding* of Satan with Satan and the beasts' *trampling* of the saints in chapter 13, even within the narrative of the book. The thousand-year reign also *follows* the judgment sequences, so would be completely out of narrative order.

Postmillennialism. In the medieval period, the idea developed that the millennium describes a period of future history, so that the return of Jesus follows (is "post-") the millennium. Joachim of Fiore in the twelfth century proposed that the kingdom of the Spirit would arrive in the year 1260, following the (then) present age of the Son. Postmillennial thinking was revived under the philosophical influence of Hegel and the social optimism of the nineteenth century, but largely disappeared in Western thinking after the catastrophe of the Great War.[42] The difficulty of this reading is making sense of the placing of the millennium *after* the coming of Jesus riding the white horse in Rev 19.

Dispensational premillennialism. Renewal of a belief in a literal thousand years came with the complex dispensational schemes created by John Nelson Darby around 1830, one of the founders of the movement known as the Plymouth Brethren. This approach takes a strictly futurist view of Revelation, and within it there are different schemes to relate the seven-year period of "tribulation," the rapture of the saints (in effect a secret first coming of Jesus involving believers being taken up to heaven)—which might come at the beginning, in the middle, or at the end of the seven years—and the final return of Jesus. The difficulty with this reading is that it does not attend to John's use of the language of

[41] Tyconius's commentary is lost and is available only through citation by others. See Weinrich, *Revelation*, xxix–xxx. For a recent critical reconstruction, see Tyconius, *Expositio Apocalypseos*, ed. Roger Gryson, CCSL 107A (Turnhout: Brepols, 2011).

[42] See Brian Stanley, *Christianity in the Twentieth Century: A World History* (Princeton, NJ: Princeton University Press, 2018), 27–32.

"tribulation" (suffering), it attempts to take the text literally but often reads it allegorically, and it imports misreadings of Paul (in the form of the "rapture") into Revelation's text. It is, nevertheless, one of the most widespread approaches within Protestantism globally.

None of these approaches is fully convincing. The textual details suggest that we should read the millennium as one of seven (unnumbered) visions of the End, each giving a different perspective on eschatology, beginning with the rider on the white horse in 19:11 and ending with the descent of the new Jerusalem in 21:1.

THEOLOGICAL THEMES

Although much popular reading of Revelation focuses on the idea of an eschatological timetable (which is lent some weight by the highly structured nature of the text), the main theological focus is a triadic vision of God.[43] This is introduced at the very beginning of the text, when we are told that this is a revelation "of Jesus Christ, which God gave ..." (Rev 1:1), but finds an immediately developed expression in the threefold epistolary greeting:

> Grace and peace to you
> from him who is, and who was, and who is to come,
> and from the seven spirits before his throne,
> and from Jesus Christ,
> who is the faithful witness,
> the firstborn from the dead,
> and the ruler of the kings of the earth.

The first element of this triad adapts the meaning of the self-revelation of God to Moses at the burning bush (Exod 3:14) by reordering the temporal elements to emphasize the present reality of God ("who is, and who was ..." rather than "who was and who is ..."), and adapting the final temporal element to give it a specific eschatological focus ("who is to come" rather than "who will be"). The threefold description of Jesus introduces a central theological theme—that of faithful witness—which both identifies the exemplary nature of his

[43] I used the term "triadic" here to avoid the suggestions of later theological developments associated with the language of "trinity." See Larry W. Hurtado, *Lord Jesus Christ: Devotion to Jesus in Earliest Christianity* (Grand Rapids, MI: Eerdmans, 2005).

atoning death and articulates the central call on John's readers.[44] The second appellation ("firstborn from the dead") alludes to Jesus's resurrection as the proleptic anticipation of the age to come, and the third points to his de jure rule over earthly powers, setting up a key narrative arc of the text which eventually leads to the final realization of this rule de facto.

The varied language of the Spirit continues to be the subject of debate.[45] But the placement of the "seven spirits" between the mention of God and Jesus in this greeting, the function of the Spirit in John's revelatory experience (at 1:10, 4:2, 17:3, and 21:10), and the close association of the Spirit or seven spirits *both* with the one seated on the throne *and* with the Lamb/Jesus (not least in the saying of Rev 19:10 "the testimony of Jesus is the Spirit of prophecy") all underscore the triadic nature of John's vision of God.

It is generally recognized that the throne, introduced as a visual metonym for the rule of God (frequently described as the *pantokrator*, "almighty," particularly in the "liturgical" sections of praise), is a central symbol in the text. It establishes central importance of the idea of the reign of God, in continuity with themes of God's kingship in the Old Testament, though by way of contrast the "one seated on the throne" is never described in anthropomorphic terms: unlike in the Old Testament, the God of Revelation has no eyes or ears, nostrils, arms, or hands. It also contributes to the triadic vision of God, as the "Lamb" takes his place on the throne with God, even to the point that John uses a singular verb to describe the Lamb and the one on the throne together in Rev 11:15. The narrative vision of Revelation is not that the Lamb and God reign severally and together, but that they reign singularly and jointly.

The symbol of the throne also functions polemically, setting the claims of God's reign against all other rival claims to power. Revelation offers a highly developed and graphic account of the forces of evil. Central to this account is the "counterfeit triad" of dragon, beast (from the sea), and beast from the land/false prophet. The multiplicity of images and complex deployment of Old Testament imagery offers a highly developed theology of evil, which is cosmic and spiritual,

[44] Hence the frequency of "Jesus" and "saints" both occurring fourteen times; see "Numerology" above.

[45] For the case that the language of "the seven spirits" and "the Spirit" are all reference to aspects of the godhead, see Richard Bauckham, *The Theology of the Book of Revelation*, New Testament Theology (Cambridge: Cambridge University Press, 1993), 109–25. For the contrary view, see Koester, *Revelation*, 216.

political and imperial, and religious and personal. This is expressed not only in the narrative symbolism of the central part of the text, but also in seven messages of chapters 2 and 3, which function as a contextualized prolegomenon to the visionary section. Within these messages, the readers of the first century are presented with the personal challenge of fidelity to Jesus as faithful witness within their social and religious context.

The repeated metaphor of sexual immorality, while problematic for many contemporary interpretive strategies, contrasts the call to the true worship of the one true God with the alternative of the idolatrous worship of other powers who make rival claims to loyalty. Although much of the imagery offers this kind of binary choice, the contrast between the power of God and the powers of evil is never dualistic. It is striking that, within the narrative episodes of conflict and combat, there is an anticlimactic omission of the contest itself. So in Rev 12, the victory won by the "blood of the Lamb" is enacted by delegation to Michael and his angels, and in the dramatic conquest by the rider on the white horse in chapter 19, the narrative passes directly from the battle array to the result of the triumph, with no description of the conflict itself. There is, throughout the text, literally no contest between God and his allies, and Satan and his.

Caught between these rival claims of power come the created order and, in particular, humanity.[46] Revelation is striking in having perhaps the most developed description of the socioeconomic stratifications of the human situation, exemplified by the cataloguing of human social groups in Rev 6:15: "kings of the earth, the magnates, the generals, the rich, the powerful, and everyone else, both slave and free." Within this, humanity is portrayed as having power as a moral agent with a qualified sense of free choice. The world is shaped by cosmic forces of good and evil and, although these are powerful, they are not in themselves determinative of human destiny. They create a world in cosmic conflict, and because of this humanity does not have absolute freedom—but does have the freedom to choose with which side to be allied. This sense of moral responsibility is reinforced by the figure of John, who is a near-model of faithful witness but who must choose to commit to this path, illustrated in his two temptations to worship an angel in Rev 19:10 and 22:8. God's perspective and insight on the way the world is and the

[46] Ian Paul, "Revelation's Human Characters and Its Anthropology," in *Anthropology and New Testament Theology*, ed. Jason Maston and Benjamin E. Reynolds (London: Continnuum, 2018), 205–24.

choices faced by the Christian communities are not expressed in unqualified autocratic terms, but must be listened to, received, and acted upon.

Humanity in Revelation is portrayed as inhabiting a specific chronological time and a specific cultural, social, and political space. But these locations are not of absolute importance. Spatially, the redeemed in some sense already inhabit the heavenly reality, so that both vertical (heaven/earth) and temporal (past/future/present) distinctions are relativized. In the narrative world of Revelation, to become a follower of the Lamb is to enter into a sense of history as the story of God's faithful dealings with his people in the past, and the eschatological story of God's redemption and renewal of the whole of creation.[47]

Selected Further Reading

Allen, Garrick, Ian Paul, and Simon Woodman, eds. *The Book of Revelation: Currents in British Research on the Apocalypse*. Wissenschaftliche Untersuchungen zum Neuen Testament 2.411. Tübingen: Mohr Siebeck, 2015.

Aune, David E. *Apocalypticism, Prophecy, and Magic in Early Christianity: Collected Essays*. Grand Rapids, MI: Baker Academic, 2008.

Aune, David E. *Revelation 1–5*. Word Biblical Commentary 52. Dallas, TX: Word, 1997.

Bauckham, Richard. *The Climax of Prophecy: Studies on the Book of Revelation*. Edinburgh: T&T Clark, 1993.

Beale, G. K. *Revelation: A Commentary on the Greek Text*. New International Greek Testament Commentary. Grand Rapids, MI: Eerdmans, 1999.

Friesen, Steven J. *Imperial Cults and the Apocalypse of John: Reading Revelation in the Ruins*. Oxford: Oxford University Press, 2001.

Howard-Brook, Wes, and Anthony Gwyther. *Unveiling Empire: Reading Revelation Then and Now*. Maryknoll, NY: Orbis, 1999.

Koester, Craig R. *Revelation: A New Translation with Introduction and Commentary*. New Haven, CT: Yale University Press, 2014.

Leithart, Peter J. *Revelation 1–11*. International Theological Commentary. New York: Bloomsbury, 2018.

O'Hear, Natasha, and Anthony O'Hear. *Picturing the Apocalypse: The Book of Revelation in the Arts over Two Millennia*. New York: Oxford, 2015.

Paul, Ian. *Revelation: An Introduction and Commentary*. Tyndale New Testament Commentaries. London: InterVarsity Press, 2018.

[47] For an extended ecological reading of Revelation, see Micah D. Kiel, *Apocalyptic Ecology: The Book of Revelation, the Earth, and the Future* (Collegeville, MN: Liturgical Press, 2017).

4 The Gnostic Apocalypses

DYLAN M. BURNS

INTRODUCTION: "APOCALYPTICISM" AND "GNOSTICISM"

One does not have to read about "apocalyptic literature" for very long to encounter its fellow unruly cousin, "Gnostic literature." Scholarship of the early to mid-twentieth century often paired "apocalypticism" and "Gnosticism," for various reasons and in various configurations.[1] One often used to read of how the "temporal" dualism of apocalypticism—emphasizing the eclipse of the present age by that of the eschaton—is mirrored by the "metaphysical" dualism of Gnosticism, ostensibly predicated on dualities like mind–matter, God–cosmos, and of course good–evil.[2] An old cliché dictates that Gnostic sources are concerned not with cosmic eschatology, but only with personal eschatology.[3] A version of this myth has even served as evidence in older theories explaining the mysterious origins of Gnostic literature as a response to the dashed hopes of apocalyptically minded Roman Jews, or other

[1] Dylan M. Burns, "Apocalypses among Gnostics and Manichaeans," in *The Oxford Handbook of Apocalyptic Literature*, ed. John J. Collins (New York: Oxford University Press, 2014), 358.

[2] Surveyed in Jaan Lahe, *Gnosis und Judentum: Alttestamentliche und jüdische Motive in der gnostischen Literatur und das Ursprungsproblem der Gnosis* (Leiden and Boston: Brill, 2012), 113–22, 140–42.

[3] John J. Collins, "Introduction: Towards the Morphology of a Genre," in "Apocalypse: Morphology of a Genre," special issue, *Semeia* 14 (1979): 13, 17; cf. George MacRae, "Apocalyptic Eschatology in Gnosticism," in *Apocalypticism in the Ancient Mediterranean World and Near East: Proceedings of the International Colloquium on Apocalypticism, Uppsala, August 12–17, 1979*, ed. David Hellholm (Tübingen: Mohr Siebeck, 1983), 317–25. For a corrective, see Malcolm Peel, "Gnostic Eschatology and the New Testament," *Novum Testamentum* 12, no. 2 (1970): 141–65, esp. 155–62; Harold W. Attridge, "Valentinian and Sethian Apocalyptic Traditions," *JECS* 8, no. 2 (2000): 173–211, esp. 175–77; Burns, "Apocalypses among Gnostics and Manichaeans," 364.

groups experiencing a crisis.[4] As scholars' working definitions of the terms "apocalypticism" and "Gnosticism" have changed over the years, the binary of the two has come increasingly into question. Influential studies have argued that "Gnosticism" is a vague term of virtually no utility.[5] Conversely, scholarship has preferred over the last forty years to focus on the primary sources in question, "apocalypses"—actual surviving texts written by actual people—rather than nebulous theological constructions.[6]

Even if it remains difficult to speak of "apocalypticism and Gnosticism" without some qualification, it is helpful—even necessary—to speak of "Gnostic apocalypses": works employing the apocalyptic genre that were written by people known in antiquity as "Gnostics" (Gk. *gnōstikoi*, "knowers"), or authors whose thought resembles that of the Gnostics. Crucial evidence regarding such people is found in the testimonies of the Christian theologian and heresiographer Irenaeus of Lyons (writing ca. 180 CE) and the Greek philosopher Porphyry of Tyre (later third century CE). Irenaeus wrote his lengthy work *Against Heresies* in part to combat the beliefs that derived from a group of individuals whom he calls "Gnostics" (*Against Heresies*, Preface, 1.11.1, 1.29). Porphyry, meanwhile, says that not long after he began studying with his teacher, Plotinus, who was probably the greatest philosopher of late antiquity, and a key influence on St. Augustine, among many others:

> there were in his (Plotinus's) time many others, Christians, in particular heretics (*hairetikoi*) who had set out from the ancient philosophy, men belonging to the schools of Adelphius and Aculinus—who possessed many texts of Alexander the Libyan and Philocomus and Demostratus of Lydia, and who produced revelations (*apokalupseis*) of Zoroaster and Zostrianos and Nicotheus and Allogenes and Messos and others of this sort who deceived many, just as they had been deceived, actually alleging

4 Critically discussed in Michael A. Williams, *Rethinking Gnosticism: Arguments for Dismantling a Dubious Category* (Princeton, NJ: Princeton University Press, 1996), 97–109, 227–29; David Frankfurter, "The Legacy of Jewish Apocalypses in Early Christianity: Regional Trajectories," in *The Jewish Apocalyptic Heritage in Early Christianity*, ed. James C. VanderKam and William Adler (Minneapolis, MN: Fortress, 1996), 150–51, 162.

5 Williams, *Rethinking Gnosticism*.

6 John J. Collins, "What Is Apocalyptic Literature?," in *The Oxford Handbook of Apocalyptic Literature*, ed. John J. Collins (New York: Oxford University Press, 2014), 2, 6–7.

> that Plato really had not penetrated to the depth of intelligible substance. Wherefore, Plotinus often attacked their position in his seminars, and wrote the book which we have entitled *Against the Gnostics.* (*Life of Plotinus* 16)[7]

Plotinus wrote a treatise against these individuals (ca. 263 CE), which Porphyry titled *Against the Gnostics*, or *Against Those Who Say that the World and Its Maker Are Evil* (*Ennead* 2.9 [33]). This writing of Plotinus survives today, and it is clear from its content that he was dealing with fellow Platonists who espoused myths in which the world is created by some kind of cosmic accident, do not identify its maker (Gk. *dēmiourgos*, "demiurge") as divine, do not acknowledge Plato as the ultimate philosophical authority, and affirm teachings such as belief in the end of the world or the superiority of humans to certain heavenly powers.[8]

While Plotinus and Irenaeus were very different individuals with very different goals, it is striking that they both encountered individuals called "knowers" who espoused myths regarding creator-gods of ambivalent or downright malevolent mores. The story is complicated by the modern discovery and publication of ancient books, all written in Coptic (the final stage of the Egyptian language), whose content appears to resemble what Irenaeus and Plotinus describe as the thought of the "Gnostics."[9] By far the most important of these books are the Coptic codices found near Nag Hammadi, Egypt (ca. December 1945).[10] With access to these Coptic sources, we may today read the writings of the Gnostics themselves, instead of relying on their ancient opponents for information about them. Although the Nag Hammadi Codices (henceforth NHC) contain a diverse selection of works—some of which are clearly not "Gnostic" in origin—key notions in many of them are that the world was not created by God, and that human beings are of a divine

[7] *Plotinus I. Porphyry on the Life of Plotinus on the Order of His Books. Enneads I. 1–9*, trans. Arthur Hilary Armstrong (Cambridge, MA: Harvard University Press, 1966), 45, trans. modified; see further Dylan M. Burns, *Apocalypse of the Alien God: Platonism and the Exile of Sethian Gnosticism* (Philadelphia: University of Pennsylvania Press, 2014), 2–3, 161–63.

[8] Burns, *Apocalypse of the Alien God*, 32–47.

[9] Bentley Layton, "Prolegomena to the Study of Ancient Gnosticism," in *The Social World of the First Christians: Essays in Honor of Wayne Meeks*, ed. L. Michael White and Larry O. Yarbrough (Minneapolis, MN: Fortress, 1995), 338; David Brakke, *The Gnostics: Myth, Ritual, and Diversity in Early Christianity* (Cambridge, MA: Harvard University Press, 2010), 29–51.

[10] James M. Robinson, *The Nag Hammadi Story*, 2 vols. (Leiden and Boston: Brill, 2014).

nature, in some sense, and are even superior to the world and its creator. It is useful to use the term "Gnosticism" to describe this complex of evidence, which is so distinctive in both ancient and modern contexts.[11] Significantly, a great many of these Gnostic texts from Nag Hammadi are apocalypses.

THE EXTANT CORPUS OF GNOSTIC APOCALYPSES

Indeed, five Nag Hammadi texts include the term "apocalypse" (*apokalupsis*, "revelation") in their titles. Some scholars limit the body of what they would like to call "Gnostic apocalypses" more or less to these documents, thus focusing on the works in NHC V and VII.[12] This chapter rather adopts the approach of Collins to what may be termed the genre "apocalypse": in short, texts where some kind of divine mediator imparts a revelation—i.e., divine knowledge—regarding a transcendent reality.[13] As Collins notes, while many works called "apocalypses" in our various manuscripts fit this bill, there are many other texts that share the content of "apocalypses" but do not have the word "apocalypse" in their title at all.[14] Similarly, while many apocalypses describe a heavenly journey or rapture during which the revelation takes place, many others take place entirely without a heavenly journey. Finally, although the revelatory content of Daniel or the Book of Revelation focuses on the end-times and world history, there are many apocalypses that are "speculative," dealing rather with

[11] Dylan M. Burns, "Providence, Creation, and Gnosticism According to the Gnostics," *JECS* 24, no. 1 (2016): 55–79.

[12] Martin Krause, "Die literarschen Gattungen der Apokalypsen von Nag Hammadi," in *Apocalypticism in the Ancient Mediterranean World and Near East: Proceedings of the International Colloquium on Apocalypticism, Uppsala, August 12–17, 1979*, ed. David Hellholm (Tübingen: Mohr Siebeck, 1983), followed by Hans-Josef Klauck, "Die Himmelfahrt des Paulus (2 Kor 12, 2–4) in der koptischen Paulusapokalypse aus Nag Hammadi (NHC V/2)," *Studien zum Neuen Testament und seiner Umwelt* 10 (1985): 151–90, esp. 160; Gregor Wurst, "Apokalypsen in den Nag Hammadi-Codices," in *Die Nag-Hammadi-Schriften in der Literatur- und Theologiegeschichte des frühen Christentums*, ed. Jens Schröter and Konrad Schwarz (Tübingen: Mohr Siebeck, 2017), 69–70.

[13] Collins, "Introduction"; Collins, "What Is Apocalyptic Literature?"; John J. Collins, "The Genre Apocalypse Reconsidered," *Zeitschrift für Antikes Christentum/Journal of Ancient Christianity* 20, no. 1 (2016): 21–40; cf. Christoph Markschies, "Editorial/Einleitung," *Zeitschrift für Antikes Christentum/Journal of Ancient Christianity* 20, no. 1 (2016): 15–17.

[14] Collins, "Introduction," 2.

cosmological and philosophical lore, such as the makeup of the heavens, the fate of souls after death, or the origin of evil.[15]

These are all important points for delimiting the corpus of Gnostic apocalypses. If we apply Collins's definition of the "genre apocalypse" to our body of extant Gnostic literature, and regard texts commonly called "revelation discourses" (featuring a post-resurrection Jesus Christ as the revelator: see further below) as "apocalypses without a heavenly journey," we count about twenty-five extant apocalypses with Gnostic features.[16] Nearly all of these are preserved in the Nag Hammadi Codices and the Berlin Gnostic Codex (henceforth BG):

The Apocryphon of John (NHC II, 1; III, 1; IV, 1; BG, 2)
The Hypostasis of the Archons (NHC II, 4)[17]
The Wisdom of Jesus Christ (NHC III, 4; BG, 3)
The Apocalypse of Paul (NHC V, 2)
The First Apocalypse of James (NHC V, 3; Codex Tchacos, 2)
The Second Apocalypse of James (NHC V, 4)
The Apocalypse of Adam (NHC V, 5)
The Paraphrase of Shem (NHC VII, 1)[18]
The Apocalypse of Peter (NHC VII, 3)
Zostrianos (NHC VIII,1)
The Letter of Peter to Philip (NHC VIII, 2; Codex Tchacos, 1)
Melchizedek (NHC IX, 1)
Marsanes (NHC X, 1*)[19]
Allogenes (NHC XI, 3)
Pistis Sophia (Codex Askewensis)
The Gospel of Mary (BG, 1)

15 Ibid., 10–12.

16 The list agrees with Attridge, "Valentinian and Sethian Apocalyptic Traditions," 208–09 (who revised in turn the lists of Francis T. Fallon, "The Gnostic Apocalypses," in "Apocalypse: Morphology of a Genre," special issue, *Semeia* 14 [1979]: 123–58, and Frankfurter, "The Legacy of Jewish Apocalypses," 157); cf. also Burns, "Apocalypses among Gnostics and Manichaeans," 360, with divergences noted. See also Michael Kaler, *Flora Tells a Story: The Apocalypse of Paul and Its Contexts* (Waterloo, Ont.: Wilfrid Laurier University Press, 2008), esp. 140–63.

17 Included only with hesitation; this work opens as a letter, but shifts abruptly to a revelatory dialogue without heavenly journey in the second half, a sort of "apocalypse of Norea." See Birger A. Pearson, "Jewish Sources in Gnostic Literature," in *The Literature of the Jewish People in the Period of the Second Temple*, ed. Michael E. Stone (Leiden: Brill, 1984), 464–65.

18 See Michel Roberge, "The Paraphrase of Shem (NH VII, 1) as an Ascent Apocalypse," *Muséon* 113 (2000): 25–54.

19 The frame-narrative here is very fragmentary, but would work well in an apocalyptic context, which is shared by its cousin-treatises *Zostrianos* and *Allogenes.*

Attridge rightly includes a group of texts he calls "revelations without a revelatory frame," i.e., works that presuppose being understood as apocalypses:

The Book of Thomas the Contender (NHC II, 7)
The Dialogue of the Savior (NHC III, 5)
Thunder: Perfect Mind (NHC VI, 2)
The Meaning of Our Great Power (NHC VI, 4)
The Second Treatise of the Great Seth (NHC VII, 2)
Trimorphic Prōtennoia (NHC XIII*, 1)
1 and *2 Jeu* (Codex Brucianus)[20]

Finally, to all these we may add hitherto unknown apocalypses, extant only in Codex Tchacos (TC), first published in 2006: *The Gospel of Judas* (TC, 3) and a very fragmentary work provisionally titled *Allogenes* (TC, 4). The Tchacos apocalypse entitled *James* (TC, 2) is a second, more complete version of the Nag Hammadi work *First Apocalypse of James*; similarly, TC includes a version of the Letter of Peter to Philip. In other words, Codex Tchacos contains almost nothing but apocalypses.[21] The same is true of Nag Hammadi Codex V, where four apocalypses follow a work on cosmology.[22] Clearly, the Gnostics very much liked to read, write, and copy apocalypses. Why?

The short answer is: Gnostics wrote apocalypses for the same reasons that other Christians and Jews wrote apocalypses, namely, to express their thoughts about something in as authoritative a way as

[20] For the latter as "revelation dialogues," see Eric Crégheur, "Édition critique, traduction et introduction des 'deux *Livres de Iéou*' (MS Bruce 96) avec des notes philogiques et textuelles" (PhD diss., Université Laval, Québec City, 2013), 97–98, re Pheme Perkins, *The Gnostic Dialogue: The Early Church and the Crisis of Gnosticism* (New York: Paulist, 1980); Kurt Rudolph, "Der gnostische 'Dialog' als literarisches Genus," in *Gnosis und spätantike Religionsgeschichte* (Leiden: Brill, 1996), 103–22.

[21] Fragments indicate that following the four apocalypses discussed in the previous note, TC also contained a Coptic translation of *Corpus Hermeticum XIII*; Gregor Wurst, "Weitere neue Fragmente aus Codex Tchacos: Zum 'Buch des Allogenes' und zu *Corpus Hermeticum XIII*," in *Judasevangelium und Codex Tchacos: Studien zur religionsgeschichtlichen Verortung einer gnostischen Schriftensammlung*, ed. Enno Edzard Popkes and Gregor Wurst (Tübingen: Mohr Siebeck, 2012), 1–12.

[22] Klauck, "Die Himmelfahrt des Paulus," 159; Françoise Morard, "Les apocalypses du Codex V de Nag Hammadi," in *Les textes de Nag Hammadi et le problème de leur classification: actes du colloque tenu à Québec du 15 au 19 Septembre 1993*, ed. Louis Painchaud and Anne Pasquier (Québec: Presses Université Laval, 1995), 341–57; Markschies, "Editorial/Einleitung," 14; Lautaro Roig Lanzillotta, "The Apocalypse of Paul (NHC V, 2): Cosmology, Anthropology, and Ethics," *Gnosis: Journal of Gnostic Studies* 1 (2016): 112; cf. Wurst, "Apokalypsen in den Nag Hammadi-Codices," 70.

possible, in the absence of a local, living authority upon whom one could fall back. The work that Gnostic apocalypses do and whatever social dynamics we might glimpse behind them are perhaps most clearly highlighted by briefly taking up two case studies.

THE *APOCRYPHON OF JOHN*: APOCALYPSE WITHOUT HEAVENLY JOURNEY OR REVELATION DIALOGUE?

Perhaps the most well-known extant Gnostic work is the *Apocryphon of John* ("secret book of John": henceforth *Ap. John*). It is prized by scholars because it offers a complete and coherent Gnostic myth, beginning with a hymn on the transcendence of the First Principle and its subsequent emanation of the heavenly realm; cosmogony, describing the birth of the monstrous world-creator (*dēmiourgos*) and his construction of the visible cosmos and its demonic administrators; anthropogony, featuring the creation of the First Man, Adam, a divine being; and salvation history, narrating the travails of Adam, his wife Eve, and their progeny, especially those belonging to the lineage of Seth, their third child and bearer of Adam's original divine nature.[23] The text was popular in antiquity, too: we possess five ancient witnesses to it, encompassing four manuscripts (NHC II, 1; III, 1; IV, 1; BG, 2), three translations, two recensions, and one exposé—Irenaeus himself, who recounts a summary of the first part of the text (*Against Heresies* 1.29).

Ap. John is an apocalypse.[24] Its frame-narrative features the titular apostle, who is taunted by Jews before the Temple following the crucifixion. John is tormented, filled with doubt about the heavenly realm from which the Lord had come and to which his followers shall return (NHC II 20–33).[25] Then the sky opens up, the world is illuminated, and:

[23] On the structure of *Ap. John*, see Michael Waldstein, "On the Relation between the Two Parts of the *Apocryphon of John*," in *Der Gottesspruch in der kopt. Literatur: Hans-Martin Schenke zum 65. Geburtstag*, Hallesche Beiträge zur Orientwissenschaft 15, ed. Walter Beltz (Halle and Wittenberg: Institut für Orientalistik der Martin-Luther-Universität, 1995), 99–112; Zlatko Pleše, *Poetics of the Gnostic Universe: Narrative and Cosmology in the Apocryphon of John* (Leiden and Boston: Brill, 2006), 47–66.

[24] Fallon, "The Gnostic Apocalypses," 130; Pearson, "Jewish Sources in Gnostic Literature," 458; Frankfurter, "The Legacy of Jewish Apocalypses," 159–60; Karen L. King, *The Secret Revelation to John* (Cambridge, MA: Harvard University Press, 2006), 183–84.

[25] All passages taken from *Ap. John* in this chapter are from the version preserved in NHC II, 1. Translations are my own, with reference to the Coptic edition of M. Waldstein and Frederick Wisse, eds. and trans., *The Apocryphon of John: Synopsis of Nag Hammadi Codices II, 1; III, 1; and IV, 1 with BG 8502, 2* (Leiden:

[I was afraid—and behold! I] saw in the light [a child, who stood] before me. When I looked [at him, he became] like an old man, and he [changed his] form again, like that of a servant. There was [not several (individuals)] before me. Rather, there was [a likeness with] many forms in the light, and [the images] mingled with one another. [And] the [visage] came to have [three] forms.

[He] said to me: "John, [John], why [do you] doubt? And why [are you] afraid? [Are you] a stranger to this form?—that is, [do not be] faint-hearted! It is I who [am with you (pl.)] always. I [am the Father; I am] the Mother; I am the [Son. I am the undefiled] one and the uncorrupted one." (1.20–33)

The revelator of heavenly knowledge is not only Jesus, but also the rest of the "trinity" of Father, Mother, and Son—as divine a heavenly mediator as can be.[26] It is a literary *topos* of ancient Jewish and Christian apocalypses for seers to be in a sorry state, and to be told by the heavenly mediator to buck up and pull themselves together before the revelation gets underway (so 2 Bar. 22:2–8, 55:4–8; *Apocalypse of Adam*, NHC V [66].17–21; Zostrianos, NHC VIII 4.8–13). There is no heavenly journey; on earth, Jesus explains the history of the entire universe. It begins with the primordial manifestation of the divine realm, a procession of different *aeons* ("ages, eternities") with the names of various cognitive and psychological faculties. In other words, the "cosmic trip" that *Ap. John* and other Gnostic myths relate is ultimately not into a heaven in the sky, but into the human mind—the true heaven, and home to God. Meanwhile, the *aeons'* praise of the transcendent God, as they emerge, recalls ancient Jewish traditions regarding the angels' praise of God before the celestial throne, in turn reflecting an idealization of the court of a Hellenistic monarch.[27] The work goes on explain the appearance of the demiurge Yaldabaoth, his creation of the world and his subjects—a perversion of the heavenly court—and the divine origin of Adam, the first human being.[28] It is worth noting that while "history" in *Ap. John* is conceived in terms of salvation history, the work defies the

Brill, 1995). Citations in parentheses are to the page and line number in the manuscript.

[26] Dylan M. Burns, "Self-Begotten, Not Equal: The Pre-existence of Christ and the Elect in the *Apocryphon of John* (NHC, II, 1 and par.)," in *Perspektiven zur Präexistenz im Frühjudentum und frühen Christentum*, ed. Jörg Frey and Ruth-Friederike Kunath (Tübingen: Mohr Siebeck, in press).

[27] Pleše, *Poetics*, 140–41.

[28] Ibid., 118–21; King, *The Secret Revelation to John*, 86, 168–71.

notion that Gnostic apocalypses have "very little interest in history or eschatological crises."[29]

Several times, the narrative breaks off for John to pose further questions regarding the story of creation, the origin of evil, and the postmortem fate of human souls,[30] including a novel rendition of the tale of the descent of angels to mate with human beings (29.17–30.11, re Gen 6:1–4; 1 En. 6–8).[31] The text concludes with Jesus telling John not to accept money or material goods in return for this revealed knowledge, and John returns to the other disciples to teach them what he has learned (31.34–32.5). Many apocalypses conclude with instructions regarding their own publication.[32] The entire frame-narrative—a persecuted follower of Jesus who receives on earth a revelation that is both visual and auditory, and who shares it by writing to an insider-group—does not only seek to supplement John's Gospel, but closely recalls the situation of John of Patmos, putative author of the Book of Revelation.[33]

The question-answer format has also led scholars to refer to *Ap. John* as a "revelation dialogue,"[34] and strictly speaking, this is not inaccurate. The phrase "revelation dialogue" recalls that of the "Gnostic dialogue" or "gospel dialogue" (*Evangeliendialog*; also *dialogische Evangelien*): works featuring Jesus's appearance after the resurrection, and his subsequent leadership of a dialogue.[35] A great deal of earlier scholarship focused on the "Gnostic" vs. "Christian" character of the "Gnostic dialogue," as well as its ostensible roots in more readily

[29] Collins, "Introduction,"13.

[30] Waldstein, "On the Relation between the Two Parts of the Apocryphon of John," 100–03.

[31] Pearson, "Jewish Sources in Gnostic Literature," 453–55; followed by Frankfurter, "The Legacy of Jewish Apocalypses," 159; more recently, Claudia Losekam, *Die Sünde der Engel: Die Engelfalltradition in frühjüdischen und gnostischen Texten* (Tübingen: Mohr Siebeck, 2010), 167–83; Christian Bull, "Women, Angels, and Dangerous Knowledge: The Myth of the Watchers in the *Apocryphon of John* and Its Monastic Manuscript-Context," in *Women and Knowledge in Early Christianity*, ed. Ulla Tervahauta et al. (Leiden and Boston: Brill, 2017), 75–107.

[32] Collins, "Introduction," 8.

[33] Karen L. King, "The *Apocryphon of John*: Genre and Christian Re-making of the World," in *Die Nag-Hammadi-Schriften in der Literatur- und Theologiegeschichte des frühen Christentums*, ed. Jens Schröter and Konrad Schwarz (Tübingen: Mohr Siebeck, 2017), 148–50, esp. n. 28, re Rev 1:4.9–20; 22:16.

[34] Judith Hartenstein, *Die zweite Lehre: Erscheinungen des Auferstandenen als Rahmenerzählungen frühchristlicher Dialoge*, Texte und Untersuchungen 146 (Berlin: de Gruyter, 2000), 68.

[35] So Rudolph, "Der gnostische 'Dialog' als literarisches Genus"; Perkins, *The Gnostic Dialogue*; Hartenstein, *Die zweite Lehre*, 1–2.

identifiable biblical or Greek genres.[36] Yet there is nothing particularly "Gnostic" about revelatory phenomena, except perhaps that all revelations connote some acquisition of very important knowledge.[37] Revelatory knowledge is not contingent on any particular type of content: it could concern anything, and the rhetorical goals of the apocalypses are diverse indeed, even within the Gnostic corpus.[38] If there is any "Gnosticism" in the "Gnostic dialogue," it is not the *revelatory setting* itself, but the *content* of the revelation: the differentiation of God and demiurge, and some kind of divine nature of at least a portion of humanity, themes absolutely central to *Ap. John*. The heavy overlap of the categories "apocalypse" and "revelation dialogue" is already evident in the terms themselves, since *apokalupsis* is simply the Greek word for "revelation," and many apocalypses employ the dialogue format.[39] Formally speaking, there is then no difference between the "Gnostic dialogue" and an "apocalypse without heavenly journey," since the risen Christ constitutes a very otherworldly being transmitting heavenly knowledge.[40]

These "revelation dialogues" often do not describe this transmission as taking place by vision,[41] a fact that leads some to argue they should not be reckoned as apocalypses.[42] Even setting aside the assumption that visionary language is essential to the genre "apocalypse," its ostensible absence in Gnostic literature should not be overemphasized.[43] Gnostic visionary texts include the *Apocalypse of Peter*, *Apocalypse of Adam*, and *Apocalypse of Paul* (henceforth *Apoc. Paul*) (see below). While the communicative medium of *Ap. John* is speech, it contains deeply vivid accounts, such as the description of the bestial appearances of the demiurge and archons. So the birth of the demiurge Yaldabaoth, son of Sophia (Wisdom):

[36] Hartenstein, *Die zweite Lehre*, 5–19, re Rudolph, "Der gnostische 'Dialog' als literarisches Genus"; Philipp Vielhauer, *Geschichte der urchristlichen Literatur. Einleitung in das Neue Testament, die Apokryphen und die Apostolischen Väter* (Berlin: de Gruyter, 1985), 690–92.

[37] Burns, "Apocalypses among Gnostics and Manichaeans," 368–69.

[38] Collins, "What Is Apocalyptic Literature?," 6; Burns, "Apocalypses among Gnostics and Manichaeans," 361–64 (respectively).

[39] Collins, "Introduction," 6.

[40] Ibid., 14; cf. Hartenstein, *Die zweite Lehre*, 13.

[41] Collins, "Introduction," 13; Fallon, "The Gnostic Apocalypses," 125; Perkins, *The Gnostic Dialogue*, 52.

[42] Krause, "Die literarschen Gattungen der Apokalypsen," 629; Vielhauer, *Geschichte der urchristlichen Literatur*, 690–91; Hartenstein, *Die zweite Lehre*, 13.

[43] *Pace* Vielhauer, *Geschichte der urchristlichen Literatur*, 488.

> he changed into the shape of a lion-faced serpent. His eyes were like fires of lightning, flashing. His mother cast him away from herself, outside of those places, so that no one among the immortals would see him, for it was in ignorance that she had created him. She surrounded him with a luminous cloud, and she placed a throne in the middle of the cloud, lest anyone see him, except for the Holy Spirit, who is called, "the mother of the living." And she (Sophia) named him Yaltabaoth; he is the first archon. (10.7–20)

In fact, *Ap. John* begins with vision, the theophany of the triune revelator (of the appearance of the revelator himself).[44] Even the apocalypses *Zostrianos* and *Marsanes*—which, together with *Allogenes*, constitute the most abstruse Gnostic apocalypses, whose discourses deal with Greek philosophy—describe the celestial "crowns" worn in heaven.[45] As throughout the Gnostic corpus, heavenly beings in these Platonizing works descend to impart revelations, seers ascend on clouds, records of the revelation are left for posterity on mountains or even in the sky, and more.[46] Most importantly, language about light and luminosity—*the raw material of vision*—is ubiquitous in this literature.

To be sure, *Ap. John* exemplifies the complexity inherent in questions of genre, insofar as it adopts not only many elements of apocalyptic literature, but extra-biblical genres such as the Greek novel.[47] All of the chief genres under which the text has been denoted—"gospel," "wisdom," and "apocalypse"—are modern scholarly constructions, not categories employed by the ancient authors in question. Their mutual permeability and overlap are notorious, and texts exhibiting their features do not exclusively belong to *any* single genre.[48] What is clear, however, is that Gnostic "revelation dialogues" are formally and thematically indistinguishable from Gnostic "apocalypses" and should be reckoned alongside them, rather than as belonging to an exclusive

44 Pleše, *Poetics*, 25–40.

45 Dylan M. Burns, "Sethian Crowns, Sethian Martyrs? Jewish Apocalyptic and Christian Martyrology in a Gnostic Literary Tradition," *Numen* 61, nos. 5–6 (2014): 555–56.

46 For a survey, see Burns, *Apocalypse of the Alien God*, 53–58.

47 Pleše, *Poetics*, 14–73; King, *The Secret Revelation to John*, 184–90; King, "The *Apocryphon of John*," 155–60.

48 *Inter alii*, King, "The *Apocryphon of John*," 150–55.

category all their own. Their segmentation obscures their many common literary elements, their shared venues of transmission and survival (the same Coptic codices), and, perhaps, a common purpose that largely hinges upon their common use of pseudepigraphy: the claim to authority where there is none for the views in question, whether from a revealing angel or from the risen Christ himself.[49]

THE NAG HAMMADI *APOCALYPSE OF PAUL* AND THE QUESTION OF VALENTINIAN APOCALYPSES

The problem of who wrote these pseudonymous Gnostic apocalypses and why may be clarified, if not exactly solved, through a brief look at *Apoc. Paul* (NHC V, 2).[50] While *Ap. John* is an apocalypse without heavenly journey, *Apoc. Paul* features a heavenly journey showcasing the judgment and punishment of souls after their death.[51] It begins with the apostle Paul himself, who, on the road to Jerusalem, meets a "holy spirit" who resembles a small boy. Standing on the mountain of Jericho,[52] Paul then begins his ascent, even gazing upon his body on earth below as he rises to the fourth heaven ([19].8–[20].5; cf. 2 Cor 12:2–4).[53] He sees an angel flogging and bringing forth a soul to the gate of the fourth heaven. A toll-collector (*telōnēs*) rebukes the soul for its sins; it pleads innocence, but witnesses to its guilt are produced, and it is "cast below … into [a] body which had been prepared [for it]" ([21].18–21).

49 Cf. Perkins, *The Gnostic Dialogue*, 19; Frankfurter, "The Legacy of Jewish Apocalypses," 152.

50 In this section I summarize points made in full in Dylan M. Burns, "Is the *Apocalypse of Paul* a Valentinian Apocalypse? Pseudepigraphy and Group Definition in NHC V, 2," in *Die Nag-Hammadi-Schriften in der Literatur- und Theologiegeschichte des frühen Christentums*, ed. Jens Schröter and Konrad Schwarz (Tübingen: Mohr Siebeck, 2017), 97–112.

51 Not to be confused with another *Apocalypse of Paul* that also deals with the postmortem fate of the soul, but is considerably longer, much better attested across a variety of languages and manuscripts, and entirely without features that recall Gnostic traditions. Given the prominence of this work in Latin manuscripts, it is commonly referred to as *Visio Pauli*. See Jan N. Bremmer and István Czachesz, eds., *The Visio Pauli and the Gnostic Apocalypse of Paul* (Leuven: Peeters, 2007).

52 On which, see Mathew Twigg, "The Mountain of Jericho in the Nag Hammadi *Apocalypse of Paul*: A Suggestion," *Vigiliae Christianae* 69 (2015): 1–21.

53 All translations of *Apoc. Paul* in this article are my own, with reference to the Coptic in the edition of William Murdock and George R. MacRae, ed. and trans., "NHC V, 2: The Apocalypse of Paul," in *Nag Hammadi Codices V, 2–5 and VI with Papyrus Berlinensis 8502, 1 and 4*, ed. Douglas M. Parrott (Leiden: Brill, 1979), 47–64.

Paul sees other punishing angels in the fifth heaven, and another toll-collector in the sixth, before coming to an "old man" in the seventh:

> And I looked at the spirit, and he was nodding his head, saying to me, "speak with him." And I said to the old man, "I shall go to the place from which I came."
>
> And the old man replied to me, "Where are you from?"
>
> But I responded, "I shall descend unto the world of the mortals, so that I might take captive the captivity which was taken captive in the captivity of Babylon."
>
> The old man said to me, "How will you be able to escape from me? Look, and see the principalities and the authorities."
>
> [The] spirit said, "Give him [the] token which is in your hand. And [he shall] open up for you."
>
> And then I gave [him] the token. He bowed his [head] to the ground, together with those who belong to him, the authorities.
>
> And [then] the <seventh> heaven opened up, and we ascended [to the] eighth (heaven). Now, I saw the twelve apostles. They greeted me (*au^{e}raspaze ^{e}mmoi*), and we went up to the ninth heaven. I greeted (*ai^{e}raspaze*) all those who were in the ninth heaven, and we ascended to the tenth heaven. And I greeted my fellow spirits. ([23].5–[2]4.8)

Apoc. Paul is a work that is brief, but full of mystery. Its description of the punishment, trial, and reincarnation of souls, and of the heavenly "toll-collector," puts it in the good company of ancient Mediterranean ascent literature offering guided tours of judgment (cf. *Testament of Abraham* 10) and punishment.[54] Paul's meeting with apostles in heaven (a heavenly "Jerusalem"; cf. Gal 2:1–9; 4:26) and with his "fellow spirits" (who are they?) leads the reader to ask whether the text aims to reconcile the apostles with their competitor Paul, or if it establishes Paul's authority as exceeding that of the Twelve?[55] Is the text "Gnostic" at all? The "old man" in the seventh heaven is clearly inspired by the Ancient of Days (Dan 7:9), but is he a malevolent demiurge to be overcome (whose "principalities and authorities" are none other than nasty archons), or is he a more

[54] Klauck, "Die Himmelfahrt des Paulus," 182–83; Lanzillotta, "The Apocalypse of Paul," 118–20; Wurst, "Apokalypsen in den Nag Hammadi-Codices," 73.

[55] Lanzillotta, "The Apocalypse of Paul," 117–18; Kaler, *Flora Tells a Story*, 217–20.

ambivalent figure?[56] Finally, why *ten* heavens, a schema more typical of Hermetic than Gnostic sources?[57]

Apoc. Paul also raises important questions about who produced Gnostic apocalypses and why. The reason for this is, once again, Irenaeus of Lyons. In a chapter of book 2 of his *Against Heresies*, he is engaged in a lengthy attack on the thought of the followers of the second-century Christian Platonist Valentinus, whose teachings Irenaeus claims to have been rooted in that of the Gnostics (*Against Heresies* 1.11.1). Irenaeus writes that there are some who maintain that the apostle Paul had knowledge of supernal realities beyond the realm of the demiurge, who is an ambivalent (if not exactly evil) figure in Valentinian thought. Irenaeus counters that 2 Cor 12:2–4 is a problematic text for such individuals, since Paul here writes that he had ascended to only the third heaven; yet in Valentinian theology as Irenaeus understands it, the third heaven is where the demiurge resides. Therefore, the Valentinians must believe that when Paul talks about ascending to a second and third heaven in 2 Cor 12, he actually is referring to heavens beyond that (*Against Heresies* 2.30.7). Irenaeus imagines other aspects of what a Valentinian exegesis of the passage might look like: would it describe the heavenly world beyond the third heaven, or how Paul could leave the body in making his ascent, his journey past the demiurge? All these features are paralleled in *Apoc. Paul*. The parallels do not show that Irenaeus knew the text, but that *Apoc. Paul* may be a translation of a text as old as the second century CE, when the sort of ideas Irenaeus had in mind were already circulating, and dialogue between Valentinians and the "proto-orthodox" was still possible.[58] While some studies have suggested parallels between elements of the theology of *Apoc. Paul* and distinctively Valentinian thought,[59] others have regarded these parallels

[56] See, e.g., Kaler, *Flora Tells a Story*, 61–63; Matthew Twigg, "Becoming Paul, Becoming Christ: The Nag Hammadi Apocalypse of Paul (NHC V, 2) in Its Valentinian Context" (PhD diss., Oxford University, 2015), 19; Lanzillotta, "The Apocalypse of Paul," 118.

[57] Klauck, "Die Himmelfahrt des Paulus," 185–87; Kaler, *Flora Tells a Story*, 168–71; Lanzillotta, "The Apocalypse of Paul," 122–25.

[58] Michael Kaler, Louis Painchaud, and Marie-Pierre Bussières, "The Coptic *Apocalypse of Paul*, Irenaeus' *Adversus Haereses* 2.30.7, and the Second-Century Battle for Paul's Legacy," *JECS* 12, no. 2 (2004): 178–87; Kaler, *Flora Tells a Story*, 49–59.

[59] Kaler, *Flora Tells a Story*, 64–73; Twigg, "Becoming Paul, Becoming Christ"; Twigg, "The Mountain of Jericho in the Nag Hammadi *Apocalypse of Paul*"; Michael S. Domeracki, "The Apocalypse of Paul (NHC V, 2) as a Valentininan Baptismal Liturgy of Ascent," *Gnosis: Journal of Gnostic Studies* 2 (2017), 212–34.

with skepticism, particularly given the striking absence of any other extant apocalypses with ostensibly Valentinian provenance (excepting perhaps the *First Apocalypse of James*, which utilizes material that has also appeared in Valentinian contexts).[60]

Thematic parallels aside, we also have little reason to expect that the well-known Valentinian teachers of the second and third centuries CE composed apocalypses at all, *precisely because they were well known.*[61] A useful comparison may be made with the Dead Sea community at Qumran that produced writings with much apocalyptic content, but no apocalypses. A possible reason for this strange fact is that, in Second Temple Judaism, the practice of pseudepigraphy seems to coincide with environments of low social cohesion, where there is an absence of living authority to which one may appeal for support for one's views.[62] Such a living authority was present in the Dead Sea sect, and so the sect's members did not need to resort to pseudepigraphy. The case may be similar to that of the Valentinian teachers like Valentinus or Ptolemy, who were highly educated. Famous in their day, they appear to have taught their interpretations of Scripture in environments resembling those of the philosophical groups in which they had trained, with an identifiable individual as head of the circle. The case is altogether different with the Gnostics, who seem to have only produced anonymous revelatory works.[63] There is

[60] See Attridge, "Valentinian and Sethian Apocalyptic Traditions," 182; Einar Thomassen, "The Valentinian Materials in *James* (NHC V, 3 and CT, 2)," in *Beyond the Gnostic Gospels: Studies Building on the Work of Elaine Pagels*, ed. Eduard Iricinschi, Lance Jenott, Nicola Denzey Lewis, and Philippa Townsend (Tübingen: Mohr Siebeck, 2013), 79–90; cf. Kaler, *Flora Tells a Story*, 67.

[61] While there is a legend reported by an anonymous heresiologist (*Refutation of All Heresies* 6.42.2) that Valentinus authorized his teachings by referring to a vision of a newborn babe identified as the Logos, there is no evidence to suggest that Valentinus actually wrote an apocalypse, or that *Apoc. Paul* is inspired by this legend. Irenaeus does note that the followers of Marcus the Magician write and circulate apocryphal texts (*Against Heresies* 1.20.1), but it is not strong evidence upon which to make any claims about a wider Valentinian approach to pseudepigrapha. On these points, see Burns, "Is the *Apocalypse of Paul* a Valentinian Apocalypse?," 101–04; cf. Kaler, *Flora Tells a Story*, 68; Twigg, "Becoming Paul, Becoming Christ," 170; Domeracki, "The Apocalypse of Paul (NHC V, 2) as a Valentininan Baptismal Liturgy of Ascent," 217.

[62] John J. Collins, "Pseudepigraphy and Group Formation in Second Temple Judaism," in *Pseudepigraphic Perspectives: The Apocrypha and Pseudepigrapha in Light of the Dead Sea Scrolls; Proceedings of the International Symposium of the Orion Center for the Study of the Dead Sea Scrolls and Associated Literature, 12–14 January, 1997*, ed. Esther G. Chazon and Michael Stone (Leiden: Brill, 1999), 56.

[63] David Brakke, "Scriptural Practices in Early Christianity: Towards a New History of the New Testament Canon," in *Invention, Rewriting, Usurpation: Discursive Fights*

no author to whom we can attribute composition of any "classic Gnostic" work like *Ap. John*, including all the Gnostic apocalypses. The anonymous character of these texts may even indicate that their authors intended for the reader to identify *themselves* with the narrator; thus, the narrator's journey into the divine mind would be a journey into one's *own* mind.[64] This may indicate that the circles in which these texts were produced resembled religious subcultures that existed within or on the fringes of larger Christian groups.[65] This seems to have been precisely the situation Porphyry reports in Rome in the 260s, where there were Christians who were very knowledgeable about Plato and were circulating "revelations," i.e., apocalypses. These Christians probably did not constitute an independent "church" founded on these apocalyptic scriptures. Rather, they were likely members of larger ecclesial communities who also happened to have more specific interests in Platonism—and in apocalypses "of Zoroaster and Zostrianos and Nicotheus and Allogenes and Messos and others of this sort."[66]

IMPORTANCE AND RECEPTION HISTORY

The Gnostic apocalypses are of great importance for our understanding of late ancient philosophy and religion, even beyond the study of apocalyptic literature. This importance lies primarily in their history of reception, particularly in the contexts of (1) later Greek philosophy, (2) Jewish mysticism, (3) Coptic literature, (4) Manichaeism, and (5) early Islam.

This reception history begins with those Platonizing Christians reading apocalypses, some of whose titles Porphyry rattles off for posterity. Among the works discovered at Nag Hammadi are apocalypses with titles identical to some of those Porphyry mentions: *Zostrianos* and *Allogenes*. These Coptic apocalypses are replete with the terminology of third-century Greek philosophy, itself a *sui generis*

over Religious Traditions in Antiquity, ed. Jörg Ulrich, Anders-Christian Jacobson, and David Brakke (Frankfurt am Main: Lang, 2011), 263–80.

64 David Brakke, "Pseudonymity, Gnosis, and the Self in Gnostic Literature," *Gnosis: Journal of Gnostic Studies* 2 (2017), 194–211; see also Dylan M. Burns, "Apophatic Strategies in *Allogenes* (NHC XI, 3)," *Harvard Theological Review* 103, no. 2 (2010): 175–77.

65 Alan B. Scott, "Churches or Books? Sethian Social Organization," *JECS* 3, no. 2 (1995), 109–22; Williams, *Rethinking Gnosticism*, 109–15; Kaler, *Flora Tells a Story*, 164; Michael Kaler, "The Cultic Milieu, the Nag Hammadi Collectors and Gnosticism," *Religious Studies* 38 (2009), 427–44.

66 Burns, "Is the *Apocalypse of Paul* a Valentinian Apocalypse?," 110.

phenomenon. Even more, *Zostrianos* includes a long segment of text that appears to share a source about the transcendent deity with the fourth-century theologian (and teacher of St. Augustine) Marius Victorinus; the content of this source resembles in turn that of the anonymous Turin *Commentary on Plato's Parmenides*, a fascinating work whose provenance and place in the Platonic tradition remain under debate. The question of the precise relationship between these sources is a vexed one about which there remains no scholarly consensus, except that these Gnostic apocalypses are of enormous importance for our understanding of the development of later Greek philosophy.[67] It is worth adding that following Plotinus's and Porphyry's conflict with the Gnostics, Greek philosophers all but ceased from citing Judeo-Christian sources; the Gnostic apocalypses appear to have catalyzed this "acute Hellenization" of the Platonic tradition.[68] Remarkably, these same "Platonizing" Gnostic apocalypses are also full of language regarding the ascension, glorification, and transformation of the seer—even into an angel—culminating in the protagonist's participation in the praise of the deity in heaven among the other celestial powers, a *Leitmotiv* of ancient and medieval Jewish mysticism.[69] Our sources for the development of Jewish mysticism in late antiquity—the period between the floruit of the ancient Jewish apocalypses and the early medieval *Hekhalot* ("palaces") literature—are very poor.[70] The Gnostic apocalypses that were composed and copied precisely in this same period thus provide us with an invaluable window into the transformation of Jewish mystical traditions in a formative stage where we have otherwise little evidence.[71]

However, within their transmission in Egypt, these apocalypses may have assumed entirely different kinds of importance. Scholarship has recently come to emphasize the importance of reading our extant

[67] On all these questions see most recently John D. Turner, "The Anonymous *Parmenides* Commentary, Marius Victorinus, and the Sethian Platonizing Apocalypses: State of the Question," in *Gnose et Manichéisme: entre les oasis d'Égypte et la Route de la Soie; hommage à Jean-Daniel Dubois*, ed. Anna van den Kerchove and Luciana Gabriela Soares Santoprete (Turnhout: Brepols, 2017), 93–126.

[68] Burns, *Apocalypse of the Alien God*, 147–54.

[69] Ibid., 112–39.

[70] Annette Yoshiko Reed, "Rethinking (Jewish-)Christian Evidence for Jewish Mysticism," in *Hekhalot Literature in Context: Between Byzantium and Babylonia*, ed. Ra'anan Boustan, Martha Himmelfarb, and Peter Schäfer (Tübingen: Mohr Siebeck, 2013), 354.

[71] Cf. Philip J. Alexander, "Comparing Merkavah Mysticism and Gnosticism: An Essay in Method," *Journal of Jewish Studies* 35, no. 1 (1984): 1–18.

Coptic Gnostic material with respect to the one context in which we know it was written and read, namely Coptic Egypt. Egyptian monasticism, which began flourishing in the early fourth century CE, may constitute an important context for the transmission of Gnostic apocalypses, because we know that many monks of the fourth and fifth centuries were very interested in revelations, visions, and other aspects of apocryphal and apocalyptic literature; the otherworldly concerns and disparagement of the body characteristic of many Gnostic texts could have been appealing in a purely ascetic context. Consequently, monks read, shared, and copied apocrypha, at times to the displeasure of their superiors.[72] It is thus also worthwhile to read our Coptic Gnostic materials as *Coptic* literature, rather than simply *Gnostic* literature, and certain aspects of the Gnostic apocalypses are sometimes most intelligible from this angle. A fine example presents itself in the greeting formulae used in *Apoc. Paul*: as we read above, "Paul" says, "they greeted me, and we went up to the ninth heaven. I greeted all those who were in the ninth heaven, and we ascended to the tenth heaven. And I greeted my fellow spirits." It is uncharacteristic of ascent literature for characters to greet one another with a kiss in heaven, as do Paul and the apostles, but it is quite normal in many Coptic texts, particularly martyrdoms.[73]

Finally, the matrix of Gnostic and apocalyptic traditions—if not actual Gnostic apocalypses—appears to have been central to the emergence of two new religions in late antiquity: Manichaeism and Islam. The miniature papyrus codex known as the Cologne Mani Codex (first published in the 1970s and 1980s) sheds invaluable new light on early Manichaean tradition about the religion's founder, particularly in sections that quote "apocalypses" of Adam, Sethel, Enosh, Shem, and Enoch in order to validate the putative revelations of Mani himself.[74] It is thus likely that Mani developed his earliest religious ideas in an environment in which apocalyptic literature circulated, and the prominence of the tale of the fall of the Watchers in his mythography,

[72] Frankfurter, "The Legacy of Jewish Apocalypses," 170–96; Hugo Lundhaug and Lance Jenott, *The Monastic Origins of the Nag Hammadi Codices* (Tübingen: Mohr Siebeck, 2015), 146–77.

[73] Julio Cesar Dias Chaves, "From the *Apocalypse of Paul* to Coptic Epic Passions: Greeting Paul and the Martyrs in Heaven," in *The Nag Hammadi Codices in the Context of Fourth-and Fifth-Century Christianity in Egypt*, ed. Hugo Lundhaug and Lance Jenott (Tübingen: Mohr Siebeck, 2018), 174–80; cf. Kaler, *Flora Tells a Story*, 214–17.

[74] John C. Reeves, *Heralds of That Good Realm: Syro-Mesopotamian Gnosis and Jewish Traditions* (Leiden: Brill, 1996).

together with the presence in the Manichaean canon of a *Book of the Giants*, evinces some kind of dependence on Enochic tradition.[75] The many parallels between Gnostic and Manichaean works, and their emergence from a similar matrix of Jewish and Christian apocalyptic traditions,[76] raise the question of whether Gnostic apocalypses were among those known to the young Mani. Meanwhile, Islam is increasingly regarded today as emerging from a late antique context dominated by religions with significant apocalyptic elements (Judaism, Zoroastrianism, and Christianity), and in which the massive war between Byzantium and Iran stoked eschatological speculations.[77] Gnostic sources appear to have been among those apocalyptic elements present in the first Islamic centuries, particularly among Shiʿite groups broadly indebted to ancient Gnostic and Manichaean ideas, such as the Ghulat ("extremists").[78] A treatment of the parts of the human body and their associations with their respective heavenly spheres found in *Ap. John* appears in an only slightly different form in the early Shiʿite apocalypse *Umm al-kitāb*, which became a significant text among the Ismāʿīlīs.[79]

The reception of ancient Gnostic literature beyond the context of the first centuries CE is among the most promising and enticing of new horizons opening up in the study of Gnosticism and apocalypticism alike. The perspective of the *longue durée* reminds us that, while our

[75] John C. Reeves, *Jewish Lore in Manichaean Cosmogony: Studies in the Book of Giants Traditions* (Cincinnati, OH: Hebrew Union College Press, 1992); Matthew Goff, Loren T. Stuckenbruck, and Enrico Morano, eds., *Ancient Tales of Giants from Qumran and Turfan* (Tübingen: Mohr Siebeck, 2016).

[76] Burns, *Apocalypse of the Alien God*, 143–45; Jason D. BeDuhn, "Secrets of Heaven: Manichaean Cosmology in Its Late Antique Context," in *Gnose et Manichéisme: entre les oasis d'Égypte et la Route de la Soie; hommage à Jean Daniel Dubois*, ed. Anna van den Kerchove and Luciana Gabriela Soares Santoprete (Turnhout: Brepols, 2017), 195–214.

[77] Robert Hoyland, "Early Islam as a Late Antique Religion," in *The Oxford Handbook of Late Antiquity*, ed. Scott Fitzgerald Johnson (Oxford: Oxford University Press, 2012), 1066–67; see also Michael Pregill, "Ahab, Bar Kokhba, Muhammad, and the Lying Spirit: Prophetic Discourse before and after the Rise of Islam," in *Revelation, Literature, and Community in Late Antiquity*, ed. Philippa Townsend and Moulie Vidas (Tübingen: Mohr Siebeck, 2011), 271–313.

[78] See Mushegh Asatryan and Dylan M. Burns, "Is Ghulat Religion Islamic Gnosticism? Religious Transitions in Late Antiquity," in *Esotérisme shiʿite: ses racines et ses prolongements*, ed. Mohammad Ali Amir-Moezzi (Turnhout: Brepols, 2016), 55–86.

[79] Einar Thomassen, "The *Melothesia* of the *Apocryphon of John* and the *Umm al-kitab*," in *Gnose et Manichéisme: entre les oasis d'Égypte et la Route de la Soie; hommage à Jean-Daniel Dubois*, ed. Anna van den Kerchove and Luciana Gabriela Soares Santoprete (Turnhout: Brepols, 2017), 161–72.

only extant ancient Gnostic texts survive for us in the Coptic codices which lay hidden in Egypt for around 1500 years, the traditions they contain did not exactly die out. They were transmitted, transformed, rediscovered, and reinvented by individuals and in ways entirely remote from the purposes of the ancient Gnostic authors and Egyptian scribes—a process of discovery and invention in which we continue to take part today when we take up these ancient Coptic texts and speak of the Gnostic apocalypses.

Selected Further Reading

Attridge, Harold W. "Valentinian and Sethian Apocalyptic Traditions." *Journal of Early Christian Studies* 8, no. 2 (2000): 173–211.

Brakke, David M. "Scriptural Practices in Early Christianity: Towards a New History of the New Testament Canon." In *Invention, Rewriting, Usurpation: Discursive Fights over Religious Traditions in Antiquity*, 263–80. Edited by Jörg Ulrich, Anders-Christian Jacobson, and David Brakke. Frankfurt am Main: Lang, 2011.

Burns, Dylan M. *Apocalypse of the Alien God: Platonism and the Exile of Sethian Gnosticism*. Divinations. Philadelphia: University of Pennsylvania Press, 2014.

Collins, John J. "Introduction: Towards the Morphology of a Genre." In "Apocalypse: The Morphology of a Genre." Edited by John J. Collins. Special issue, *Semeia* 14 (1979): 1–19.

Frankfurter, David. "The Legacy of Jewish Apocalypses in Early Christianity: Regional Trajectories." In *The Jewish Apocalyptic Heritage in Early Christianity*, 129–200. Edited by James C. VanderKam and William Adler. Minneapolis, MN: Fortress, 1996.

Hartenstein, Judith. *Die zweite Lehre: Erscheinungen des Auferstandenen als Rahmenerzählungen frühchristlicher Dialoge*. Texte und Untersuchungen zur Geschichte der altchristlichen Literatur 146. Berlin: de Gruyter, 2000.

Kaler, Michael. *Flora Tells a Story: The Apocalypse of Paul and Its Contexts*. Waterloo, Ont.: Wilfrid Laurier University Press, 2008.

Pregill, Michael. "Ahab, Bar Kokhba, Muhammad, and the Lying Spirit: Prophetic Discourse before and after the Rise of Islam." In *Revelation, Literature, and Community in Late Antiquity*, 271–313. Edited by Philippa Townsend and Moulie Vidas. Tübingen: Mohr Siebeck, 2011.

Reeves, John C. *Heralds of That Good Realm: Syro-Mesopotamian Gnosis and Jewish Traditions*. Leiden: Brill, 1996.

Wurst, Gregor. "Apokalypsen in den Nag Hammadi-Codices." In *Die Nag-Hammadi-Schriften in der Literatur- und Theologiegeschichte des frühen Christentums*, 69–78. Edited by Jens Schröter and Konrad Schwarz. Tübingen: Mohr Siebeck, 2017.

5 Exegeting the Apocalypse with the Donatist Communion

JESSE A. HOOVER

INTRODUCTION

When assessing the apocalyptic perspectives of minority movements in late antiquity—indeed, in every era—it is all too easy to succumb to caricature. We should be on guard against the temptation to rely on contemporary accounts uncritically, often composed as they are by hostile authors with their own reasons for highlighting the eschatological oddities of their opponents. Unfortunately, such has often been the case when in evaluations of the apocalyptic exegesis of the Donatist church of North Africa. Following the lead of Augustine of Hippo, who was not above portraying his rivals as apocalyptic fanatics when it suited him,[1] twentieth-century historians often characterized the dissident communion as a movement obsessed with the end. Notice, for instance, the assessment of W. H. C. Frend, "A dissenting church whose members lived in a world of prophetic and apocalyptic hopes,"[2] or Gerald Bonner, "Characterized by an ascetic hostility to the social order ... and an urgent expectation of the end of the world."[3] Similarly, the dissident communion's millenarian tendencies have often been taken for granted,[4] despite the fact that the only two references to the

[1] See, for instance, Augustine, Letter 76.2, in *The Works of Saint Augustine: A Translation for the 21st Century* (*WSA*), ed. and trans. John Rotelle and Boniface Ramsey (New York: New City Press, 1990–), 2.1:299.

[2] W. H. C. Frend, "'And I Have Other Sheep'—John 10:16," in *The Making of Orthodoxy: Essays in Honour of Henry Chadwick*, ed. Rowan Williams (Cambridge: Cambridge University Press, 1989), 31.

[3] Gerald Bonner, "Quid imperatori cum ecclesia? St. Augustine on History and Society," *Augustinian Studies* 2 (1971): 237.

[4] See for example, Jean-Paul Brisson, *Autonomisme et christianisme dans l'Afrique romaine: de Septime Sévère à l'invasion vandale* (Paris: Éditions E. de Boccard, 1958), 398–99; W. H. C. Frend, "Popular Religion and Christological Controversy in the Fifth Century," in *Popular Belief and Practice*, ed. G. J. Cumming and D. Baker (Cambridge: Cambridge University Press, 1971), 20; Bonner, "Quid imperatori cum ecclesia?," 237.

thousand-year rule in extant Donatist literature are both negative: while Tyconius's reinterpretation of the critical passage in Rev 20 as a reference to the present era of the church is widely known,[5] it is also mirrored by an anonymous Donatist prophecy-list entitled *Prophecies Compiled from All Books*, which warns its readers that Isaac's blessing upon Jacob "was fulfilled in his own time: one should avoid using this passage with regard to the thousand year reign."[6] This is not to imply that millenarian theology did not exist within the Donatist communion, but its complete absence from extant Donatist writings should give us pause.

Donatist apocalyptic exegesis was certainly more complex than such reductionist interpretations allow. And yet we should not err in the opposite extreme and argue, as some have, that the movement was therefore devoid of an eschatological dimension.[7] Testimony from Donatist sources survives which demonstrates that the dissident community did indeed possess a vibrant apocalyptic vision: in the Donatist martyrology *The Passion of the Holy Martyrs Isaac and Maximian*, for instance, the soon-to-be executed Isaac has a vision in which he hears a voice from above, "like that of an old man, saying 'Woe to you, world, for you are perishing!'"[8] Lest we misinterpret its intent, the narrator takes care to explain the meaning of this phrase: "What could be plainer than this vision? ... he had prophesied annihilation for the world, and we all know he was not lying."[9] In another representative example, this time from an early fifth-century Donatist chronology entitled *The Genealogy Book*, the sign given to Cain after the murder of his brother foreshadows the apocalyptic mark of the beast: "For after Cain had been cursed by God, in order that no one would kill him he gained an evil sign, which if anyone now accepts on his forehead or his right hand, he

5 Tyconius, *Expositio Apocalypseos*, ed. Roger Gryson, CCSL 107A (Turnhout: Brepols, 2011), 7.15; in English, see *Tyconius: Exposition of the Apocalypse*, trans. Francis X. Gumerlock, FC 134 (Washington, DC: Catholic University of America Press, 2017), 179.

6 Adalbert Hamman et al., eds., *Prophetiae ex omnibus libris collectae*, Patrologiae Latinae Supplementum 1 (Paris: Éditions Garnier Frères, 1958), 177–80, 1738–41, at 177. All translations are my own unless otherwise indicated.

7 Cf. Maureen Tilley, *The Bible in Christian North Africa: The Donatist World* (Minneapolis, MN: Fortress, 1997), 54, 63, 111–12.

8 *Passio Isaac et Maximiani* 9, in *Le dossier du Donatisme*, vols. 1–2, ed. Jean-Louis Maier (Berlin: Akademie-Verlag, 1989), 1:259–75; English translation from Maureen Tilley, trans., *Donatist Martyr Stories* (Liverpool: Liverpool University Press, 1996), 69–70.

9 *Passio Isaac et Maximiani* 10 (Tilley, *Donatist Martyr Stories*, 70).

too will 'drink of the wine of the wrath of God mixed in the bowl of his wrath and be punished in the sight of his holy angels.'"[10]

CONTEXTUALIZING THE APOCALYPSE

The key, then, is to walk a middle path. Rather than depicting the Donatist church as a millenarian cult or, conversely, minimizing the eschatological motifs present within its surviving texts, we ought to place the dissident movement's apocalyptic exegesis firmly within its fifth-century context. Too often we read the world of late antiquity through the lens of Augustine, whose skepticism towards an imminent end is well known. But Augustine is not the only voice of his era, nor necessarily a representative one. To the contrary, this was a world which lived in the shadow of the end: as Rome crumbled, apocalyptic speculation thrived. Jerome would write in 409 to the widow Ageruchia, "*That which holds back is taken from the midst*, and we do not recognize the approach of Antichrist! ... everything between the Alps and the Pyrenees, all the lands between the Rhine and Ocean, have been devastated."[11] Even those within Augustine's immediate orbit—his mentor Ambrose of Milan and his disciple Quodvultdeus of Carthage, for instance—did not shy away from identifying the invading Goths with the prophesied armies of Gog and Magog.[12] The recognition of a genuinely apocalyptic trajectory within Donatist theology, therefore, is not necessarily a pronouncement of fanaticism or credulity: rather, it correctly situates the dissident communion within the context of its own era.

In many ways, the surviving snippets of apocalyptic speculation within Donatist exegetical writings mirror those of their contemporaries. Like their African and transmarine counterparts, including Ambrosiaster, Chrysostom, and even Augustine,[13] Donatist texts like the *Prophecies Compiled from All Books* consider the rise of Manichaeism a direct fulfillment of Paul's warning in 1 Tim 4:1–4: "This prophecy

[10] *Liber genealogus* (Sangallensis), 38, MGH: Auctores Antiquissimi 9 (Berlin, 1892), 162–63.

[11] Jerome, Letter 123.16, PL 22, 1057.

[12] See Ambrose, *De fide* 2.16.135–38, CSEL 78, 105; Quodvultdeus, *Liber promissionum et praedictorum Dei* D.13.22, CCSL 60, 207.

[13] See Ambrosiaster, *Ad Timotheum prima* 4.5.2, CSEL 81, 272; Chrysostom, Homily 12 on 1 Tim 4:1–3, PG 62, 557–58; Augustine, *Contra Faustum* 15.10, CSEL 25 (Vienna, 1891), 437.

very clearly rebukes Mani."[14] Indeed, the dissident controversialist Fulgentius goes further, linking his Catholic opponents—or, as we might call them more neutrally, Caecilianists—to the apocalyptic Whore of Babylon on the basis of its alleged reception of Manichaean baptism.[15] While terse, a Donatist *capitula* series on Ezekiel parallels widespread early Christian speculation regarding the eschatological conversion of the Jews and their return to their homeland: "The Lord promises the restoration of all the Jews to their land," and elsewhere: "Concerning Christ the Lord, that they will receive him in the last days and that he will be sanctified in him."[16]

Furthermore, like their Caecilianist opponents Quintus Julius Hilarianus, Quodvultdeus, or the anonymous *Carthaginian Computus of 455*,[17] Donatist sources often assert the idea of a "cosmic week"—the idea that the world's age mirrors the days of creation. Tyconius, for example, will insist that "just as [God] made the world in six days, so he makes the spiritual world, which is the church, in the course of six thousand years; and he will stop on the seventh day, which he has blessed and made eternal."[18] According to the Donatist *Genealogy Book*, the world's age as of 427 CE was precisely 5,879 years,[19] meaning that the year 6000 would occur in 548—a date that is actually further removed in time than the dates predicted by Quintus Julius Hilarianus (498), Quodvultdeus (510), or the *Carthaginian Computus of 455* (535). Similarly, the *Genealogy Book*, following long-established precedent, identifies the two witnesses of Rev 11 with Enoch and Elijah and the Antichrist as a revivified Nero,[20] a claim paralleled by Sulpicius Severus, Martin of Tours, and, according to Augustine, many within his own Caecilianist communion.[21]

[14] Hamman et al., *Prophetiae ex omnibus libris collectae*, 179.

[15] *Contra Fulgentium* 1.12, in *Le dossier du Donatisme*, 2:253.

[16] Ezekiel *capitula* 97, 99, in *Biblia sacra iuxta latinam vulgatam versionem*, vol. 15, *Liber Hiezechielis* (Rome: Libreria Editrice Vaticana, 1978), 26. Cf. Augustine, *De civitate Dei*, ed. B. Dombart and A. Kalb (Leipzig: Teubner, 1927); in English, see St. Augustine, *City of God*, trans. Henry Bettenson (London: Penguin, 2003).

[17] Quintus Julius Hilarianus, *De cursu temporum* 17, PL 13, 1105; Quodvultdeus, *Liber promissionum et praedictorum Dei* D.4.6, CCSL 60, 193; the *Carthaginian Computus* of 455, 2.8; Bruno Krusch, *Studien zur christlich-mittelalterlichen Chronologie* (Leipzig: Verlag der Akademie der Wissenschaften, 1880), 289.

[18] Tyconius, *Liber regularum* 5.3.1; in English, *Tyconius: The Book of Rules*, ed. and trans. William S. Babcock (Atlanta, GA: Scholars Press, 1989), 91.

[19] *Liber genealogus* (Sangallensis), explicit (MGH 9, 158).

[20] *Liber genealogus* (Sangallensis), 614 (MGH 9, 194).

[21] Sulpicius Severus: *Chronica* 2.29, CSEL 1, 83–84; Martin of Tours: in Sulpicius Severus, *Dialogi* 2.14, CSEL 1, 197; Augustine's congregation: Augustine, *De civitate Dei* 20.29.

KEY DIVERGENCES

Nevertheless, the same passage in the *Genealogy Book* alerts us to a fascinating divergence between Donatist eschatological assumptions and that of their contemporaries, albeit one more likely rooted in a differing textual tradition than in conscious opposition. The *Genealogy Book* supports its identification of Nero with the Antichrist by appealing to a simple gematric calculation: by multiplying the numerical equivalent of the Latin word *Antichristus* (154) by the number of letters in Nero's name (4), the number of the beast may be obtained. But it is not 666, as both we and the larger world of late antiquity would have assumed: rather, 616 serves as the dread number.[22] As demonstrated by Irenaeus and several Greek and Latin biblical manuscripts, 616 is a known textual variant of Rev 13:18;[23] but it is interesting that apart from Irenaeus's unnamed opponents, the only Christian sources who utilize the 616 alternative in their exegesis are Donatists or authors dependent on them. Perhaps the most well known example is Tyconius, who in his *Exposition of the Apocalypse* interprets 616 (χιϛ in Greek) as a diabolical parallel to the Christogram (χρϛ).[24] Later African and European authors who incorporate this interpretation, such as Caesarius of Arles and the anonymous *De monogramma XPI*,[25] are clearly dependent on Tyconius. There is, however, a third witness to the number's use within a Donatist context. In a Donatist *capitula* series for the Book of Daniel, the four beasts of Dan 7:1–8 are introduced as follows: "Where Daniel saw four beasts, symbolizing 154 kings."[26] As the number 154 is not found within the biblical text, nor is the political significance of "154 kings" elsewhere attested, we are likely encountering another gematric puzzle. Like the *Genealogy Book*, the author of the Daniel *capitula* appears to be intending for us to multiply the two numbers together to reach the number 616: the mark of the beast. The number of

[22] *Liber genealogus* (Sangallensis), 615 (MGH 9, 194).

[23] Irenaeus, *Adversus haereses* 5.30.1, PG 7b, 1203–04. See also the third-century manuscript P115 (Greek) and the fifth-century *Codex Ephraemi rescriptus* (Greek), as well as the ninth-century Düsseldorf Universitätsbibliothek, Ms. B 3 (Latin).

[24] Tyconius, *Expositio Apocalypseos* 4.46 (FC 134, 139).

[25] Caesarius of Arles, *Expositio in Apocalypsim*, in *Sancti Caesarii Arelatensis opera omnia*, ed. G. Morin (Maredsous: [Abbey], 1942); in English, see William C. Weinrich, trans., *Latin Commentaries on Revelation*, ACT (Downers Grove, IL: InterVarsity Press, 2011), Homily 11; *De monogramma*, ed. Roger Gryson, CCSL 107.

[26] Daniel *capitulum* 16, in *Biblia sacra iuxta latinam vulgatam versionem*, vol. 16, *Liber Danihelis* (Rome: Libreria Editrice Vaticana, 1981), 23.

human kings is thus what Tyconius might call a "perfect number,"[27] in that it implies that *all* human kings are in some sense complicit in the rise of Antichrist.

Donatists do not appear to have used the 616 variant as a selfconscious identity marker. An updated recension of the *Genealogy Book* which appeared in 438, for instance, appears genuinely confused with the fact that its predecessor was at odds with the majority view: "But this seems to disagree with reliable calculations when compared with what other teachers have discussed concerning the number of the beast."[28] Nevertheless, the near unanimity in Donatist interpretations of the number and its clear divergence from more mainstream apocalyptic calculations is worth noting.

REMNANT ECCLESIOLOGY

A more deliberate example of divergence, on the other hand, is the role that many Donatists seem to have believed that their communion—and its opponents—would play in the coming apocalypse: an exegetical interpretation that we will designate as "remnant ecclesiology." Likely appearing in the aftermath of the enforced suppression of the dissident church from 347 to 361, a period often referred to as the "Macarian Persecution,"[29] remnant ecclesiology posited that the hostility of the wider ecclesiastical world towards the Donatist cause constituted a fulfillment of prophecy. In assessing such an interpretation, we must be careful: we should not assume that all Donatists held to this position, nor that its contours were sharply defined. Nevertheless, an apocalyptic form of remnant ecclesiology appears to have been a relatively popular way to account for the failure of the dissident communion to achieve recognition by the European churches.

We can find hints of this tendency in the same passage from the *Prophecies Compiled from All Books* already discussed above in connection with the Manichaeans. That the author views the end as very near is evident: in his interpretation of 2 Tim 3:1–5, in which Paul warns that "in the last days distressing times will come," he states that "it is

27 See Tyconius, *Liber regularum* 5.4.3 (trans. Babcock, 97); and *Expositio Apocalypseos* 1.21 (FC 134, 45).

28 *Liber genealogus* (Florentini), 616 (MGH 9, 194–95).

29 See Parmenian, in Augustine, *Contra epistulam Parmeniani* 1.3.4, *Oeuvres de St Augustin* (*OSA*), vol. 28, ed. Guy Finaert (Paris: Descleé, 1963), 217; Fortunianus, in Augustine, Letter 44.3 (*WSA* 2.1:175–76); Tyconius, *Expositio Apocalypseos* 1.38 (FC 134, 42).

perfectly clear that this prophecy was declared about our own times."[30] But Manichaeans are not the only ones to haunt the church in fulfillment of the prophecy: commenting on Paul's warning to the Ephesians that "savage wolves will come in among you, not sparing the flock,"[31] the Donatist writer warns his audience that "In this passage it should be clearly understood that he is talking about the *traditores*."[32]

That this is merely the edge of a much larger phenomenon is evident from the witness of Tyconius. In his *Exposition of the Apocalypse*, likely written during the mid-370s, Tyconius preserves for us the basic outlines of a common Donatist argument: "If Philadelphia alone, or now Africa, *kept the word of* God's *patience*, to whom afterward in the whole world does he promise the testing that is going to come? ... For Antichrist, as some think, will not persecute the church in [only] one place, since he will rule as the last king over the whole earth."[33] According to the remnant ecclesiology advanced by his opponents, in other words, the falling away of the church outside North Africa was eschatologically significant: "They say that the church is dwindling and is able to be reduced to the number of the household of Noah, with many losing their crown."[34]

The interpretation hinted at in Tyconius and the *Prophecies* is corroborated by other Donatist voices that emerge from Augustine's writings. In the bishop of Hippo's 397 work *On Christian Combat*, we find a succinct encapsulation of a Donatist claim that pairs well with our previous witnesses:

> There are many other passages, in the books of both the Old and New Testaments, which have been written to make it perfectly evident that the Church has been spread over the world. When we confront them with this objection, they answer that all those prophecies were already fulfilled before the rise of the Donatist sect. Afterwards, so they say, the whole Church became extinct, and the remains of it have been preserved only within the Donatist sect.[35]

30 Hamman et al., *Prophetiae ex omnibus libris collectae*, 179.

31 Acts 20:29.

32 Hamman et al., *Prophetiae ex omnibus libris collectae*, 179.

33 Tyconius, *Expositio Apocalypseos* 1.41 (FC 134, 56).

34 Tyconius, *Expositio Apocalypseos* 1.41 (FC 134, 57).

35 Augustine, *De agone christiano* 29.31, *OSA* 1:373–435; in English, *St. Augustine: Letters 165–203*, trans. Wilfred Parsons, FC 4 (Washington, DC: Catholic University of America Press, 1956). See also Augustine, *Enarrationes*, Ps 101(2):8 (*WSA* 3.19:68).

What we are seeing here, I argue, is the outline of a tripartite apocalyptic interpretation intended to buttress the legitimacy of the Donatist communion in the face of Caecilianist allegations that its geographical insularity undermined its claims to be the true church in North Africa.

The Spread of the Gospel

The first part of this argument hinges on the crucial assertion that the gospel had already been preached throughout the world. In other words, despite the bishop of Hippo's constant insinuations to the contrary (a classic example: "The clouds of heaven thunder their witness that God's dwelling is being constructed throughout the world, and yet all the while [these] frogs are croaking from the swamp, 'We are the only Christians!'"[36]), Donatists would have agreed with Augustine that the church must increase until it fills the whole earth. This much is clear from Donatist sources including a *capitula* series for Isaiah, which includes numerous references "concerning the new people who will come out of all the nations."[37]

Where proponents of remnantism would have parted ways with Augustine, however, revolved around the timing of this event: while Augustine usually insisted that Christianity had not *yet* reached the remotest nations of the world, a least some Donatists claimed that it had. And while Augustine's interpretation was not unprecedented, it was by no means representative of the wider church as a whole. In a letter written to Augustine in 420, for instance, the Dalmatian bishop Hesychius argued that "once the emperors became Christian, the gospel of Christ spread everywhere in a short time."[38] Significantly, Hesychius made this claim in order to support his contention that the end of the world was imminent. Nor was he alone: Jerome too, writing in 398 regarding the proper interpretation of Matt 24:14, believed that the "proclamation of the Gospel in the whole world ... is either already completed or will be completed in a short time. For I do not think any nation remains that is ignorant of the name of Christ,"[39] while John

[36] Augustine, *Enarrationes*, Ps 95:11 (*WSA* 3.18:433).

[37] Isaiah *capitulum* 116; see also Isaiah *capitula* 16, 64, 85, 125, 132, 136, 141, and 161, in *Biblia sacra iuxta latinam vulgatam versionem*, vol. 13, *Liber Isaiae* (Rome: Libreria Editrice Vaticana, 1969), 13–29.

[38] Hesychius, in Augustine, Letter 198.6 (*WSA* 2.3:326).

[39] Jerome, *Commentariorum in Matheum* 24:14, CCSL 77; in English, *St. Jerome: Commentary on Matthew*, trans. Thomas P. Scheck, FC 117 (Washington, DC: Catholic University of America Press, 2008), 271.

Chrysostom, commenting on the same verse, claimed that the gospel had actually reached all nations prior to the fall of Jerusalem in 70 CE.[40]

The Apostasy of the Church

As long as this crucial preliminary aspect of the Donatist scenario is granted, the second point follows naturally: once the entire world had been exposed to the Christian message, significant elements of it would then fall away from the faith before the end. In Augustine's *Letter to the Catholics on the Sect of the Donatists*, we find a rendition of the verses most commonly used to support this claim. Luke 18:8 holds pride of place: "They also say that the Lord was talking about the falling away of the world when he said: 'When the Son of Man comes, do you think he will find faith on the earth?'"[41] That this was a very popular—and rather compelling—proof-text is evidenced by the number of times it is addressed by Augustine in his corpus.[42] Other verses, such as Matt 24:12–13 and 1 Tim 4:1, also make an appearance in the *Letter*:

> Here are the dregs: "Because iniquity has increased, the love of many will grow cold." Here is the good seed: "He who endures to the end will be saved." (Matt 24:12–13) Where is Donatist Africa named? Here are the dregs: "But the Spirit," he says, "plainly states that in the last times some shall certainly depart from the faith, paying attention to seducing spirits, and doctrines of demons," etc. (1 Tim 4:1) Where again is Donatist Africa named?[43]

Elsewhere, in a letter to the leader of a Donatist splinter group, Augustine reproduces an entire catena of passages which he claims Donatists used to support their belief that the world had apostatized:

> And so, *the whole world has been placed in the power of the evil one* (John 5:19) ... But *the love of many grows cold* (Matt 24:12) ... the Lord also says, *Amid the abundance of sinfulness he who perseveres up to the end will be saved* (Matt 24:13) ... this passage was also written, *When the Son of Man comes, do you suppose he will find faith on earth*? (Luke 18:8).

[40] Chrysostom, Homily 75 on Matt 2, PG 58, 688–89.

[41] Augustine, *Epistula ad Catholicos de secta Donatistarum* 15.38 (*OSA* 28:502–707).

[42] See Augustine, Letter 93.9.32–33 (*WSA* 2.1:397–98); Sermon 88.21 (*WSA* 3.3:433–44); *Enarrationes*, Ps 31(2):11 (*WSA* 3.15:374–75); *Contra gaudentium Donatistarum episcopum* 2.6.6 (*OSA* 32:510–685).

[43] Augustine, *Epistula ad Catholicos* 17.43.

Notice the prominent role of Matt 24:12–13 in both of these writings: when linked to the prophecy in the very next verse that the end would come once the "good news of the kingdom will be proclaimed throughout the world,"[44] it provided explicit evidence that the worldwide church had, in Tyconius's paraphrase, "dwindled … to the number of the household of Noah."[45]

In their belief that a mass apostasy had *already* occurred, Donatist proponents of remnant ecclesiology were necessarily out of sync with the majority of Christians in late antiquity. Significantly, however, they are not quite unique: we find similar parallels in a western "Arian," or better, Homoian, homily collection entitled *The Incomplete Commentary on Matthew* and, to a lesser extent, in a late fourth- or early fifth-century Catholic document called *The Discussion of Zacchaeus the Christian and Apollonius the Philosopher*. In the homily series, written by a member of a Homoian community undergoing persecution similar to the Donatists, the proclamation to the world is envisioned as substantially complete by the time of Constantine;[46] since then, "the church was vanquished as many were either seduced or forced to lie; now it only remains for the end to occur."[47] The pro-Nicene *Discussion*, in contrast, does not locate the prophesied "falling away" in the past: but, citing Luke 18:8 and 2 Tim 3:2–3, it assumes that the only way for the future Antichrist to emerge in a world now dominated by Christianity is for a future mass apostasy to so weaken the church that it is unable to prevent his rise.[48]

The Significance of the South

Easily the most controversial element of Donatist remnant ecclesiology, however, was its final component: the claim that the biblical text had predicted the geographical location of the remnant who would remain faithful in the midst of prophesied apostasy. The verse most often appealed to in support of this argument was Song 1:7, in which the beloved asks her lover, "Tell me, you whom my soul loves, where do you pasture your flock? Where do you make it lie down?" As evidence

44 Matt 24:14.

45 Tyconius, *Expositio Apocalypseos* 1.41 (FC 134, 57).

46 *Opus imperfectum in Matheum*, Homily 46, 23.25, PG 56, 611–946; in English, *Ancient Christian Texts: Incomplete Commentary on Matthew*, trans. James Kellerman (Downers Grove, IL: InterVarsity Press, 2010), 379.

47 *Opus imperfectum in Matheum*, Homily 48, 24.6 (Kellerman, *Ancient Christian Texts*, 375).

48 *Consultationes Zacchei et Apolloni* 3.7.3–4, SC 402, 208–10.

throughout the Augustinian corpus testifies, the lover (Christ) then identifies the true home of his flock: "In the south."[49] It was the last word, of course, that proved controversial: while modern translations usually render the word as "noon," the word used in both the Vulgate and its Old Latin predecessors is "meridie," which can mean either "noon" or "south." Augustine's exasperated summary in Sermon 138 captures the Donatist interpretation of this verse well:

> Whenever we begin to press them by the light of the unity of the Church spread throughout the whole world, and request them in their turn to point to some testimony from the scriptures where God foretold that the Church would exist only in Africa, with the rest of the nations seemingly lost to it, this is the testimony they usually have on the tips of their tongues, saying that Africa is in the noon day, or south. "So," they say, "when the Church asks the Lord where he grazes his flock, where he lies down, he answers *In the noon day*, or *south*; so that it's as if the questioner's voice goes, *Tell me, you whom my soul has loved, where you graze your flock, where you lie down*, and the answerer's voice says, *In the south*, that is, in Africa."[50]

Augustine is not, in fact, our only witness to the willingness of at least some elements within the Donatist communion to use this verse as a weapon against Caecilianists. In the *Book of Rules*, Tyconius cites Song 1:7 as well, agreeing with his colleagues about its geographical significance: "There are two parts in the church, one of the south and one of the north. The Lord abides in the southern part, as it is written: 'where you graze your flock, where you abide in the south.' But the devil abides in the north."[51] His own interpretation of this crucial verse, however, differs from theirs: rather than identifying the "south" with a particular location, Tyconius recasts it as a universal metaphor: "The southern part, certainly, is the Lord's, as it is also written in Job: *from the southern part will your life sprout forth*; the north is the devil's. And *both* parts appear in all the world."[52]

Song 1:7 was not the sole piece of scriptural evidence that Donatists used to reinforce their interpretation. Despite claiming that "this is the

49 See Augustine, Letter 93.8.24, 25 (*WSA* 2.1:392–93); Sermon 46.33, 35 (*WSA* 3.2:286, 287); Sermon 138.9 (*WSA* 3.4:391–92); Sermon 147A.3 (*WSA* 3.4:454), among others.

50 Augustine, Sermon 138.9 (*WSA* 3.4:390–91).

51 Tyconius, *Liber regularum* 7.4.2 (trans. Babcock, 121).

52 Tyconius, *Liber regularum* 7.4.3 (Babcock, *Tyconius*, 125). Emphasis mine.

only testimony they can come up with that even remotely appears to refer to them" in the *Letter to the Catholics*,[53] Augustine mentions at least two further exegetical underpinnings in a sermon preached around 414. Citing the Old Latin text of Hab 3:3, "God will come from the Afric" (in context, a synonym for the south), at least some Donatists believed that the actual location of the remnant had in fact been explicitly named in the Bible: "of course where *the Afric* is, there is Africa."[54] A second proof, likely garbled in Augustine's transmission of it, has to do with the man who carried Christ's cross, Simon of Cyrene: "'A Cyrenaean,' they say, 'a certain Simon was compelled to carry the Lord's cross.' We've read about it, but how does it help you, I would like to know? 'A Cyrenaean,' he says, 'is an African. That's why he was the one who was compelled to carry the cross.'"[55] Taken out of context, of course, these proofs appear far-fetched. We must remember that we are hearing them only second-hand, through a hostile witness.

Even here, however, the Donatist eegetical tradition is not entirely without precedent. As Karl Shuve noted in his 2016 book *The Song of Songs and the Fashioning of Identity in Early Latin Christianity*, the earliest known Latin commentary on the Song of Songs (written in the early 350s by Gregory of Elvira) preserves a strikingly similar interpretation of Song 1:7:

> *Make known to me, you who love my soul, where do you graze? Where do you abide in the south?* Surely this is said about the church, which, as if it did not know, it asks of him. Surely no one may doubt that "the south" [*meridianum*] refers to Egypt, and parts of Africa, since there the infant Christ was taken when Herod sought to kill him, just as it is written in the Gospel what an angel of the Lord [said], in order that the infant might be preserved and withdraw to Egypt, so that what was written might be fulfilled: *out of Egypt I will call my son*, and elsewhere: *God will come from Egypt*.[56]

[53] Augustine, *Epistula ad Catholicos* 16.40.

[54] Augustine, Sermon 46.39 (*WSA* 3.2:290–91).

[55] Augustine, Sermon 46.41 (*WSA* 3.2:292).

[56] Gregory of Elvira, *Tractatus de epithalamio* 2.5; *Gregorius Eliberritanus: epithalamium sive explanatio in Canticis canticorum*, ed. Eva Schulz-Flügel (Freiburg: Herder, 1994), 195–97. Cf. Karl Shuve, *The Song of Songs and the Fashioning of Identity in Early Latin Christianity* (Oxford: Oxford University Press, 2016), 48.

Gregory clearly did not have Donatist Africa in mind when he wrote this text, and his specific geographic referent differs from the Donatist exegetes mentioned above: here, "the south" is Egypt and parts of Africa because he views Song 1:7 as a prophecy regarding Christ's flight to Egypt. Nevertheless, it is striking that Gregory appeals to the same catena of verses as do the Donatists: the reading "God will come from Egypt" is almost certainly a reference once more to Hab 3:3. At the very least, Gregory's willingness to identify both Hab 3:3 and Song 1:7's reference to "the south" as a specific geographical location suggests the existence of a prior hermeneutical tradition used by Donatist exegetes as well. In other words, if the Donatist appropriation of these verses for Roman North Africa is unprecedented, the underlying exegetical theory it is based on is not.

To sum up, Augustine's constant objections to what I have called Donatist remnant ecclesiology are strenuous for a reason: the apocalyptic scenario that emerges from them is, at least within its late antique and North African context, disconcertingly plausible. As I have sought to demonstrate, none of the key components of this interpretation are unprecedented in Christian literature: many Christians believed that the gospel had spread to all nations, and while few outside other dissident communions would have claimed that worldwide apostasy had *already* occurred, at least some were willing to entertain the possibility of the faith's future collapse. Even where Donatists appear at their most idiosyncratic—their localizing of "the south" to North Africa—the underlying framework appears to have been modified from a pre-existing exegetical tradition. The resulting synthesis likely served as an effective response to Caecilianist polemic, and a credible condemnation of the wider transmarine church for its support of the *traditores*.

TYCONIUS AND THE APOCALYPSE

Remarkably, however, this is not the only apocalyptic trajectory to have originated from within the Donatist communion. Throughout this chapter, I have mentioned the "rogue" Donatist theologian Tyconius, whose pointed critiques of his colleagues have given us valuable insight into their thought. But Tyconius was no mere critic of his own party's apocalyptic claims. His *Exposition of the Apocalypse*, a commentary on the Book of Revelation recently reconstructed by Roger Gryson, strongly affected the early medieval commentary tradition, influencing such diverse writers as Primasius of Hadrumetum, Caesarius of Arles, the Venerable Bede, and Beatus of Liébana. In his continuation of

Jerome's *On Illustrious Men*, Gennadius of Marseilles commends him for his radical reinterpretation of the thousand-year reign, and indeed Tyconius is principally remembered today for his anti-millenarian exegesis. I submit, however, that this is in fact tangential to the *Exposition*'s true purpose: rather than functioning primarily as a condemnation of chiliasm, the text is best understood as a reaction to the growing popularity of the Donatist remnant apocalyptic position discussed above.

We have already noticed that the *Exposition* contains passages directed against unnamed opponents within the Donatist communion who "say that the church is dwindling and is able to be reduced to the number of the household of Noah."[57] Elsewhere, Tyconius strongly condemns those who argue regarding "the door of the church, which God opens in the whole world, that someone is able to shut it up in a certain part of the world."[58] I argue that it is this critical background that provides the key to understanding Tyconius's distinctive apocalyptic theory. Throughout his two surviving works, Tyconius consistently defends his belief that prior to the end, both the righteous and the wicked will be mixed together within the church; indeed, this is why Augustine found him so useful.[59] In the *Book of Rules*, for instance, Tyconius uses the story of Jacob and Esau's struggle within their mother's womb as an allegory for the church: "Lest anyone think, as a result, that the two peoples would be sharply separated, it was made plain that both would be in one body ... Jacob, i.e., the church, never comes for blessing without concomitant deceit, i.e., without false brethren."[60] These "false brothers," whom he will elsewhere identify as the "mystery of iniquity" referred to in 2 Thess 2:7, are therefore hidden inside the church at present. But this state of affairs is not permanent. At the time of the end, the true church and the false brothers within it will finally separate: one to suffer the last persecution, the other to inflict it. This "separation," or *discessio* in Tyconius's Latin text, is derived from 2 Thess 2:3: "Let no one deceive you in any way: for that day will not come unless the separation (ἀποστασία) comes first and the lawless one is revealed, the one destined for destruction." In Tyconius's thought, the *discessio* is in fact the catalyst behind the lawless one's unveiling: "this will go on," he claims, referring to the presence of the

[57] Tyconius, *Expositio Apocalypseos* 1.41 (FC 134, 57).
[58] Tyconius, *Expositio Apocalypseos* 1.38 (FC 134, 55).
[59] See Augustine, *Contra epistulam Parmeniani* 1.1.
[60] Tyconius, *Liber regularum* 3.26 (trans. Babcock, 51).

false church within the true, "from the time of the Lord's passion until the church, which keeps it in check, withdraws from the midst of this mystery of lawlessness so that godlessness may be unveiled in its own time, as the apostle says."[61] At the separation, the false brothers will finally be revealed for who they are.

Up to this point, Tyconius's argument could be easily embraced by Christians outside his own communion, and indeed often was. Augustine, for example, seems to have adapted his often-referenced interpretation of the parable of the wheat and weeds from Tyconius: it was the Donatist theologian, after all, who first utilized the parable as evidence that "the good are mixed with the evil in the church up until the end of time."[62] But the Donatist communion is not absent from Tyconius's apocalyptic narrative; in fact, it occupies a privileged place within it. While the hardships suffered by the dissident communion do not in themselves constitute the eschatological persecution, they do serve as a typological foreshadowing of the last era, a facet of his theology often lost when Tyconius is read through an Augustinian lens. While he does not agree with his colleagues that the rest of the world has been tainted by the crime of *traditio*, he does believe that there is only one true church in North Africa—and it is not Caecilianist.

We first encounter this alternate vision in the *Exposition*'s discussion of the Philadelphian church of Rev 3:7–13. Earlier, we noted that Tyconius uses this passage to castigate his more insular Donatist opponents for their restriction of the church to Africa: "If Philadelphia alone, or now Africa, *kept the word of* God's *patience*, to whom afterward in the whole world does he promise the testing that is going to come?" And yet the Donatist–Caecilianist schism is not completely devoid of significance, for the passage continues: "For just as was done in Africa, so it is necessary that Antichrist is to be revealed in the whole world, and in the same way to be overcome everywhere by the church, where he was overcome by her in part for the purpose of showing the way that the last struggle will happen."[63] What Tyconius appears to be claiming here is that the "separation" of the Donatist church from the *traditores* is, in fact, eschatologically significant, though in a more subtle way than the interpretation favored by his rivals.

61 Tyconius, *Liber regularum* 7.4.3 (trans. Babcock, 123).

62 Tyconius, *Expositio Apocalypseos* 1.11 (FC 134, 39). For Augustine's use of the parable, see Letter 76.2 (*WSA* 2.1:299); Sermon 47.6 (*WSA* 2.2:302); *Contra litteras Petiliani* 2.78.174, CSEL 52, 108–09; *Epistula ad Catholicos* 15.38; and *De civitate Dei* 20.9, among others.

63 Tyconius, *Expositio Apocalypseos* 1.41 (FC 134, 56).

Elsewhere, the Donatist–Caecilianist divide is even granted a specific location within the recapitulative structure of Revelation. Within the Tyconian system, the first three seals stand for three parties, who appear in roughly chronological order. The first seal and its attendant white horse, for instance, stand for Christ and the establishment of his church; the second seal for the onslaught of pagan persecution, the third for the rise of the "false brothers" within the church. The fourth seal, however, introduces a new character to the story: "Before the 'man of sin' is revealed everywhere and the 'son of perdition' is manifested publicly," Tyconius warns his readers, "he has already been revealed from one part: and where three parts were seen [i.e., the church, the pagans, and 'false brothers'], now a fourth is manifested. For the church will not spew out every evil person, but only some, for the purpose of showing to the world what the last persecution will be like."[64] In other words, the fourth seal functions as a dress rehearsal for the future eschatological separation, but one that is limited to a specific part of the world. We do not have to wait long to discover the location of this prequel *discessio*. It is "in Africa ... [where] they were revealed already a short time ago when they were expelled from the church."[65] Tyconius's commentary on the fourth seal concludes with an explicit affirmation of the Donatist church's typological relevance: "what is taking place in Africa is a figure of the future revelation of Antichrist throughout the world, who now, under the scale in his outstretched hand, performs works of iniquity."[66]

Thanks to the recapitulative nature of Revelation in Tyconian hermeneutics, we encounter this "fourth part" again in the sounding of the fifth trumpet (Rev 9:1–11), John's eating of the "bitter scroll" in Rev 10:10, and the angel "flying in the midst of heaven" in Rev 14:6–7. Each case solidifies my contention that Tyconius is deliberately positioning African Donatism as a major player within the book of Revelation, albeit as a typological prequel of the main event. The events of the fifth trumpet, for instance, are specifically linked to "the whole time of the five-year persecution that happened principally in Africa."[67] The unique role that the Donatist communion will therefore play in alerting the worldwide church to its imminent peril is referenced in Tyconius's interpretation of the puzzling command given to John to "preach again"

[64] Tyconius, *Expositio Apocalypseos* 2.35 (FC 134, 75).
[65] Tyconius, *Expositio Apocalypseos* 2.35 (FC 134, 76).
[66] Ibid.
[67] Tyconius, *Expositio Apocalypseos* 3.35 (FC 134, 99).

after ingesting the "bitter scroll": "He said *again* because he describes the time that will come after the African persecutions, that he might show that the last preaching and refreshment from the contest will be like this one."[68]

The significance of Tyconius's achievement is worth noticing: in the *Exposition*, he has sidelined his opponents' apocalyptic interpretation by effectively incorporating it into his own. Like his more mainstream rivals within the Donatist communion, Tyconius strongly believes that the Donatist–Caecilianist divide was no mere outworking of history: rather, Donatists have a role to play at the time of the end. While they will not face Antichrist alone in the final drama, their experience does stand as an example and a warning to the wider church of the nations concerning what will shortly befall it: "For this reason it happens in one place, in Africa, that it might be known what will happen in every nation—and so that the church, which preaches in part in Africa, therefore might also preach in every nation when she will have come out of the midst of this world, Babylon."[69]

CONCLUSION

To return once more to the opening lines of this chapter, it is all too easy to caricature the Donatist communion as an example of apocalyptic fanaticism run amok, or conversely to downplay eschatological elements within the dissident communion in order to rehabilitate their image. The truth is more complicated. While, as I have sought to demonstrate, apocalyptic exegesis did play a significant role in Donatist thought, such themes are only to be expected given the dissident church's position among the Christian communities that ringed the western Mediterranean in the late fourth and early fifth centuries. If its apocalyptic preoccupations were therefore unexceptional within their late antique context, the Donatist church was noticeably innovative in how it deployed eschatological themes in order to counter Caecilianist polemic. Whether one follows the trajectory of Tyconius's *Exposition of the Apocalypse* or the remnant ecclesiology of mainstream Donatists, it is clear that apocalyptic exegesis served as an effective foil to Caecilianist charges of insularity. And whether we, from the perspective of two millennia later, respond to it as curiously persuasive or merely idiosyncratic, it is hard to deny that such a strategy was

[68] Tyconius, *Expositio Apocalypseos* 3.60 (FC 134, 108).

[69] Tyconius, *Expositio Apocalypseos* 5.2 (FC 134, 141).

remarkably effective in its own time—and in the case of Tyconius, profoundly influential on the developing eschatological trajectories of the early medieval era.

Selected Further Reading

Augustine. *Epistula ad Catholicos de secta Donatistarum.* In *Oeuvres de St Augustin*, vol. 28, 502–707. Paris: Descleé de Brouwer, 1963.

Donatist capitula series. *Biblia sacra iuxta latinam vulgatam versionem*, vol. 13, 11–31 (Isaiah), vol. 15, 11–30 (Ezekiel), vol. 16, 21–25 (Daniel). Rome: Libreria Editrice Vaticana, 1969–81.

Fulgentius. *Libellus de baptismo.* In *Aduersus Fulgentium Donatistam.* In Jean-Louis Maier, ed., *Le dossier du Donatisme*, vol. 2, 239–72. Berlin: Akademie-Verlag, 1989. Reconstructed in Paul Monceaux, *Histoire littéraire de l'Afrique chrétienne*, vol. 5, 335–39. 1920; Brussels: Culture et Civilisation, 1963.

Hamman, Adalbert, et al., eds. *Prophetiae ex omnibus libris collectae.* Patrologiae Latinae Supplementum 1, 177–80, 1738–41. Paris: Éditions Garnier Frères, 1958.

Hoover, Jesse. *The Donatist Church in an Apocalyptic Age.* Oxford: Oxford University Press, 2018.

Liber genealogus. Monumenta Germaniae Historica: Auctores Antiquissimi 9, 160–96. Berlin, 1892.

Passio SS. martyrum Isaac et Maximiani. In Jean-Louis Maier, ed., *Le dossier du Donatisme*, vol. 1, 259–75. Berlin: Akademie-Verlag, 1989. In English in Maureen Tilley, trans., *Donatist Martyr Stories*, 63–75. Liverpool: Liverpool University Press, 1996.

Shuve, Karl. *The Song of Songs and the Fashioning of Identity in Early Latin Christianity.* Oxford: Oxford University Press, 2016.

Tilley, Maureen. *The Bible in Christian North Africa: The Donatist World.* Minneapolis, MN: Fortress, 1997.

Tyconius. *Expositio Apocalypseos.* Corpus Christianorum Series Latina 107A. Turnhout: Brepols, 2011. In English as *Exposition of the Apocalypse.* Translated by Francis X. Gumerlock. Fathers of the Church 134. Washington, DC: Catholic University of America Press, 2017.

Tyconius. *Liber regularum.* In English as *Tyconius: The Book of Rules.* Edited and translated by William S. Babcock. Atlanta, GA: Scholars Press, 1989.

6 Tests of Faith, Rebirth out of Corruption, or Endless Cycles of Regeneration: Experiments in the Restoration of the Late Roman Empire

BRIAN DUVICK

After the conversion of Constantine, apocalyptic chronography demonstrates conflicted expectations about the end-time. The traditional view that less than 200 years remained was challenged by the historian Eusebius, who rejuvenated the world by another 300 years.[1] Although Eusebius's calculation had little immediate influence in the east, the theory was used to temper fears of impending doom in the west following the Battle of Adrianople (378), the sack of Rome (410), and subsequent disasters that threatened the Western Roman Empire. We shall see that, reflecting hopes of recovery as well as current anxieties, apocalyptic literature of the early fifth century demonstrates renewed awareness of impending catastrophe, divine judgment, and a wide variety of possibilities for sociopolitical and cosmic transformation or restoration.[2] While our analyses will focus on specific cases of systems-collapse in North Africa and southern Gaul, there is a growing

[1] For Eusebius's role in the development of an alternative to the *anno mundi* (AM) chronology, which originated in both Jewish and Christian circles ca. 100–250 CE, see Richard Landes, "Lest the Millennium Be Fulfilled: Apocalyptic Expectations and the Pattern of Western Chronography 100–800 CE," in *The Use and Abuse of Eschatology in the Middle Ages*, ed. Werner Verbeke, Daniel Verhelst, and Andries Welkenhuysen (Leuven: Leuven University Press, 1988), 137–211, esp. 149–56; and now Richard W. Burgess and Michael Kulikowski, *Mosaics of Time: The Latin Chronicle Traditions from the First Century BC to the Sixth Century AD*, vol. 1, *A Historical Introduction to the Chronicle Genre from Its Origins to the High Middle Ages* (Turnhout: Brepols, 2012). For general background see James T. Palmer, *The Apocalypse in the Early Middle Ages* (New York: Cambridge University Press, 2014), 25–54.

[2] For background on *restoratio/apokatastasis* see Ilaria L. E. Ramelli, *The Christian Doctrine of Apokatastasis: A Critical Assessment from the New Testament to Eriugena* (Leiden: Brill, 2013), esp. 4–10; and Ilaria L. E. Ramelli, "The Debate on Apokatastasis in Pagan and Christian Platonists: Martianus, Macrobius, Origen, Gregory of Nyssa, and Augustine," *Illinois Classical Studies* 33–34 (2008–09): 201–34. For a discussion of the relationship between Apocalypse/Revelation, millennialism, and eschatology in spiritual, political, and cosmic reform see James T. Palmer and Matthew Gabriele, "Introduction: Reform and the Beginning of the

bibliography of similar studies on frontier regions across the empire, ranging from the Middle East and eastern Europe to the Atlantic seaboard.[3]

INKLINGS OF THE END: ADRIANOPLE AND THE SACK OF ROME

When the Huns swept across central Europe and drove the Goths south of the Danube into Thrace, the Romans greeted the immigrants with a policy of neglect and exploitation. The Goths finally reacted with widespread violence and marched on the city of Adrianople. Valens rushed from the east to meet them and, fearing to lose credit for the victory, engaged his troops before Gratian could arrive with western reinforcements. Valens's army was devastated, and the empire was left virtually defenseless. In desperation, Gratian appealed to Theodosius to come out of retirement, to rebuild the army, and to save the Republic. This he did as much by incorporating the Goths into the Roman military as by bringing them to bay. Theodosius's strategy was unprecedented (and is still controversial today)[4] not for filling the Roman ranks with *barbari*, a practice as ancient as Rome itself, but for permitting the Goths to maintain their traditional military and political conventions while serving in the Roman armed forces. The most famous example of this dual sense of ethno-political identity may be found in Alaric, who was appointed both commander of the Goths and commander-in-chief (*magister militum*) of the Roman armies in Illyricum. After the western emperor, Honorius, executed his barbarian general Stilicho, however, imperial relations with the Goths deteriorated until they finally sacked

End," in *Apocalypse and Reform from Late Antiquity to the Middle Ages*, ed. Matthew Gabriele and James T. Palmer (London: Routledge, 2019), 1–9.

[3] A. H. Merrills, ed., *Vandals, Romans and Berbers: New Perspectives on Late Antique North Africa* (New York: Routledge, 2016); Anathea E. Portier-Young, *Apocalypse against Empire: Theologies of Resistance in Early Judaism* (Grand Rapids, MI: Eerdmans, 2011); Veronika Wieser, "The Chronicle of Hydatius: A Historical Guidebook to the Last Days of the Western Roman Empire," in *Apocalypse and Reform from Late Antiquity to the Middle Ages*, ed. Gabriele and Palmer, 11–30.

[4] Noel Lenski, "Initium mali Romano imperio: Contemporary Reactions to the Battle of Adrianople," *Transactions of the American Philological Association* 127 (1997): 144–45. Lenski notes that a total victory was within Theodosius's power, but, according to Themistius, the emperor believed it better to fill Thrace with Gothic farmers than with corpses (Themistius, *Orationes* 16.211a). This positive spin soon deteriorated, however, into what Lenski calls "doleful recollections of a disaster that could neither be forgotten nor fully overcome."

Rome in 410.[5] Contemporary writers already described the military and political upheavals of the late 370s as the end of the world. Pagans blamed Christians, and Orthodox Christians blamed Arian heretics; some claimed that the Christian God had punished the heterodox Valens, others that the pagan gods were angry about the unavenged death of Julian.[6] At stake was the ideal of political, religious, and cultural harmony (*concordia*), which had served as a model of Roman identity since the beginning of the empire. The ensuing culture war continued to destabilize traditional Roman institutions and belief systems for over one hundred years, beyond the end of the Western Empire (476 CE).[7]

HOME AWAY FROM HOME: NORTH AFRICA

Events in North Africa in the late fourth and early fifth centuries provide an interesting variation on those following the Battle of Adrianople in Thrace. When Africa revolted in 371, Theodosius was charged again, after restoring peace in Britain, to find a solution to frontier destabilization produced by the rising tide of barbarian incursions.[8] As Vanderspoel points out, Theodosius established quasi-independent prefectures along portions of the African frontier, with defense works positioned in the interstices between them, probably to control the numbers of migrating peoples rather than to ward them off. The measure created a buffer zone of Roman and barbarian cultural exchange, which eventually developed into eight autonomous kingdoms each ruled by a "Roman king" (*rex Romanorum*).[9] When Alaric sacked Rome in 410, Augustine was already intimately aware of a present danger of foreign invasion and social turmoil in North Africa. In response to pagan claims that Christians were responsible for the destruction of Rome because of their neglect of the traditional Roman gods, to say nothing

[5] See J. H. W. G. Liebeschuetz, "Alaric's Goths: Nation or Army?" in *Fifth-Century Gaul: A Crisis of Identity?*, ed. John Drinkwater and Hugh Elton (Cambridge: Cambridge University Press, 2002), 75–83.

[6] Lenski, "Initium mali," 145–52.

[7] See Guy Halsall, *Barbarian Migrations and the Roman West, 376–568* (Cambridge: Cambridge University Press, 2007).

[8] See R. A. Markus, *Saeculum: History and Society in the Theology of St. Augustine* (Cambridge: Cambridge University Press, 1970).

[9] John Vanderspoel, "From Empire to Kingdoms in the Late Antique West," in *A Companion to Late Antiquity*, ed. Philip Rousseau (Malden, MA: Wiley-Blackwell, 2012), 437–38. For background on the successor kingdoms, see Christian Courtois, *Les Vandales et l'Afrique* (Paris: Arts et Métiers Graphiques, 1955).

of the ongoing culture wars, Augustine began writing *City of God* in 413 and finished it by 429, the year the Vandals invaded North Africa.[10] Like the Goth Alaric, Geiseric, king of the Vandals, was capable of both full cooperation with and strategic designs against the Roman administration. In fact, Boniface, the Roman governor of Africa, had recruited the Vandals to invade the province in defense against what Boniface wrongly believed to be a plot on his life by the empress, Galla Placidia. Upon his arrival from Spain, Geiseric turned against Boniface and mounted a campaign across North Africa that would result in an extensive Vandalic empire and cultural renaissance, which included adoption of Arian Christianity and the cultivation of traditional pagan literature and art.[11]

When Augustine died in 430, North Africa had already navigated war and socioreligious conflict for about sixty years. He did not expect or teach imminent apocalypse but, going further than Eusebius and Jerome, developed a rich interpretation of apocalyptic millennialism without the chronological calculations that had been performed since the early third century to date the age of the world and to predict its end.[12] The system was based on six millennial ages corresponding with the six days of creation known as the *hexameron*, which had generated extensive exegesis in its own right.[13] The belief was that the incarnation of Christ occurred somewhere in the sixth millennium, and a fervent computational dispute developed over how many centuries remained until the coming of the Antichrist. In the third century, Hippolytus and Julius Africanus argued that the incarnation occurred 5,500 years after creation, which meant that fewer than 300 remained until the end.[14] In the early fourth century, however, Eusebius reset the chronology 300 years back, thereby giving the empire a new lease on life, and

10 See J. Kevin Coyle, "Augustine and Apocalyptic: Thoughts on the Fall of Rome, the Book of Revelation, and the End of the World," *Florilegium* 9 (1987): 1–34.

11 See A. H. Merrills, "Introduction: Vandals, Romans and Berbers: Understanding Late Antique North Africa," in *Vandals, Romans and Berbers: New Perspectives on Late Antique North Africa*, ed. A. H. Merrills (New York: Routledge, 2016), 3–28.

12 For a summary of the tradition see Immo Warntjes, "The Final Countdown and the Reform of the Liturgical Calendar in the Early Middle Ages," in *Apocalypse and Reform from Late Antiquity to the Middle Ages*, ed. Gabriele and Palmer, 51–75. Warntjes calls the tradition "Chronological Millennialism."

13 See Andrew Sibley, "Creationism and Millennialism among the Church Fathers," *Journal of Creation* 26, no. 3 (2012): 95–100.

14 See *Julius Africanus Chronographiae: The Extant Fragments*, ed. Martin Wallraff, with Umberto Roberto and, for the Oriental sources, Karl Pinggéra, trans. William Adler, *Die griechischen christlichen Schriftsteller der ersten Jahrhunderte*, Neue Folge 15 (Berlin: de Gruyter, 2007).

Jerome, who translated and continued Eusebius's *Chronicle* to 379, was opposed to millennialism altogether. A major reversal occurred at the end of the century when the North African bishop Hilarianus calculated that only 101 years remained until the completion of the sixth era.[15] In fact, works of apocalyptic millennialism spike in frequency following the disaster at Adrianople, the sack of Rome, and the invasion of North Africa, which are specific instances of the broader barbarian incursions into the western Mediterranean basin throughout the fifth century.[16] Augustine's militant response was that history does indeed reflect the model of the millennial hexameron, but the radical difference between the history of the earthly city and that of the heavenly city precludes the prediction of the former by calculation of the latter, which in fact reveals God's providential guidance in a discontinuous economy of salvation.[17]

The notion of a less imminent apocalypse marked a break from the Jewish tradition, where the genre had long been associated with repression by foreign powers: the Assyrian exile, the Babylonian captivity, occupation by the Persian, Ptolemaic, and Seleucid regimes, and, ironically, the destruction of the Second Temple and the diaspora under Roman rule.[18] Eusebius was not concerned about liberating Christians from persecution but meant to celebrate the joint victory of Christianity and the Roman Empire in the conversion of Constantine, which entailed demonstrating that the Judeo-Christian tradition was more ancient than that of the Greeks and Romans. While Augustine's eschatology by no means arrested computational millennialism altogether, it shifted the historiographic focus away from imminent and deepening crisis to the unpredictable reconciliation of God and his people as promised in the postexilic literature. Written amid widespread incursions of Visigoths, Vandals, Alans, Suebi, and Huns into virtually every corner of imperial territory, Augustine's *City of God* invites direct

[15] Quintus Julius Hilarianus, *De cursu temporum* 16–17, PL 13, 1104–05.

[16] See Landes, "Lest the Millennium," 137–56 and 208–11. Landes uses the expression "Sabbatical Millennialism."

[17] For the parallel history of the earthly city and the heavenly city see Augustine, *De civitate Dei* 15–18, ed. B. Dombart and A. Kalb (Leipzig: Teubner, 1927); in English see St. Augustine, *City of God*, trans. Henry Bettenson (London: Penguin, 2003). For Augustine's discontinuous economy of salvation see J. Patout Burns, SJ, "The Economy of Salvation: Two Patristic Traditions," *Theological Studies* 37, no. 4 (1976): 600.

[18] Adela Yarbro Collins, "The Political Perspective of the Revelation to John," *Journal of Biblical Literature* 96, no. 2 (1977): 241–56.

political and historical interpretation of the conflicted interface between the earthly city and the heavenly city.[19]

THE CHALLENGE OF PAULUS OROSIUS

The Gallaecian priest Paulus Orosius, after fleeing barbarian invasion in northwestern Hispania, visited Augustine in Hippo soon after the sack of Rome and was invited to write a universal history that supported Augustine's economic millennialism against the pagan claim of contemporary historical decline.[20] Orosius was to demonstrate not only that Christians were not responsible for recent crises, but that the human condition had steadily improved from the earliest times through the four empires described in Dan 2:31–44 to the sack of Rome in 410, which, according to the logic of the cycle of empires, should have marked the end of history. It was because of Roman conversion and repentance that God had intervened directly and saved the empire, if only temporarily.[21] After a brief voyage to the Holy Land, where he conferred with Jerome about his *Chronicle* and the current Pelagian controversy, Orosius completed his *History against the Pagans* (ca. 416), which concludes with striking optimism.[22] In his discussion of events following the sack of Rome, Orosius explains that, after the death of his brother-in-law Alaric, Athaulf married Galla Placidia because he preferred to fight loyally for her brother, the emperor Honorius, rather than "to blot out the Roman name and to make all Roman territory a Gothic empire." Athaulf had realized, according to Orosius, that the Goths were "incapable of obeying laws because of their unbridled barbarism," and, "since a state is not a state without laws," he decided to become a *restorer* of the Roman Empire rather than its transformer.[23] While seeking to bring peace, however, he was

[19] Augustine, *De civitate Dei.*

[20] For the pagan model of historical decline see Hesiod's "Five Ages of Man" in *Works and Days,* trans. Stanley Lombardo (Indianapolis, IN: Hackett, 1993), 109–201. For its adaptation to cyclical history followed by restoration (*apokatastasis*) see Proclus, *Commentary on Plato's Timaeus,* vol. 1, ed. and trans. Harold Tarrant (Cambridge: Cambridge University Press, 2007), 87.30, 101.1.

[21] Peter Van Nuffelen, *Orosius and the Rhetoric of History* (Oxford: Oxford University Press, 2012), 50–52.

[22] Orosius, *Historiarum adversum paganos libri VII,* ed. H. P. Arnaud-Lindet, 3 vols. (Paris: Les Belles Lettres, 1990–91); in English see *Orosius: Seven Books of History against the Pagans,* trans. A. T. Fear, TTH (Liverpool: Liverpool University Press, 2010).

[23] Orosius, *Historiarum adversum paganos* 7.43.2–18.

murdered in Barcelona by his own men, who elected Wallia in turn to make war. It seems that God had another plan, since Wallia went on to return Galla Placidia to her brother and to defeat the other barbarian tribes for the Romans, all with "little bloodshed and no real struggle." Orosius says nothing about the murder of Athaulf and Galla Placidia's infant son, who represented a potential Romano-Gothic dynasty. With the barbarians in check, complete unification of the empire required only that pagan opponents repent and convert to the one true God. The peace and political concord that Orosius depicts are grossly distorted, as he well knew from his experience in Hispania. We shall see that pagans had their own ways to cultivate the *topoi* of post-traumatic, sociopolitical recovery.[24]

THE FICTION OF HISTORY: *PROBUS* IN THE *HISTORIA AUGUSTA*

It is now generally accepted that the biographies in the collection known as the *Historia Augusta*, which include works on imperial statesmen from Hadrian to Diocletian, were written near the beginning of the fifth century.[25] It is also likely that a single author, not the six specified in the text, wrote all thirty biographies and forged virtually all the cited documents. That author is believed to have been a pagan who composed the pieces as a blend of *jeux d'esprit* and serious political criticism of his own times, much as Orosius used the fall of Babylon and the Trojan War as symbolic parallels to current Roman affairs.[26] The concealment of the author's identity and intentions likely reflects the repression of Theodosius's anti-pagan legislation. His portrait of Probus (276–82) is especially dear to its fictional author, Flavius Vopiscus, both for what the emperor meant to Rome and for how Vopiscus constructed that meaning, since "the virtues of men are as great as they are made to appear by the genius of those who tell their story."[27] To underline the

[24] For background on this approach see Dereck Daschke, "Apocalypse and Trauma," in *The Oxford Handbook of Apocalyptic Literature*, ed. John J. Collins (New York: Oxford University Press, 2014), 457–72.

[25] Hermann Peter, ed., *Historia Augusta*, 2 vols. (Leipzig: Teubner, 1884); in English see *Historia Augusta*, 3 vols., trans. David Magie, Loeb Classical Library (Cambridge, MA: Harvard University Press, 1921–32). See David Rohrbacher, *The Play of Allusion in the Historia Augusta* (Madison: University of Wisconsin Press, 2016).

[26] Like Plutarch, the author likely wrote his biographies for a small circle of friends (cf. Rohrbacher, *The Play of Allusion in the Historia Augusta*, chap. 2).

[27] *Historia Augusta* III, "Probus," ed. Jeffrey Henderson, trans. David Magie (Cambridge, MA: Harvard University Press, 1932), I.1.

importance of both roles, Vopiscus compares the emperor and himself with the most famous pagan cultural monuments—Achilles and his Homer, Pompey and his Cicero and Livy—and all the Scipios and the famous and obscure historians who honored them in writing. Probus deserves it, Vopiscus explains, because he has restored the world to perfect order after fifty years of continuous civil war and barbarian invasion. Made emperor by divine mandate and election by the conscript fathers, he recovered the rogue Palmyrene and Gallic empires, is said to have killed some 400,000 barbarians who had seized Roman lands, and drove the rest across the Rhine where he raised frontier forts. These he manned with barbarian recruits, which he distributed along the *limes*, since "barbarian aid is to be felt but not seen."[28] Probus's treatment of the barbarians reads like a checklist of pagan complaints about what the Christian Theodosius had failed to do after Adrianople. According to Vopiscus, Probus had put all barbarian nations under his feet and made the universe itself Roman. There would be no need for arms or war; peace and the law of Rome would reign. He had promised a golden age (*aureum saeculum*), which hearkens back to Hesiod's five ages of man and Stoic millennialism, not the Christian millennial hexameron. Unfortunately, Probus was tragically killed by his own men, much like Athaulf, while draining a marsh for his people in Sirmium. But like Orosius, Vopiscus spent little time lamenting the fallen hero. As Athaulf prepared the way for the reforms of Wallia, Probus finished the work of Aurelian and set the stage for the reunification of the state under the pagan Diocletian. Probus's part would be celebrated by his divinization. This world has been disciplined, Orosius says, by alternating periods of good and bad times.[29] If the author of the *Historia Augusta* sees the crisis of the third century as parallel to that of the fifth, he may be heralding an imminent recovery. Little did he know that the Goths would soon march on Rome.

QUODVULTDEUS AND THE PILGRIMAGE TO HEAVEN

Orosius's optimism about "la marche ascendante de l'histoire"[30] also varied with current affairs. When he met Augustine in Hippo after the sack of Rome, he signed on to help restore confidence in the future of

28 Ibid., XIV.7.

29 Orosius, *Historiarum adversum paganos* 1.10.

30 Pierre Courcelle, "Quodvultdeus redivivus," *Revue des études anciennes* 67 (1965): 166.

both church and state by promoting hope in reconciliation with the barbarians under Roman rule. Augustine would complete *City of God* just before the Vandals invaded North Africa, and he died in 430 during the siege of Hippo. Quodvultdeus, bishop of Carthage and spiritual companion of Augustine, was arrested during the invasion of Carthage a decade later and deported with fellow clergy to Naples, where he spent the rest of his life evangelizing heretics, pagans, and lukewarm Christians. His *Book of the Promises and Predictions of God* (henceforth *Liber*) is Quodvultdeus's direct response to these crises and reflects both his mission and his reservations about Augustine's concept of economic millennialism.[31] The work has been criticized for its simple style and theology but, on the basis of its long popularity, seems to have suited both his purpose and audience. The *Liber* contains 153 chapters, which correspond with the number of fish caught by the disciples of the resurrected Christ in the second miraculous catch of John 21:1–14, and reinforce the evangelical intention of the work.[32] Although it may be classified as universal history, since it begins with creation itself and extends to God's promise to renew all things in eternity, its narrative development works systematically to collapse the gap between Old Testament, New Testament, and church history, which produces an effect exactly opposite to Augustine's emphasis on the radical difference between the earthly city and the heavenly city.

The title of the work also serves to unify the individual chapters, since each is introduced as either a promise (*promissio*) or a prediction (*praedictio*), establishing a typological association between events of the Old Testament and the advent of Jesus Christ. The two types of speech act operate reciprocally between the testaments and construct an ideal worldview intended to give hope and faith in the divine plan for the volatile city of man. Although the *Liber* is constructed as a closed analytical epistemology, Quodvultdeus attempts to demonstrate its historicity as well by identifying each promise and prediction as

[31] See Quodvultdeus, *Livre des promesses et de prédictions de Dieu*, trans. René Braun, SC 101–02 (Paris: Cerf, 1964).

[32] For Quodvultdeus the number 153 also symbolizes the structure of salvation history, which he divides into three eras: *Ante legem*, *Sub lege*, and *Sub gratia*, that is, from the Patriarchs to Moses, from Moses to Jesus Christ, and from Jesus Christ to the glory of the saints. He dedicates forty chapters to each of these, then adds twenty on the *Demidium tempus* (see Dan 7:25 and Rev 12:14), the period of the Antichrist, and concludes with thirteen chapters on the *Gloria regnumque sanctorum*. He also cites the six-age theory (see *Liber* 1.11).

"believed and seen" (*credita et visa*) or "to be believed" (*credenda*).[33] Its dialectical structure also contributes to the internal integrity of the work by constructing a parallel between the narrative logic of the history of the patriarchs and the typological logic of its promised relations with the salvation history of Jesus Christ.[34] At the beginning of the "Prologue," Quodvultdeus explains how the structure of the treatise reflects the believer's personal pursuit of God through the theological virtues. "Every account of faith," he says, "concludes in hope and love. In fact, it is by loving the promise, which he believes, that each person lends his faith to it until he obtains everything that he hopes for."[35] In other words, faith, hope, and charity direct the subject to the promise as object. But he then suggests that faith extends even further to a conviction in the reality of invisible things, ultimately God himself (see Heb 11:1).[36] The closed system of the *Liber*, which draws individual, community, and church into a single sacred history grounded in and leading to final reconciliation with ineffable divinity, is the most creative feature of the work.

Reconciliation is central to Quodvultdeus's worldview in two radical and complementary ways: eschatology and the cult of saints. Again, to emphasize personal spiritual investment in the living faith, Quodvultdeus follows Jerome in attempting to calculate the date of the apocalypse on the basis of the seventy-weeks model in Dan 9:20–27.[37] Although he arrives at two possible dates, depending on whether one

[33] For examples see Quodvultdeus, *Livre* I.158, 162, 164, etc.

[34] Leo I echoes this interpretation at Sermon 24.1 and 54.1. *Leo I Magnus, Sermones XCVI*, CCSL 138–138A (Turnhout: Brepols, 1973); in English *Leo the Great: Sermons*, trans. J. P. Freeland and A. J. Conway, FC 93 (Washington, DC: Catholic University of America Press, 1995).

[35] Quodvultdeus, *Livre* I.154. The translation is my own.

[36] Jean-Luc Marion's notion of the saturated phenomenon is relevant here. See Jean-Luc Marion, "The Saturated Phenomenon," in *The Visible and the Revealed* (New York: Fordham University Press, 2008), 18–48; Jean-Luc Marion, *Being Given: Toward a Phenomenology of Givenness* (Stanford, CA: Stanford University Press, 2002), 199–220; for context see Dominique Janicaud, "The Theological Turn in French Phenomenology," trans. Bernard G. Prusak, in Dominique Janicaud et al., *Phenomenology and the "Theological Turn": The French Debate* (New York: Fordham University Press, 2000), 62–65.

[37] Augustine challenges this method of dating the end, arguing that the weeks of Daniel may refer to the first coming of Christ, the Second Coming, or both. See Augustine's *Epistle to Hesychius* 199, chaps. 19–21, in *Sancti Aurelii Augustini Opera: S. Aureli Augustini Hipponiensis episcopi epistulae*, Ep. CLXXXV–CCLXX, sect. 2, pars 4, CSEL 57 (Vienna: Akademie der Wissenschaften, 1911). In English see Augustine, *Letters*, vol. 4 (letters 165–203), trans. Sister Wilfrid Parsons, FC 30 (Washington, DC: Catholic University of America Press, 1955), 356–401.

starts from the incarnation or the Passion, he concludes that Satan would be freed sixty to ninety years from his own day, sometime between 510 and 540, and use Gog and Magog, that is, the Goths and Moors, to devastate the church.[38] "*Venio cito*, blessed is he who is vigilant and keeps his vestments so that he not walk naked."[39] By vestments, Quodvultdeus means baptism in Christ,[40] which along with the incarnation and Epiphany was considered a prefiguration of Revelation itself. Many first experienced this baptism through the mediation of local saint cults and sacred relics. The cult of Quodvultdeus is still celebrated on three separate feast days corresponding with the calendars of Naples, Carthage, and Rome.[41] A mosaic portrait of Quodvultdeus was also discovered in the catacombs of San Gennaro in northern Naples.[42] In fact, large numbers of orthodox Christians fled persecution under the Vandalic occupation of North Africa and left traces of their movements in catacomb artifacts, martyrologies, liturgical calendars, and sermons, which demonstrate the influence of saint and martyr cults across the Mediterranean but especially in southern Italy and Spain. In a homily commemorating the sack of Rome by Alaric, Leo I celebrates local saints for protecting citizens who took refuge at their shrines during the occupation.[43] The eschatological expectations of the desert fathers, thousands of whom withdrew to the hinterlands ranging from Egypt up into Syria, also play a prominent role in the cultivation of regional loci of personal interaction with the other world.[44] Peter

[38] See *Liber* Demidium 22; see also *Liber* Demidium 16 on Nero and the Antichrist.

[39] Cf. Rev 16:15. This is my translation.

[40] *Liber* Demidium 23. For eschatology as baptism see Ellen Swift and Anne Alwis, "The Role of Late Antique Art in Early Christian Worship: A Reconsideration of the Iconography of the 'Starry Sky' in the 'Mausoleum' of Galla Placidia," *Papers of the British School at Rome* 78 (2010): 193–217, esp. 196–97.

[41] February 19 (Naples), January 8 (Carthage), October 26 (Rome).

[42] The catacomb comprises three cemeteries: one is dedicated to St. Gaudiosus, another fifth-century African bishop who fled the Vandals, the others to SS. Severus and Januarius (Gennaro). See Jonathan P. Conant, "Europe and the African Cult of Saints, Circa 350–900: An Essay in Mediterranean Communications," *Speculum* 85, no. 1 (January 2010): 1–46.

[43] Leo I, Sermon 84. According to tradition, Leo received the epithet "the great" from Pope Nicholas I for imitating the "Lion of the Tribe of Judah" (Rev 5:5), who, on opening his mouth, shook the whole world and the emperors themselves; Ep. 88, cited by Bronwen Neil, *Leo the Great* (New York: Routledge, 2009), 49. This is usually taken as a reference to Jesus Christ opening the seven seals of the scroll of Revelation.

[44] At its height desert monasticism is said to have attracted 10,000 monks and 20,000 nuns. See Benedicta Ward, trans., *The Desert Fathers: Sayings of the Early Christian Monks*, (London: Penguin, 2003). For its development through the sixth century see

Brown's *The Cult of the Saints* explores various ways Christians attempted to join "heaven and earth at the grave of a dead person," whose presence the faithful experienced directly. St. Eulalia of Merida, for example, was said to make trees bloom around her tomb and to heal the sick, Paulinus believed that he had been reborn with St. Felix through baptism and ascetic withdrawal, and Macrina felt she had been reborn a second St. Thecla when the latter renamed her.[45] Pilgrims traveled long distances to hear desert fathers utter a word, which was treated as a revelation from God, "a sacrament to live by."[46]

PILGRIMAGE OR ODYSSEY? RUTILIUS NAMATIANUS ON COMING HOME

The world of the ascetic looks very different through pagan eyes. Rutilius Namatianus, a Gallic aristocrat who served as prefect of the city of Rome in 414, wrote a poem of rich cultural allusion on his voyage to Gaul in 417, about the same time that Orosius published his *History against the Pagans*. Composed in elegiac couplets, *On His Return Home* (*De reditu suo*) plays with several literary genres simultaneously.[47] In recounting Rutilius's journey, it makes repeated allusions to the *nostos* of Odysseus and Aeneas's return to Italy from Troy to sow the seeds of the future Roman Empire. Rome herself is characterized as the mother of both men and gods, as the city that unified the world and gave a single fatherland (*patria*) to disparate nations. She also shares the senatorial power (*imperium*) of the state and the divine spirit (*genius*) of the Romans with people like Rutilius, from all parts of the empire, on the model of the celestial council under the supreme divinity: Jupiter. Rome is the most beautiful empire, superior to those of the Assyrians, Medes, Parthians, or Macedonians. This recalls the cycle of empires but in the Stoic tradition, not that of Daniel.[48] Like Orosius, Rutilius is deeply concerned about the widespread destruction wrought by the

Peter Brown, *The Rise of Western Christendom: Triumph and Diversity, A.D. 200–1000* (Oxford: Blackwell, 2003).

45 Peter Brown, *The Cult of the Saints: Its Rise and Function in Latin Christianity* (Chicago: University of Chicago Press, 2015), 57.

46 Ward, *The Desert Fathers*, 526.

47 Rutilius, *De reditu suo sive Iter Gallicum*, ed. E. Doblhofer, 2 vols. (Heidelberg: Winter, 1972–77).

48 Especially the *Chronicle* of Castor of Rhodes, but Varro also used it. Cf. Ernst Breisach, *Historiography: Ancient, Medieval and Modern* (Chicago: University of Chicago Press, 1994), 59. See Rutilius, *De reditu*, lines 83–85.

recent Gothic invasions and recounts a series of military disasters, not that diminish in severity, but that the Romans turn to their own advantage. Brennus after Allia, the Samnites, Pyrrhus, Hannibal: they all mourned their temporary success. The Romans have always prevailed. In fact, they trace their ancestry back to divine origins: Venus is the mother of Aeneas, Mars the father of Romulus. Like Orosius, Rutilius too calculates the age of Rome. Following Vergil's concept of an empire without end (*imperium sine fine*), however, Rutilius asserts that the time remaining has no bounds (*meta*).[49] The difference between *finis* and *meta* here is important, the latter denoting the turning point or goal in the circus as well as an end-time. For Rutilius there will be no more millennial turn, no goal, but a series of historical cycles characterized by periodic success and failure. "What restores you destroys the other regimes. The order of rebirth is to be able to grow from evil deeds."[50] The future of Rome is as divine as its origin.

Yet the elegiac couplet slips easily into satire and permits Rutilius to develop the irony of treating a short voyage from Rome to Gaul as a Homeric adventure or Aeneas's mission to plant the seeds of the future Roman Empire. Rutilius is merely returning to reclaim his home and rebuild after the Gothic invasion. He describes many of his experiences en route in epic language, but I will focus on two passages that highlight Rutilius's perspective on the Christian ascetic. In the first, he describes his experience on the island of Capraria, a squalid place full of men who flee the light, who call themselves monks because they want to live alone. They fear both the rewards and the penalties of fortune, living in misery to avoid misery. He compares them with prisoners who demand a fitting penalty for their crimes and suggests that their misanthropy, like that of Bellerophon, is due to some cruel suffering.[51] Far from the *umbilicus mundi* where pilgrims may collapse heaven and earth to commune with Christ through the cult of a saint, Rutilius's monks parody the tragic hero, since they refuse to engage in the natural cycle of life and history. In the second passage, Rutilius describes a similar approach to the island of Gorgon with Pisa and Corsica on either side. He avoids the cliffs, reminders of a young man who was recently lost there in a living death (*vivo funere*). He was descended from great ancestors and had wealth and a marriage to match, but impelled by

[49] *De reditu*, line 137.

[50] "illud te reparat quod cetera regna resolvit: ordo renascendi est crescere posse malis" (*De reditu*, lines 139–40). This is my translation.

[51] *De reditu*, lines 439–52.

madness the credulous exile entered a foul hideout. According to Rutilius, the unhappy fellow thinks the celestial beings feast on filth, and he treats himself more cruelly than the offended gods. Is not this sect worse than the poisons of Circe? Then, it was bodies that were transformed; now it is souls.[52] Rutilius here establishes a contrast between the values of elite Roman society—state religion, family, wealth, reason—and what he considers the mad superstition of those who willingly choose to live like the dead in foul exile. For Christians the daily bread (*epiousios*) of the Eucharist was believed to be both the simplest fare and superessential, sanctifying the earthly city with heavenly food, a foretaste of the messianic feast on the last day.[53] For Rutilius the encounter with the monks is indeed liminal, but he experiences it like Odysseus on the island of Circe, an uncanny encounter at the edge of the world where men are turned to swine by black magic—even worse since now it is their souls that are dehumanized.

SALVIAN OF MARSEILLES AND THE SPREADING DISEASE

If Rutilius was able to return home to Gaul in 417 because the Visigoths had pacified the local Vandal and Alan threat, by 439 the Goths had firmly established themselves in Aquitaine and southern Gaul, with their own capital and law courts at Toulouse, when the Vandal Geiseric seized Carthage.[54] The same year, a little to the east of Toulouse at the monastery of Lérins, Salvian of Marseilles began writing his famous treatise *On the Governance of God* (*De gubernatione Dei*), which offers another perspective on recent crisis and recovery both regionally and throughout the empire.[55] Convinced that Roman society is sick, Salvian

[52] Ibid., lines 515–26. "Infelix putat illuvie caelestia pasci / seque premit laesis saevior ipse deis" (523–24) suggests the body and blood of the Eucharistic sacrifice.

[53] See Gregory of Nyssa, "Sermon 4: Thy Will Be Done, on Earth as It Is in Heaven. Give us This Day Our Daily Bread," in *St. Gregory of Nyssa: The Lord's Prayer, The Beatitudes*, trans. Hilda C. Graef (New York: Paulist, 1978), 63. Brant Pitre, "Jesus, the Messianic Banquet, and the Kingdom of God," *Letter and Spirit* 5 (2009): 145–66.

[54] For background see T. S. Burns, "The Settlement of 418," in *Fifth-Century Gaul: A Crisis of Identity?*, ed. Drinkwater and Elton, 53–63.

[55] *Salvien de Marseilles, Oeuvres II: Du gouvernement de Dieu*, ed. and trans. Georges Lagarrigue, SC 220 (Paris: Cerf, 1975); in English *Salvian, Presbyter of Marseilles, On the Government of God*, trans. Eva M. Sanford (New York: Columbia University Press, 1930); I. N. Wood, "Continuity or Calamity? The Constraints of Literary Models," in *Fifth-Century Gaul: A Crisis of Identity?*, ed. Drinkwater and Elton, 9–18.

writes *Governance* as a remedy intended to persuade his elite Christian audience that the only way to reverse the current decline of the state is to repent and convert.[56] Starting with a refutation of the Epicurean claim that the gods do not intervene in human affairs, Salvian constructs an elaborate argument demonstrating that God has been directly involved in the judgment and correction of his people since the beginning of time. Tracing his universal Christian history through the line of patriarchs to the kingdom of David, Salvian recognizes a cyclical pattern in the relationship between God and his people. As Adam transgressed the sacred law, was judged, was exiled from paradise, and suffered damnation, so people paid the price again at the time of Noah and at Sodom and Gomorrah. Abraham was sent into exile to become rich and powerful, but God still tested him with periodic adversity. He faced the sacrifice of Isaac and troubles with Abimelech and the Philistines but in each case was compensated with equal consolations. All these events, Salvian explains, where God sent Gehenna down out of heaven upon an impious people, "prefigure that coming judgment" when the wicked will be punished in flames.[57] To avoid recounting an entire history of divine judgment and salvation, Salvian cites the ten times that Pharaoh rebelled and was punished, which he contrasts with a description of the Israelites wandering the desert for forty years, as God himself guided their uncharted ways, delighted them with food and drink, spared them the natural processes of growth and decay, and descended to earth to instruct his people in sacred intimacy, "in a school of heaven and earth commingled." His people learn to expect both immediate judgment as well as the judgment to come for how they respect God's law.[58]

Salvian's history of divine judgment lays the groundwork for his interpretation of the ongoing transformation of the Western Empire. At the beginning of book 3 he raises the question, why are the barbarians doing so much better than the Romans? His first response, echoing that of the Israelites following the Babylonian captivity, is that he does not know the secrets of God.[59] At 7.13, however, he explains that the Vandals had followed a divine command to invade North Africa. Like the king of the Assyrians, who devasted the land of Israel, they acted against their will and are compared with Nebuchadnezzar, king of

[56] For background see Susanna Elm, "2016 NAPS Presidential Address, New Romans: Salvian of Marseilles on the Governance of God," *JECS* 25, no. 1 (2017): 1–27.

[57] *Governance* 1.8.

[58] Ibid. 2.6.

[59] Cf. Job 23.

Babylon, who is called the servant of God. The purpose of the Vandal invasion was part of God's plan to punish and correct the Romans. Salvian's second response modifies this pattern, demonstrating a Roman exceptionalism exactly opposite to Rutilius's *sine fine* model. The Romans receive the immediate judgment of God because they break his law in every way. As Salvian has already demonstrated, justice means health and salvation. Without justice, coupled with repentance, there can be no recovery. The cycle has flattened out, as Rutilius had said, but here it is divine vengeance that continues unabated. The practical consequences of the breakdown of the legal system touch every aspect of Roman life. To fill the depleted coffers, the rich shift the bulk of the taxes onto the poor, which drives those with the means to seek asylum in barbarian territory where no such practice exists. Those who do not flee, Salvian says, simply cannot move their little property, so they seek protection from the rich and thereby pass into their power. Although they end up handing over most of their goods, they are still held liable for their taxes and find themselves ruined between private invasion and public harassment.[60] The whole Roman state is implicated, including judges, priests, and the curial class. Even the educated seek refuge with the barbarians, who now show Roman mercy while the Romans have become barbarously merciless. According to Salvian, the Romans are paying what they owe. They showed no mercy to exiles; they are now the exiles, beginning to live on foreign soil. The reason why it continues, he adds, is that they refuse to reform, to be corrected. They treasure up wrath against the day of wrath.[61] Although Salvian points here to the judgment to come, he describes God's immediate judgment and punishment, the ongoing transformation of the Western Empire, and its restoration under Gothic and Vandal rule.

Salvian's cultural motivation for writing *Governance* was the Epicurean claim that the gods do not intervene in human affairs. Like Lucretius, he hopes to allay people's fear and suffering with a literary remedy.[62] Whereas Lucretius lines the cup of his bitter philosophy with the honey of verse, Salvian rejects the use of rhetoric for personal glory.

[60] See Walter Goffart, "Salvian of Marseille, *De gubernatione Dei* 5.38–45 and the Colonate Problem," *Antiquité Tardive* 17 (2009): 269–88. See Salvian, *Governance* 5.28–43.

[61] *Governance* 5.9.

[62] For ancient references and modern discussions see Jacob L. Mackey, "Saving the Appearances: The Phenomenology of Epiphany in Atomist Theology," Princeton/Stanford Working Papers in Classics Paper No. 050601 (2006); Owen Barfield, *Saving*

His intention is "not to please idle ears but to benefit the minds of the sick."[63] The pagan tradition offered many alternatives to Epicurean thought, and Salvian cites Pythagoras, Plato, the Stoics, Vergil, and Cicero in defense of the Christian doctrine of divine providence. There still remained, however, the broader cultural problem of pagan education and entertainment. The role of the arts in the construction and transformation of political culture had been hotly debated for over a thousand years—in archaic Sparta and classical Athens, in the Hellenistic kingdoms and Roman Empire, and now in the culture wars between Christians and pagans. Writing in the tradition of Plato's *Republic*, Augustine had attacked both pagan *paideia* and the deleterious moral effects of its various types of performance.[64] If Roman culture is disintegrating like the legal and economic systems, it is because of the pollution, Salvian explains, caused by the theater, circus, games, parades, rope dancers, and mimes.[65] Drama, for example, corrupts actor and spectator alike in both mind and body because they both approve and take pleasure in the performance. They therefore also share the guilt for such crimes as homicide, robbery, adultery, and sacrilege. In contrast with Aristotle's theory of tragic catharsis, which describes a process of emotional purging and purification,[66] Salvian describes pagan drama as corrupt. He associates it with the worship of idols, since Christians have no god of theater,[67] and compares its pursuit with trying to scale the

the Appearances: A Study in Idolatry (Middletown, CT: Wesleyan University Press, 1957).

63 See "Preface to Salonius," in Salvian, *Governance*, trans. Sanford, 37. For philosophical therapy see Martha C. Nussbaum, *The Therapy of Desire: Theory and Practice in Hellenistic Ethics* (Princeton, NJ: Princeton University Press, 1994), 484–510.

64 See Daniel G. Van Slyke, "The Devil and His Pomps in Fifth-Century Carthage: Renouncing Spectacula with Spectacular Imagery," *Dumbarton Oaks Papers* 59 (2005): 53–72. Yet Honorius and Arcadius still made provisions for public entertainment. See Richard Miles, "The *Anthologia Latina* and the Creation of Secular Space in Vandal Carthage," *Antiquité Tardive* 13 (2005): 305–20, esp. 308. Proclus's *Commentary on the Republic* provides a pagan apology on many of these issues.

65 *Governance* 6.3.

66 See Constance Eichenlaug, "Aristotelian *Katharsis* as Ethical Conversion in Plotinian Aesthetics," *Dionysius* 17 (1999): 57–82; Hilaire Kallendorf and Craig Kallendorf, "Catharsis as Exorcism: Aristotle, Tragedy, and Religio-Poetic Liminality," *Literary Imagination* 14, no. 3 (2012): 296–311; Adela Yarbro Collins, *Crisis and Catharsis: The Power of the Apocalypse* (Philadelphia: Westminster, 1984).

67 Since Salvian considers Dionysus a false god, he need not mention his role as savior and liberator in the contemporary Orphic mystery cult. See M. L. West, *The Orphic*

heavens to make war on God. If drama has now become relatively uncommon in Gaul and Spain, it is because the barbarians have no theater. Local Romans have not given up the practice thanks to moral improvement but because the imperial treasury is bankrupt and they can no longer afford it. Quoting the apocalyptic passage Jer 44:21–22, Salvian states that the Lord could no longer bear "the abominations that you have committed. Your land is therefore a desolation, an astonishment and a curse." The Romans have not repented, but "constantly add evils to evils and pile sins upon sins" to complete their own destruction.[68] They are living revelation. Instead of the pagan spectacles, which he considers a violation of the Christian creed and sacraments, Salvian proposes the incarnation, the manger, and the cross, all mapping the route into exile and the return home through conversion, all prefiguring revelation and the hope of salvation.[69] The creed and the sacrament complete the bond between the city of God and the city of man, in Christ.[70]

PETER CHRYSOLOGUS ON NEW BEGINNINGS

Salvian is not the only contemporary writer who attests to the general collapse of the imperial system. Peter Chrysologus, archbishop of Ravenna with close ties to Galla Placidia and Valentinian III, often preached about the inefficiency and corruption of the Roman legal system, government bureaucracy, and military machine.[71] By 439 Roman law had been revised to eliminate contradictions in rulings and proceedings and to establish a universal standard for the entire empire. Written in Constantinople between 429 and 437, the Theodosian Code was presented

Poems (Oxford: Clarendon, 1984). For late antique syncretism of Dionysus/Christ see G. W. Bowersock, *Hellenism in Late Antiquity* (Ann Arbor: University of Michigan Press, 1996), 41–53.

[68] *Governance* 6.9, trans. Sanford.

[69] For background on the relationship between apocalyptic literature and tragic drama see James L. Blevins, "The Genre of Revelation," *Review and Expositor* 77, no. 3 (1980): 393–408. For an ancient example of the tragedy of the Passion see Leo I, Sermon 55. Also see Kevin Taylor, *Christ the Tragedy of God: A Theological Exploration of Tragedy* (London: Routledge, 2018).

[70] Peter Brown notes the connection between the *spectaculum* of the martyr festival and the Eucharist. This he describes as a "*heilbringende Schau*, a sight which in and of itself unleashed salvation" ("Enjoying the Saints in Late Antiquity," *Early Medieval Europe* 9, no. 1 (2000): 9).

[71] Peter Chrysologus, *Collectio sermonum*, CCSL 24, 24A, 24B (Turnhout: Brepols, 1982); in English *St. Peter Chrysologus, Selected Sermons*, trans. George E. Ganss, SJ, FC (Washington, DC: Catholic University of America Press, 1953).

to the Roman senate in 438 and immediately implemented throughout the provinces, though not without dissent.[72] Composed of soldiers and farmers as well as lawyers and members of the imperial court, including Galla Placidia herself, Peter's congregation is representative of a wide range of current interests and anxieties, which his sermons address both directly and figuratively. The legal revisions had removed many rituals and formulae derived from archaic religious practices, whose authority was now replaced by extensive archives of what many considered inhuman, even evil written documents. To resist the new conventions, people resorted to oaths, relics, and curse tablets, which described the specified case in detail, including the name of the plaintiff and the supporting documentation. Aware of their problems with debtors, tax collectors, and corrupt bureaucrats, Peter consoles his congregation by raising the stakes from debt and freedom to sin and redemption. According to Peter, the true Christian has no need of law. It is necessary only because of sin, and the devil himself owns the legal documents that indenture people to him. Righteousness is the debt that Christians owe to God, and the document that assures their salvation is the Apostles' Creed.[73] The mixing of metaphors is not merely rhetorical. In contrast with the growing numbers of certified imperial advocates, the bishops themselves had begun ruling civil cases through the expansion of the duties of the *audientia episcopalis*.[74] Unlike his imperial counterpart, however, Peter recognizes that the bishop is also indebted to his congregation, that clerics and laity share a mutual obligation, which "it is a joy to repay." Ristuccia points out that Peter uses the language of the Jewish Jubilee, the general liberation from debt-slavery and the restoration of leased lands to their original owners, to describe the redemption of humanity by Jesus Christ. In contrast to the fifty-year cycle of periodic restoration celebrated in Jewish law, however, Peter looks forward to the final destruction of all written law and the resurrection of the debtor.[75]

Peter describes kings as low-level administrators, stewards of God tasked to ensure only that the bureaucracy run smoothly and the

[72] Nathan J. Ristuccia, "Law and Legal Documents in the Sermons of Peter Chrysologus," *Journal of Late Antiquity* 4, no. 1 (2011): 126–27.

[73] Ibid., 125.

[74] Ibid., 129. Decretals of Popes Siricius, Celestine, Innocent I, and Leo I were published in several collections, which influenced Canon Law through the Middle Ages. See D. Jasper and H. Fuhrmann, *Papal Letters in the Early Middle Ages* (Washington, DC: Catholic University Press of America, 2001), 1–133.

[75] Ristuccia, "Law and Legal Documents in the Sermons of Peter Chrysologus," 140.

republic remain secure. On the last day they will be held accountable with everyone else: judges, governors, and generals alike. The rigid complexity of the Jewish and Roman legal systems reflects that of their governments. When Herod failed, Christ was born to restore order for his people. At his second coming, he will restore order for the entire world.[76] In the end it is not the Roman military but Christ, through the church, that stems the tide of barbarian conquest. The lack of clerical support for the military defense of the empire is a striking feature of Christian literature from the fifth to seventh centuries.[77] Prosper of Aquitaine criticizes generals and usurpers as jealous murderers and oppressors of the church.[78] Since large numbers of barbarians now served in the Roman armies, and the barbarians were for the most part Arians, the church criticized the military as much for its heresy as for its violence. Although Rome had grown from its many victories and had extended imperial law by land and sea, "what the labors of war subjected to [her] is less than what the peace of Christ subdued."[79] If the Huns were stopped (452) and the Vandals tempered in their sack of Rome (455), it was thanks to Pope Leo I, who defended the state by the grace of God, not the force of arms. These events may be taken as consequences of Leo's controversial doctrine of universal salvation offered by Christ throughout the church, where the central unity represented by St. Peter the apostle in Rome extended to the Pentecostal assembly of nations represented by St. Paul.[80] The feast of the

[76] Peter Chrysologus, Sermon 156.5; Ristuccia, "Law and Legal Documents in the Sermons of Peter Chrysologus," 142.

[77] Steven Muhlberger, "War, Warlords, and Christian Historians from the Fifth to the Seventh Century," in *After Rome's Fall: Narrators and Sources of Early Medieval History; Essays Presented to Walter Goffart*, ed. Alexander Callander Murray (Toronto: University of Toronto Press, 1998), 83. For Prosper's service to Leo I see N. W. James, "Leo the Great and Prosper of Aquitaine: A Fifth Century Pope and His Adviser," *JTS* 44, no. 2 (1993).

[78] See Muhlberger, "War, Warlords, and Christian Historians from the Fifth to the Seventh Century," 88.

[79] Leo I, Sermon 82.1, in *St. Leo the Great Sermons*, trans. Jane Patricia Freeland and Agnes Josephine Conway, FC, Patristic Series (Washington, DC: Catholic University of America Press, 2004), 353. In 450 both Valentinian III and Marcian recognized the primacy of the bishop of Rome over the entire church, east and west (Leo I, Ep. 73), but the eastern emperor soon asserted power over his church. Gelasius attempted to resolve the tension between church and state power with his doctrine of the two powers (see Gelasius, *Duo sunt*, PL 187, 458Dff.). Ecclesial resistance also continued in the east, less in the west (see Neil, *Leo the Great*, 42–43).

[80] R. A. Markus, "Chronicle and Theology: Prosper of Aquitaine," in *The Inheritance of Historiography, 350–900*, ed. Christopher Holdsworth and T. P. Wiseman (Exeter: Exeter University Publications, 1986), 37–39.

Concordia apostolorum, which replaced the Republican ideology of the *Concordia ordinum*, celebrated the harmony of the extension of the empire within the Body of Christ.[81] The feast also promoted a *renovatio urbis*, a new beginning for Rome, not based on the fratricide of Romulus and Remus, but on the love and unity of Peter and Paul, as depicted in medallions and gilded glasses discovered in catacombs and cemeteries throughout Rome.[82] Worshipers had visual access to the apostles' relics by way of *confessions*, recesses excavated in front of the altar down to the tomb. During the Hun and Vandal threats of 452–55, martyr cults became important models of military and spiritual heroism.[83]

It is worth noting that, according to an apocryphal tradition, Sixtus III appointed Peter Chrysologus archbishop of Ravenna only after St. Peter himself and Apollinaris, the first bishop of Ravenna, appeared to Sixtus in a dream and revealed their choice, not the man elected by the people of Ravenna, but Peter Chrysologus.[84] St. Peter's relationship to Paul was parallel to that with Apollinaris and presumably those with all subsequent bishops of the city until the appointment of Peter Chrysologus. Ultimately, the unity and plurality celebrated in the *Concordia apostolorum* are traced back to the feasts of Easter and Pentecost, which provide the most universal model for both the reconciliation of the human with the divine and the dissemination of the gospel news of salvation among the nations.[85] It is not coincidental that, at the Ecumenical Council of 451, Leo I advocated the perfect union of two natures, divine and human, in the one person (*hypostasis*) of Jesus Christ. Neither the Nestorians, who argued for two distinct natures in the one person, nor the Miaphysites, who recognized only one divine nature in the one person, could adequately explain how faith in the resurrection of Jesus Christ could offer a way to rebirth and salvation.[86]

[81] A. Temelini, "Cicero's Concordia: The Promotion of a Political Concept in the Late Roman Republic" (PhD diss., McGill University, 2002).

[82] Charles Pietri, "Concordia apostolorum et renovatio urbis (Culte des martyrs et propagande pontificale)," *Mélange d'archéologie et d'histoire* 73 (1961): 278ff.

[83] Neil, *Leo the Great*, 58–59.

[84] Roman Breviary, December 4.

[85] See Leo I, Sermon 63.6; 75.2.

[86] See Aloys Grillmeier, SJ, "The Council of Chalcedon," in *Christ in Christian Tradition: From the Apostolic Age to Chalcedon (451)* (Louisville, KY: Westminster John Knox, 1975), 543–54.

CONCLUDING REMARKS

The crises of the fifth century generated a long process of sociopolitical transformation in the Western Empire, whose identity contemporary witnesses contested with a rich variety of traditional and innovative ideology and with a literary verve equal to the intensity of the times. A sense that impending and repeated disaster was a sign of divine judgment and some type of imminent end-time stimulated speculation about the possibilities of personal, political, and cosmic restoration or transformation. While some see the crises as tests of faith in God's unpredictable plan of salvation, others attempt to calculate the exact date of the Parousia. Some give current events a positivist spin, where crises diminish in intensity until all are reconciled under the leadership of Rome. Others recognize both a future Last Judgment and an ongoing cycle of sin and punishment, which fuel a consequent escape from Roman rule and rebirth in a Gothic Gaul and Vandal North Africa. Interpreting the crises through their own cultural lenses, some pagans see a contemporary parallel with the end of the crisis of the third century. Others see it as an opportunity to exploit a temporary setback. Later, to counteract a general systems-collapse in the west, a Christian ideology is constructed to absorb the entire empire, including the pagans, heretics, and all the nations, by conversion into the single body of Jesus Christ, which is resurrected universally and at every level. While these views have had profound historical impact, the cultural debates of the fifth century attest to many other interpretations of contemporary sociopolitical transformation. Such writers as Dracontius, another refugee from Vandal North Africa, Victor of Vita, who documents the persecution there, and the letters of Sidonius, Ennodius, and Ruricius all present prolific perspectives on the meaning and prospects of the end of the Western Roman Empire.

Selected Further Reading

Brown, Peter. *The Rise of Western Christendom: Triumph and Diversity, A.D. 200–1000*. Oxford: Blackwell, 2003.

Burgess, Richard W., and Michael Kulikowski, *Mosaics of Time: The Latin Chronicle Traditions from the First Century BC to the Sixth Century AD*. Vol. 1, *A Historical Introduction to the Chronicle Genre from Its Origins to the High Middle Ages*. Turnhout: Brepols, 2012.

Collins, Adela Yarbro. *Crisis and Catharsis: The Power of the Apocalypse*. Philadelphia: Westminster, 1984.

Drinkwater, John, and Hugh Elton, eds. *Fifth-Century Gaul: A Crisis of Identity?* Cambridge: Cambridge University Press, 2002.

Gabriele, Matthew, and James T. Palmer, eds. *Apocalypse and Reform from Late Antiquity to the Middle Ages*. London: Routledge, 2019.
Halsall, Guy. *Barbarian Migrations and the Roman West, 376–568*. Cambridge: Cambridge University Press, 2007.
Merrills, A. H., ed. *Vandals, Romans and Berbers: New Perspectives on Late Antique North Africa*. New York: Routledge, 2016.
Palmer, James T. *The Apocalypse in the Early Middle Ages*. New York: Cambridge University Press, 2014.
Portier-Young, Anathea E. *Apocalypse against Empire: Theologies of Resistance in Early Judaism*. Grand Rapids, MI: Eerdmans, 2011.
Ramelli, Ilaria L. E. *The Christian Doctrine of Apokatastasis: A Critical Assessment from the New Testament to Eriugena*. Leiden: Brill, 2013.

7 Latin Reception of the Apocalypse in the Early Middle Ages*

E. ANN MATTER

The last book of the Christian Scriptures, the Apocalypse (or Revelation) of John, has one of the most interesting histories of interpretation in the Christian tradition. In modern Christianity, the book is primarily understood as a literal prophecy of the tribulations to come in the end-times, when Christ will return and the world will come to an end. *Left Behind*, a wildly popular series of sixteen Christian novels published between 1995 and 2007, sets the events of the biblical Apocalypse in twentieth-century America, in a strictly Christian dispensationalist reading.[1] Although the Apocalypse may seem to many modern Christians a clear description of the end-times, one of the many paradoxes of the reception of this book is the fact that, for much of Christian history, it was interpreted as looking backward rather than forward; that is, as an explanation of travails already overcome by the church rather than as a prophecy of things impending.

Although the Apocalypse was among the first biblical texts to be systematically explicated in the Latin tradition, one interesting feature of its reception in the early medieval period is the doubtful orthodoxy of the first Latin interpretations, which emerged in the third and fourth

* This chapter has been adapted from my essay "The Apocalypse in Early Medieval Exegesis," in *The Apocalypse in the Middle Ages*, ed. Richard K. Emmerson and Bernard McGinn (Ithaca, NY: Cornell University Press, 1992), 38–50. Here I have updated all references and focused more closely on the reasons for this exegetical choice. I am grateful to Colin McAllister for his advice and his patience. All translations herein are my own unless otherwise indicated.

[1] Tim LaHaye and Jerry B. Jenkins, *Left Behind* (Wheaton, IL: Tyndale House, 1995) is the first novel in the series. Dispensationalism is a theory of biblical interpretation that understands world history as divided into epochs (or dispensations) as revealed in the Bible that lead to the end of time. Although this idea is found in some early Christian writings, it has had its greatest moment in the nineteenth and twentieth centuries, especially among American Fundamentalist Protestants; see Charles Caldwell Ryrie, *Dispensationalism* (Chicago: Moody Press, 1995). I thank Anthea Butler for her advice about modern American dispensationalism.

centuries. Also interesting is the way in which the orthodox tradition transformed the seeming apocalyptic fervor of the text into an extended allegory of the church. This essay will illustrate these developments through an overview of Latin Apocalypse commentary to the ninth century, keeping in focus how each author adapted received material into new forms in response to the particular concerns of the church of his age.

The earliest known Latin interpretation of the Apocalypse was the commentary written by Victorinus of Pettau (in the Pannonia region of modern Steiermark, Austria) about 260 CE.[2] This was adapted and revised for orthodoxy in three forms by the noted biblical scholar Jerome; so, even though its interpretation was repudiated by later Latin exegetes, it remained a standard for many centuries.

Victorinus took his clue from the opening statement that the revelation to John shows "the things that must soon take place" (Rev 1:1). Perhaps understandably for one who lived (and died) in the persecutions of Diocletian, he understood the promises and threats of the Apocalypse as a literal representation of the church in his age. Victorinus's interpretation of the Apocalypse was essentially chiliastic, that is, it was based on the expectation that there would be a thousand-year reign of Christ which would constitute a sign of the end-times. This was a problematic reading for the Christian society of the post-Constantinian world in which the church grew into more solid institutional forms and developed more complicated (and safer) relationships to the temporal power of the empire.

It was therefore Jerome's task to mold the exegesis of Victorinus into a form that better reflected a church at peace with the empire, if not always with the world. This he partially accomplished, as later exegetes noted with approval, by transforming a literal reading of the text to one with an allegorical framework, suggesting a series of meanings for Victorinus's chiliasm. In the prologue to his revision, for example, Jerome explains that Victorinus's expectation of a thousand-year reign of Christ as an historical event is an overliteral reading of Rev 20, necessitating a series of corrections.[3]

[2] Victorini Poetovionensis, *Opera quae supersunt*, ed. Roger Gryson, CCSL 5 (Turnhout: Brepols, 2017). Until this recent publication, the best edition was edited by Johannes Haussleiter, CSEL 49 (Vienna and Leipzig: Corpus Scriptorum Ecclesiasticorum Latinorum, 1916). See William C. Weinrich, trans., *Latin Commentaries on Revelation*, ACT (Downers Grove, IL: InterVarsity Press, 2011).

[3] "de mille annorum regno ita ut Victorinus senserunt. Et quia me litteris obtestatus es, nolui differre ... A principio libri usque ad crucis signum quae ab imperiti<i>s erant

Within this framework of multiple meanings, Jerome was able to save a concept that Victorinus (influenced by the earlier authors Tertullian and Irenaeus) had applied to the Apocalypse in classic form: the theory of recapitulation. As understood through recapitulation, the Apocalypse presents a series of typological events that have already occurred—beginning from the time of the Patriarchs—and will reoccur in sacred history through the unknown future of the church on earth, to the Parousia. This theological concept of the "already/not yet" has become a major interpretative key of Christian theology, keeping a creative tension between the historical past and the expectation of the Second Coming of Christ. An example of this can be seen in the fact that, for Victorinus, the seven trumpets of Rev 8 echo from the empire of Babylon into the future, and Antichrist can be seen in the history of the Roman emperors as well as the one who will come in the last days.[4] This approach to New Testament prophecy—the linking of a specific historical moment to a transcendent purpose—was the insight for which the commentary of Victorinus was preserved by Jerome; this in turn gave later exegetes the freedom to interpret the text in congruence with the specific tribulations of their broadly variant ecclesiastical worlds.

The commentary of Victorinus/Jerome is therefore significant for the history of Apocalypse exegesis because it opened up some important themes of interpretation and emphasis. An easily evident example, and one that shows the complexity of the textual traditions, is the interpretation of Rev 13:18, "This calls for wisdom: let anyone with understanding calculate the number of the beast, for it is the number of a person. Its number is six hundred and sixty-six." The "Y" version of the text, Jerome's first revision, reckons the number of the beast by ascribing Pythagorean number equivalences to the Greek word *antemos*, meaning "contrary to honor," which, when broken down to letter-by-letter numerical equivalences and added up, totals 666. This reckoning may have originated with Victorinus, but a later hand is visible in the additional computation of the name Gensericus (king of the Vandals, d. 477) as also equivalent to 666. Jerome's later (post-Vulgate) redaction of Victorinus instead calculates the 666 from the Greek name *Teitan*,

scriptorum vitiata, correximus, exinde usque ad finem voluminis addita esse cognosce." CCSL 5, 109.

[4] See Victorinus on chap. 8 and chaps. 13–17 in CCSL 5, 190–96, 228–42, and Wilhelm Bousset, *Die Offenbarung Johannis*, 6th ed. (Göttingen: Vandenhoeck & Ruprecht, 1906), 53–55.

numerically equivalent to the Latin *Diclux*, the false sun, the Antichrist. The later composite recension conflates the two explanations. Combinations of these explanations are found over and over again in early medieval Apocalypse commentaries, often with elaborations bringing the examples up to date.[5]

Another influential, although also problematic, source from the late antique period of Latin exegesis was the sevenfold interpretation of the Apocalypse by Tyconius.[6] As a member of the Donatist church of North Africa, Tyconius presented an obvious cause for suspicion. Yet Augustine's guarded admiration for his exegetical schemes, and his careful response to Tyconius's rules in *De doctrina Christiana*, ensured that the Apocalypse exegesis of Tyconius would be taken seriously. The complicated relationship between Tyconius and Augustine left the two intrinsically linked in Apocalypse exegesis of the early Middle Ages.[7] Augustine was the obvious "antidote" for Tyconius, as Jerome was for Victorinus.

A "catholicized" version of Tyconius on the Apocalypse, extant in a manuscript from the Italian monastery of Bobbio, shows that a version of the text survived independently as late as the eleventh century.[8] Tyconius also seems to have been used by Jerome in his revision of Victorinus.[9] Tyconius had a direct influence on exegetes in widely diverse early medieval intellectual environments, such as Primasius in North Africa,[10]

[5] CCSL 5, 236–39. See below for how this text was used. Gryson's list of manuscripts shows that the text was widely available, in various regions, before 1100.

[6] Tyconius, *Expositio Apocalypseos*, ed. Roger Gryson, CCSL 107A (Turnhout: Brepols, 2011); in English *Tyconius: Exposition of the Apocalypse*, trans. Francis X. Gumerlock, FC 134 (Washington, DC: Catholic University of America Press, 2017). See also Pamela Bright, *The Book of Rules of Tyconius: Its Purpose and Inner Logic* (Notre Dame, IN: University of Notre Dame Press, 1988).

[7] For studies of Augustine's response to Tyconius, see Paula Fredriksen [Landes], "Tyconius and the End of the World," *Revue des études Augustiniennes* 28 (1982): 59–75; and Paula Fredriksen, "Tyconius and Augustine on the Apocalypse," in *The Apocalypse in the Middle Ages*, ed. Emmerson and McGinn, 20–37.

[8] This manuscript is now Turin, Biblioteca Nazionale MS 882 [F. IV. 1]; see Francesco Lo Bue, ed., *The Turin Fragment of Tyconius' Commentary on Revelation* (Cambridge: Cambridge University Press, 1963). A new edition of the Turin Fragment is edited by Roger Gryson in CCSL 107A, 347–86.

[9] For Jerome's use of Tyconius, see Haussleiter's edition of Victorinus in CSEL 49, xlii–xlv; also Fredriksen [Landes], "Tyconius and the End of the World," 74.

[10] Primasius, *Commentarius in Apocalypsin*, ed. A. W. Adams, CCSL 92 (Turnhout: Brepols, 1985). The best available study of Primasius is still Johannes Haussleiter, *Leben und Werke des Bischofs Primasius von Hadrumentum: Eine Untersuchung* (Erlangen: E. Th. Jacob, 1887).

Caesarius in Gaul,[11] Bede in Northumbria,[12] and Ambrosius Autpertus in the Lombard kingdom of Benevento.[13] There are also two early medieval Hiberno-Latin commentaries: a seventh-century preacher's handbook falsely attributed to Jerome (and in one manuscript to Isidore), known as the Pseudo-Jerome *Handbook on the Apocalypse of the Apostle John*,[14] and an eighth-century treatise *On the Mysteries of the Apocalypse of John* (part of the large Hiberno-Latin text known as *The Reference Bible*).[15] Both of these texts are anonymous, and both have recently been translated into English by Francis X. Gumerlock.[16] Gumerlock's introduction points out that the *Handbook* cites the Apocalypse commentaries of Victorinus, Tyconius, and Primasius—as well as works of Jerome, Gregory the Great, and Isidore—but not Bede's great commentary. Since Bede's commentary dates to the early eighth century, and since the *Handbook* displays many Irish characteristics, Gumerlock agrees with previous scholars that it must predate Bede's work.[17] The *Reference Bible* commentary on the Apocalypse dates from the eighth century. It seems to be heavily dependent on a now-lost Hiberno-Latin Apocalypse commentary from the first half of the eighth century, but evidently not on the *Handbook*, although it may share some unknown sources with the earlier text. The *Reference Bible* also draws also on Tyconius, and perhaps on Bede.[18] There is also a Hiberno-Latin *Glossa in Apocalypsin* found only in one Cambridge manuscript. This commentary draws from Tyconius, apparently directly, but not, it seems, from the later commentators Primasius and Bede.[19]

[11] Caesarius Arelatensis, *Expositio in Apocalypsim*, ed. G. Morin (Maredsous: [Abbey], 1942), repr. in LLT, Series A (Turnhout: Brepols, 2010), 210–77. See English translation in Weinrich, *Latin Commentaries on Revelation*.

[12] Bede, *Explanatio Apocalypseos*, ed. Roger Gryson, CCSL 121A (Turnhout: Brepols, 2001). Cf. Weinrich, *Latin Commentaries on Revelation*. In English see Bede, *Commentary on Revelation*, trans. Faith Wallis, TTH 58 (Liverpool: Liverpool University Press, 2013).

[13] Ambrosius Autpertus, *Expositionis in Apocalypsim*, ed. R. Weber, CCCM 27, 27A (Turnhout: Brepols, 1975).

[14] *Commemoratorium de Apocalypsi Iohannis Apostoli*, in *Commentaria minora in Apocalypsin Iohannis*, ed. Roger Gryson, CCSL 107 (Turnhout: Brepols, 2003), 191–229. See also Joseph T. Kelly, "Early Medieval Evidence for Twelve Homilies by Origen on the Apocalypse," *Vigiliae Christianae* 39 (1985): 273–79.

[15] *De enigmatibus ex Apocalypsi Johannes*, in *Commentaria minora in Apocalypsin Iohannis*, ed. Gryson, CCSL 107, 231–95.

[16] Francis X. Gumerlock, ed., *Early Latin Commentaries on the Apocalypse*, TEAMS Commentary Series (Kalamazoo, MI: Medieval Institute Publications, 2016).

[17] Ibid., 1–3.

[18] Ibid., 13–15.

[19] *Glossa in Apocalypsin e codice Bibliothecae Vniuersitatis Cantabrigiensis Dd.X.16 (Exegetica)*, ed. Roger Gryson, CCSL 108G (Turnhout: Brepols, 2013); English

Through these intermediaries, Tyconius's themes of Apocalypse interpretation, including a clear rejection of chiliasm, the emphasis on the incarnation as defined in the great councils of his century, and a theory of recapitulation expounded within his seven rules, are used by many medieval authors who were probably not directly aware of Tyconius. For example, Ambrosius Autpertus, at the end of the eighth century, acknowledges that Primasius put together Tyconius and Augustine into one commentary; perhaps a decade later, a treatise attributed to Alcuin, whose author probably did not know Tyconius, repeats this information verbatim.[20] The commentary of Primasius thus marks the second stage of early medieval Apocalypse exegesis.

The later tradition is, in fact, so indebted to Primasius that it could be argued that he—rather than Victorinus or Tyconius—is the start of medieval Latin Apocalypse exegesis. Primasius's text on the Apocalypse is essentially a synthesis of the two influential but heterodox exegetes of the fourth century, read, of course, through the lenses of their orthodox redactors.

Primasius was the bishop of Justiniapolis (Hadrumentum) in the North African province of Numidia from 527 to 565. A staunch supporter of Justinian, Primasius lived through both the Byzantine reconquest of the Arian Vandal kingdom in North Africa and the collapse of this imperial enterprise. His role as a Catholic ecclesiastical leader in a tumultuous time and place is at least partially responsible for his interest in the Apocalypse. Primasius follows the lead of his expurgated sources, however, in presenting a spiritual reading of the text. His prologue explains at some length his relationship to the interpretation of Tyconius and praises Jerome for the insight that "in these single words [of the Apocalypse] lie multiple understandings."[21]

Primasius's commentary is quite original in its interpretation, for it is here that the problem of dividing the text for the purpose of interpretation is addressed for the first time. This structural problem is especially interesting in early medieval exegesis because biblical texts had not yet been shaped into standardized chapters and verses. One manuscript tradition, for example, divides the Apocalypse into forty-eight

translation by Colin McAllister forthcoming in the series CCT (Brepols). I thank Colin McAllister for making the prologue to his forthcoming translation available to me.

20 Compare the prologue of the treatise attributed to Alcuin in *Commentariorum in Apocalipsin Libri Quinque*, PL 100, 1087A–1156C, with that of Ambrosius Autpertus, CCCM 27, 5–7, for identical lists of sources.

21 "In verbis singulis multiplices latent intelligentiae" (CCSL 92, 3).

chapters; others present the text with essentially no numerical headings.[22] This gave exegetes freedom from the a priori interpretation latent in divided texts, and allowed for a spontaneous selection and matching of passages. Primasius divided his commentary into five books, which discuss (1) the seven churches; (2) the seven seals; (3) the seven trumpets and the woman clothed with the sun; (4) the beasts from the land and the sea, the seven plagues, the seven bowls; and (5) the Lamb on the throne, the new heaven, and the new earth. His sense of the rhythm of the text was enormously influential and is very possibly evident in the fact that his books 2–5 essentially mark the beginnings of chapters 5, 8, 13, and 18 in the later standard division of the received Apocalypse text.[23] As becomes evident, however, later Latin exegetes were by no means bound to Primasius's division when structuring their own commentaries. Nor was the popularity of this commentary affected by the fact that it used a text of the Apocalypse which can be placed squarely in North Africa, one that differs at points from the text of Tyconius, agreeing sometimes with Tyconius against the Vulgate, and at other points going its own way.[24]

The trust later interpreters placed in Primasius's explanation of the Apocalypse is evident from its influence on the tradition. All later commentaries were influenced by this one, either directly or indirectly. The way in which Primasius was filtered through later commentators is especially evident in the ease with which his original addition to Jerome's numeric symbolism of Rev 13:18 is cited by later exegetes. Primasius added a breakdown of the Greek *arnoyme*, meaning "I deny" (in Latin, *nego*), which equals 666, while, in contrast, *Cristei* totals 1,225. The difficulty of tracing textual influences through this increasingly dense filter of sources is evident from the fact that few commentators (for example, Bede) tend to distinguish which example came from which source.

[22] For a recent discussion of chapter and verse divisions of the Latin Bible, see P. Saenger, "The Anglo-Hebraic Origins of the Modern Chapter Division of the Latin Bible," in *La fractura historiografica: Edad Media y Renacimento desde el tercer milenio*, ed. F. Javier Burguillo and L. Meier (Salamanca: Seminario de Estudios Medievales y Renacentistas, 2008), 177–202.

[23] See Yves Christe, "Traditions littéraires et iconographiques dans l'interprétation des images apocalyptiques," in *Apocalypse de Jean: traditions exégétiques et iconographiques; IIIe–XIIIe siècles*, ed. Yves Christe (Geneva: Droz, 1979), 134ff.

[24] Johannes Haussleiter gives a comparison of the Apocalypse texts of Primasius, Tyconius, and the Vulgate in "Die lateinische Apokalypse der alten afrikanischen Kirche," in *Forschungen zur Geschichte des neutestamentlichen Kanons und der alkirchlichen Literatur*, ed. T. Zahn, vol. 4 (Erlangen: E. T. Jacob, 1891), 197–99.

Finally, the commentary of Primasius, in its interpretation of the Apocalypse as a text about the church on earth, shares a concern about orthodoxy with the fourth-century redactors of Victorinus and Tyconius and in a way that marks a path for later exegetes. Primasius understands the woman of Rev 12:1 as the Virgin Mary and pauses to give a list of heretics (ancient and contemporary, famous and obscure) who misunderstand the incarnation: Valentinus, Bardezanes, Apollinaris, Nestorius, Eutyches, Timotheus Hilarius.[25] Near the end of the treatise, Primasius shows his hand a bit more clearly in an open polemic against the heretics who really presented the greatest challenge to his church: the Arians. His interpretation of Rev 22:13, "I am the Alpha and the Omega, the first and the last, the beginning and the end," uses numeric symbolism to show the consubstantiality of the Father and the Son and the unity of the Holy Spirit, the third person of the Trinity. The letters alpha and omega have the same value as *peristera*, the Greek word for dove, the form in which, according to the Synoptic Gospels, the Holy Spirit appeared in the baptism of Jesus.[26] Therefore the Arians, who assert alien natures of the Father and the Son, are refuted by biblical warrant, since the numbers show that all three persons of the Trinity are equal.

The importance of Primasius can also be measured by contrast with the other commentaries of the sixth century: those of Apringius of Béja, Cassiodorus, and Caesarius of Arles. Apringius, who wrote under the Visigothic (and Arian) King Theudis in the part of the Iberian Peninsula that is now Portugal, seems to have been inspired by the same forces that moved Primasius. His commentary survives in only one copy, a twelfth-century manuscript of Barcelona, now in Copenhagen, which conflates an original commentary on three sections of the Apocalypse (1:1–5:7, 18:6–19:21, and 20:1–end) with sections from the commentary of Victorinus/Jerome.[27] Apringius's interpretation of the Apocalypse may have originally been a set of homilies intended for the liturgical season between Easter and Pentecost, when selections from the Apoca-

[25] For these "*heretici male de Christi incarnatione sentientes*," see Primasius, *Commentarius in Apocalypsin* 3.12 (CCSL 92, 179–90).

[26] Matt 3:16, Mark 1:10, Luke 3:22; see Primasius, *Commentarius in Apocalypsin* 5.22 (CCSL 92, 307–08).

[27] For Apringius on the Apocalypse, see *Variorum auctorum commentaria minora in Apocalypsin Johannis, Apringi Pacensis Tractatus fragmenta*, ed. R. Gryson, CCSL 107, 33–97, and the English translation of Weinrich in *Latin Commentaries on Revelation*, 23–62.

lypse were read in the Visigothic church.[28] The influence of this text seems to have been limited to the Iberian Peninsula, as the only later author to cite it is Beatus of Liébana. The *Complexiones in Apocalypsin* of Cassiodorus also survives in only one manuscript, a sixth-century copy from northern Italy. It is a largely original work in thirty-three sections, each providing an allegorical comment on a short pericope of the biblical text.[29] In contrast, the Apocalypse sermons of Caesarius of Aries circulated widely throughout the Middle Ages, but under the name of Augustine.[30] As the specific interpretations of these homilies are drawn from the treatises of Victorinus/Jerome and Tyconius, it can be difficult to measure their influence on the later tradition of Apocalypse exegesis. Nevertheless, it is clear that no Apocalypse commentary from the sixth century was equal to that of Primasius in influence on medieval authors.

All three of the commentaries of the eighth century, the next great flowering of Apocalypse exegesis, depend heavily on Primasius, although they also draw directly from earlier commentaries. The interpretation of Beatus of Liébana, probably the latest of the three to be written, quotes lavishly from four of its predecessors: Victorinus/Jerome, Tyconius, Primasius, and Apringius, as well as from a number of other sources.[31] The commentary of Beatus has a rather peculiar fame among twentieth-century scholars because of the stunning full-page illustrations of the surviving manuscripts, all from the tenth century

[28] Cf. B. Altaner's review of an edition of Apringius by A. C. Vegas in *Theologische Revue* 4 (1942): 119–20. Altaner cites Canon 17 of the Fourth Council of Toledo (633), for which see J. D. Mansi, *Sacrorum conciliorum nova, et amplissima collectio* (Florence, 1795–98), 10:624.

[29] CCSL 107, 99–129. See also James J. O'Donnell, *Cassiodorus* (Berkeley: University of California Press, 1979), 224–25; also see p. 226, where the meaning of *complexiones*, a sequential commentary, is distinguished from Cassiodorus's *breves*. O'Donnell's contention that the work is "resolutely literal," with "virtually no allegorical interpretation" (227), is open to debate, and certainly depends on what might count as a literal interpretation of the Apocalypse.

[30] PL 35, 2417–52, as Augustine, and *Sancti Caesarii episcopi Arelatensis*, ed. G. Morin (Maredsous: [Abbey], 1942). See also G. Morin, "Le commentaire homilétique de S. Césaire sur l'Apocalypse," *Revue Bénédictine* 45 (1933): 43–61.

[31] Beatus of Liébana, *Tractatus in Apocalipsin*, ed. Roger Gryson, CCSL 107C (Turnhout: Brepols, 2012), and *Commentarius in Apocalypsin/Beatus Liebanensis*, LLT, Series A (Turnhout: Brepols, 2010), based on the edition of H. A. Sanders, Papers and Monographs of the American Academy in Rome 7 (Rome: American Academy in Rome, 1930). Beatus also cites Irenaeus, Augustine, Fulgentius, Gregory of Elvira, Gregory the Great, and Isidore of Seville. See also M. Del Alamo, "Los Commentarios de Beato al Apocalipsis y Elipando," in *Letteratura medioevale*, vol. 2: *Miscellanea Giovanni Mercati*(Vatican City: Vatican Library, 1946), 16–33.

or later.[32] In the Middle Ages, however, the text was relatively little known and, it would seem, known not at all outside Spain. Perhaps this is because of the extremely dense character of the commentary, or perhaps because of its equally extreme topicality. The commentary of Beatus is divided into twelve books, each with an extensive prologue; the titles of the books make evident the major themes of the treatise: the sanctity of the church and the defense of the divinity of Christ against the Adoptionist theology of the followers of Bishop Elipandus of Toledo. As John Williams has pointed out, the promises of the triumph of the true church over all enemies may have also struck a comforting note with Beatus because of the increasing threat of Muslim domination of Christian Spain. Although no open reference to Islam can be discerned in the text,[33] concerns about the Islamic domination of Iberia may be assumed from the fact that in books 1, 2, 6 and 12 Beatus deals explicitly with the church, whereas books 3 and 11 deal with specific issues about the divinity of Christ. At any rate, the particular combination of ecclesiological and christological exegesis in this treatise reflects early medieval Latin exegesis of the Song of Songs. Beatus quotes lengthy passages from the Song of Songs at several key points, borrowing interpretations from the *Moralia* of Gregory the Great, the letters of Jerome, and the commentary on Luke by Ambrose of Milan.

It is, in fact, in the eighth century that the link between exegesis of the Apocalypse and the standard readings of the Song of Songs becomes clearly visible. Of the exegetes on the Apocalypse up to this point, only the shadowy Victorinus is said to have written on the Song of Songs as well; but from this period on, the Apocalypse and the Song of Songs seem to attract the same exegetes.[34] In the period covered by this chapter alone, there are extant commentaries on both books by Bede, Alcuin, and Haimo, while Ambrosius Autpertus is credited with a Song

[32] See John Williams, "The Beatus Commentaries and Spanish Bible Illustration," in *Actas del Simposio para el estudio de los códices del "Commentario al Apocalipsis" de Beato de Liébana*, vol. 1 (Madrid: Joyas Bibliográficas, 1978), 201–19; and John Williams, *Visions of the End in Medieval Spain: Catalogue of Illustrated Manuscripts and Study of the Geneva Beatus*, ed. Therese Martin, Late Antique and Early Medieval Iberia (Amsterdam: Amsterdam University Press, 2017).

[33] Williams, "The Beatus Commentaries," 219.

[34] For Late Antique Latin treatments of the Song of Songs, see Karl Shuve, *The Song of Songs and the Fashioning of Identity in Early Latin Christianity* (Oxford: Oxford University Press, 2016). For connections between exegesis of the Song of Songs and the Apocalypse in early medieval exegesis, see E. Ann Matter, *The Voice of My Beloved: The Song of Songs in Western Medieval Christianity* (Philadelphia: University of Pennsylvania Press, 1990), 89–92.

of Songs commentary that does not survive.[35] The association of the Apocalypse and the Song of Songs, on first consideration perhaps rather unlikely, derives from the tradition of allegorical exegesis in the ecclesiological mode (the "allegoria" of John Cassian), which had become a standard tool of monastic exegesis by the eighth century. An assumption that the most mysterious books of the Bible could and ought to be explained by means of a ready-made hermeneutic (that is, that the texts are "really" about the story of the church on earth, whatever they may seem to be about) emphasizes the central importance of ecclesiology. The Early Middle Ages in Latin Christianity were marked by a sharp concern for the survival of the church, even to the point of draining the Apocalypse of its apocalyptic fervor.

Eighth-century commentaries on the Apocalypse also mark a turning point in the transmission of sources. Just as Primasius had become a filter for earlier interpretation, so the commentaries of Bede and Ambrosius Autpertus incorporate Primasius and his sources and become in turn the major sources of Apocalypse exegesis for the Carolingian age. The *Explanatio Apocalypseos* of the Venerable Bede is a sophisticated analysis of the Apocalypse, one that carries on a reading of the text as the history of the church on earth while keeping a watchful eye on the larger picture of cosmic history. In the dedicatory epistle, Bede makes use of the seven rules of Tyconius to describe the seven ages (*periochae*) of the world reflected in seven movements of the text.[36] First, after a lengthy preface, the Apocalypse speaks of the seven churches of Asia that are really the one church of Christ (1:1–3:21); the second period, marked by the four animals and the opening of the seven seals, reveals the future conflicts and triumphs of the church (4:1–8:1); the third, under the form of seven angels blowing trumpets, describes future happenings of the church (8:2–11:19); the fourth opens

35 The commentaries on the Song of Songs are: Bede, *In Cantica Canticorum*, ed. D. Hurst, CCSL 119B (Turnhout: Brepols, 1985); Alcuin, *Commento al Cantico dei cantici/Alcuino; con i commenti anonymi Vox ecclesie, vox antique* ecclesie, ed. Rossana E. Gugielmetti, Millennio Medievale 53, Testi 13 (Florence: SISMEL, Edizioni del Galluzzo, 2004); and Haimo of Auxerre, *Commentaria in Cantica Canticorum*, PL 117, 295–358 (and as Cassiodorus, PL 70, 1055–1106). For the possibility that Ambrosius Autpertus wrote on the Song of Songs, see R. Weber's introduction to *Expositio in Apocalypsin*, CCCM 27. The Song of Songs is quoted more than forty times in this Apocalypse commentary.

36 Gerald Bonner has shown the relationship between Bede's *periochae* in this work and the stages of universal history developed in his other writings: see *Saint Bede in the Tradition of Western Apocalyptic Commentary* (Jarrow: St. Paul's Church, 1966), 14–15.

the works and victories of the church under the figure of the woman giving birth and the dragon pursuing her (12:1–15:4); the fifth is the *periocha* of seven plagues that will infest the earth (15:5–16:21); the sixth is the damnation of the great harlot, that is, the impious city (17:1–20:15); and the seventh will see Jerusalem, adorned as the bride of the Lamb, descend from heaven (21–22). The commentary that follows, made up of three books, conforms closely to this scheme. The aspect of Bede's commentary on the Apocalypse that proved most interesting to later medieval exegetes was this working-out of the text in accordance with a broad scheme of the church moving through universal history into sacred time—and it is especially useful of Bede to have left the *periochae* undefined. Latin Christians of later centuries, reading or commenting on the Apocalypse, had Bede's framework—a result of the distillation of earlier commentary—ready to plug in to the interpretation of particular events of the life of the church in the world.

The commentary of Ambrosius Autpertus, in contrast, provides an exhaustive spiritual reading of the Apocalypse for future generations. Written between 758 and 767 in the Lombard duchy of Benevento, the ten books of this treatise absorb the Apocalypse commentaries of Victorinus/Jerome, Tyconius, and Primasius, as well as large sections of Augustine's *De civitate Dei* and the *Moralia* of Gregory the Great. By far the most visible source for this commentary is Primasius, who is quoted literally hundreds of times. It is clear that one motivation for Ambrosius Autpertus was to create a smooth conflation of his sources; yet his own selection of biblical texts—particularly from epithalamic writings such as Song of Songs, Psalms, Lamentations, and Ephesians—focuses the commentary on a special theme: Christ's incarnation and his spiritual marriage with the church. This focus is especially evident in the long prologues to books 5 and 9, books that cover Apocalypse 10:1–12:12 (the opening of the seventh seal and the persecution of the woman by the dragon), and 19:11–21:8 (the binding of the dragon and the rise and fall of Gog and Magog).

Although the Apocalypse commentaries of Victorinus/Jerome, Tyconius, and Primasius still circulated—and were even recopied—after the eighth century, the particular selections from this earlier tradition compiled and arranged by Bede and Ambrosius Autpertus became the major sources for Carolingian commentary. An excellent example of the weaving together of Bede and Ambrosius Autpertus can be seen in the incomplete Apocalypse commentary attributed to Charlemagne's schoolmaster, Alcuin, a text written around the turn of the ninth century.[37] This is a late addition to the Alcuinian canon, not part of the collection of Alcuin texts printed by Johannes Froben in sixteenth-century Basel, but edited only in 1837 by Angelo Mai from a tenth-century manuscript in the Vatican Library.[38] Scholars now think this is a compendium of Ambrosius Autpertus, perhaps from late ninth-century Italy.[39] A second treatment of the Apocalypse attributed to Alcuin is found in one ninth-century manuscript from Sankt Emmeram, Regensburg.[40] This is a question-and-answer text on the Apocalypse, which the nineteenth-century editor E. Dümmler assigned to Alcuin, perhaps because the manuscript he used also contains Alcuin's *Quaestiones et responsiones in Genesin*.[41] Here, the "questions" are all verses of the Apocalypse largely "answered" by selections from Bede's commentary. Thomas MacKay argues for the authenticity of this text based on the way it uses, and distinguishes from, Bede, although Michael Gorman attributes it to Alcuin's *dubia*, apparently because it lacks a dedicatory epistle.[42] Michael Fox deems the evidence for Alcuin's authorship of the Apocalypse commentary preserved in the Sankt Emmeram manuscript inconclusive, but adds, "Without doubt, the commentary is not far removed from Alcuin's circle," and says a complete study of the text is in progress.[43]

There is yet another anonymous, unpublished text on the seven seals of the Apocalypse that has been associated with Alcuin, but is probably from Visigothic Spain.[44] The fact that three different treatises on some

37 Alcuin, *Commentariorum in Apocalypsin*, PL 100, 1087–1156.

38 The manuscript is in Biblioteca Apostolica Vaticana, lat. 651, first published in Angelo Mai, ed., *Scriptorum veterum: nova collectio e Vaticanis codicibus*, vol. 9 (Rome: Typis Vaticanis, 1837), 257–338. The text is known from one other manuscript, Benevento 9; see M. M. Gorman, "Alcuin before Migne," *Revue Bénédictine* 112 (2002): 101–30, at 127–28.

39 See Gorman, "Alcuin before Migne," 129, and Michael Fox, "Alcuin's Expositio in epistola ad Hebraeos," *Journal of Medieval Latin* 18, no. 2 (2006): 329.

40 Munich, Bayerische Staatsbibliothek, clm 13581.

41 E. Dümmler, ed., *Karolini aevi II*, MGH, Epistolarum 4 (Berlin: Weidmann, 1895), 5, Codex D.

42 T. W. MacKay, "Apocalypse Comments by Primasius, Bede, and Alcuin. Interrelationship, Dependency and Individuality," in *Papers Presented at the Thirteenth International Conference Held in Oxford, 1999*, Studia Patristica 36 (Leuven: Peeters, 2001), 28–34; Gorman, "Alcuin before Migne," 129.

43 Fox, "Alcuin's Expositio in epistola ad Hebraeos," 327 n. 8.

44 E. A. Matter, ed., "The Pseudo-Alcuinian 'De Septem Sigillis': An Early Latin Apocalypse Exegesis," *Traditio* 36 (1980): 111–37. The one manuscript that attributes the text to "Albinus" is in Biblioteca Apostolica Vaticana, lat. 5096, from eleventh-century Italy. Its text is close to that of Munich, Staatsbibliothek, clm 6407, copied ca. 800 in Verona, but then sent to Freising. The Munich

part of the Apocalypse are attributed in some way to Alcuin is evidence of both the importance of the Apocalypse to Carolingian exegesis and the stature of Alcuin as the consummate teacher of that era. Thomas MacKay and Michael Fox agree that the question-and-answer text preserved in the Sankt Emmeram manuscript is the closest to Alcuin and his circle, but all three pseudo-Alcuinian texts are important testimony to the interpretation of the Apocalypse among Carolingian scholars.

The commentary of Haimo of Auxerre is also a conflation of Bede and Ambrosius Autpertus.[45] It is organized in seven books, showing the influence of Bede, but these divisions are adapted from the ten books of Ambrosius Autpertus. Haimo characterizes the Apocalypse as an "intellectual vision" about the present and future church, a vision that can be related to the prayer said every Sunday (at the least) by Christians: "thy kingdom come."[46] Haimo's commentary shows clearly the distance between effective apocalyptic expectation and the Latin Apocalypse exegesis that had become standard by the ninth century.

All of the Apocalypse commentaries from the Carolingian world thus show the continuing assumption that this book of the Bible is an allegory of the church, and a continuing process of filtering specific interpretations from earlier commentaries to support that assumption. There is little in these texts that shares the radical assumption of the imminent end that seems so evident in interpretations of the Apocalypse after the nineteenth century. Instead, early medieval exegesis presents the Apocalypse as a book about the integrity and purity of the church on earth. Tyconius's insistent rejection of chiliasm led to an interpretation of the Apocalypse that understood the book not as a warning of the imminent end of the world, but as a guide for the church on earth in expectation of the final joining of the spiritual and physical churches. Cassian's term "anagogic" (having to do with the moral realm) is perhaps more appropriate than "apocalyptic" (having to do with end times) in characterizing this literature.

manuscript contains catechetical works of Alcuin, which may explain the attribution in the Vatican manuscript. This text is available in English in Francis X. Gumerlock, ed. and trans., *The Seven Seals of the Apocalypse: Medieval Texts in Translation*, TEAMS Commentary Series (Kalamazoo, MI: Medieval Institute Publications, 2009), 30–31.

45 Haimo of Auxerre (under Haimo of Halberstadt), *Expositionis in Apocalypsin B. Joannis Libri Septem*, PL 117, 937–1220.

46 "Haec omnis Ecclesia loquitur in Joanne, optans ut veniat Christus ad judicium. Unde et quotidie in Dominica oratione postulat suppliciter: *Adveniat regnum tuum*. Et illud: *Ostende nobis faciem tuam et salvi erimus*." PL 117, 1220C.

This is not to argue, though, that there was no apocalyptic thought in the early Middle Ages. On the contrary, these centuries give evidence of a definite tradition of apocalyptic literature, in which the Apocalypse played a decisive role, one that centers around a figure whose advent is spoken of in the Apocalypse: the Antichrist. Antichrist actually comes from an ancient (certainly pre-Christian) tradition; in Jewish apocalyptic literature he is spoken of as Belial, "the lawless one." In canonical Scripture besides the Apocalypse, medieval Christians found references to Antichrist in Daniel (especially the evil king of Dan 11:36), and Second Thessalonians (especially 2:3–4).[47] Commentaries on these biblical texts develop the apocalyptic expectation of the advent of Antichrist far more than do the commentaries on the Apocalypse; a glance at Jerome's commentary on Daniel confirms this, as does a comparison of Haimo's two discussions of Antichrist: the first in his commentary on 2 Thessalonians, the second his mere repetition of the etymologies derived from Primasius when discussing the Antichrist in his Apocalypse commentary.[48]

An even more impressive testimony to early medieval apocalyptic is the tenth-century *De ortu et tempore Antichristi*, a text written by Adso of Montier-en-Der at the request of Queen Gerberga.[49] This handbook on the Antichrist drew from many sources, including Jerome on Daniel, Haimo on 2 Thessalonians, and Bede on the Apocalypse; it was so popular that it circulated in at least seven versions and was attributed to Alcuin, Augustine, Methodius, and Anselm of Canterbury. The most significant thing about Adso's treatise is that it coexisted with a tradition of Apocalypse exegesis that continued spiritual and anagogic readings of the last book of the Bible for centuries to come. In the twelfth century, for example, both the *Glossa ordinaria* and the popular commentary of Rupert of Deutz on the Apocalypse are far more ecclesiological than eschatological in their focus.[50]

47 For an overview, see Bernard McGinn, *Antichrist: Two Thousand Years of the Human Fascination with Evil* (New York: HarperSanFrancisco, 1994).

48 Haimo, *In Epistolam II ad Thessalonicenses*, PL 117, 777–83. English translation by Kevin L. Hughes in *Second Thessalonians: Two Early Medieval Apocalyptic Commentaries*, TEAMS Commentary Series (Kalamazoo, MI: Medieval Institute Publications, 2001).

49 Adso, *De ortu et tempore Antichristi*, ed. D. Verheist, CCCM 45 (Turnhout: Brepols, 1976); English translation by Bernard McGinn in *Apocalyptic Spirituality*, Classics of Western Spirituality (Mahwah, NJ: Paulist, 1979), 81–96.

50 *Glossa ordinaria Apocalypsis B. Johannis*, PL 114, 709–52; see also *Biblia Latina cum glossa ordinaria: facsimile reprint of editio princeps Adolph Rusch of Strassburg 1480/81*, ed. Karlfried Fröhlich and Margaret Gibson (Turnhout: Brepols,

Yet it is also in the twelfth century that the future of Apocalypse exegesis begins to change, when the apocalyptic themes of Christian symbolism gain precedence over the ecclesiological symbolism that dominated the earlier period. The earlier Latin exegesis I have examined here used allegorical interpretation to avoid both an overliteral reading of the end of the world and the perception that the Roman Empire was the enemy of the Christian church. But, as Robert Lerner has pointed out, "literal millennialism did return."[51] Lerner suggests that Bede's understanding of the opening of the seven seals as successive stages in the development of the church and his use of the term "Sabbath" to describe the opening of the seventh seal "actually prove a fruitful source for millennialism in ways he may not have considered ... once an earthly Sabbath was present in an authoritative Apocalypse commentary, it was there for other exegetes to employ in ways that Bede himself had resisted."[52] Bede's comments on the seven seals were included in the *Glossa ordinaria*, where they were seen by Richard of Saint Victor (d. 1173), whose commentary on the Apocalypse—although still resisting strict millenarianism—linked the opening of the seven seals more closely to historical ages.[53] This opened the possibility for other commentators to "advance toward millennialism," culminating in the Apocalypse exegesis of Joachim of Fiore.[54] Thus by the twelfth century, the subtle changes in understanding of the Bedan *periochae*, and the changing historical attitudes to the apocalyptic that encouraged these changes, begin to affect even Latin commentary on the Apocalypse.

Selected Further Reading

Bright, Pamela. *The Book of Rules of Tyconius: Its Purpose and Inner Logic.* Notre Dame, IN: University of Notre Dame Press, 1988.

1992), and Lesley Smith, *The Glossa ordinaria: The Making of a Medieval Bible Commentary*, Commentaria, vol. 3 (Leiden: Brill, 2009). Rupert's *Commentarium in Apocalypsim Iohannis apostoli* is published in PL 169, 825–1214, and LLT, Series A (Turnhout: Brepols, 2010). See also John Van Engen, *Rupert of Deutz* (Berkeley: University of California Press, 1983), 175–82.

51 Robert E. Lerner, "The Medieval Return to the Thousand-Year Sabbath," in *The Apocalypse in the Middle Ages*, ed. Emmerson and McGinn, 51–71, at 51.

52 Ibid., 54–55.

53 Richard of Saint Victor, *In Apocalypsim Joannis Libri Septem*, PL 196, 683–888, discussed by Lerner, "The Medieval Return to the Thousand-Year Sabbath," 55–56.

54 Scholarship on Joachim is enormous, but a good place to start is E. Randolph Daniel, "Joachim of Fiore: Patterns of History in the Apocalypse," in *The Apocalypse in the Middle Ages*, ed. Emmerson and McGinn, 72–88.

Gumerlock, Francis X., ed. *Early Latin Commentaries on the Apocalypse*. TEAMS Commentary Series. Kalamazoo, MI: Medieval Institute Publications, 2016.

Gumerlock, Francis X., ed. and trans. *The Seven Seals of the Apocalypse: Medieval Texts in Translation*. TEAMS Commentary Series. Kalamazoo, MI: Medieval Institute Publications, 2009.

Matter, E. Ann. *The Voice of My Beloved: The Song of Songs in Western Medieval Christianity*. Philadelphia: University of Pennsylvania Press, 1990.

McGinn, Bernard. *Antichrist: Two Thousand Years of the Human Fascination with Evil*. New York: HarperSanFrancisco, 1994.

Shuve, Karl. *The Song of Songs and the Fashioning of Identity in Early Latin Christianity*. Oxford: Oxford University Press, 2016.

Tyconius. *Exposition of the Apocalypse*. Translated by Francis X. Gumerlock. Fathers of the Church 134. Washington, DC: Catholic University of America Press, 2017.

Weinrich, William C., trans. *Latin Commentaries on Revelation*. Ancient Christian Texts. Downers Grove, IL: InterVarsity Press, 2011.

Williams, John. *Visions of the End in Medieval Spain: Catalogue of Illustrated Manuscripts and Study of the Geneva Beatus*. Late Antique and Early Medieval Iberia. Edited by Therese Martin. Amsterdam: Amsterdam University Press, 2017.

8 Exegesis of the Apocalypse in the Tenth Century[*]

FRANCIS X. GUMERLOCK

This essay examines three texts on the Apocalypse produced in the tenth century: the *Commentary on the Apocalypse* by Arethas of Caesarea, the *Catechesis Celtica*, and an anonymous *Gloss on the Apocalypse of John*.[1] After discussing a few features of tenth-century exegesis of the Apocalypse, it provides information, when possible, about the author, date, provenance, sources, and contents of each of these texts. Since no complete English translations of any of these texts have been published, the essay includes a number of quotations from these writings and concludes with a translation of the entire *Gloss on the Apocalypse of John*.

TENTH-CENTURY EXEGESIS OF THE APOCALYPSE

An examination of the writings on the Apocalypse in the tenth century reveals three characteristic features. These are described below under their paucity, their utilization of earlier exegesis, and their lack of millennial fears and anxieties.

Paucity

In comparison with the twenty-five or more exegetical texts on the Apocalypse composed during the thirteenth century, relatively few were written in the tenth century. What accounts for this? In the Latin-speaking West the answer is likely related to the Carolingian

[*] I wish to thank Jean Rittmueller of Memphis for carefully reading this essay and giving helpful suggestions. All translations of the texts herein are mine unless otherwise noted.

[1] Two texts not included in this essay are a Latin version of the Book of Revelation with glosses in Old High German, found in a manuscript transcribed about 900 CE: Paris, Bibliothèque Nationale, n.a.lat. 1132, fols. 1r–35v; and a question-and-answer text on the Old and New Testament contained in Lyons, Bibliothèque Municipal, 447 (376), fols. 106r–152. The contents on the Book of Revelation are near its end.

literary *renovatio* that occurred in the eighth and ninth centuries. In the eighth century, Irish teachers on the continent composed *On the Mysteries of the Apocalypse of John* and the *Cambridge Gloss on the Apocalypse*.[2] Later that century Alcuin of York wrote both an *Exposition on the Apocalypse* and another *Exposition of the Apocalypse through Question and Answer*.[3] Ambrose Autpert, an abbot in northern Italy in the late eighth century, wrote a massive *Exposition on the Apocalypse*; and in the ninth century both Otfrid of Weissenburg and Haimo of Auxerre wrote systematic explanations of the Apocalypse.[4] The effectiveness of Carolingian production of exegetical works on the Apocalypse seems to have made commentary on this book in the tenth century unnecessary.[5]

Utilization of Earlier Exegesis

Tenth-century exegetical works on the Apocalypse to a great extent reconfigured texts composed in previous centuries, repurposing them for contemporary audiences. Arethas's *Commentary on the Apocalypse* is mainly a selective reworking of exegesis found in the sixth- and seventh-century Apocalypse commentaries of Oecumenius and Andrew of Caesarea. Both the *Catechesis Celtica* and the *Gloss on the*

[2] *On the Mysteries of the Apocalypse of John* is edited by Roger Gryson in *Commentaria minora in Apocalypsin Johannis*, CCSL 107 (Turnhout: Brepols, 2003) and translated in Francis X. Gumerlock, ed., *Early Latin Commentaries on the Apocalypse*, TEAMS Commentary Series (Kalamazoo, MI: Medieval Institute Publications, 2016). The *Cambridge Gloss on the Apocalypse* is edited by Roger Gryson as *Glossa in Apocalypsin e codice Bibliothecae Vniuersitatis Cantabrigiensis Dd.X.16 (Exegetica)*, in *Incerti avctoris glossa in Apocalypsin*, CCSL 108G (Turnhout: Brepols, 2013). An English translation by Colin McAllister is forthcoming and will be published in the series CCT (Brepols).

[3] The *Exposition on the Apocalypse* is in PL 100, 1085–1156. The *Exposition of the Apocalypse through Question and Answer* is in Municch, Bayerische Staatsbibliothek, Clm 13581, fols. 3r–31r. The attribution of both to Alcuin is probable but uncertain. English translations of both texts are in *Alcuin of York on Revelation*, trans. Sarah Van Der Pas, CCS (West Monroe, LA: Consolamini, 2016).

[4] Ambrosius Autpertus, *Expositionis in Apocalypsim*, ed. Robert Weber, CCCM 27 and 27A (Turnhout: Brepols, 1975); Otfrid of Weissenburg, *Glossed Apocalypse*, Wolfenbüttel, Herzog August Bibliothek, Weissenburg 59; Haimo of Auxerre, *Exposition of the Apocalypse*, PL 117, 843–1058 (under the name Haimo of Halberstat).

[5] E. Ann Matter, "Exegesis and Christian Education: The Carolingian Model," in *Schools of Thought in the Christian Tradition*, ed. Patrick Henry (Philadelphia: Fortress, 1984), 102; Richard Landes, "Introduction: The *Terribles espoirs* of 1000," in *The Apocalyptic Year 1000: Religious Expectation and Social Change, 950–1050*, ed. Richard Landes, Andrew Gow, and David C. Van Meter (New York: Oxford University Press, 2003), 32.

Apocalypse of John drew from Hiberno-Latin exegetical traditions on Revelation to explain the seven seals; and the aforementioned *Gloss* made very ample use of Bede's early eighth-century *Exposition of the Apocalypse.*

In their utilization of earlier traditions, tenth-century commentators on the Apocalypse often viewed the visions as symbols of Christian truths relevant for life in the present age. They also saw in the visions depictions of past history. According to Arethas, the 144,000 in Rev 7 were Jewish people who escaped the destruction of Jerusalem by the Romans; and the visions of Rev 12 recounted the early life of Jesus, including the attempt on his life by Herod and his flight to Egypt. For the authors of the *Catechesis Celtica* and the *Gloss on the Apocalypse of John* the seven seals of Rev 5–8 were symbols of seven major events in the life of Christ.

In addition, tenth-century expositors of the Apocalypse saw in the visions references to events that they believed would occur in the last days. These include the return of Enoch and Elijah, the appearance of Antichrist, the general resurrection, the Second Coming of Christ, the damnation of the wicked, and the entrance of the saints into their heavenly inheritance. However, none of the commentaries hint that the very last days were imminent.

Lack of Millennial Anxieties

In the tenth century there was no lack of expectation that the world would end soon.[6] Some of these expectations of the end were related to a particular interpretation of the thousand years mentioned in Rev 20:1–7. Some believed that around the turn of the millennium, or the year 1000, Satan would be loosed from his prison onto the earth. This meant that the Antichrist would make his appearance soon, followed by the Second Coming of Christ and the Last Judgment. For example, in the first half of the tenth century, Niketas the Paphlagonian wrote a letter to bishops in the West who had approached him concerning the meaning of the thousand-year reign and whether the millennium was coming to completion.[7] In the late tenth century Abbo of Fleury related:

[6] Francis X. Gumerlock, *The Day and the Hour: Christianity's Perennial Fascination with Predicting the End of the World* (Powder Springs, GA: American Vision, 2000), 47–50; James Reston, Jr., *The Last Apocalypse: Europe at the Year 1000 A.D.* (New York: Random House, 1998); Richard Erdoes, *A.D. 1000: Living on the Brink of Apocalypse* (San Francisco: Harper and Row, 1988).

[7] James T. Palmer, *The Apocalypse in the Early Middle Ages* (New York: Cambridge University Press, 2014), 200.

> When I was a young man I heard a sermon about the end of the world preached before the people in the cathedral of Paris. According to this, as soon as the number of a thousand years was completed, the Antichrist would come and the Last Judgment would follow in a brief time. I opposed this sermon with what force I could from passages in the Gospels, the Apocalypse and the Book of Daniel.[8]

In Byzantium a scribe noted that the Antichrist was born in the year 995. Some in Bulgaria in the tenth century taught that the number of years allotted for world history would expire in the year 1000.[9] However, no such interpretation of the thousand years of Rev 20 is mentioned in the works on the Apocalypse featured in this essay.[10] This is not surprising, since most biblical commentators in that time held that the thousand years were figurative. For if the thousand years were to be understood literally, and they began with either the birth or passion of Jesus, then the date for the end of the world could be calculated. However, the official position of clerics and theologians in the tenth century was that the date of the end of the world was known only to God, and any claim to know that date was regarded as contradictory to the words of Jesus in Acts 1:7: "It is not for you to know the times or the periods that the Father has set by his own authority."

THREE TEXTS ON THE BOOK OF REVELATION

Arethas of Caesarea, *Commentary on the Apocalypse*

Author

Arethas (ca. 850–932 or 860–940[11]) was born in Peloponnesian Patra, and is said to have been a student of Photius in Constantinople. Raised to the diaconate in 895, he became archbishop of Caesarea in

[8] Abbo of Fleury, *Apologetic Work*, PL 139, 471. Translation from Bernard McGinn, *Antichrist: Two Thousand Years of the Human Fascination with Evil* (New York: HarperSanFrancisco, 1994), 210 n. 100.

[9] Palmer, *The Apocalypse in the Early Middle Ages*, 192; Anissava Miltenova, "Historical Apocalypses in Medieval Bulgarian Literature (10th–14th Centuries)," in *The Armenian Apocalyptic Tradition: A Comparative Perspective*, ed. Kevork B. Bardakjian and Sergio La Porta (Boston: Brill, 2014), 711 n. 29.

[10] Henri Focillon, *The Year 1000* (San Francisco: Harper and Row, 1969), 60, observed similarly that there is no trace of millennial terrors "in the official documents" of the church near the end of the tenth century.

[11] For his dates as ca. 850–932 see Robert Osculati, "*Hic Romae:* Cornelio a Lapide commentatore dell'*Apocalisse* al Collegio Romano," in *Storia e figure dell'Apocalisse fra '500 e '600* (Rome: Viella, 1996), 327. For his dates as 860–940

Cappadocia about 902. Sometime after 913 he wrote a Greek commentary on Revelation.[12] No English translation of it has yet been published.

Sources and Purpose

Many of Arethas's comments are taken from the seventh-century Greek commentary on the Apocalypse by Andrew of Caesarea.[13] However, Arethas did not simply copy or abridge Andrew's work. Rather, on many passages Arethas chose to ignore Andrew's remarks and instead preferred the sixth-century Greek commentary of Oecumenius.[14] Because most of Arethas's comments are based on either Andrew or Oecumenius, his purpose seems to have been to provide a commentary that reflected earlier Greek interpretive traditions regarding the Book of Revelation. In doing this, however, Arethas does not seem to have known of the commentary of Didymus of Alexandria,[15] the discourses on Revelation by Basil of Caesarea,[16] the twenty-four discourses on Revelation by Gregory of Nyssa,[17] or the Greek

see Karl Staab, *PaulusKommentare aus der griechischen Kirche* (Münster: Ashendorff, 1984), xlvii.

[12] One is in PG 106, ed. Jacques-Paul Migne (Paris: Petit-Montrouge, 1863), 485–786, with a parallel Latin translation. Some of the information on the life of Arethas was gathered from Thomas Hilary Oller, "The Nikol'skij Apocalypse Codex and Its Place in the Textual History of Medieval Slavic Apocalypse Manuscripts" (PhD diss., Brown University, 1993), 669. Robert W. Thomson, *Nerses of Lambron: Commentary on the Revelation of Saint John* (Leuven: Peeters, 2007), 15, however, says that Arethas wrote his commentary around the year 895.

[13] *Andrew of Caesarea: Commentary on the Apocalypse*, trans. Eugenia Scarvelis Constantinou, FC 123 (Washington, DC: Catholic University of America Press, 2011); William C. Weinrich, trans., *Greek Commentaries on Revelation: Oecumenius and Andrew of Caesarea*, Ancient Christian Texts (Downers Grove, IL: InterVarsity Press, 2011).

[14] For example, Arethas follows Oecumenius, among other places, on most of Rev 12 and on Rev 19:7–10. Oecumenius, *Commentary on the Apocalypse*, trans. John N. Suggit, FC 112 (Washington, DC: Catholic University of America Press, 2006); Weinrich, *Greek Commentaries on Revelation.*

[15] In his commentary on Zechariah, Didymus of Alexandria mentioned that he had written a commentary on Revelation. However, it has been lost. *Didyme l'Aveugle sur Zacharie: texte inédit d' après un papyrus de Toura*, ed. and trans. Louis Doutreleau, SC 244 (Paris: Cerf, 1978), 83:123; 84:654–55.

[16] The discourses on Revelation by Basil of Caesarea, now lost, are mentioned by Oecumenius, *Commentary on the Apocalypse*, FC 112, 203.

[17] On the twenty-four discourses on Revelation by Gregory of Nyssa, now lost, see Nicetas Seides, *Synopsis of Holy Scripture*, 1, cited in Panayiotis Tzamalikos, *An Ancient Commentary on the Book of Revelation: A Critical Edition of the Scholia in Apocalypsin* (New York: Cambridge University Press, 2013), 20.

Scholia in Apocalypsin attributed variously to Origen and Cassian the Sabaite.[18]

Methodology and Content

Arethas follows Andrew in dividing the Book of Revelation into seventy-two short chapters. After quoting short passages from the biblical text, each citation is followed by commentary. In keeping with his purpose, Arethas often gives two or more interpretations of a particular word or phrase. For example, regarding the "hour of affliction" in Rev 3:10, Arethas states that it could refer to either the persecution stirred up under Domitian or that persecution which will be stirred up by the Antichrist before the end of the world (PG 106, 558; hereafter only column numbers). Arethas says that the "four angels who are bound at the great river Euphrates" in Rev 9:14 could be the divine angels Michael, Gabriel, Raphael, and Uriel, an opinion of Oecumenius; or they could be demons (630–31). On Rev 13:18, Arethas follows Andrew and Oecumenius in giving several names that equal the number of the beast: Lampetis, Teitan, Lateinos, and common nouns like "victor" and "evil leader" (682). He writes that some interpret the harlot of Babylon (Rev 17:1–3) as Old Rome, while others see her as representing all the kingdoms of the present world up to the Second Coming of Christ (715). On Rev 19:20–21, Arethas writes that "some interpret the beast as the devil, but others as the Antichrist" (747). On the date of the writing of the Book of Revelation, Arethas repeats Oecumenius at two places, on Rev 1:9 and 3:10, that John was exiled to Patmos under the Emperor Domitian, who reigned from 81 to 96 CE (514, 558). However, on Rev 7:4–8, Arethas claims that "when John received the oracles, the devastation of the Jews by the Romans had not yet happened" (606). This latter comment seems to indicate that Arethas believed John wrote the Apocalypse before the First Jewish–Roman War of 67–70 CE. Consequently, Arethas has been cited by some as an external witness for an early dating of the Book of Revelation.[19]

[18] Adolf Harnack attributed the scholia to Origen. See Joseph A. Robinson, "Origen's Comments on the Apocalypse," *JTS* 13 (1912): 295–97; Cuthbert H. Turner, "The Text of the Newly Discovered Scholia of Origen on the Apocalypse," *JTS* 13 (1912): 386–87; Cuthbert H. Turner, "Origen Scholia in Apocalypsin," *JTS* 25 (1923): 1–16. Tzamalikos (*An Ancient Commentary on the Book of Revelation*) attributes the scholia to Cassian the Sabaite.

[19] For example, Steve Gregg, ed., *Revelation: Four Views; A Parallel Commentary* (Nashville, TN: Nelson, 1997), 40; Kenneth L. Gentry, Jr., *Before Jerusalem Fell: Dating the Book of Revelation*, rev. ed. (Powder Springs, GA: American Vision,

Following Andrew, Arethas interprets the opening of the seven seals and sounding of the seven trumpets in Rev 6–10 tropologically, as containing information relevant for Christian morality. The trees and grass that are burned up (Rev 8:7) represent sinners; and the five months of torture (Rev 9:5) indicate people sinning through their five senses (615, 623). On Rev 9:1, "the star which fell from heaven is the devil" (622). The marks on people's forehead and hand (Rev 14:9) represent their words and deeds (690). In addition, Arethas puts forth other symbolic interpretations of the visions of John. Jesus's garment in Rev 19:15–16 represents his flesh (743); and the twelve gates and twelve angels of the New Jerusalem in Rev 21:12 represent the apostles (767).

However, Arethas does not view all of the visions of Revelation as moral metaphors or symbols of various Christian teachings. Some of them he refers to historical events, which either will occur in the future or have already passed. The forty-two months in Rev 11:2 and elsewhere are a future time of the Antichrist in which the faithful will be tested and suffer persecution (647, 675, 690). The Antichrist, whom Arethas sees in Rev 11:7 and Rev 13, will rule in Jerusalem as king of the Jews and will perform miraculous signs (671, 675, 678, 722). The two witnesses of Rev 11:3–6 will be Enoch and Elijah. On the other hand, following Oecumenius, Arethas interprets almost the entirety of Rev 12 as a record of the past. The woman is Mary the Mother of God (659, 662). The dragon urged King Herod to kill the infants in Bethlehem but the holy family fled to safety into the desert, which is Egypt (663). The two wings of an eagle were the oracle given to the Magi saying that they should not return to Herod and the oracle given to Joseph urging him to flee to Egypt. The water coming forth from the mouth of the serpent represents the affliction Mary suffered when she witnessed the passion of her Son (670). The 144,000 in Rev 7 are Jewish people who had escaped the first-century destruction of Jerusalem (602–03).

On the identification of Babylon in Rev 17 and 18, Arethas realizes that some believe it represents Jerusalem or Constantinople (714), but he prefers to understand the city as "this whole corrupt world" (730, 734–35). On Jesus having a name "that no one knows but himself" (Rev 19:12), Arethas, like Andrew, lists various biblical names for Jesus including Shepherd, Sun, Light, Life, Sanctification, and Redemption (739). On the thousand years of Rev 20, Arethas again follows Andrew,

1998), 107–08; and Francis X. Gumerlock, *Revelation and the First Century: Preterist Interpretations of the Apocalypse in Early Christianity* (Powder Springs, GA: American Vision, 2012), 100–01.

writing on verses 1–3: "Let us understand the number one thousand to signify either multitude or perfection. Therefore the thousand years are those which flow from the coming of Christ up to the coming of the Antichrist, which are not known exactly to us, because it is given to no mortal *to know the times and seasons which the Father has placed in his own authority* (Acts 1:7)" (750).

Following Andrew, Arethas rejects Oecumenius's preterist interpretation of the thousand years, which portrayed them as a symbol of the time of the ministry of Jesus. Arethas also distances himself from a futuristic chiliast reading of the thousand years, quoting a Gospel and a Pauline epistle in refutation. On these views, followed by his own, he writes:

> Some interpret, I know not how, the aforementioned time of the thousand years as the three and half years from the baptism of Christ up to his ascension into heaven, after which they understand the devil is loosed. But others say that after the completion of the six thousand years, the first resurrection is to be given to the saints alone, so that on this earth in which they displayed endurance, they enjoy a thousand years in delights and glory, and after this there will be the universal resurrection not only of the just but also of sinners. And so since the church receives none of these things, it is even vain to say it. Therefore, let us hear with the Lord what he says to the Sadducees: *Just like the angels of God in heaven, so also are the saints* (Matt 22:30), also when the Apostle said: *The kingdom of God is not food and drink* (Rom 14:17), and interpret the time of the thousand years as the duration of evangelical preaching. (755)

On Rev 21:19–20, Arethas gives a detailed description of the gemstones. This description was inherited from Andrew, who in turn was dependent upon *On the Gems* of Epiphanius.[20]

Arethas's *Commentary on the Apocalypse* provided explanations of the visions of John gathered mainly from earlier exegetical traditions. He supplied this for tenth-century Greek readers and hearers.

Catechesis Celtica

Manuscript and Editions

From the late tenth century is a collection of homiletical material designated by André Wilmart as "Catéchèses celtiques" and often

[20] See Robert P. Blake and Henri de Vis, *Epiphanius de Gemmis* (London: Christophers, 1934).

referred to as the *Catechesis Celtica.* The collection comprises the manuscript Vatican City, Biblioteca Apostolica Vaticana, Reg. lat. 49. Wilmart edited about a third of the material in his *Analecta Reginensia* (Studi e Testi 59, Vatican City: Biblioteca Apostolica Vaticana, 1933, 29–112). Jean Rittmueller is editing the entire compilation for the Scriptores Celtigenae sub-series of Corpus Christianorum Series Latina to be published jointly by Brepols and the Royal Irish Academy. She is also preparing an English translation.

Provenance

The *Catechesis Celtica* appears to be the product of a scriptorium in a Brythonic-speaking area; and locations in Wales, Cornwall, and Brittany have been suggested.[21] Although it is likely to have been compiled outside Ireland, its many Irish elements and affiliations are discussed in a number of publications.[22]

Exegesis of the Apocalypse

The collection includes several sections that contain exegesis of passages from the Apocalypse. Folio 45r (Wilmart, *Analecta Reginensia,* no. 29; *Catechesis Celtica,* 70–71), within a homily on many mansions in heaven,[23] contains commentary on the vision of one like the Son of Man in Rev 1:13–16. The Son of Man's white hair and shining face represent his divinity. "His eyes are the two laws, which burn up sinners like fire ... and which illuminate the saints." His feet, similar to brass, represent the saints who experience martyrdom; his voice is the sound of preaching; and the sharp sword proceeding from his mouth is the divine word. The seven stars in his right hand represent the seven churches, the seven steps mentioned in Ezek 40:22, 26, and the seven gifts of the Holy Spirit listed in Isa 11:2.

21 Benjamin Hudson, "Time Is Short: The Eschatology of the Early Gaelic Church," in *Last Things: Death and the Apocalypse in the Middle Ages,* ed. Caroline Walker Bynum and Paul Freedman (Philadelphia: University of Pennsylvania Press, 2000), 109.

22 Diarmuid Ó Laoghaire, "Irish Elements in the *Catechesis Celtica,*" in *Ireland and Christendom: The Bible and the Missions,* ed. Próinséas Ní Chatháin and Michael Richter (Stuttgart: Klett-Cotta, 1987), 146–64; Martin McNamara, "The Irish Affiliations of the *Catechesis Celtica,*" *Celtica* 21 (1990):291–334; Jean Rittmueller, "MS Vat. Reg. lat. 49 Reviewed: A New Description and a Table of Textual Parallels with the *Liber questionum in evangeliis,*" *Sacris Erudiri* 33 (1992–93): 259–305; Martin McNamara, "Sources and Affiliations of the *Catechesis Celtica* (MS Vat. Reg. lat 49)," *Sacris Erudiri* 34 (1994):185–237.

23 See John 14:1–2.

Folio 45rb–va (Wilmart, *Analecta Reginensia*, no. 30; *Catechesis Celtica*, 71 n. 8) contains exegesis of Rev 4:5, interpreting the lightning, voices, and peals of thunder that proceed from the heavenly throne. Divine preaching, the author writes, imitates all of these. For example, preaching is like lightning in that it "comes suddenly, penetrates swiftly, illuminates dark hearts, lessens bodily desires through abstinence, and frightens the righteous along with sinners." Preaching sometimes pierces the heart as thunder, which "strikes inward terror in the soul."

Exegesis of Rev 5:1–3 about a scroll "sealed with seven seals" is on folio 40va–b (Wilmart, *Analecta Reginensia*, no. 26).[24] The seven seals are correlated with seven events in the life of Christ: his conception, nativity, passion, burial, resurrection, ascension, and Second Coming.

The twelve gates of the heavenly city described in Rev 21:12–14 are explained on folio 35ra–vb (Wilmart, *Analecta Reginensia*, no. 29; *Catechesis Celtica*, 56–58). After a short comparison of the colors of the precious stones on the walls of the city with actions of the saints, the text continues:

> The twelve patriarchs whom John saw on the gates of the city, these are the teachers who guard [the precepts] of the old law. Likewise the twelve apostles whom John saw are the lawgivers who keep the new law. Likewise the twelve angels whom John saw, these are the ministers and guardians of the Catholic Church, as the psalmist says: *Since he entrusted his angels concerning you, to guard you,* etc. (Ps 91:11), because the angels of heaven guard the souls of each person from the day of his birth up to the day when he leaves his body. Therefore, sinners will go before Christ in judgment to suffer judgment. Therefore, the gates of the kingdom of heaven will be closed to them because of the merits of their evil deeds. And they will be cast forth to eternal punishments with the army of demons, through the testimony of the apostles and patriarchs and angels. And it will be said to them from the mouth of God alone: *Go, accursed ones,* etc. (Matt 25:41). But the saints will ascend with Christ to his kingdom and the gates of the kingdom of heaven will

[24] Martin McNamara published this text in "The Affiliations and Origins of the *Catechesis Celtica*: An Ongoing Quest," in *The Scriptures and Early Medieval Ireland*, ed. Thomas O'Loughlin (Turnhout: Brepols, 1999), 199–200. In English, see F. X. Gumerlock, ed. and trans., *The Seven Seals of the Apocalypse: Medieval Texts in Translation* (Kalamazoo, MI: Medieval Institute Publications, 2009), 34–35.

be opened before them. And these three, whom we have mentioned before, will be their guides and guards. And the voice of God alone will call them in the sight of the apostles and patriarchs and angels, saying: *Come, blessed ones*, etc. (Matt 25:34).

The text then gives allegorical interpretations of the gates. The three gates on the east represent faith, hope, and love, and the apostle Peter is their key holder. The three southern gates represent virginity, penance, and marriage, and the apostle John has watch over them. The three gates on the west are deeds, words, and thoughts, and the apostle Thomas is their gatekeeper. The northern gates represent baptism, repentance, and martyrdom, and the apostle James watches over them.

The comments in the *Catechesis Celtica* on various passages from the Apocalypse provide a small glimpse of how it was explained and understood in the tenth century by this particular compiler, his community, and the recipients or audience for which it was written.

Gloss on the Apocalypse of John

Manuscripts and Purpose

A short, anonymous Latin gloss on the Apocalypse is found in two tenth-century manuscripts: Fulda, Hessische Landesbibliotek, Aa 2, folios 105v–107v; and Bern, Burgerbibliothek, 258, folios 42r–43r. Both manuscripts were edited in P. Vaciago, ed., *Glossae Biblicae, Pars II*, CCCM 189B (Turnhout: Brepols, 2004), 355–60, 673–77. This gloss is especially concerned with explaining the meanings of certain Latin words in the Apocalypse.

Content

The gloss provides the meaning of various words and names which perhaps those reading the Book of Revelation in the tenth century may not have known. For example, on Rev 1:13, it informs the reader that a *poderis* is a linen tunic worn by priests similar to what they know as a "camisole." On Rev 2:11, it explains that a *romphea* is a sword and on Rev 9:17 that "hyacinth" has a color similar to smoke. The gloss also clarifies biblical weights with Latin equivalents. For example, a "quart" (Rev 6:6), it says, equals two pounds; and a "talent" (Rev 16:21) seventy-two pounds. Since a tenth-century reader of the Apocalypse might not have been familiar with the various gemstones mentioned in Rev 21:19–20, a description of each stone is given, followed by a Christian virtue that each stone signifies.

Sources

Many of the explanations are abridgements of Bede's *Exposition of the Apocalypse* (ca. 700),[25] including the lengthy description of the stones on the foundation of New Jerusalem in Rev 21:19–20. Some of the explanations of the names derive from Jerome's *On Hebrew Names*, but came to the author of the gloss through Bede. The seven seals of Rev 5:1 are interpreted as seven events in the life of Jesus, that is, his nativity, baptism, cross, burial, resurrection, ascension, and judgment. This interpretation follows Hiberno-Latin exegesis.[26] Other material seems to be original to the author.

An English translation of this *Gloss on the Apocalypse of John* is provided below. The enumeration of chapters and verses, corresponding to our modern organization of the Book of Revelation, was added by the present writer.

ON THE APOCALYPSE OF JOHN

Chapter One

1 "Moreover, Apocalypse is interpreted from Greek into Latin as Revelation. A revelation is said to be a manifestation of those things which had been hidden, according to which also John himself said: *The Apocalypse of Jesus Christ which God gave to him to make plain to his servants.*"[27]

11 For, in these [names],[28] I. Ephesus is interpreted both "great fall" and "my will."

II. Smyrna is called Myra which designates the "mortification of the flesh."

[25] The *Exposition of the Apocalypse* by Bede is edited by Roger Gryson in *Bedae Presbyteri Expositio Apocalypseos*. CCSL 121A (Turnhout: Brepols, 2001). Recent English translations are in William Weinrich, trans., *Latin Commentaries on Revelation* (Downers Grove, IL: InterVarsity Press, 2011) and Bede, *Commentary on Revelation*, trans. Faith Wallis, TTH 58 (Liverpool: University of Liverpool Press, 2013).

[26] This is the interpretation of the seals in the eighth-century Hiberno-Latin *On the Mysteries of the Apocalypse of John* and in the *Catechesis Celtica*.

[27] Isidore of Seville, *Etymologies* 6.2, 49; in English, see *The Etymologies of Isidore of Seville*, trans. Stephen A. Barney, W. J. Lewis, J. A. Beach, and Oliver Berghof (New York: Cambridge University Press, 2006), 138.

[28] The interpretation of the names of the seven cities of Asia is based upon comments on Rev 2–3 in Bede, *Exposition of the Apocalypse*. They in turn are based on Jerome's *On Hebrew Names*, Apoc., CCSL 72 (Turnhout: Brepols, 1959), 160.

III. Pergamum is interpreted "the dividing of their horns."
IV. Thyatira is translated into "sacrifice of the saints," for they *present* their *bodies as a living sacrifice* (Rom 12:1).
V. Also *the angel of the church of Sardis* (Rev 3:1). This angel, that is, the priest, was less skilled in correcting evils. Nevertheless he made known that he praises some for walking in white garments.[29] The name of the sardis stone, which is everywhere precious, corresponds to these.
VI. Philadelphia is interpreted "brotherly love."
VII. Laodicea "tribe beloved of the Lord," or "they were in vomit."[30]

13 *Poderis* is a linen tunic of a priest worn tight on his body. Accordingly they commonly call it a "camisole."

Chapter Two

6 *Of the Nicolaitans,* named from the deacon Nicholas, who was established with Stephen and the others by Peter.[31] He taught, among other things, that things sacrificed to idols were to be eaten and that all things[32] were to be done commonly in public.

7 *From the tree of life.* "Christ is the tree of life."[33]

11 *Romphea,* a sword.

13 *Antipas my witness.* "Some understand him to be a martyr who suffered in Pergamum. Others understand him to be Christ the Lord."[34]

16 *Or else.* Or, in another interpretation "surely" or "without doubt."

17 *Hidden manna* is about that which he said: *I am the living bread which comes down from heaven* (John 6:51).[35] *White stone,* a shiny rock.

20 *Because you allow the woman Jezebel, who says that she is a prophetess, to teach.* In fact in this church which is called Thyatira,

[29] See Rev 3:4.
[30] See Rev 3:16.
[31] See Acts 6:5.
[32] That is, sexual relations.
[33] Bede, *Exposition of the Apocalypse,* on Rev 2:7.
[34] Ibid., on Rev 2:13.
[35] See Tyconius, *Exposition of the Apocalypse,* on Rev 2:17; *Tyconius: Exposition of the Apocalypse.,* trans. Francis X. Gumerlock, FC 134 (Washington, DC: Catholic University of America Press, 2017), 46; Irish Reference Bible, *On the Mysteries of the Apocalypse of John,* on Rev 2:17 (Gumerlock, *Early Latin Commentaries,* 50).

they say there was a woman of this name who taught and persuaded people to fornicate and to eat things sacrificed to idols.[36] The name Jezebel sounds like the "flow of blood."[37]

Chapter Three

12 "*I shall write upon him the name of my God,* that is, we are *called sons of God* (Matt 5:9; 1 John 3:1) through adoption.[38] *The name of the city of my God, Jerusalem,* the unity of the church. *My new name,* that is, the name 'Christian.'"[39]

14 "*Amen* is interpreted 'truly' or 'faithfully.'"[40]

15 "*Neither cold nor hot,* that is, you are neither fervent in faith nor entirely unfaithful."[41]

Chapter Four

3 *Jasper and sardonyx.* "Jasper is the color of water; sardonyx signifies fire."[42] *Rainbow,* a bow in the clouds appears. *Emerald,* a stone having a green color.

5 *Seven spirits of God.* "He speaks of the septiform Spirit."[43]

Chapter Five

1 *Seven seals.* Some say the first seal [is] the nativity, the second [his] baptism, the third the cross, the fourth the burial, the fifth the resurrection, the sixth the ascension, the seventh the judgment.[44]

36 See Bede, *Exposition of the Apocalypse,* on Rev 2:20; *On the Mysteries of the Apocalypse of John,* on Rev 2:20.

37 See Bede, *Exposition of the Apocalypse,* on Rev 2:20, from Jerome, *On Hebrew Names,* Apoc., CCSL 72, 160.

38 The author makes the common theological distinction between Christ, the Son of God by nature, and his people, sons of God by adoption.

39 Bede, *Exposition of the Apocalypse,* on Rev 3:12.

40 Bede, *Exposition of the Apocalypse,* on Rev 3:14, from Jerome, *On Hebrew Names,* Apoc., CCSL 72, 159.

41 Bede, *Exposition of the Apocalypse,* on Rev 3:15.

42 Bede, *Exposition of the Apocalypse,* on Rev 4:3, from Primasius, *Commentary on the Apocalypse,* on Rev 4:2–3; Primasius, *Commentarius in Apocalypsin,* ed. A. W. Adams, CCSL 92 (Turnhout: Brepols, 1985), 47.

43 Bede, *Exposition of the Apocalypse,* on Rev 4:5. See Isa 11:2.

44 See Apringius of Beja, *Explanation of the Revelation,* on Rev 5:1 (ed. and trans. in Weinrich, *Latin Commentaries on Revelation*); *On the Mysteries of the Apocalypse of John,* on Rev 5:1–3.

Chapter Six

6 *A quart*, two pounds.[45] *Three quarts*, six pounds.

13 *Its figs*, that is, the fruit of a fig tree. *Unripened*, "useless and frail,"[46] which fall off in the movement of the winds.

Chapter Nine

16 *Two hundred thousand thousand.* "Another translation has it this way: two myriads of myriads."[47]

17 *Breastplates of hyacinth.* Hyacinth is said to have the color of smoke.

21 *Sorcerers*, those who give poison, whether those skilled in herbs or enchanters.[48] *Because time will be no more.* [There are] varieties of times. In the last trumpet[49] it will cease.

Chapter Eleven

1 *Measure*, take a measurement.

Chapter Thirteen

16 *Written character*, a mark.

Chapter Fourteen

19 *Pool.*[50] In this passage it signifies a winepress.

Chapter Fifteen

1 *Seven last plagues*, that is, "because the wrath of God always strikes stubborn people."[51]

Chapter Sixteen

2 *Grievous*, severe.

16 "*Armageddon* is interpreted 'rising up in former things,' or 'spherical mountain.'"[52]

21 *Talent*, among the Romans seventy-two pounds.

45 Cf. Isidore of Seville, *Etymologies* 16, 26, which says that a pint, not a quart, equals two pounds (trans. Barney et al., 334).

46 Bede, *Exposition of the Apocalypse*, on Rev 6:13.

47 Ibid., on Rev 9:16. The other translation to which he refers is found in Tyconius, *Exposition of the Apocalypse*, on Rev 9:16.

48 Lat. *malefici*, probably meaning *malefactores* or those who cast spells or put curses on people.

49 See 1 Cor 15:52; Rev 11:15.

50 Lat. *Lacum*.

51 Bede, *Exposition of the Apocalypse*, on Rev 15:1.

52 Ibid., on Rev 16:16, from Jerome, *On Hebrew Names*, Apoc., CCSL 72, 159.

Chapter Seventeen

2 *Of fornication*, of debauchery, since a prostitute is called a harlot.

3 *Scarlet*, red.

Chapter Eighteen

12 *Thyine wood*, the particular name of that wood.

13 *Fine flour*, the kernel of a grain.

19 *Desolate*, deserted or abandoned.

Chapter Twenty

6 "*Blessed and holy is the one who has a part in the first resurrection*, that is, the one who will have preserved that which was born anew."[53]

7 *Gog and Magog*. "According to the interpretation of the names, which are said [to mean] 'covering'[54] and 'out from the covering,' he indicates hidden and visible enemies."[55]

Chapter Twenty-One

8 *Abominable*, accursed or detestable.

17 *The measure, that is, of an angel.* Indeed the quantity is understood literally. "He signifies that the angel appeared to him in the form of a man."[56]

The Names of the Stones[57]

19

I. *The first foundation, jasper.* There are many kinds of jaspers. For one is of a green color and appears as if dipped in flowers. Another has similarity to an emerald, but of an uncultured color with which, they assert, all [kinds of] phantasms are formed. Another has the appearance of snow and foam of sea waves, as if mixed with blood.[58]

[53] Tyconius, *Exposition of the Apocalypse*, on Rev 20:6, probably via Bede, *Exposition of the Apocalypse*, on Rev 20:6.

[54] Lat. *tectus* or "roof."

[55] Bede, *Exposition of the Apocalypse*, n Rev 20:7, from Jerome, *On Hebrew Names*, Apoc., CCSL 72, 160.

[56] Bede, *Exposition of the Apocalypse*, on Rev 21:17.

[57] From here to the end of the gloss, the author provides an abridged version of Bede's comments. See Bede, *Exposition of the Apocalypse*, on Rev 21:19–20. On the sources of the comments of Bede on the twelve stones, see Bede, *Explanatio Apocalypseos*, ed. Roger Gryson, CCSL 121A (Turnhout: Brepols, 2001), 173–77, and Wallis in Bede, *Commentary on Revelation*, 267 n. 1072.

[58] The entire comment on jasper has its basis in Jerome's *Commentary on Isaiah*, 15,7 (Thomas P. Scheck, trans., *St. Jerome-Origen:Commentary on Isaiah; Origen Homilies 1–9 on Isaiah*, Ancient Christian Writers 68 [New York: Newman, 2015], 691), via Bede.

II. *Sapphire.* Moses explained the color of, as well as the mystery of, this stone when describing the dwelling of God. He said: *Under his feet was like a work of sapphire stone and like the sky when it is clear* (Exod 24:10). And Ezekiel also says that the place, in which the throne of the Lord is, has a similarity to sapphire.[59]

III. *Chalcedony.* Chalcedony has an appearance like the pale fire of a lamp, and has a brightness under daylight [but] not in the house.

Emerald is very green to the point that it surpasses green plants and leaves. Also, covering every [emerald] gem all around is the green color of hammered brass, which approaches pure and green oil, as much as it is colored by nature. There are many kinds of them, but the Scythian ones are the most noble. The Bactrian hold second place, and in third place are the Egyptian.[60]

20 *Sardonyx.* Drawing its whiteness from onyx and its redness from sardion, it received the name sardonyx from both.[61] Moreover, there are many kinds of them. For one has the likeness of red earth.[62] Another appears as if the color of blood shining through a human fingernail. Another consists of three colors: black on the bottom, white in the middle, and red on top.[63]

I. *Sardion* is the color of pure blood.

II. The *chrysolite* stone shines like gold having fiery sparks.

III. *Beryl* is as, if you would imagine, water struck by the brightness of the sun, giving off a beautiful and red color. But it does not shine unless by polishing it, it is shaped into a six-sided form. For it is from the reflection of the angles that its brightness is accentuated.[64]

Topaz stone. Since it is rarely found, the [small] quantity of such a commodity makes it very pricey.[65] It is said to have two

[59] Ezek 10:1.

[60] The entire comment on emerald has its basis in Isidore of Seville, *Etymologies* 16.7, 1–2 (trans. Barney et al., 322), via Bede.

[61] The description is from Isidore, *Etymologies* 16.8, 4 (trans. Barney et al., 323), via Bede.

[62] This sentence is from Gregory the Great, *Moral Teaching on Job*, 18.75 (*Morals on the Book of Job by St. Gregory the Great*, no translator listed [London: Rivington, 1844], 597), via Bede.

[63] These last two sentences have their basis in Isidore, *Etymologies* 16.8, 3–4 (trans. Barney et al., 323), via Bede.

[64] These last two sentences have as their basis Isidore's *Etymologies* 16.7, 5 (trans. Barney et al., 322), via Bede.

[65] This sentence is from Cassiodorus, *On the Psalms*, Ps 118 (PL 70, 881), via Bede.

colors, one of very pure gold and the other shining with an ethereal brightness.

Chrysophrase has a mixture of green and gold, even bringing forth a certain purple gleam interspersed with gold spots. Moreover, it is found in India.

Hyacinth is found in Ethiopia. Having a blue color, the best is that which is neither scanty[66] nor dull from its density, but shines moderately between both qualities and resembles a sweetly purified flower. Moreover, it does not gleam the same way all the time, but changes with the appearance of the sky. For, when [the day] is serene, it is clear and pleasing; but when it is cloudy, it vanishes and become weak before the eyes.[67]

Amethyst is purple and mixed with a violet color, like the luster of a rose, and lightly emitting certain sparks. But in fact even in its purple, there appears something not entirely fiery but like red wine.[68]

What is signified through the stones?

I. Therefore, in *jasper* is designated the greenness of faith.

II. In *sapphire* the height of heavenly hope.

III. In *chalcedony* is signified the flame of inner love.

IV. Moreover, in *emerald* the greenness [symbolizes] the bold confession of the same faith through adversities.

In *sardonyx* the humility of the saints amid their virtues.

V. In *sardion* is expressed the revered blood of the martyrs.

VI. But in *chrysolite* spiritual preaching accompanied by miracles.

VII. In *beryl* the perfect work of those preaching.

VIII. In *topaz* is shown their fervent contemplation.

X [*sic*]. In *chrysophrase* the work of the blessed martyrs and equally their reward.

XI. In *hyacinth* the heavenly elevation of teachers to high places and their humble descent to human things on account of the weak.

XII. In *amethyst* is designated the contemplation of the heavenly kingdom, always in the mind of the humble.

66 Lat. *rarus*, the opposite of dense.

67 The comment on hyacinth has its basis in Isidore, *Etymologies* 16.9, 3 (trans. Barney et al., 324), via Bede.

68 The comment on amethyst has its basis in Isidore, *Etymologies* 16.9, 1 (trans. Barney et al., 324), via Bede.

And so each of the precious stones was assigned to one of the foundations. This is, because although everyone is perfected,[69] by whom the city of our God on his holy mountain is adorned and established, nevertheless they [all] shine with the light of their [particular] spiritual grace.[70]

Selected Further Reading

Andrew of Caesarea. *Commentary on the Apocalypse.* Translated by Eugenia Scarvelis Constantinou. Fathers of the Church 123. Washington, DC: Catholic University of America Press, 2011.

Arethas of Caesarea. *Commentarius in Apocalypsin.* Patrologia Graeca 106, 485–786. Paris: Petit-Montrouge, 1863.

Bede. *Commentary on Revelation.* Translated by Faith Wallis. Translated Texts for Historians 58. Liverpool: University of Liverpool Press, 2013.

Gumerlock, Francis X., ed. and trans. *Carolingian Commentaries on the Apocalypse by Theodulf and Smaragdus.* Kalamazoo, MI: Medieval Institute Publications, 2019.

McNamara, Martin. "The Irish Affiliations of the *Catechesis Celtica.*" *Celtica* 21 (1990): 291–334.

Oecumenius. *Commentary on the Apocalypse.* Translated by John N. Suggit. Fathers of the Church 112. Washington, DC: Catholic University of America Press, 2006.

Palmer, James T. *The Apocalypse in the Early Middle Ages.* Cambridge: Cambridge University Press, 2014.

Rittmueller, Jean. "MS Vat. Reg. lat. 49 Reviewed." *Sacris Erudiri* 33 (1992–93): 259–305.

Vaciago, P., ed. and trans. *Glossae Biblicae, Pars II.* Corpus Christianorum: Continuatio Mediaevalis 189B. Turnhout: Brepols, 2004.

Wilmart, André, ed. *Analecta Reginensia.* Studi e Testi 59. Vatican City: Biblioteca Apostolica Vaticana, 1933.

[69] In the New Jerusalem. If the author refers to the church now, he is making the distinction between the common redemption that all believers share in Christ and the diversity of individual graces. If he refers to the eschaton, he is making the distinction between the common beatitude of all the elect in heaven and the diversity of individual rewards.

[70] Lat. *gratie*, or "gift." Bede goes on to quote 1 Cor 12:8–10 about the diversity of spiritual gifts given to the members of Christ's one body.

9 The End of the World at the Ends of the Earth: Apocalyptic Thought in Medieval Ireland

JOHN CAREY

Christians have been concerned with the final times ever since Christ's disciples asked him about the signs of "the end of the age" (τῆς συντελείας τοῦ αἰῶνος).[1] St. Patrick, laboring to spread the gospel in an Ireland still largely pagan, spoke of himself as living "in the last days" (*in novissimis diebus*), shortly before the Second Coming (*expectamus adventum ipsius mox futurum*).[2] Indeed, he believed that his own work was directly preparing the eschaton: by preaching "as far as the place beyond which there is no one" (*usque ubi nemo ultra est*), he was fulfilling Christ's prophecy that the gospel would be proclaimed "in the whole inhabited world ... and then will come the end" (ἐν ὅλῃ τῇ οἰκουμένῃ ... καὶ τότε ἥξει τὸ τέλος).[3]

One of the oldest surviving Hiberno-Latin hymns is *Altus Prosator*, probably composed on the island of Iona early in the seventh century. Of its twenty-three stanzas, fifteen describe the wonders of the cosmos, the sixteenth speaks of Moses as the only human to have seen God directly, and the remaining seven are devoted to eschatology. The supreme importance of this concluding theme is evoked in a coda:

> Quis potest Deo placere · novissimo in tempore,
> variatis insignibus · veritatis ordinibus,
> exceptis contemptoribus · mundi praesentis istius?
>
> Who can satisfy God in the last times,
> when the noble rules of truth have been changed,
> save for those who scorn the present world?[4]

1 Matt 24:3. All translations are my own unless indicated otherwise.

2 Ludwig Bieler, *Libri epistolarum Sancti Patricii episcopi* (Dublin: Irish Manuscripts Commission, 1952), 1.59, 76.

3 Ibid., 1.76; Matt 24:14.

4 Text and translation from John Carey, *King of Mysteries: Early Irish Religious Writings*, 2nd ed. (Dublin: Four Courts Press, 2000), 48–49.

Taken as a sequence, the eschatological stanzas provide a masterly concatenation of images and phrases drawn from both the Old and the New Testaments, reflecting the close attention with which the author trawled the entirety of Scripture in search of hints concerning the End.[5]

Treatments of this subject were popular in all periods of Irish literature thereafter, throughout the Middle Ages and beyond.[6] These reflect various influences, most notably that of the *Apocalypse of Thomas*: several of the witnesses to the many versions of this apocryphon are in fact preserved in manuscripts with Irish associations.[7] Over time, the account of the world's final week in the *Apocalypse of Thomas* evolved into a list of fifteen signs of the approaching end, versions of which are attested across much of Europe; in an extended study of this tradition, W. W. Heist argued that it had originated in Ireland, and in the tenth century.[8] Subsequent research has revised some of Heist's conclusions, indicating that the signs were known in Ireland considerably earlier than he thought.[9] Thus an eighth-century date and an Irish authorship have tentatively been proposed for the pseudo-Bedan tract *De quindecim signis*;[10] and the poems attributed to Blathmac mac Con Brettan,

[5] For the hymn's main sources see Thomas Owen Clancy and Gilbert Markús, *Iona: The Earliest Poetry of a Celtic Monastery* (Edinburgh: Edinburgh University Press, 1995), 54–67.

[6] A collection of material is contained in J. Carey, E. Nic Cárthaigh, and C. Ó Dochartaigh, eds., *The End and Beyond: Medieval Irish Eschatology* (Aberystwyth: Celtic Studies Publications, 2014), 547–760, with a survey by Bernard McGinn, "Medieval Visions of the End: The Irish Contribution," ibid., 11–36. Editions of several further key texts are forthcoming in parts 2:2 and 2:3 of the Apocrypha Hiberniae subseries of CCSA.

[7] Our understanding of this text has evolved significantly in recent years, thanks primarily to the important work of Charles D. Wright: his two key publications are "*The Apocalypse of Thomas*: Some New Latin Texts and their Significance for the Old English Versions," in *Apocryphal Texts and Traditions in Anglo-Saxon England*, ed. K. Powell and D. G. Scragg (Cambridge: D. S. Brewer, 2003), 27–64; and "Rewriting (and Re-editing) *The Apocalypse of Thomas*," in *Écritures et réécritures: la reprise interprétative des traditions fondatrices par la littérature biblique et extra-biblique*, ed. C. Clivaz et al., Bibliotheca ephemeridum theologicarum lovaniensium 248 (Leuven: Peeters, 2012), 441–53.

[8] W. W. Heist, *The Fifteen Signs before Doomsday* (East Lansing: Michigan State College Press, 1952).

[9] See for instance Ó Dochartaigh's observations in John Carey and Caitríona Ó Dochartaigh, "Introduction to 'The Judgement and Its Signs,'" in *The End and Beyond*, ed. Carey, Nic Cárthaigh, and Ó Dochartaigh, 558–61; and the important collection of relevant texts forthcoming in Apocrypha Hiberniae 2:3 (see n. 6 above).

[10] Martha Bayless and Michael Lapidge, *Collectanea Pseudo-Bedae*, Scriptores Latini Hiberniae 14 (Dublin: Dublin Institute for Advanced Studies, 1998), 178 (§§356–71), with remarks on provenance on p. 9.

discovered since Heist wrote and also assigned to the eighth century, contain some of the same signs.[11] Whatever the details, there can be no doubt that enumerations of eschatological signs emerged early, and remained important, among the medieval Irish.

Besides transmitting and embellishing earlier apocalyptic doctrines, the Irish formulated eschatological expectations that appear to be peculiar to the Gaelic world. Thus the "Additamenta" (later eighth century?) in the Book of Armagh already state that one of the favors granted by God to Patrick was that "none of us—that is, of the Irish—will live beyond seven years before the Day of Judgment, because they will be destroyed by the sea seven years before the Judgment."[12] This association of the national saint with a specifically Irish eschaton invites comparison with the statement of the seventh-century writer Tírechán that the druids had their own word (hence, presumably, their own conception) for the Day of Judgment;[13] and perhaps with Patrick's ideas about the link between his preaching in Ireland and the approaching end.[14] This inundation is mentioned repeatedly in later sources: in the late Middle Irish poem *Éistea riom, a Bhaoithín bhuain*, for instance, St. Colum Cille joins Patrick in foretelling "that seven years before the Judgment | the sea will cover Ireland in a single hour."[15]

Before it is engulfed by the sea, however, Ireland is fated to endure other tribulations: a vast invading fleet that is to land at Malahide Bay, Co. Dublin; and the more mysterious, but even more devastatingly lethal, "Broom out of Fánat" and "Fiery Arrow."[16] Such disasters are often forecast for the feast of John the Baptist. The most bizarre among them is the "Rowing Wheel" or *Roth Rámach*, an enormous and elaborate weapon and/or vehicle said to have been constructed by the druid Mug Roith when he was assisting Simon Magus in his struggles against

[11] Martin McNamara, "The (Fifteen) Signs before Doomsday in Irish Tradition," *Warszawskie Studia Teologiczne* 22, no. 2 (2007): 231–33; cf. the discussion by Ó Dochartaigh in John Carey and Caitríona Ó Dochartaigh, "Introduction to 'The Judgement and Its Signs.'"

[12] Ludwig Bieler, *The Patrician Texts in the Book of Armagh*, Scriptores Latini Hiberniae 10 (Dublin: Dublin Institute for Advanced Studies, 1979), 164; discussion of date on p. 49.

[13] Ibid., 132.

[14] I discuss these possibilities in John Carey, "Saint Patrick, the Druids, and the End of the World," *History of Religions* 36, no. 1 (1996): 42–53.

[15] John Carey, "Colum Cille's Warning to Baíthín," in *The End and Beyond*, ed. Carey, Nic Cárthaigh, and Ó Dochartaigh, 703 §62.

[16] I provide some references in Carey and Ó Dochartaigh, "Introduction to 'The Judgement and Its Signs,'" 550.

the apostles.[17] There was a tradition, traces of which can be found as far back as the glossary *Sanas Cormaic* (ca. 900), that Mug Roith's daughter brought a part of the wheel with her to Ireland, and set it up as a pillar stone at Cnámchaill; in the final days the wheel itself will come out of the east and smash against the stone, causing untold destruction.[18] It is said of the wheel that "everyone who will see it will be blind, everyone who will hear it will be deaf, everyone against whom it will strike will be dead."[19] Interpretations of this terrible but enigmatic object range from T. F. O'Rahilly's view, that it represents the destructive power of the sun-god, to the proposal of Nicholas O'Kearney that it is a prophecy of the use of paddle-wheel steamers in naval warfare.[20] Its true origins remain obscure.

Bernard McGinn has described the genre "apocalypse" with useful concision as "a form of revelation in which an angelic figure conveys a message from God to a seer and his community, the message concerning heavenly secrets about history and its end, as well as about cosmology and the fate of souls."[21] So far, I have considered the first of these concerns; I shall not be directly dealing with the second of them, even though I shall be making some use below of the remarkable Irish cosmological work *In Tenga Bithnúa* or *The Ever-New Tongue*. Concerning the fate of souls, there is an abundant literature in Irish. In what remains of this chapter I will briefly consider this literature's most essential background; I will then give more detailed attention to two aspects of the subject which, while not necessarily peculiar to Irish accounts of the afterlife, are certainly characteristic of it.

The most important literary source for descriptions of the afterworld in Ireland, as elsewhere in Europe, was without question *Visio Sancti Pauli*, described by Anthony Hilhorst as "a receptacle of earlier traditions and at the same time a fountainhead of ideas and images in

17 According to some sources, doom is to strike Ireland on the feast of John the Baptist because it was Mug Roith who was the saint's executioner.

18 Kuno Meyer, *Sanas Cormaic (Cormac's Glossary)*, Anecdota from Irish Manuscripts 4 (Halle: Max Niemeyer, 1912), 49 §598.

19 M. A. O'Brien, *Corpus genealogiarum Hiberniae*, 2nd ed. (Dublin: Dublin Institute for Advanced Studies, 1976), 280.

20 T. F. O'Rahilly, *Early Irish History and Mythology* (Dublin: Dublin Institute for Advanced Studies, 1946), 520–21; Nicholas O'Kearney, *The Prophecies of Saints Colum-cille, Maeltamlacht, Ultan, Senan, Bearcan, and Malachy* (Dublin: Duffy, 1856), 53 n. 2, 54 n. 2, 55 n. 3.

21 McGinn, "Medieval Visions of the End," 13. For more detailed discussion, he cites John J. Collins, ed., "Apocalypse: The Morphology of a Genre," special issue, *Semeia* 14 (1979).

later texts."[22] This account of the apostle's travels in the beyond, inspired by his cryptic reference to a visit to "the third heaven" in 2 Cor 12:2–4, provided a basis for imitation and creative elaboration throughout the medieval centuries. It is generally held that its original form is best reflected in the version known as the "Long Latin."[23] Here it is related how Paul, after having witnessed souls being judged after death, was taken by an angel to the third and the second heavens, then to the "land of promise" and the "city of Christ," thereafter to the regions of punishment, and at last to paradise, before being obliged to return to the mortal world. There are also several "Redactions": abbreviated forms of the vision that concentrate, often exclusively, on its infernal component.[24] Although they omit much of what is found in the Long Latin, the Redactions supply further elements of their own.

Both the Long Latin and the Redactions were known in the British Isles, and notably in Ireland, from an early date. Thus Aldhelm of Malmesbury († 709) refers disparagingly to the Long Latin *Visio* in his *De laudibus virginum*;[25] and at roughly the same time it provided a model for the out-of-body experiences of the Irish saint Fursa (to be discussed below). The Long Latin's continuing influence in Ireland is evident from one of the most elaborate and magnificent accounts of the afterlife, *Fís Adomnáin* (*The Vision of Adomnán*, ca. 1000): this work derives not only much of its structure from the *Visio*, but also several of its details.[26]

[22] Anthony Hilhorst, "The Apocalypse of Paul: Earlier History and Later Influence," in *Apocalyptic and Eschatological Heritage: The Middle East and Celtic Realms*, ed. M. McNamara (Dublin: Four Courts, 2003), 62.

[23] Theodore Silverstein and Anthony Hilhorst, eds., *Apocalypse of Paul: A New Critical Edition of Three Long Latin Versions* (Geneva: Patrick Cramer, 1997).

[24] The system for categorizing the Redactions formulated by Theodore Silverstein, and further developed by subsequent scholars, puts their number at eleven: Silverstein, *Visio Sancti Pauli: The History of the Apocalypse in Latin Together with Nine Texts*, Studies and Documents 4 (London: Christophers, 1935); Mary E. Dwyer, "An Unstudied Redaction of the *Visio Pauli*," *Manuscripta* 32 (1988): 121–38. A new and considerably more sophisticated scheme of classification has been proposed by Lenka Jiroušková, *Die Visio Pauli: Wege und Wandlungen einer orientalischen Apokryphe im lateinischen Mittelalter unter Einschluß der alttschechischen und deutschsprachigen Textzeugen* (Leiden: Brill, 2006).

[25] Rudolf Ehwald, *Aldhelmi opera*, MGH, Auctores Antiquissimi 15 (Berlin: Weidmann, 1919), 256.

[26] David N. Dumville, "Towards an Interpretation of *Fís Adamnán*," *Studia Celtica* 12–13 (1977–78): 75, notes the *Visio*'s influence but does not seem to me to go far enough in acknowledging its extent; I endeavor to deal with this question more fully in my own edition of the text, forthcoming in Apocrypha Hiberniae 2:2. For a translation, see meanwhile Carey, *King of Mysteries*, 261–74.

Evidence of the influence of the Redactions is more extensive: this is not surprising, as they appear to have been considerably more popular. Several of the Redactions have strong Insular associations, and a case can indeed be made for regarding some of them as Irish compositions.[27] Theodore Silverstein noted that what he called Redaction VI contains several additional elements that can be paralleled in *Fís Adomnáin*, as well as in other Irish texts (*The Vision of Laisrén*, *Immram Curaig Úa Corra*, and *Udhacht Mhuire*);[28] and I have discussed further evidence that the Redactions served as sources for the account of hell in the late-tenth-century *Saltair na Rann*.[29] In the later Middle Ages, two Irish translations were made of Silverstein's Redaction IV.[30]

In the remainder of this chapter I shall consider the treatment in early Irish sources of two topics: the nature of the embodiment or disembodiment of the visionary; and the extent to which the regions of the afterlife are imagined as belonging to earthly geography. For both questions, *Visio Sancti Pauli* and its impact on the Irish imagination will provide us with our starting point.

Paul himself was resolutely noncommittal as to the physicality or otherwise of the visit to the third heaven, stating twice that only God knows "whether [it was] in the body or outside of the body" (εἴτε ἐν σώματι εἴτε ἐκτὸς τοῦ σώματος; 2 Cor 12:3, cf. 2). The testimony of *Visio Sancti Pauli* on this point is also not entirely clear: the Paris manuscript of the Long Latin version has Paul say that he was addressed by God "when I was in the body in which I was snatched up to the third heaven" (*dum in <cor>pore essem in qua raptus sum usque ad tercium celum*); but this phrase is missing from the only other manuscript that contains this section of the text.[31] In Ireland, as mentioned above, *Fís Adomnáin* bases much of its framework on the *Visio*; but it differs from the Paris manuscript in stating unequivocally that Adomnán went to the afterworld "when his soul passed out of his body," and that at the end of his travels his soul was commanded "to come back to the same

27 Thus Charles D. Wright, "Next-to-Last Things: The Interim State of Souls in Early Irish Literature," in *The End and Beyond*, ed. Carey, Nic Cárthaigh, and C. Ó Dochartaigh, 339.

28 Silverstein, *Visio Sancti Pauli*, 82–90.

29 Carey, "*Visio Sancti Pauli* and the *Saltair*'s Hell," *Éigse* 23 (1989): 39–44.

30 These have been edited by J. E. Caerwyn Williams, "Irish Translations of the Visio Sancti Pauli," *Éigse* 6 (1960): 127–34; new editions by Caoimhín Breatnach are forthcoming in Apocrypha Hiberniae 2:2.

31 Silverstein and Hilhorst, *Apocalypse of Paul*, 68–69 §3.

body out of which it had passed."[32] We are however told nothing concerning the circumstances by which the visionary's soul and body were first separated and then reunited.

It is otherwise in *Transitus beati Fursei* (*The Passage of the Blessed Fursey*): the earliest account of the life of St. Fursa, and another work which, as already noted, clearly drew much of its inspiration from *Visio Sancti Pauli*. The *Transitus* was composed between the middle of the seventh century (the date of Fursa's death) and the early decades of the eighth (when Bede drew on it when writing his *Historia ecclesiastica*). Fursa is said to have had two visions, each preceded by an attack of acute physical debility: on both occasions his vision darkened and he lost the ability to move his limbs, then lost consciousness, and was at length taken to have died by those who were tending him.[33] From his own perspective, the darkness that had surrounded him was lightened by the radiance of angels who came to protect him, and to convey him to heaven. (He seems himself to have had no power of locomotion during his visions.) This supernatural light enabled him to see the faces of the angels, but only partially, as it dazzled him; analogously, it was difficult for him to see the faces of the devils whom he also encountered because of the "horror of darkness" that surrounded them.[34] His sight penetrated the walls of buildings; indeed, the only physical object that he appears to have been able to perceive was his own body.[35] In the course of the first vision, it was not until he was told that he must return to it that Fursa realized "that he had left his body" (*se corpore exutum*);[36] on both occasions he was acutely reluctant to resume a corporeal existence. At the conclusion of the first vision, we are told that Fursa "could not understand how the soul had entered the body" (*qualiter anima in corpus intraverit ... intellegere non potuit*); towards the end of the second, looking down from the roof of the house, he saw that "his body opened in the chest" (*pectore illius corpus aperiri*), apparently to afford him entry.[37] Especially noteworthy is the

[32] §§10 and 54 in my forthcoming edition.

[33] Fursa's companions say that, throughout the night, they had watched over his body, which was lifeless in their midst (*corpus exanime in medio servassent*); I cite Claude Carozzi's edition in *Le voyage de l'âme dans l'Au-delà d'après la littérature latine (Ve–XIIIe siècles)*, Collection de l'École Française de Rome 189 (Rome: École Française de Rome, 1994), 680 §4.6–7.

[34] Ibid., 681 §6.11–13.

[35] Ibid., 681 §6.2–3, 692 §17.2–3.

[36] Ibid., 680 §3.12.

[37] Ibid., 680 §4.1–2, 692 §17.8.

circumstance that a burn which he had suffered in the spirit, when a damned soul had been hurled against him, appeared on his body after he had returned to it: "In a wondrous manner, what the soul alone had experienced was made manifest in the flesh" (*Mirumque in modum quod anima sola sustinuit in carne demonstrabatur*).[38]

The Vision of Laisrén, probably composed in the eighth century and in any case not later than the ninth, survives in fragmentary form in a single manuscript. Even though only the beginning has been preserved, it is still of considerable importance as the earliest attested vision of the afterworld that is written in the Irish language. Besides the influence of Redaction VI of *Visio Sancti Pauli*, noted by Silverstein,[39] the text also exhibits indebtedness to *Transitus beati Fursei*.[40] The absence of the conclusion means that we do not know how Laisrén's soul returned to his body; but there is a vivid account of how it left it. After Laisrén had fasted for nine days in a church:

> sleep overcame him in the oratory. In his sleep he heard a voice addressing him: "Arise!" He did not move the first time. He heard the voice again. Thereupon he raised his head, and made the sign of the cross upon his face. He saw that the church in which he was was bright; and a portion of the night still remained. And he saw a radiant shape between the chancel rail and the altar. The shape said to him, "Come to me!" The cleric's whole body trembled, from crown to sole, at that voice. He suddenly saw that his soul was above the crown of his head, and he did not know by what way it had gone out of the body. He saw that the church was open, up to heaven. He saw that two angels took him between them, and raised him into the air.[41]

Several elements in this description recall the experiences of Fursa: Laisrén sees by means of a light that is not the light of this world, and with a vision that can pierce through the physical structure of a

[38] Ibid., 692 §17.17–18. Cf. the roughly contemporary *Vita Sancti Columbae* iii.6 (A. O. Anderson and M. O. Anderson, *Adomnán's Life of Columba*, 2nd ed. [New York: Oxford University Press, 1991], 190–91): in a vision (*in extasi mentis*) St. Columba is struck by an angel, the blow leaving a mark which he bears on his body for the rest of his life (*livorosum in eius latere vestigium omnibus suae diebus permansit vitae*).

[39] See Silverstein, *Visio Sancti Pauli*, 82–90; also St John D. Seymour, *Irish Visions of the Other-World: A Contribution to the Study of Mediæval Visions* (London: SPCK, 1930), 28–31.

[40] Thus Seymour, *Irish Visions*, 23; also John Carey, "The Vision of Laisrén," in *The End and Beyond*, ed. Carey, Nic Cárthaigh, and Ó Dochartaigh, 430–31.

[41] Carey, "The Vision of Laisrén," 434–35 §§1–2.

building; and his discarnate soul has no power of movement of its own, being dependent on angels to transport it. But there are also conspicuous differences. While the circumstances of Fursa's visions are involuntary, being attendant on an acute illness, Laisrén's soul leaves his body after a nine-day fast that he has voluntarily undertaken;[42] and whereas Fursa's soul appears to return to the body via an opening in the chest, Laisrén's soul exits via the crown of the head (*mullach*). There are other accounts of the soul either leaving the body through the *mullach*,[43] or—amounting presumably to the same thing—doing so when the head is struck against the lintel of a door;[44] such episodes are evidently to be associated with the teaching in a passage added to the legal treatise *Bretha Déin Chécht*, which places the *mullach* of the head first in a list of the "twelve doors of the soul."[45]

If the soul can leave the body at God's behest, and through angelic agency, might it not be possible for it to do so on its own initiative as well? We find this being accomplished with sinister intent in two related texts, dating probably from the eleventh or twelfth century: the Irish prose work *De Ingantaib Érenn* ("On the Wonders of Ireland") and the Latin poem *De mirabilibus Hibernie*, written by one Patrick.[46] According to both, certain men in Ireland (in *De Ingantaib Érenn*, those of the region of Ossory) are able to leave their bodies; having done so, they ravage the countryside in the form of wolves. If the wolves are wounded, these wounds will appear on the human bodies that they have left behind, and traces of the flesh of their prey can be found in their mouths. During their time as wolves, their bodies must not be moved, or they will not be able to return to them.[47] That injuries sustained

[42] Fixed periods of fasting are also associated in Irish sources with altered states of consciousness in nonecclesiastical contexts; see ibid., 429.

[43] John Carey, "The Dialogue of the Body and Soul," in *The End and Beyond*, ed. Carey, Nic Cárthaigh, and Ó Dochartaigh, 54–55.

[44] John Carey, "The Two Clerical Students and the Next Life," in *The End and Beyond*, ed. Carey, Nic Cárthaigh, and Ó Dochartaigh, 140–41. In the short tale *Aided Lóegairi Búadaig*, set in the pagan period, the hero Lóegaire meets his death in the same fashion: Kuno Meyer, *The Death-Tales of the Ulster Heroes*, Todd Lecture Series 14 (Dublin: Hodges, Figgis, 1906), 22–23.

[45] D. A. Binchy, "*Bretha Déin Chécht*," *Ériu* 20 (1966), 24–25 §2A.

[46] For the date of *De Ingantaib Érenn* see my discussion in "The Finding of Arthur's Grave: A Story from Clonmacnoise?," in *Ildánach Ildírech: A Festschrift for Proinsias Mac Cana*, ed. J. Carey, J. T. Koch, and P. Y. Lambert (Andover and Aberystwyth: Celtic Studies Publications, 1999), 9–11.

[47] I give text and translation of the relevant passage from Trinity College Dublin MS 1336 in "Werewolves in Medieval Ireland," *Cambrian Medieval Celtic Studies* 44 (Winter 2002): 54; for the corresponding section of the poem see Aubrey Gwynn, *The*

while out of the body leave physical traces is reminiscent of the story of Fursa. It is curious that neither text specifies that it is the *souls* of these men that leave their bodies: this may reflect the teaching of Augustine, who held that such extracorporeal experiences involve not the soul but what he called the *phantasticum*, the illusion of a physical self that we have in dreams.[48]

Oddly resembling these accounts of out-of-body werewolves is a brief anecdote concerning St. Brendan, dating perhaps from the tenth or eleventh century: "Brendan went to bring the soul of his mother from hell. His soul was battling against demons from one hour until the same time the next day, until he fetched his mother from the demons. And the bishop Moínenn was keeping his body in the meantime. Then his soul came to his body, and he heaved a sigh."[49] Here we see again the need for someone to watch over the vacated body; but now it is explicitly stated that it is the soul that has parted from it. Brendan's soul has gone into the next world, like the souls of Adomnán and Fursa and Laisrén; but it needs no angels to guide or convey it. Unaided, it journeys to hell on a mission of its own. This is a remarkable little story, having more in common with the healing rituals of Siberian shamans than with conventional hagiography.[50]

These are by no means the only texts that deal with the soul's separation from the body; in most cases, however, this is described in the context of death rather than of vision.[51] It is interesting that Irish apocalyptic literature is so frequently concerned not only with the knowledge revealed through such an experience, but also with the state of being and the powers of awareness of the visionary.

While some of the regions visited by Paul in *Visio Sancti Pauli*, such as the second and third heavens, clearly exist beyond this world, others can be notionally linked with earthly geography. Thus we are told that Paul was conducted by an angel to the firmament, and then to "the

Writings of Bishop Patrick 1074–1084, Scriptores Latini Hiberniae 1 (Dublin: Dublin Institute for Advanced Studies, 1955), 62–63.

48 Discussion and references in Carey, "Werewolves in Medieval Ireland," 47–48.

49 John Carey, "Saint Brendan on the Fear of Death," in *The End and Beyond*, ed. Carey, Nic Cárthaigh, and Ó Dochartaigh, 447. The (admittedly very slight) indications of date are discussed on p. 446.

50 Cf. for instance Waldemar Jochelson's description of a spirit journey undertaken to rescue a soul by the Yukaghir shaman Samsonov in 1896: *The Yukaghir and the Yukaghirized Tungus*, part 2, The Jesup North Pacific Expedition 9 (New York: Stechert, 1924), 196–99.

51 For editions of several of these texts, with discussion, see Carey, Nic Cárthaigh, and Ó Dochartaigh, eds., *The End and Beyond*, 43–151.

gates of heaven" which are "founded upon a river that irrigates the whole earth. And I asked the angel and said: 'Lord, what is this river of water?' And he said to me: 'This is the Ocean.'" Next Paul was taken to the "land of promise" (*terra repromissionis*), a paradisal country where the soil is seven times brighter than silver, and the trees bear fruit in extraordinary profusion. Inhabited by the souls of the just, this will be the dwelling of the saints following the destruction of the "first earth" by God at the end of days.[52] After Paul had seen this place's many beauties, the angel guide led him further:

> I went with the angel and he took me to the setting of the sun. And I saw the beginning of heaven founded on a great river of water, and asked: "What is this river of water?" And he said to me: "This is the Ocean, which encircles the whole earth." And when I was at the outer places of the Ocean, I looked; and there was no light in that place, but darkness and sorrow and sadness, and I sighed.

The next thing that Paul saw was a river of fire, the first of a series of torments that he encountered in the region set aside for the souls of sinners.[53]

Paul is accordingly described as having come to the Ocean just before reaching the place of the blessed, and then as having come to it again immediately preceding his visit to the place of punishment. It would be a natural inference that both places are situated in or beyond the Ocean; and this is in fact what we find in various Irish sources.

Prominent among these is the hagiographic narrative *Navigatio Sancti Brendani*, probably composed in the eighth or ninth century.[54] The goal of St. Brendan's protracted voyaging is the "land promised to the saints (*terra repromissionis sanctorum*), which God will give to those who will come after us in the last times"; this is depicted as an island in the Atlantic Ocean. It is never night there, the ground consists of precious stones, and the trees are full of fruit.[55] Whatever other

[52] Silverstein and Hilhorst, *Apocalypse of Paul*, 114–15 §21.

[53] Ibid., 136–37 §31.

[54] On the question of date, see the recent discussions by Jonathan M. Wooding, "The Date of *Navigatio S. Brendani abbatis*," *Studia Hibernica* 9 (2011): 9–26; and Donnchadh Ó Corráin, *Clavis litterarum Hibernensium: Medieval Irish Books & Texts (ca. 400–ca. 1600)*, Corpus Christianorum Claves 1 (Turnhout: Brepols, 2017), 304 §231.

[55] Giovanni Orlandi and Rossanna E. Guglielmetti, *Navigatio Sancti Brendani: alla scoperta dei segreti meravigliosi del mondo*, Per Verba 30 (Florence: Edizioni del Galluzzo, 2014), 4–7, 108–11.

sources it may have,[56] I think that there can be no doubt that this description is primarily based on that of the *terra repromissionis* in *Visio Sancti Pauli*.[57] As Charles D. Wright observes, the *Navigatio* "seems to be the earliest Christian-Latin text that specifically identifies the earthly paradise as an island."[58] At another point in the text, Brendan and his companions approach a smoking mountain "in the Ocean towards the north" (*in oceano contra septentrionem*), where one of the monks is carried off by demons; they later learn that within the mountain is hell itself.[59] In *Visio Sancti Pauli* as well, Paul had found the entrance to the final hell—even more terrible than the places of punishment that he had seen already—in the north.[60]

The *Navigatio*'s adaptation of *Visio Sancti Pauli*'s *terra repromissionis* had a curious twofold destiny. On the one hand, the literary success enjoyed by the *Navigatio* throughout the Middle Ages familiarized a European public with the idea of a paradise in the Atlantic: the eschatological region was conceived as having physical actuality, and "Brendan's island" found a place on maps. It has been claimed, indeed, that a desire to follow Brendan's example may have been one of the motivations for the voyages of Columbus.[61] In Ireland itself, on the other hand, the "Land of Promise" or *Tír Tairngire* is attested from the eleventh century onward as a name for the realm of the immortal *Túatha Dé* or "Tribes of the Gods": the old divinities of the Irish, as they survived in medieval legend and belief. Usually called the people of the *síde* or hollow hills, and thought of as dwelling beneath the earth or as

[56] Thus Thomas O'Loughlin has noted several elements that clearly derive from the account of the New Jerusalem in the Book of Revelation; see his *Celtic Theology: Humanity, World and God in Early Irish Writings* (London: Continuum, 2000), 195.

[57] This has been tentatively suggested by Martin McNamara, "*Navigatio Sancti Brendani*: Some Possible Connections with Liturgical, Apocryphal and Irish Tradition," in *The Brendan Legend: Texts and Versions*, ed. G. L. Burgess and C. Strijbosch (Leiden: Brill, 2006), 182–85; I have put the case rather more strongly in "The Reception of Apocryphal Texts in Medieval Ireland," in *The Other Side: Apocryphal Perspectives on Ancient Christian Orthodoxies*, ed. T. Nicklas et al., Novum Testamentum et Orbis Antiquus 117 (Göttingen: Vandenhoeck & Ruprecht, 2017), 267–69.

[58] Wright, "Next-to-Last Things," 331.

[59] Orlandi and Guglielmetti, *Navigatio Sancti Brendani*, 88–89, 92–93.

[60] Silverstein and Hilhorst, *Apocalypse of Paul*, 154–55.

[61] Thus Isabelle Lecoq has noted that islands derived from the *Navigatio* are included on a map that is attributed to Columbus himself: "Saint Brandan, Christophe Colomb, et le paradis terrestre," *Revue de la Bibliothèque Nationale de France* 25 (1992): 14–21. For the claim that Columbus actually used the *Navigatio* in charting his own routes, see Paul H. Chapman, *The Man who Led Columbus to America* (Atlanta, GA: Judson, 1973).

being associated with other elements in the immediate landscape, these beings could also be imagined as inhabitants of a radiant otherworld, sometimes described as lying remote beyond the sea: it was to this realm that the name *Tír Tairngire* was given.[62]

In Tenga Bithnúa, composed in the ninth or perhaps the tenth century, is a cosmological apocalypse, in which the soul of the apostle Philip undertakes to "make plain" to an assembly of Hebrew sages "the wondrous tale which the Holy Spirit related by means of Moses son of Amram, concerning the making of heaven and earth, together with the things which are in them. ... For the making of the world's form is opaque and very obscure to you, as it has been related since ancient times."[63]

One of the most intriguing of the cosmic mysteries thus revealed is the path followed by the sun between its setting and its rising—a journey, evidently, across the underside of the world, described as "twelve plains beneath the edges of the earth." The sun's nocturnal passage begins with "the stream beyond the sea,"[64] after which it comes to "the lofty sea of fire, and ... the seas of sulphurous flame which surround the red peoples." I take this stream and these seas to correspond to the world-encircling river of the Ocean, with a river of flame beyond it, described in *Visio Sancti Pauli*.[65] *In Tenga Bithnúa* accordingly appears to follow the *Visio* in using the Ocean, at the outer edge of the world, as a point of transition between the realm of the living and the infernal regions.[66] And indeed the antipodean landscape traversed by the sun at night has a decidedly infernal character, with "streams of fire," a "valley of torments," and—recalling the northern location of hell in both *Visio Sancti Pauli* and *Navigatio Sancti Brendani*—"the terrible populous enclosure which has closed around the hell-dwellers

62 Discussion in my essay "The Old Gods of Ireland in the Later Middle Ages," in *Understanding Celtic Religion: Revisiting the Pagan Past*, ed. K. Ritari and A. Bergholm (Cardiff: University of Wales Press, 2015), 55–56.

63 John Carey, *In Tenga Bithnua: The Ever-New Tongue*, Apocrypha Hiberniae II: Apocalyptica 1, CCSA 16 (Turnhout: Brepols, 2009), 113–15, 119 §§12, 15.

64 This is the rendering that I have proposed for *a sruth n-allmuirede*. The adjective *allmuirede* does not appear to be otherwise attested, but is related to *allmarda* "foreign, strange"; I follow Whitley Stokes, the text's first editor, in understanding it as a calque on Latin *transmarinus*.

65 Discussion in Carey, *In Tenga Bithnua*, 340–41.

66 While it is presumably no more than a coincidence, it is intriguing that Odysseus too finds the approaches to the regions of the dead beside the stream of Ocean (παρὰ ῥόον Ὠκεανοῖο; *Odyssey* xi.21).

to the north."[67] At last, traveling always towards the place of its rising, the sun comes to paradise, traditionally believed to lie in the easternmost part of the world.[68]

Another feature in the sun's night journey is eschatological in a different sense: in the regions "beneath the edges of the earth" there is a "mountain of fire which was formed from the fire of Judgment, to triumph over every created thing." This appears to reflect the influence of the *Apocalypse of Thomas*, which includes a prophecy that "there will be loosed the bond of the fire of paradise, since paradise is girt about with fire (*clausura ignis paradysi, quoniam ex igne paradysus cinctus est*). For this is a perpetual fire, which consumes the earth and all the elements of the world (*universa mundi elementa*)."[69]

In a fashion analogous to what we have seen with the "land of promise" in *Navigatio Sancti Brendani*, then, it is not only the afterworld of souls that lies beyond the Ocean, but also those things which God has prepared for the present world's ending, and for the time thereafter.

The same passage in the *Apocalypse of Thomas* evidently inspired a detail in *Immram Snédgusa ocus Maic Ríagla* (*The Voyage of Snédgus and Mac Ríagla*): a tale, written in both prose and verse and assigned by its most recent editor to the later Middle Irish period,[70] of a voyage undertaken by two monks of Iona to a series of fantastic islands in the Ocean. The next to the last of these, inasmuch as it is the "holy country in which are Enoch and Elijah," appears to be a version of paradise;[71] and

[67] Elsewhere in the text, a list of rivers includes a stream of water which goes across the island of torments (Carey, *In Tenga Bithnua*, 147 §40). This too is presumably a place in the afterworld; but it is here grouped together with sources of water in Libya and the Holy Land.

[68] Ibid., 177–83 §66. I have given a more detailed analysis of this remarkable passage, taking into account further sources besides *Visio Sancti Pauli*, in "The Sun's Night Journey: A Pharaonic Image in Medieval Ireland," *Journal of the Warburg and Courtauld Institutes* 57 (1994): 14–34. For the doctrine of the eastern location of paradise, going back ultimately to the rendering of *miqqedem* in the Hebrew of Gen 2:8 as κατὰ ἀνατολὰς in the Septuagint, see e.g. Isidore of Seville, *Etymologiae* xiv.3.2: *Paradisus est locus in orientis partibus constitutus.*

[69] P. Bihlmeyer, "Un text non interpolé de l'Apocalypse de Thomas," *Revue Bénédictine* 28 (1911): 273. Discussion in Carey, *In Tenga Bithnua*, 348–49.

[70] More precisely, he proposes that the verse component was composed ca. 1000, and the bulk of the prose in the latter part of the eleventh century or in the early twelfth: Kevin Murray, "The Voyaging of St Columba's Clerics," in *The End and Beyond*, ed. Carey, Nic Cárthaigh, and Ó Dochartaigh, 762–66.

[71] An early example of this widely attested belief is the *Gospel of Nicodemus* §25: Constantinus Tischendorf, *Evangelia apocrypha*, 2nd ed. (Leipzig: Hermann Mendelssohn, 1876), 404–05.

here too there are stored up eschatological forces of annihilation: "This is a terrible thing, two lakes, their advance was prophesied, a violent creation, a lake of water which will not provide produce, a strong lake of fire. They would have come to Ireland long ago as God's flood, were it not for Martin and Patrick beseeching them."[72] Here the eschatological fire adjoining paradise appears to be combined with the deluge of water which, as we have seen above, was foretold as the peculiar doom of Ireland.

Another Middle Irish voyage tale, somewhat later in date, is *Immram Curaig Úa Corra*. Here regions of punishment are found not beyond the Ocean, but within it: among other wonders, the voyagers encounter (1) an island where those who did not fulfil their penances in life are condemned to exist until the judgment on "a flagstone of the flagstones of hell," tormented by fiery seas and pierced by fiery spits;[73] (2) flocks of birds, who are souls released from hell on Sunday;[74] (3) individual sinners being tormented by fire in the midst of the sea for having engaged in inappropriate activities on a Sunday;[75] (4) an island of dishonest metalworkers, whose tongues are on fire and who are mutilated by monstrous birds;[76] and (5) a fiery sea, called "an abode of death" by one of the voyagers, filled with human heads that are striking against one another.[77]

From the range of texts surveyed in this brief chapter, it will be evident that medieval Irish apocalyptic thought was rooted in such widely influential works as the *Apocalypse of Thomas* and *Visio Sancti Pauli*; at the same time, the Irish made the perennial themes of eschatology very much their own. When the whole of the mortal world meets its cataclysmic end, this will happen in Ireland in a specifically Irish

[72] Murray, "The Voyaging of St Columba's Clerics," 796–97 §§62–63, citing the verse. The prose has: "There are two lakes in this country, a lake of water and a lake of fire; and they would have come over Ireland long ago were it not for Martin and Patrick praying with regard to them" (790–91).

[73] Whitley Stokes, "The Voyage of the Húi Corra," *Revue celtique* 14 (1893): 46–47 §53. Charles D. Wright's reinterpretation of this episode ("Next-to-Last Things," 327–28) is undermined by the fact that the stone is a *lecc* "flagstone, slab," not a *lía* "pillar-stone" as he states.

[74] Stokes, "The Voyage of the Húi Corra," 48–51 §§55–57.

[75] Ibid., 50–55 §§61, 63, 65. As Silverstein notes, one of these individuals (who stole a horse and rode it on Sunday) has a counterpart in Redaction VI of the *Visio*: *Visio Sancti Pauli*, 86; cf. 217 §9.

[76] Stokes, "The Voyage of the Húi Corra," 52–55 §64. Burning tongues and abusers of iron tools are both found in Redaction VI, but there they are not associated with one another: Silverstein, *Visio Sancti Pauli*, 82–84; cf. 215 §3, 217 §10.

[77] Stokes, "The Voyage of the Húi Corra," 54–55 §66.

fashion; and the Irish set the joys of paradise, and the horrors of the hells, in the depths of the Ocean that washed their western shores. Just as Patrick himself seems to have believed that, by coming to "the place beyond which there is no one," he had also come to the end of mortal time, his spiritual descendants saw their existence on the rim of the known world as situating them on the knife-edge between one state of being and another, or indeed between being and annihilation. This is the place of apocalypse.

Selected Further Reading

Boswell, C. S. *An Irish Precursor of Dante: A Study on the Vision of Heaven and Hell Ascribed to the Eighth-Century Irish Saint Adamnán*. London: David Nutt, 1908.

Carey, John. *The Ever-New Tongue: The Text in the Book of Lismore*. Apocryphes 15. Turnhout: Brepols, 2018.

Carey, John. *King of Mysteries: Early Irish Religious Writings*. 2nd ed. Dublin: Four Courts Press, 2000.

Carey, John, Emma Nic Cárthaigh, and Caitríona Ó Dochartaigh, eds. *The End and Beyond: Medieval Irish Eschatology*. Aberystwyth: Celtic Studies Publications, 2014.

Heist, W. W. *The Fifteen Signs before Doomsday*. East Lansing, MI: Michigan State College Press, 1952.

Herbert, Máire, and Martin McNamara. *Irish Biblical Apocrypha: Selected Texts in Translation*. Edinburgh: T&T Clark, 1989.

McNamara, Martin. *The Apocrypha in the Irish Church*. Dublin: Dublin Institute for Advanced Studies, 1975.

McNamara, Martin, ed. *Apocalyptic and Eschatological Heritage: The Middle East and Celtic Realms*. Dublin: Four Courts, 2003.

O'Meara, John J. *The Voyage of Saint Brendan: Journey to the Promised Land*. Dublin: Dolmen, 1978.

Seymour, St John D. *Irish Visions of the Other-World: A Contribution to the Study of Mediæval Visions*. London: SPCK, 1930.

10 Byzantine Apocalyptic Literature

ANDRÁS KRAFT

Apocalyptic writings formed a marginal yet significant part of Byzantine literature. They complement the Scriptures and the church tradition, which are overly reticent on eschatological matters. To fill this gap, late antique and medieval authors produced a wide range of pseudonymous texts that professed to supplement the ancient prophetic tradition by disclosing the developments of what was anticipated to be the near future, and concomitantly to advance socio-political as well as moral criticism about the contemporary conditions of their respective audiences. Elements of apocalyptic literature appear in various literary genres, and first and foremost in historiographical and ecclesiastical writings. The histories of such eminent authors as "Theophanes Continuatus" (tenth century), Nikētas Chōniatēs († 1217), and Nikēphoros Grēgoras († ca. 1360) contain numerous motifs and interpretations from the apocalyptic tradition. Hagiographies, too, are saturated with apocalyptic references. In order to fully appreciate the meaning of these references it is necessary to understand the evolving tradition of apocalyptic literature. Apocalypses were constantly reproduced, compiled, and revised. Although many texts and oral traditions have been lost to oblivion, the remnants that have survived constitute an indicative corpus from which the Byzantines' rich apocalyptic imagination can be reconstructed.

This contribution surveys medieval Greek apocalyptic literature written for Christian audiences. Jewish and Muslim apocalyptic texts have not been considered here. Likewise, neighboring linguistic traditions, first and foremost the Syriac, Slavonic, and Armenian traditions, have been omitted as well.[1] However, it needs to be stressed

[1] For surveys of apocalyptic literature within the wider "Byzantine commonwealth," see Lorenzo DiTommaso, *The Book of Daniel and the Apocryphal Daniel Literature* (Leiden: Brill, 2005); Vassilka Tapkova-Zaimova and Anissava Miltenova, *Historical and Apocalyptic Literature in Byzantium and Medieval Bulgaria* (Sofia: Исток-Запад, 2011); Julian Petkov, *Altslavische Eschatologie: Texte und Studien zur apokalyptischen Literatur in kirchenslavischer Überlieferung* (Tübingen: Narr

that although Byzantine apocalyptic literature largely comprises *apocalyptica* written in Greek, it is not limited to them. Furthermore, the focus of this study rests with narrative texts, which are mostly concerned with describing the signs of the end. Alternatively, some apocalyptic texts focus on chronological calculations presaging the precise date of the end. End-time calculations have been disregarded here, since they do not feature prominently among apocalyptic narratives.[2]

Modern apocalyptic studies began in the late nineteenth century, when German (Wilhelm Bousset, Franz Kampers, Ernst Sackur, et al.) and Russian (Vasilij Istrin, Alexander Vassiliev, Alexander Veselovsky, et al.) scholars edited and analyzed Greek, Latin, and Slavonic redactions of medieval apocalypses. Arguably, the interest of these scholars reflected the political climate in the two countries on the eve of the First World War. In the aftermath of the defeat of the German and Russian empires, scholarly interest in apocalypticism abated. It was revived in the second half of the twentieth century by European and American researchers—most notably Gerhard Podskalsky, Paul Alexander, and Agostino Pertusi—who can be seen as the pioneers of the field, as their studies have remained foundational until today.[3] Moreover, it was this second wave of scholarship that conclusively established the academic merit of investigating Byzantine apocalypticism. In recent decades, scholarly work has been focused on continuing their interpretative work while paying less attention to the edition of still unexplored literary sources. Although a few new editions

Francke Attempto, 2016); and Kevork B. Bardakjian and Sergio La Porta, eds., *The Armenian Apocalyptic Tradition: A Comparative Perspective; Essays Presented in Honor of Professor Robert W. Thomson on the Occasion of His Eightieth Birthday* (Leiden: Brill, 2014). Much work still remains to be done on Christian apocalypses written in Arabic. Curiously, the Georgian tradition does not seem to have been receptive of Byzantine apocalypticism.

2 On the topic of end-time calculations, see Paul Magdalino, "The End of Time in Byzantium," in *Endzeiten: Eschatologie in den monotheistischen Weltreligionen*, ed. Wolfram Brandes and Felicitas Schmieder (Berlin: de Gruyter, 2008), 119–33.

3 Gerhard Podskalsky, *Byzantinische Reichseschatologie: Die Periodisierung der Weltgeschichte in den vier Grossreichen (Daniel 2 und 7) und dem tausendjährigen Friedensreiche (Apok. 20); Eine motivgeschichtliche Untersuchung* (Munich: Fink, 1972); Paul J. Alexander, *The Byzantine Apocalyptic Tradition*, ed. Dorothy deF. Abrahamse (Berkeley: University of California Press, 1985); Agostino Pertusi, *Fine di Bisanzio e fine del mondo: significato e ruolo storico delle profezie sulla caduta di Costantinopoli in Oriente e in Occidente*, ed. Enrico Morini (Rome: Nella sede dell'Istituto Palazzo Borromini, 1988). The latter two works remained unfinished and had to be published posthumously.

have been published at the turn of the millennium,[4] the majority of available source material was edited during the first and second waves of scholarship.

As will be shown below, much of Byzantine apocalyptic literature is closely related to historiography. For this reason, scholars have often read apocalypses as historical sources and have "mined" them for new, otherwise unknown information. Although the historicist approach is potent in establishing new factual and chronological insights, it does not exhaust the functions of the apocalyptic genre. Medieval Greek *apocalyptica* can also be read from literary, sociological, or aesthetical perspectives. The approach of this contribution is to survey Byzantine apocalypses from a literary point of view.

DEFINITORY APPROACH AND GENERIC CHARACTERISTICS

What is a Byzantine apocalypse? This seemingly plain question bears considerable difficulty. The issue of defining the genre of Byzantine apocalypses has received little notice. In all likelihood, this is partly due to the silence of our sources. Ancient rhetorical handbooks do not discuss this genre, nor do Byzantine apocalypses themselves suggest any definition. At the same time, it is tempting to apply the classical definition of the apocalyptic genre, as formulated by John J. Collins, to the Byzantine period. This definition classifies apocalypses as a group of narrative texts that (1) convey revelatory information concerning either the end of history or the otherworld and (2) are necessarily mediated by otherworldly beings.[5] The definition was established on the basis of a comprehensive survey of late antique apocalypses. When reading medieval Greek apocalypses, however, it becomes apparent that references to angelic mediation (criterion 2 above) were generally omitted. That is to say, if Collins's definition

[4] Willem J. Aerts and George A. A. Kortekaas, eds., *Die Apokalypse des Pseudo-Methodius: Die ältesten griechischen und lateinischen Übersetzungen*, 2 vols. (Leuven: Peeters, 1998); Paul Magdalino, "Une prophétie inédite des environs de l'an 965 attribuée à Léon le Philosophe (MS Karakallou 14, f.253r–254r.)," *Travaux et mémoires* 14 (2002): 391–402; Ihor Ševčenko, "Unpublished Byzantine Texts on the End of the World about the Year 1000 AD," *Travaux et mémoires* 14 (2002): 561–78; Antonio Rigo, "La profezia di Cosma Andritzopoulos," in *Καίσκιν: studi in onore di Giuseppe Spadaro*, ed. Anna di Benedetto Zimbone and Francesca R. Nervo (Soveria Mannelli: Rubbettino, 2002), 195–201.

[5] John J. Collins, "Introduction: Towards the Morphology of a Genre," in "Apocalypse: The Morphology of a Genre," ed. John J. Collins, special issue, *Semeia* 14 (1979): 1–20, at 9.

were to be applied, various Byzantine apocalyptic narratives could not be properly called "apocalypses."[6] Alternatively, one may argue that the genre underwent some degree of historical development and that Byzantine apocalypses therefore require their own definition.

A major challenge for any definitory approach to medieval Greek apocalypses lies in the fuzzy boundaries of the genre. Apocalyptic narratives possess a wide variety of stock motifs and compositional methods, few of which are used in every single representative of the genre. Moreover, numerous apocalyptic components are not exclusive to the genre; they also appear in other literary forms such as homilies and hagiographies. It seems unfeasible to identify essential and genre-specific attributes that are necessary to demarcate this literary type clearly. Therefore, a nonessentializing approach is needed to accommodate the ambiguity of Byzantine apocalypses. A prototypical approach lends itself to such generic fuzziness. Accordingly, membership of the apocalyptic genre is not merely dependent on containing particular elements or features; it rather depends on how elements relate to one another in the *gestalt* structure of a given text. As a result, membership is a matter of degree depending on the relative distance from the prototype.[7]

Byzantine apocalypses consist of a number of typical motifs and techniques. Although these alone are not what trigger recognition of the genre, the compositional methods are important building blocks of apocalyptic narratives. Typical literary devices are the use of word pictures (e.g., "the lion and the whelp will pursue together the wild ass"),[8] particular *topoi* (e.g., the savior-emperor or the Antichrist), and oracular formulae.[9] Moreover, characteristic is the prevalent use of demotic Greek, a language register that was closer to the spoken

6 This view is taken by Lorenzo DiTommaso, "Biblical Form, Function, and Genre in the Post-Biblical Historical Apocalyptica," in *The Reception and Interpretation of the Bible in Late Antiquity: Proceedings of the Montréal Colloquium in Honour of Charles Kannengiesser, 11–13 October 2006*, ed. Lorenzo DiTommaso and Lucian Turcescu (Leiden: Brill, 2008), 145–62, esp. 151–52.

7 This approach has been proposed by Carol A. Newsom, "Spying Out the Land: A Report from Genology," in *Seeking Out the Wisdom of the Ancients: Essays Offered to Honor Michael V. Fox on the Occasion of His Sixty-Fifth Birthday*, ed. Ronald L. Troxel, Kelvin G. Friebel, and Dennis R. Magary (Winona Lake, IN: Eisenbrauns, 2005), 437–50. It should be noted that the prototype does not need to be an historical artefact; it can also be an ideal type.

8 On this word picture, see Alexander, *The Byzantine Apocalyptic Tradition*, 172–74.

9 Oracular formulae are larger coherent units of motifs. See Lorenzo DiTommaso, "The Armenian Seventh Vision of Daniel and the Historical Apocalyptica of Late Antiquity," in *The Armenian Apocalyptic Tradition: A Comparative Perspective; Essays Presented in Honor of Professor Robert W. Thomson on the Occasion of His*

vernacular than to the stylized model of Atticism. This allowed for the general intelligibility of apocalyptic narratives, at least in terms of language. Byzantine apocalyptic literature was, for the most part, comprehensible by every layer of society: the learned and uneducated, clergy and laity, emperors and commoners.

Further characteristics are the rationale of retributive justice, the notion of apocalyptic urgency, periodic shifts in verb tenses, and typological exegesis. Apocalypses are governed by the dualistic rationale of good fighting evil. The emotive descriptions of misery and hardship are resolved by images of climactic vengeance when the forces of the good finally vanquish their antagonistic counterparts. This struggle is framed by a timeline that anticipates the relatively near end. However, for the most part Byzantine apocalyptists were eager to postpone cautiously the ultimate end to the next generation. This notion of relative proximity must have evoked a sense of urgency to act while tempering the fear of immediate death. Another characteristic is the frequent alteration of verbal tenses and moods. Usually, verbs stand in the future tense or aorist subjunctive, which together with the pervasive use of temporal conjunctions convey a diachronic narrative. The diachronicity of historical developments is contrasted by the use of the present indicative and the aorist imperative, which are generally reserved for divine actions and direct speech. Arguably, such changes in verbal forms do not portray the lack of the author's erudition but rather convey different notions of time. On the one hand stands the diachronic progression of earthly time, and on the other stands the synchronous stasis of divine eternity. Furthermore, shifts in verbal tenses are potent to suggest that the orderly flow of worldly time is going to be unraveled once the world undergoes gradual destruction. The remaining aspect of typology requires some more explanation.

Typology is an exegetical technique that is best known from the Bible.[10] The Old and especially the New Testament present numerous

Eightieth Birthday, ed. Kevork B. Bardakjian and Sergio La Porta (Leiden: Brill, 2014), 126–48, esp. 134–40, who proposes the designation of "apocalyptic oracles." See further Zaroui Pogossian and Sergio La Porta, "Apocalyptic Texts, Transmission of Topoi, and Their Multi-Lingual Background: The Prophecies of Agat'on and Agat'angel on the End of the World," in *The Embroidered Bible: Studies in Biblical Apocrypha and Pseudepigrapha in Honour of Michael E. Stone*, ed. Lorenzo DiTommaso, Matthias Henze, and William Adler (Leiden: Brill, 2017), 824–51, esp. 825–26, who coin the descriptive appellation of "text-blocks."

[10] On biblical typology, see Leonhard Goppelt, *Typos: The Typological Interpretation of the Old Testament in the New*, trans. Donald H. Madvig (Grand Rapids, MI: Eerdmans, 1982) and Jean Daniélou, *From Shadows to Reality: Studies in the*

characters and events as the fulfillment of earlier adumbrations. Biblical texts construct correspondences among past, present, and future moments in salvation history, whereby earlier characters or events (*types*) are said to prefigure their subsequent counterparts (*antitypes*). Famously, Christ is characterized as a new Adam (Rom 5:14), as a new David (Matt 1:1–17, Acts 2:29–32), as a new Jonah (Matt 12:39–42, Luke 11:29–32), and the like. Since salvation history is unilaterally directed towards the Last Judgment, the later the corresponding counterpart, the higher its eschatological significance and value. Christian historiography is inherently typological in structure, and Byzantine *apocalyptica* faithfully accommodate this Christian heritage. Medieval Greek apocalypses are replete with typological reasoning that employ not only biblical types like Moses and Christ, but also extra-biblical ones like Alexander and Constantine the Great. Typological structures were pivotal hermeneutical stratagems in (re)constructing the history of the apocalyptic future. On the basis of the belief that history is purposeful, apocalyptists were convinced that by looking into the past they could anticipate the future with some amount of accuracy. It would be difficult to find any Byzantine apocalypse that did not employ typologies. Yet typology is not specific to apocalypses. Typological reasoning appears in every genre that conveys the Christian notion of salvation history. Put differently, while typology typically belongs to the apocalyptic genre, it is not an exclusive feature that could serve as a differentiating hallmark in a definition.

With that being said, Collins's definition is far from being irrelevant for the Byzantine period. The distinction between historical and moral apocalypses (criterion 1 above) does apply. Moral apocalypses (also called otherworldly visions or celestial journeys) are revelatory texts that disclose what happens to the individual soul in the ambiguous state of postmortem existence.[11] Historical or political apocalypses, on

Biblical Typology of the Fathers (London: Burns & Oates, 1960). See also Erich Auerbach, "Figura," in *Scenes from the Drama of European Literature* (Minneapolis: University of Minnesota Press, 1984), 11–76.

[11] On moral apocalypses, see Evelyne Patlagean, "Byzance et son autre monde: observations sur quelques récits," in *Faire croire: modalités de la diffusion et de la réception des messages religieux du XIIe au XVe siècle; actes de table ronde de Rome (22–23 juin 1979)* (Rome: École Française de Rome, 1981), 201–21; Jane Baun, "The Moral Apocalypse in Byzantium," in *Apocalyptic Time*, ed. Albert I. Baumgarten (Leiden: Brill, 2000), 241–67; Jane Baun, *Tales from Another Byzantium: Celestial Journey and Local Community in the Medieval Greek Apocrypha* (Cambridge: Cambridge University Press, 2007), 30–33. Concerning the related notion of the afterlife, see Vasileios Marinis, *Death and the Afterlife in*

the other hand, prognosticate the political fortunes of the entire community in anticipation of the Last Judgment. Byzantine apocalyptists composed numerous pseudepigraphical texts in both subgenres. Yet it is noteworthy that these subgenres did not always enjoy equal popularity. The composition of moral apocalypses was in vogue during the ninth to the eleventh and twelfth centuries. The most notable exemplars are the *Apocalypse of the Theotokos*, the *Life of St. Basil the Younger*, the *Vision of the Monk Kosmas*, the *Life of St. Niphon*, and the *Apocalypse of Anastasia*. Curiously enough, it seems that no new moral apocalypse was composed thereafter—a fact that has not yet been explained. Be that as it may, the manuscript tradition of these middle Byzantine texts testifies to their unabating popularity, which eventually reached its climax in the post-Byzantine period.

It is intriguing to observe that while interest in composing moral apocalypses was high during the middle Byzantine period, interest in writing historical apocalypses was markedly low. Apocalyptic narratives with historico-political agendas boomed during periods of political crisis, like the seventh century, which saw the Arab expansion, the eighth and ninth centuries, which saw the iconoclast controversy, or the thirteenth and fifteenth centuries, which saw the repeated conquest of Constantinople. During times of imperial prosperity, however, the fate of the individual soul took precedence over the fate of the empire. The surviving manuscript material suggests that moral apocalypses, on the whole, enjoyed more widespread circulation and presumably more popularity in Byzantium than historical apocalypses. Starting in the fifteenth century, historical apocalypses became the dominant literary type, to judge from the increasing number of distinct texts as well as the staggering amount of manuscript witnesses thereof. Yet both types, historical and moral apocalypses, constitute the apocalyptic genre in Byzantium.

HISTORICAL APOCALYPSES AND THEIR NARRATIVE SEQUENCE

Two kinds of historical apocalyptic literature can be distinguished: one that is composed in prose and the other in poetry.[12] The vast majority of medieval Greek apocalypses were written in prose, emulating the

Byzantium: The Fate of the Soul in Theology, Liturgy, and Art (New York: Cambridge University Press, 2017).

[12] See John Wortley, "The Literature of Catastrophe," *Byzantine Studies/Études byzantines* 4 (1977): 5–6.

prophetic books of the Bible, especially the Book of Daniel. A few apocalyptic texts followed another paradigm. In imitation of the Judeo-Hellenistic tradition of Sibylline oracles, some texts were versified. The most renowned collection of Byzantine apocalyptic poems is the *Oracles of Leo the Wise*.[13] The *Oracles* are famed for their images. Each oracle is placed next to a depiction, to which it closely relates. It can be debated whether this oracular collection qualifies as apocalyptic literature or not, given its linguistic, textual, and pictorial idiosyncrasy. This largely depends on how one defines the genre. A prototypical approach to apocalyptic literature could readily incorporate them.

The *Oracles of Leo the Wise* exerted great influence in Byzantium and beyond. Initially, the collection does not seem to have enjoyed wide circulation before the thirteenth century. In fact, our first reliable textual testimony of the *Oracles* comes from the court official and historian Nikētas Chōniatēs. Chōniatēs informs us that the *Oracles* were consulted by virtually every emperor of the twelfth century, who sought to learn from them the significance and the prophesied length of their respective reigns. The *Oracles* belonged to the genre of *basileiographeia*, texts with regnal lists that specify years of reign. Imperial legislation prohibited public access to such texts. The dissemination or sheer possession thereof was a capital offense punishable by death.[14] The fact that Chōniatēs could quote from the *Oracles* testifies to his privileged access and his intimate knowledge of imperial decision-making. The Latin conquest of Constantinople spurred an even greater interest in the *Oracles*. They were amended with further oracular pronouncements that clearly relate events surrounding the fateful year of 1204. Furthermore, the *Oracles* inspired the composition of a series of poems in demotic Greek as well as a compilation of various text-blocks

[13] For the edition and English translation of the Amsterdam version of the *Oracles of Leo the Wise*, see Pseudo-Leo the Wise, *The Oracles of the Most Wise Emperor Leo & The Tale of the True Emperor (Amstelodamensis graecus VI E 8)*, ed. and trans. Walter G. Brokkaar et al. (Amsterdam: Universiteit van Amsterdam, 2002). A critical edition (with Dutch translation) can be found in Jeannine Vereecken, "Τοῦ σοφωτάτου βασιλέως Λέοντος χρησμοί: De Orakels van de zeer wijze keizer Leo; Editio princeps van de Griekse tekst en van de Latijnse bewerking, de Vaticinia Pontificum," 3 vols. (PhD diss., Ghent University, 1986), vol. 3. For an expert study of the *Oracles*, see Nikos Kastrinakēs, "Εικονογραφημένοι χρησμοί του Λέοντος του Σοφού: Από τη βυζαντινή εποχή στην πρώτη έντυπη έκδοση (1596)," 2 vols. (PhD diss., University of Crete, 2018).

[14] See Wolfram Brandes, "Kaiserprophetien und Hochverrat: Apokalyptische Schriften und Kaiservaticinien als Medium antikaiserlicher Propaganda," in *Endzeiten: Eschatologie in den monotheistischen Weltreligionen*, ed. Wolfram Brandes and Felicitas Schmieder (Berlin: de Gruyter, 2008), 157–200.

concerning the savior-emperor. Both texts show dependence on the *Oracles* and were compiled during the course of the thirteenth century.[15] By the end of the century, the *Oracles* had also been rendered into Latin. This translation came to exert tremendous influence in the West as an ever-expanding collection of papal prophecies, generally referred to as *Vaticinia de summis pontificibus* (Prophecies of the Supreme Pontiffs).[16] Although the dependence of the Latin *Vaticinia* on the Greek *Oracles* has been securely established, the context and process of the transmission remain to be elucidated.

There are a number of other apocalyptic narratives—written in prose—that were formative for the Byzantine apocalyptic tradition. Without any doubt, the most significant apocalyptic narrative, not only in Byzantium but also in the Latin West as well as in the Christian East, was the *Apocalypse of Pseudo-Methodios*. Originally composed in Syriac at the end of the seventh century, the *Apocalypse of Pseudo-Methodios* was quickly translated into Greek and thereupon repeatedly updated, leading to four Greek redactions.[17] The importance of this apocalypse can hardly be overestimated. It provided a firm condemnation of nascent Islam and interpreted its political successes as an apocalyptic—and thus final—divine test to separate the faithful from the impious. Furthermore, it prophesied the imminent reversal of fortunes, with Christians gaining the final victory at the hands of a messianic Byzantine emperor. The irredentist vision to recover lost lands became

[15] For the respective text editions, see Erich Trapp, "Vulgärorakel aus Wiener Handschriften," in *Ἀκροθίνια: Sodalium Seminarii Byzantini Vindobonensis Herberto Hunger oblata*, ed. Johannes Koder and Erich Trapp (Vienna: Institut für Byzantinistik der Universität Wien, 1964), 83–120, and *The Oracles of the Most Wise Emperor*, ed. and trans. Brokkaar et al., 90–101. See further the still relevant study by Cyril Mango, "The Legend of Leo the Wise," *Zbornik radova Vizantološkog instituta* 6 (1960): 59–93; repr. in *Byzantium and Its Image* (London: Variorum, 1984), no. XVI.

[16] See, among others, Bernard McGinn, *Visions of the End: Apocalyptic Traditions in the Middle Ages* (New York: Columbia University Press, 1979), 188–89, 194–95, and Martha H. Fleming, *The Late Medieval Pope Prophecies: The Genus nequam Group* (Tempe: Arizona Center for Medieval and Renaissance Studies, 1999).

[17] The four redactions have been critically edited in Anastasios Lolos, ed., *Die Apokalypse des Ps.Methodios* (Meisenheim am Glan: A. Hain, 1976) and Anastasios Lolos, ed., *Die dritte und vierte Redaktion des Ps.Methodios* (Meisenheim am Glan: A. Hain, 1978). Only the first redaction has received scholarly attention, while the later ones still remain to be dated and analyzed. An English translation of the first redaction is available in *Apocalypse of Pseudo-Methodius: An Alexandrian World Chronicle*, ed. and trans. Benjamin Garstad, Dumbarton Oaks Medieval Library 14 (Cambridge, MA: Harvard University Press, 2012), 1–71.

a hallmark of subsequent Byzantine apocalypticism. Before the Arab conquests, Byzantine apocalyptic thought was rather optimistic in tone.[18] The Christian Roman Empire was believed to realize Christ's kingdom on earth. This interpretation made good sense in view of the continuous deferment of the Last Judgment, the global spread of Christianity, and the military successes of the sixth-century (Eastern) Roman Empire. The rise of Islam called into question the latter two aspects and thereby shocked the optimistic view of Roman imperial eschatology. The *Apocalypse of Pseudo-Methodios* set the stage for an alternative eschatology that was pessimistic and defensive in character, focusing on irredentist and retributive claims vis-à-vis Muslims and other foreign conquerors.

Another important apocalypse had been integrated in the *Life of St. Andrew the Fool*.[19] This text is peerless, as it presents the only historical apocalypse in Byzantine hagiography. Its content follows the irredentist ideology laid out by Pseudo-Methodios: the Muslims would be vanquished and the Byzantine Empire reconstituted before political power would ultimately disintegrate, climaxing in an imperial abdication that would allow the Antichrist to come forth. But the *Apocalypse of St. Andrew the Fool* does more than reiterate the Pseudo-Methodian narrative. It reinforces the usage of the Book of Revelation in the apocalyptic tradition by weaving key references into the saint's end-time vision. Most notably, it identifies Constantinople with the harlot of Babylon. While most of the *Life* equates the imperial capital with the new Jerusalem, the apocalyptic section is explicit in portraying the final destruction of Constantinople in unmistakable reminiscence of Rev 18, which describes the devastation of Babylon in graphic detail.[20] The ambiguity of being the saintly Jerusalem while at the same time the wicked Babylon developed into a standard conviction during the middle Byzantine period. Apocalyptists increasingly turned Constantinople

[18] See Alice Whealey, "The Apocryphal Apocalypse of John: A Byzantine Apocalypse from the Early Islamic Period," *JTS* 53, no. 2 (2002): 536–37, and Paul Magdalino, "'All Israel Will Be Saved'? The Forced Baptism of the Jews and Imperial Eschatology," in *Jews in Early Christian Law: Byzantium and the Latin West, 6th–11th Centuries*, ed. John Tolan, Nicholas de Lange, Laurence Foschia, and Capucine Nemo-Pekelman (Turnhout: Brepols, 2014), 239–42.

[19] Lennart Rydén, ed. and trans., *The Life of St Andrew the Fool*, 2 vols. (Uppsala: Almqvist & Wiksell, 1995), 2:258–85.

[20] The *Apocalypse of St. Andrew the Fool* was not the first apocalypse to apply Rev 18 to Constantinople. Yet this hagiographical account lent substantial support to the authenticity of the Book of Revelation, whose canonical status was not undisputed in Byzantium.

into the focal point of the Byzantine apocalyptic imagination. Not only historical apocalypses but also otherworldly visions expressed the conviction that the end-time drama was expected to be largely played out in a Constantinopolitan setting. The apocalyptic sections in the *Life of St. Basil the Younger* are well known for their depictions of the afterlife as a passage through celestial tollhouses (τὰ τελώνια): an image that recalls procedural law courts in Byzantium. Likewise, the *Vision of the Monk Kosmas* imagines the heavenly city to be encircled by a wall system that is reminiscent of the Theodosian Walls, while the *Apocalypse of the Theotokos* characterizes the heavenly arbiter in close likeness to his earthly equivalent, the emperor.

The *Last Vision of the Prophet Daniel* was another extremely popular apocalypse, to judge from the amount of surviving manuscript copies and the fact that it was translated several times into Slavonic. This apocalypse seems to have revived the type of historical apocalypses that were written in the guise of the prophet Daniel and that had been particularly popular in the eighth and ninth centuries.[21] The fact that we do not possess Pseudo-Danielic prophecies from the tenth through twelfth centuries may reflect a lessened concern about political developments. Yet it may also be the result of more effective censorship or of a transmission history that filtered out these prophecies. The *Last Vision* comes down in two recensions. The latter one was redacted in the aftermath of the Ottoman conquest of Constantinople in 1453, while the original version was composed in reaction to the Latin conquest in 1204. Its language and structure are typically apocalyptic. It uses various word pictures like "the sleeping snake" (ὁ ὄφις ὁ κοιμώμενος) or "the savage-looking wolf" (ὁ λύκος ὁ ἀγριοειδής) and employs numerous typological correspondences, for instance, between Constantinople and Jerusalem, between the Latin conquerors and the Old Testament King Ahab, or between the savior-emperor and Constantine the Great.[22] In terms of content, the text contains one

[21] See the Pseudo-Danielic apocalypses edited in Hans Schmoldt, ed. and trans., "Die Schrift 'Vom jungen Daniel'und 'Daniels letzte Vision': Herausgabe und Interpretation zweier apokalyptischer Texte" (PhD diss. University of Hamburg, 1972), 202–37. See also Klaus Berger, ed. and trans., *Die griechische Daniel-Diegese* (Leiden: Brill, 1976).

[22] See András Kraft, "Typological Hermeneutics and Apocalyptic Time: A Case Study of the Medieval Greek Last Vision of the Prophet Daniel," in *Όψεις του Βυζαντινού Χρόνου: Πρακτικά Διεθνούς Συνεδρίου, 29–30 Μαΐου 2015, Αθήνα*, ed. Elenē G. Saradē, Aikaterinē Dellaporta, and Theōnē Kollyropoulou (Kalamata: Πανεπιστήμιο Πελοποννήσου/Χριστιανικό και Βυζαντινό Μουσείο, 2018), 180–94.

of the earliest references to the capture and occupation of Constantinople, a notion that had been thought absurd before 1204. Otherwise, it presents the usual account of imperial irredentism, which is followed by the final and irreversible destruction of the empire and the arrival of the Antichrist. The primary purpose of this apocalypse is to integrate the apparent catastrophe of 1204 into the narrative of salvation history and to demonstrate thereby its purpose within the divine plan. Byzantine apocalypses persistently argue that even if outside forces challenge the fortunes of the empire, they are unable to usurp Byzantium's honor of being God's elect nation.

Another end-time revelation, the *Apocalypse of Leo of Constantinople*, is much harder to contextualize historically.[23] Its main narrative revolves around the struggle between a pious monk and a villainous emperor who orders his imperial image to be venerated together with the icon of Christ. This dispute has been interpreted by its modern editor to mirror the iconoclast controversy. Yet the notion, mentioned in passing, that the use of unleavened bread (ὁ ἄζυμος ἄρτος) will be established in Constantinople points to the Latin occupation in 1204 and can be read as a *vaticinium ex eventu*, a prophecy after the event.[24] Apocalypses use *vaticinia ex eventu* in order to bolster their authenticity and authority by claiming that since their alleged predictions concerning present events are accurate, their genuine predictions about the future are reliable. Such *vaticinia* are often the only means to date a given apocalypse, since their pseudonymity and their usually late manuscript transmission inhibits a secure dating. Although the reference to the unleavened bread seems to refer to the Latin rule of Byzantium, it may simply be a later interpolation. Apocalypses are prone to subsequent insertion and addition, which served to update a prophecy and to render it meaningful in a new historical context. In any event, the final text that has come down to us seems to have been redacted in the thirteenth century, while various sections of it may well have been composed centuries beforehand. The main narrative is positively concluded when angels intervene and righteously slay the immoral emperor. The remainder of the *Apocalypse of Leo* discusses the alternation of good and bad rulers before expounding the workings of the Antichrist. The

[23] Riccardo Maisano, ed. and trans., *L'apocalisse apocrifa di Leone di Costantinopoli* (Naples: Morano Editore, 1975).

[24] Ibid., 71, lines 58–59.

apocalypse closes with a rare description of the Last Judgment, a topic that is usually not dealt with in historical apocalypses, which is another indication of its compiled nature.

There are many more historical apocalypses from Byzantium.[25] These prophecies were most commonly attributed to the prophet Daniel, the church father Methodios of Olympos († 311), and from the late Byzantine period onwards to the Emperor Leo VI († 912). The pseudonymous nature of apocalyptic literature ought to be seen as an honest exegetical approach that aims to interpret and to supplement traditional prophetic material. Given the undisputed canonicity of the Book of Daniel, it is not surprising that Byzantine apocalyptists saw in the prophet Daniel the greatest authority to be emulated. Consequently, Byzantine apocalypticism consists to a large extent of Pseudo-Danielic texts, some of which still remain to be edited.[26]

Typically, Byzantine historical apocalypses follow a standard narrative that revolves around three major groups of protagonists: the ideal emperor(s), the eschatological peoples of the north, and the Antichrist. The narrative customarily starts with a period of hardship that is overcome through the intervention of a messianic ruler or a series of rulers, who carry out a set of eschatological tasks that include the defeat of all foreign enemies, the inauguration of peace and posterity, and the abdication of the imperial dignity to Christ in Jerusalem. The abdication is followed by the arrival and malicious deeds of the Antichrist. Woven into this sequence are the eschatological peoples of Gog and Magog (Ezek 38–39; Rev 20:8), whose identity was an issue of constant dispute, with speculations ranging from the Huns and the Göktürks to the Rus' and the Bulgars. Medieval Greek apocalypses also often prophesied that Constantinople would be besieged yet saved from conquest before being destroyed by a deluge. Given these motifs, the following narrative scheme can be drawn up:

[25] For a useful survey of the most prominent Byzantine apocalyptic texts (supplemented with extracts in French translation), see Marie-Hélène Congourdeau, "Textes apocalyptiques annonçant la chute de Constantinople," in *Constantinople 1453: des Byzantins aux Ottomans; textes et documents*, ed. Vincent Déroche and Nicolas Vatin (Toulouse: Anacharsis, 2016), 983–1024. See also the excellent survey by Paul Magdalino, "The History of the Future and Its Uses: Prophecy, Policy and Propaganda," in *The Making of Byzantine History: Studies Dedicated to Donald M. Nicol*, ed. Roderick Beaton and Charlotte Roueché (Aldershot: Variorum, 1993), 3–34.

[26] For a survey of the various Pseudo-Danielic texts, see DiTommaso, *The Book of Daniel*.

Source	Narrative succession of motifs					
(Greek) *Apocalypse of Pseudo-Methodios*	**A** (XIII.11–18)	**B** (XIII.19–21)	**C** (XIV.2–6)	–	**E** (XIV.1, 6–13)	**F** (XIV.14)
Apocalypse of St. Andrew the Fool	**A** (lines 3824–58)	**C** (lines 3913–20)	**D** (lines 3989–99)	**B** (lines 4050–65)	**E** (lines 4069–101)	**F** (lines 4118–27)
Last Vision of the Prophet Daniel	**B** (§§34–39)	**A** (§§47–59)	**C** (§§60–61)	**D** (§§69–70)	**E** (§§74–78)	**F** (§§83–85)
Apocalypse of Leo of Constantinople	**B** (§14)	**A** (§15)	–	–	**E** (§§16–21)	**F** (§§22–29)

Key

A motif: savior-emperor's victory and benefactions
B motif: arrival of the eschatological peoples
C motif: imperial abdication
D motif: destruction of Constantinople
E motif: arrival and deeds of the Antichrist
F motif: resurrection / Last Judgment

THE MANUSCRIPT TRADITION AND OTHER SOURCE MEDIA

It is important to note that Byzantine apocalypses have been preserved, for the most part, in late manuscripts. According to a rough estimation, about 70 percent of manuscripts containing Byzantine apocalyptic sources date to the fifteenth century or later.[27] The Ottoman conquest of Constantinople in 1453 can be seen as the main reason why interest in Greek apocalyptic texts peaked in the fifteenth through seventeenth centuries. Apocalypses professed to render intelligible the Muslim subjugation of Byzantium within a providential plan that promised the eventual restoration of the orthodox body politic. They fed salvific hopes and irredentist confidence that fell on sympathetic ears. Moreover, many prophecies that had been written in reaction to the fall in 1204 seemed to perfectly apply to the second fall in 1453. This apparent congruence was believed to confirm the veracity of the Byzantine apocalyptic tradition. For instance, the *Last Vision of the Prophet Daniel* was believed to have adequately foretold the Ottoman conquest. That is why Nestor-Iskinder extensively quotes from the work in his account of the capture (*halōsis*) of 1453.[28] Around the year 1470, the *Last Vision of the Prophet Daniel* was subjected to a textual revision; it was shortened and slightly updated into a new Pseudo-Danielic prophecy entitled the *Vision of Daniel on the Seven-Hilled City*.[29] The intrinsic ambiguity of prophetic narratives facilitated their repeated reinterpretation.

Another pivotal cause for the unparalleled proliferation of apocalyptic speculation in the fifteenth century can be seen in the disappearance of imperial censorship. Apocalyptic narratives were frequently instrumentalized to advance *Kaiserkritik*, that is, to reproach imperial policies and incumbents. As a result, apocalypses were rigorously censored throughout the Byzantine millennium. Conversely,

[27] András Kraft, "An Inventory of Medieval Greek Apocalyptic Sources (c. 500–1500 AD): Naming and Dating, Editions and Manuscripts," *Millennium-Jahrbuch* 15 (2018): 69–143, at 141–43.

[28] For the respective passage in the *Tale on the Conquest of Constantinople* (Повесть о взятии Царьграда), see Walter K. Hanak and Marios Philippides, eds. and trans., *The Tale of Constantinople (of Its Origin and Capture by the Turks in the Year 1453) by Nestor-Iskander* (New Rochelle, NY: Aristide D. Caratzas, 1998), 94–97 (= §§86–87). See further Pertusi, *Fine di Bisanzio*, 76–81.

[29] Edition and German translation in Schmoldt, "Die Schrift 'Vom jungen Daniel,'" 190–99.

apocalypses could flourish during periods of crisis when imperial censorship was curtailed or altogether abrogated.

In the wake of 1453, various workshops (especially in Constantinople, Crete, Rome, and Venice) produced a large number of anthologies that compiled and updated the Byzantine apocalyptic material at their disposal. Consequently, most of our textual witnesses belong to a post-Byzantine context that was selecting and filtering Byzantine apocalypticism. The historical filter inherent in the manuscript tradition still needs to be investigated in order to differentiate, as much as possible, the original Byzantine layers from the post-Byzantine additions and omissions.

Our knowledge of Byzantine apocalyptic literature, however, is not solely dependent on the manuscript tradition of medieval Greek apocalypses. We find additional source material in the patriographic tradition, in exegetical works, and in art history. Patriographic writings collected legends about Constantinople and its monuments. This genre was particularly popular during the middle Byzantine period. Its most well-known exemplar, the *Patria Kōnstantinoupoleōs*, was compiled in the late tenth century and contains numerous apocalyptically connoted legends.[30] Furthermore, exegetical literature provides an abundance of information about Byzantine apocalyptic traditions. Of particular significance are the commentaries on the Book of Revelation. Altogether four Byzantine commentaries are known, which were penned by Oikoumenios, Andrew of Caesarea, Arethas of Caesarea, and Neophytos the Recluse respectively.[31] The early seventh-century commentary by Andrew of Caesarea was by far the most influential.[32] Among others,

[30] For the Greek text with English translation, see Albrecht Berger, trans., *Accounts of Medieval Constantinople: The Patria* (Cambridge, MA: Harvard University Press, 2013). For supplementary studies, see among others Albrecht Berger, "Das apokalyptische Konstantinopel: Topographisches in apokalyptischen Schriften der mittelbyzantinischen Zeit," in *Endzeiten: Eschatologie in den monotheistischen Weltreligionen*, ed. Wolfram Brandes and Felicitas Schmieder (Berlin: de Gruyter, 2008), 135–55, and Albrecht Berger, "Magical Constantinople: Statues, Legends, and the End of Time," *Scandinavian Journal of Byzantine and Modern Greek Studies* 2 (2016): 9–29.

[31] See Cyril Mango, "Le temps dans les commentaires byzantins de l'Apocalypse," in *Le temps chrétien de la fin de l'Antiquité au Moyen Âge, IIIe–XIIIe siècles, Paris 9–12 mars 1981*, ed. Jean-Marie Leroux (Paris: Éditions du CNRS, 1984), 431–38, and Stephen J. Shoemaker, "The Afterlife of the Apocalypse of John in Byzantium," in *The New Testament in Byzantium*, ed. Derek Krueger and Robert S. Nelson (Washington, DC: Dumbarton Oaks, 2016), 301–16.

[32] For an English translation, see Eugenia S. Constantinou, trans., *Andrew of Caesarea: Commentary on the Apocalypse* (Washington, DC: Catholic University of America Press, 2011).

it represents one of the earliest witnesses to the identification of Constantinople with Babylon and repeatedly expresses the anxiety that the Antichrist would be a Roman emperor. Other exegetical works deserve attention as well, such as the *Commentary on Daniel* by Basil of Neopatras (tenth century). Unfortunately, this text remains unpublished.[33] Likewise, the Greek pseudepigraphical corpus attributed to Ephraem the Syrian († 373) awaits much needed editorial and commentary work.[34] Fortunately, the eschatological treatise by Pseudo-Hippolytos entitled *On the End of the World* (probably from the seventh or eighth century) has been recently reedited.[35] This largely exegetical work was widely disseminated, as testified by its copious manuscript tradition and its influence on neighboring apocalyptic literature. In addition to textual sources, one should not forget about the contributions of Byzantine art. In the aftermath of the iconoclast controversy, artists began to depict the Last Judgment in manuscript illuminations and mural paintings. Notable examples are found in Paris, Bibliothèque Nationale de France, cod. gr. 923, folio 68v (ninth century), and cod. gr. 74, folios 51v and 93v (eleventh century), as well as in the wall paintings in the Church of St. Stephanos in Kastoria, Greece (tenth century), in the Church of St. Peter and St. Paul at Tatev Monastery, Armenia (tenth century), in the Yılanlı Kilise (Snake Church) in Cappadocia, Turkey (ninth to eleventh centuries), and, most famously, the Last Judgment mosaic in the Torcello Cathedral, Italy (twelfth century).

The Byzantine apocalyptic imagination found expression in various visual, oral, and textual media. Only a fraction thereof has been preserved, with apocalyptic literature making up the greatest part. The fragmentary material needs to be studied with care since the genre required texts to undergo constant revision in order to remain relevant. Any given text is likely to contain multiple layers of redaction and interpolation. Apocalyptic literature should be seen as a continuous project in textual interpretation, a project that is still ongoing. Scholars contribute to this project by presenting critical editions of texts whose

[33] An edition is currently in preparation by Caroline Macé and Pablo Ubierna.

[34] For a recent discussion, see Emmanouela Grypeou, "Ephraem Graecus, 'Sermo In Adventum Domini': A Contribution to the Study of the Transmission of Apocalyptic Motifs in Greek, Latin and Syriac Traditions in Late Antiquity," in *Graeco-Latina et Orientalia: Studia in honorem Angeli Urbani heptagenarii*, ed. Samir K. Samir and Juan P. Monferrer-Sala (Cordóba: Oriens Academic, 2013), 165–79.

[35] Panagiotis C. Athanasopoulos, ed., *Ψ.-Ἱππολύτου Περὶ τῆς συντελείας τοῦ κόσμου—Κριτικὴ Ἔκδοση* (*Ps.-Hippolytus's De consummatione mundi—a Critical Edition*), 2nd ed. (Ioannina: Carpe Diem, 2016).

original form is often untraceable. This is not to belittle editorial work, which is gravely needed in apocalyptic studies. Numerous short oracles and full-length apocalypses remain to be discovered in manuscripts scattered across Europe. I only wish to call attention to the hermeneutical responsibility scholarship holds and to incite methodological humility in view of the fuzziness of the genre and the textual openness of Byzantine apocalypses.

Selected Further Reading

Alexander, Paul J. *The Byzantine Apocalyptic Tradition.* Edited by Dorothy deF. Abrahamse. Berkeley: University of California Press, 1985.

Baun, Jane. *Tales from Another Byzantium: Celestial Journey and Local Community in the Medieval Greek Apocrypha.* Cambridge: Cambridge University Press, 2007.

Magdalino, Paul. "The Year 1000 in Byzantium." In *Byzantium in the Year 1000*, 233–70. Edited by Paul Magdalino. Leiden: Brill, 2003.

Pseudo-Leo the Wise. *The Oracles of the Most Wise Emperor Leo & The Tale of the True Emperor (Amstelodamensis graecus VI E 8).* Edited and translated by Walter Brokkaar et al. Amsterdam: Universiteit van Amsterdam, 2002.

Pseudo-Methodius. *Apocalypse of Pseudo-Methodius: An Alexandrian World Chronicle.* Edited and translated by Benjamin Garstad. Dumbarton Oaks Medieval Library 14. Cambridge, MA: Harvard University Press, 2012.

Rydén, Lennart. "The Andreas Salos Apocalypse: Greek Text, Translation, and Commentary." *Dumbarton Oaks Papers* 28 (1974): 197–261.

Treadgold, Warren. "The Prophecies of the Patriarch Methodius." *Revue des études byzantines* 62 (2004): 229–37.

Turner, Christopher J. G. "An Oracular Interpretation Attributed to Gennadius Scholarius." *Hellēnika* 21 (1968): 40–47.

Zervos, George T. "Apocalypse of Daniel (Ninth Century A.D.): A New Translation and Interpretation." In *The Old Testament Pseudepigrapha*, vol. 1, *Apocalyptic Literature and Testaments*, 755–70. Edited by James H. Charlesworth. Garden City, NY: Doubleday, 1983.

11 Joachim of Fiore and the Apocalyptic Revival of the Twelfth Century

BRETT EDWARD WHALEN

Not long after the year 1200 CE an anonymous monk from northern France carefully copied some unusual materials into the last few spare folios of a manuscript containing Isidore of Seville's *Etymologies*.[1] First, he included a table showing the history of the Old and New Testaments, organized on the left by the generational descent of biblical figures from Adam to Christ, and on the right by the line of Roman popes from Christ until the present, just two generations away from Christ's return in Final Judgment (Fig. 1). After that, he included a short work on the "genealogy of the ancient fathers," covering much of the same ground as the table described above and describing historical concords between the sixty-three generations from Adam to Christ, and the matching sixty-three generations from King Uzziah of Judah to the end of history. Next, he reproduced a short tract on the seven seals from the Book of Revelation, linking the seals to parallel sets of successive persecutions against the Jews and the Christian church (Fig. 2). Finally, he transcribed a letter from the author of all these works, "Brother Joachim, called abbot," addressed to "all the faithful of Christ," warning them about the approaching apocalypse and the need to repent while there was still time.

In the history of Christian apocalyptic literature few names attract more attention and controversy than that of the so-called Calabrian

[1] Paris, Bibliothèque Nationale de France (hereafter BNF), Lat. 11864, fols. 151v–152v. On the contents and provenance of this manuscript see Leone Tondelli, Marjorie Reeves, and Beatrice Hirsch-Reich, eds., *Il libro delle figure dell'abate Gioachino da Fiore*, 2 vols. (Turin: Società Editrice Internazionale, 1953), 1:34; and Marjorie Reeves and Beatrice Hirsch-Reich, *The Figurae of Joachim of Fiore* (Oxford: Clarendon, 1972), 109. Translations are my own unless otherwise indicated.

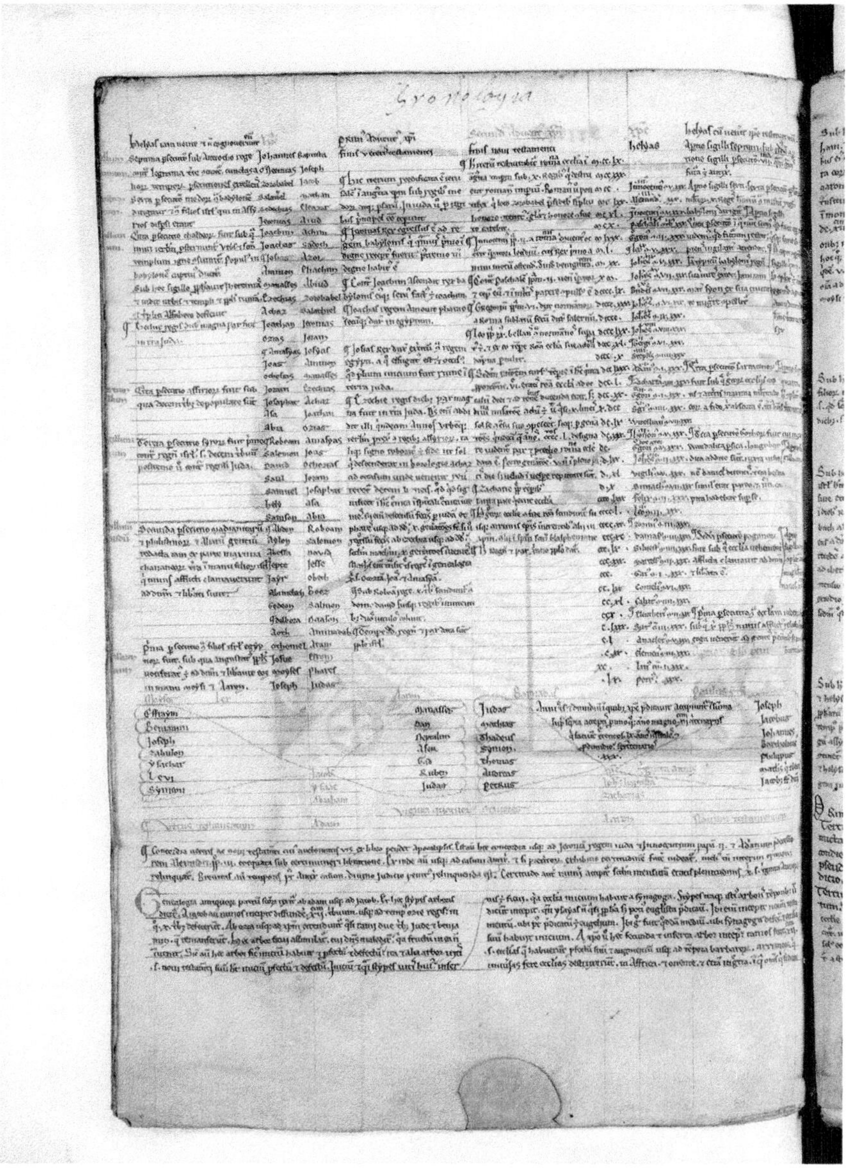

Figure 1. Paris, Bibliothèque Nationale de France, Lat. 11864, fol. 151v: The *Table of Concords* and the opening of the *Genealogy*

Figure 2. Paris, Bibliothèque Nationale de France, Lat. 11864, fol. 152r: *On the Seven Seals* (with text from the *Genealogy* across the bottom)

abbot, Joachim of Fiore (1135–1202 CE).[2] Joachim remains best known for his groundbreaking claim that the course of history reflected the nature of the Trinity, distinguishing between three temporal eras (*status*): that of the Father, from Adam to Christ; that of the Son, from King Uzziah of Judah until the abbot's own present times; and that of the Holy Spirit, doubly proceeding from the *status* of the Father under the prophet Elisha and from the *status* of the Son under Benedict of Nursia. That final era of the Holy Spirit, Joachim proclaimed, was about to "flower" within or just after his lifetime, inaugurating a terrestrial Sabbath age of spiritual fulfillment, peace, and perfection. Eagerly embraced by his posthumous followers, especially among the Franciscans, the third *status* became the vehicle for envisioning radical transformations in the offices, institutions, and sacraments of the Roman church, as the clerical order of the second *status* gave ground to the monastic "spiritual" men of the third *status*. While Joachim's genuine and pseudo-epigraphical works remained irrepressibly popular, conservative authorities denounced the proponents of such dangerous millennialist fantasies. The fact that the Fourth Lateran Council had condemned certain aspects of Joachim's Trinitarian theology in 1215 only seemed to confirm suspicions that the abbot of Fiore, although considered orthodox in his lifetime, was actually a source of heresy.[3]

When the unknown French monk arranged his selection of Joachim's works, namely the *Table of Concords*,[4] the *Genealogy*

[2] There is a vast and constantly expanding bibliography on Joachim of Fiore. Key studies include Herbert Grundmann, *Studien über Joachim von Floris* (1927; Darmstadt: Springer Fachmedien Wiesbaden, 1966); Herbert Grundmann, *Aufsätze*, Schriften der Monumenta Germaniae Historica 25/2 (Stuttgart: Hiersemann, 1977); Marjorie Reeves, *The Influence of Prophecy in the Later Middle Ages* (Oxford: Oxford University Press, 1969; repr., Notre Dame, IN: University of Notre Dame Press, 1994); Marjorie Reeves, *Joachim of Fiore and the Prophetic Future* (New York: Harper & Row, 1977; repr., Stroud: Sutton, 1999); Bernard McGinn, *The Calabrian Abbot: Joachim of Fiore in the History of Western Thought* (New York: Macmillan, 1985); and Gian Luca Potestà, *Il tempo dell'apocalisse: vita di Gioacchino da Fiore* (Rome: Laterza, 2004). See also Matthias Reidl, ed., *A Companion to Joachim of Fiore* (Leiden: Brill, 2018), including Brett Whalen, "Joachim the Historian and Theorist of Society," 88–108.

[3] Reeves, *The Influence of Prophecy*, 45–74. See also Fiona Robb, "The Fourth Lateran Council's Definition of Trinitarian Orthodoxy," *Journal of Ecclesiastical History* 48 (1997): 22–43.

[4] For a similar table to the one featured in BNF, Lat. 11864, fol. 151v, see Tondelli, Reeves, and Hirsch-Reich, *Il libro delle figure*, vol. 2, plates IX–X.

(*Genealogia*),[5] *On the Seven Seals* (*De septem sigllis*),[6] and the *Letter to All the Faithful* (*Epistola universis fidelibus*),[7] that sense of scandal associated with Joachite millennialism still lay in the future. Depending upon when the scribe wrote, he might have known about the Fourth Lateran Council's condemnation of the abbot, but that carefully circumscribed judgment had little immediate bearing on Joachim's overall reputation. Indeed, this early consumer of the abbot's apocalyptic ideas probably did not much associate him with the Trinity in one way or another. None of the works he reproduced contain any explicit discussion of the three *status* or the coming millennial era of the Holy Spirit. Like the rest of Joachim's productions, the materials described above dwell mainly on the past and its significance building to the present rather than on the future. After all, by Joachim's calculations, after the sixty-three generations of the Old Testament and the forty generations of the New Testament since Christ, only two generations of history remained. There was a lot of the past to remember and only a little of the future still ahead. When the abbot did look beyond the present to discern the shape of things to come he focused especially on the imminent trials of the faithful under the forces of Antichrist. The promised time of rest and renewal for the church would only come after these horrific tribulations.

"The past," Amos Funkenstein once observed, "is the remembered past, just as the future is the anticipated present: memory is always derived from the *present* and from the contents of the present."[8] What did the present look like for Joachim of Fiore? How did it shape what we might call his apocalyptic memory: his remembrance of the past and anticipation of the future, framed by his presentist reading of Scripture? For all of his immense ingenuity, Joachim participated in the wider revival of Latin apocalypticism during the twelfth century, including figures such Rupert of Deutz, Honorius Augustodunensis, Anselm of

[5] Gian Luca Potestà, "Die Genealogia: Ein frühes Werk Joachims von Fiore und die Anfänge seines Geschichtsbildes," *Deutsches Archiv für Erforschung des Mittlealters* 56 (200): 55–101.

[6] Julia Eva Wannenmacher, *Hermeneutik der Heilsgeschichte:* De septem sigillis *und die sieben Siegel im Werk Joachims von Fiore* (Leiden: Brill, 2004).

[7] Jeanne Bignami-Odier, "Notes sur deux manuscrits de la bibliothèque du Vatican contenant des traités inédits de Joachim de Fiore," *Mélanges d'archéologie et d'histoire* 54 (1937): 220–23.

[8] Amos Funkenstein, "Collective Memory and Historical Consciousness," *History and Memory* 1 (1989): 9 (emphasis his).

Havelberg, and Gerhoh of Reichersberg.[9] Before Joachim began to write down his scriptural insights, these "speculative exegetes" had turned to the Bible to decipher the meaning of history in present times. From this perspective, the Old Testament remained a record of literal history describing the historical fortunes of the Jews and a source of allegories foreshadowing the spiritual truths of the New Testament. Scripture, however, also suggested historical patterns and contained prophecies that might have bearing for the contemporary age.[10] These historically minded theologians sensed that the end-times, while not necessarily imminent, might be sooner than later. They also highlighted the possibility that the conclusion of history might feature forms of earthly improvement or at least a brief "refreshment" for the faithful before Final Judgment.[11]

The reasons for this intensified interest in apocalypticism were complex and cannot be reduced to a single cause. In broad terms, the twelfth century witnessed an overall intellectual "renaissance," to put it in somewhat old-fashioned terms, including the fields of biblical exegesis and history writing. Some of that interest in Scripture and history took an apocalyptic turn. Specific developments during this era, moreover, seemed to suggest that current events were rushing towards the end of history, for better or for worse. The First Crusade's capture of Jerusalem followed by further—generally disappointing—crusades provided an especially dramatic example of prophecy apparently realized in living

9 See Wolfgang Beinert, *Die Kirche-Gottes Heil in der Welt: Die Lehre von der Kirche nach den Schriften des Rupert von Deutz, Honorius Augustodunensis, und Gerhoh von Reichersberg; Ein Beitrag zur Ekklesiologie des 12 Jahrhunderts*, Beiträge zur Geschichte der Philosophie und Theologie des Mittelalters 13 (Münster: Aschendorff, 1973); Marjorie Reeves, "The Originality and Influence of Joachim of Fiore," *Traditio* 36 (1980): 296–316; Peter Classen, "*Res Gestae*, Universal History, Apocalypse: Visions of Past and Future," in *Renaissance and Renewal in the Twelfth Century*, ed. Robert L. Benson and Giles Constable (Cambridge, MA: Harvard University Press, 1982), 387–417; Amos Funkenstein, *Theology and the Scientific Imagination from the Middle Ages to the Seventeenth Century* (Princeton, NJ: Princeton University Press, 1986), 243–71; and Bernard McGinn, "Ratio and Visio: Reflections on Joachim of Fiore's Place in Twelfth-Century Theology," in *Gioacchino da Fiore tra Bernardo di Clairvaux e Innocenzo III*, ed. Roberto Rusconi (Rome: Viella, 2001), 27–46.

10 On the "senses of Scripture," see Henri Lubac, *Exégèse médiévale*, 2 vols. (Paris: Aubier, 1961). See also Marie-Dominique Chenu, "Theology and the New Awareness of History," in *Nature, Man, and Society in the Twelfth Century*, ed. and trans. Jerome Taylor and Lester K. Little (Chicago: University of Chicago Press, 1968), 162–201.

11 Robert Lerner, "Refreshment of the Saints: The Time after Antichrist as a Station for Earthly Progress in Medieval Thought," *Traditio* 32 (1976): 97–144.

memory.[12] The rapid emergence of new religious orders, upsetting centuries of ostensible stability in monastic life, convinced others that history was changing in profound, possibly apocalyptic ways.[13] Last but not least, contemporaries reacted to the clashes between "reformist" popes and emperors, struggling since the days of the Investiture Controversy to determine the balance of power between the "priesthood" (*sacerdotium*) and worldly rulership (*regnum*).[14]

For Joachim of Fiore, the emblematic figure of the twelfth century's apocalyptic revival, the patterns of history remembered in their totality rendered the end-times significance of the present legible for the followers of the Roman church. After an era of relative peace granted to them by God, Latin Christians had entered into the fifth seal, the new "Babylonian Captivity," suffering from the oppression of German rulers, papal schisms, and abuses of the church's liberty (*libertas*). Only two more, urgent generations of history remained. Orienting his readers on the moving edge of the apocalyptic present, the abbot braced them for the imminent opening of the sixth seal that would bring a double persecution of the faithful, the worst that God's people would ever experience. While Joachim sometimes hedged about the ability to measure the course of the future in precise terms, he expressed no uncertainty about the imminence of those apocalyptic trials before the church could hope to enjoy the promised Sabbath age before history's consummation. The question remained how to decode and recognize the historical signposts provided by the Bible, preparing oneself spiritually before the end of all things.

* * * *

The basic facts of Joachim of Fiore's life are well known. Born around 1135 in Calabria, he experienced a conversion to religious life in his mid-thirties, followed by a series of divine revelations into the meaning

[12] Jay Rubenstein, *Armies of Heaven: The First Crusade and the Quest for Apocalypse* (New York: Basic Books, 2011). See also Rubenstein's recent study *Nebuchadnezzar's Dream: The Crusades, Apocalyptic Prophecy, and the End of History* (New York: Oxford University Press, 2019).

[13] Giles Constable, *The Reformation of the Twelfth Century* (Cambridge: Cambridge University Press, 1996), 125–67.

[14] Brett Whalen, *Dominion of God: Christendom and Apocalypse in the Middle Ages* (Cambridge, MA: Harvard University Press, 2009), 72–99. See also E. Randolph Daniel, "Joachim of Fiore: A Reformist Apocalyptic," in *Fearful Hope: Approaching the New Millennium*, ed. Christopher Kleinhenz and Fannie J. LeMoine (Madison: University of Wisconsin Press, 1999), 40–72.

of Scripture and their application to the course of history.[15] Over the following years, while serving as the abbot of Corazzo and eventually founding his own monastic order at Fiore, he composed a substantial body of exegetical works that revealed the divine mysteries linking the Bible and time.[16] These included his three principal books, the *Concordance of the New and Old Testament* (*Concordia de novi ac veteris testamenti*),[17] the *Exposition on the Apocalypse* (*Expositio in Apocalypsim*),[18] and the *Ten-Stringed Psaltery* (*Psalterium decem cordarum*).[19] In addition to the *Genealogy* and *On the Seven Seals*, he wrote numerous tracts explaining his scriptural and historical insights, including *On an Unknown Prophecy* (*De prophetia ignota*),[20] *Treatise Explaining the Life and Rule of St. Benedict* (*Tractatus in expositionem vite et regule beati Benedicti*),[21] *Introduction to the Apocalypse* (*Praephatio super Apocalipsim*),[22] *Enchiridion on the Apocalypse* (*Enchiridion super Apocalypsim*),[23] *Exhortation to the Jews* (*Exhortatorium Iudeorum*),[24] *An Understanding of the Fig-Baskets* (*Intelligentia super calathis*),[25] and *On the Final Tribulations* (*De ultimis*

[15] On these revelations (ca. 1183–84), see Robert E. Lerner, "Joachim of Fiore's Breakthrough to Chiliasm," *Cristianesimo nella storia* 6 (1985): 489–512. See also Robert E. Lerner, "Ecstatic Dissent," *Speculum* 67 (1992): 33–57.

[16] On Joachim's monastic career, see Stephen E. Wessley, *Joachim of Fiore and Monastic Reform* (New York: Peter Lang, 1990).

[17] *Concordia novi ac veteris testamenti*, ed. Alexander Patschovsky, 4 vols., MGH: Quellen zur Geistesgeschichte des Mittelalters 28 (Wiesbaden: Harrassowitz, 2017). This edition supersedes the long-serviceable, if incomplete, one by E. Randolph Daniel, *Abbot Joachim of Fiore: Liber de concordia novi ac veteris testament*, Transactions of the American Philosophical Society 73 (Philadelphia: American Philosophical Society, 1983).

[18] The only printed edition remains, for now, *Expositio in Apocalypsim* (Venice, 1527; repr., Frankfurt: Minerva, 1964).

[19] *Psalterium decem cordarum*, ed. Kurt-Victor Selge, MGH: Quellen zur Geistesgeschichte des Mittelalters 20 (Hanover: Hahnsche Buchhandlung, 2009).

[20] *De prophetia ignota: Eine frühe Schrift Joachims von Fiore*, ed. Matthias Kaup, MGH: Studien und Texte 19 (Hanover: Hahnsche Buchhandlung, 1998).

[21] *Tractatus in expositionem vite et regule beati Benedicti*, ed. Alexander Patschovsky, Fonti per la storia dell'Italia medievale: antiquitates 29 (Rome: Istituto Storico Italiano per il Medioevo, 2008).

[22] Kurt-Victor Selge, "Eine Einführung Joachims von Fiore in die Johannesapokalypse," *Deutsches Archiv für Erforschung des Mittlealters* 46 (1990): 85–131.

[23] *Enchiridion super Apocalypsim*, ed. Edward Kilian Burger, Studies and Texts 78 (Toronto: Pontifical Institute of Mediaeval Studies, 1986).

[24] *Exhortatorium Iudeorum*, ed. Alexander Patschovsky, Fonti per la storia dell'Italia medievale: antiquitates 26 (Rome: Istituto Storico Italiano per il Medioevo, 2006).

[25] *Intelligentia super calathis*, in *Gioacchino da Fiore: aspetti inediti della vita e delle opera*, ed. P. de Leo (Rome: Rubbetino, 1988), 135–48.

tribulationibus).[26] He also prepared a number of sermons and a program of designs that visualized his historical ideas, compiled in the *Book of Figures* (*Liber figurarum*).[27] He was composing another substantial work, the *Tract on the Four Gospels* (*Tractatus super quatuor evangelia*), when he died in 1202.[28]

As is evident from this selective list of his writings, Joachim was a truly prodigious thinker and author. In the space allotted here one cannot hope to do justice to the kaleidoscope of his apocalyptic exegesis, produced and revised across the course of decades. Instead, taking a cue from the collection of his texts compiled by the unknown French monk described above, we might discern the main outlines of Joachim's apocalypticism by considering the *Genealogy*, *On the Seven Seals*, and the *Letter to All the Faithful*. Taken together, this collection of texts represents a not atypical digest of the abbot's writings from the years soon after his death, offering a quick-and-ready guide to his amazingly sophisticated view of history.[29]

The *Genealogy* was Joachim's earliest known work, written in 1176.[30] Its interpretation of history relies upon a relatively straightforward

[26] E. Randolph Daniel, "Abbot Joachim of Fiore: The *De ultimis tribulationibus*," in *Prophecy and Millenarianism: Essays in Honour of Marjorie Reeves*, ed. Ann Williams (Harlow: Longman, 1980), 165–90.

[27] *Sermones*, ed. Valeria de Fraja, Fonti per la storia dell'Italia medievale: antiquitates 18 (Rome: Istituto Storico Italiano per il Medioevo, 2004). On the *Book of Figures*, in addition to Tondelli, Reeves, and Hirsch-Reich, *Il libro delle figure*, and Reeves and Hirsch-Reich, *The Figurae of Joachim of Fiore*, see Marco Rainini, *Disegni dei tempi: Il "Liber figurarum" e la teologia figurativa di Gioacchino da Fiore* (Rome: Viella, 2006).

[28] *Tractatus super quatuor evangelia*, ed. Francesco Santi, Fonti per la storia dell'Italia medievale: antiquitates 17 (Rome: Istituto Storico Italiano per il Medioevo, 2002).

[29] As pointed out by Morton Bloomfield and Marjorie Reeves, "The Penetration of Joachimism into Northern Europe," *Speculum* 29 (1954): 772–93, the earliest evidence for the circulation of the abbot's works showed little awareness of the three *status*, focusing instead on his concords, vision of the seven seals, and predictions of Antichrist.

[30] Disagreeing with Tondelli, Reeves, and Hirsch-Reich, *Il libro delle figure*, 1:37, Reeves and Hirsch-Reich, *The Figurae of Joachim of Fiore*, 83–84, considered the *Genealogy* (also known as the *Epistola subsequentium figuarum*) to be one of the first spurious, pseudo-Joachite works. However, Stephen E. Wessley, "A New Writing of Joachim of Fiore: Preliminary Observations," in *Prophecy and Eschatology*, ed. Michael Wilks, Studies in Church History 10 (Oxford: Blackwell, 1994), 15–28, followed by Potestà, "Die Genealogia," 55–61, have convincingly argued not just for the *Genealogy*'s authenticity, but for its status as Joachim's earliest surviving work. It seems clear from internal evidence this short tract was intended from the outset to accompany the figure of "two trees," depicting the genealogies of the Old and New Testaments, as the text typically does in later manuscripts. Potestà, "Die Genealogia," 97–101, provides an edition of those

premise, positing parallels between the "genealogies" of the Old and New Testaments, envisioned in the tract's opening as a matching set of trees, that of the New Testament "grafted" onto the Old. As Joachim explained, the trunk of the Old Testament ran from Adam to Jacob, where it extended twelve branches (i.e., the twelve tribes of the Jews) that lasted until the era of King Uzziah of Judah (ca. 790–740 BCE). At that point, the ten tribes of Israel failed, leaving just Benjamin and the tribe that really mattered, Judah. The trunk of the New Testament ran from the time of Uzziah and the prophet Isaiah until Christ, when twelve branches flourished (i.e., the earliest twelve churches). These lasted until Arian barbarians like the Goths and Vandals destroyed nearly all the churches of Africa and the east. Only the Roman church survived, honoring Christ without the stain of heresy, just as the tribe of Judah gave birth to Christ.[31] Clarifying these genealogies, Joachim identified sixty-three "carnal" generations in the Old Testament from Adam to Christ, and sixty-three "spiritual" generations in the New Testament from King Uzziah until the end of time. The final twenty-one generations of the Old Testament and the first twenty-one of the New Testament thereby overlapped, mixed between flesh and spirit. In duration, the generations of the Old Testament were of uneven length, but those of the New Testament lasted thirty years each, symbolized by the fact that Christ began his ministry at the age of thirty. Writing in the year 1176, Joachim specified that forty generations had passed since the birth of Christ. This left just two more generations—sixty years—which would start soon, although the abbot qualified that the precise end of time would happen by God's will.[32]

Making this argument, Joachim did not dismiss the long-standing division of history into seven ages, based on the seven days of creation. As he reviewed them, the ages ran as follows:

1. Adam to Noah
2. Noah to Abraham
3. Abraham to David

diagrams, which appear much like the *Table of Concords* featured in BNF, Lat. 11864, fol. 151v.

31 Potestà, "Die Genealogia," 91–92 (lines 3–24).

32 Ibid., 93 (lines 33–38). In his later elaborations of the concordance, trying among other things to reconcile the time periods of the Old and New Testaments (the *prima diffinitio*) with his Trinitarian model of the three *status* (the *secunda diffinitio*), Joachim identified two lines of descent from Jacob to the final kings of Judah, one through the "fathers" (starting with Judas and Phares) and the other through the "judges" (starting with Joseph and Moses), e.g. book 2.1.16–29, *Concordia novi ac veteris testament*, 2:93–127.

4. David to the Babylonian Captivity
5. The Babylonian Captivity to Christ
6. Christ until Final Judgment
7. The quiet of souls

This presentation of history placed the seventh age after the end of time, matching God's rest on the seventh day after creation—not really an age at all, but the eternal Sabbath.[33] Anyone with a basic knowledge of Christian theology would have recognized this seven-ages scheme, popularized by Augustine of Hippo among others. Augustine had likewise measured the duration of those ages by generations of uneven length, not years. Such an interpretation of history was sufficiently vague and orthodox, just the way Augustine wanted things, featuring the sixth age of history as an indeterminable stretch of time when nothing of consequence would happen in terms of the divine plan for earthly events linked to salvation.[34]

Diverging from Augustine, Joachim took the consequential step of subdividing the sixth age of history—from the Incarnation up to the present—into six "little ages" (*etatulis*), each distinguished by a "battle" (*prelia*), "struggle" (*certamen*), or "tribulation" (*tribulatio*). From the time of Jacob until Christ, or from Moses to John the Baptist, there were seven tribulations of the Old Testament, peoples who oppressed the sons of Israel:

1. The Egyptians
2. The Canaanites
3. The Syrians
4. The Assyrians
5. The Chaldeans
6. The Medes
7. The Greeks

These seven tribulations, he declared, were revealed by the seven seals from the Book of Revelation (Rev 5–8), "hidden signs of the future."

[33] On the patristic seven-ages scheme of history, see Auguste Luneau, *Histoire du Salut chez les pères de l'église: la doctrine des âges du monde* (Paris: Beauchesne, 1964).

[34] For a discussion of Augustine's "historical agnosticism" and its implications for medieval apocalypticism, see Paula Fredriksen, "Tyconius and Augustine on the Apocalypse," in *The Apocalypse in the Middle Ages*, eds. Richard K. Emmerson and Bernard McGinn (Ithaca, NY: Cornell University Press, 1992), 20–37; and Richard Landes, "The Fear of an Apocalyptic Year 1000: Augustinian Historiography, Medieval and Modern," *Speculum* 75 (2000): 97–145.

Like the sons of Israel, he continued, the church experienced its own comparable battles:

1. Against the Jews
2. Against the pagans
3. Against the Persians, Goths, Vandals, and Lombards
4. Against the Saracens
5. Against the New Chaldeans and Babylonians
6. The destruction of Babylon (i.e., Rome)
7. Under Antichrist

Joachim was far from the first Christian exegete to invoke the seven seals in broadly historical terms, viewing them as a prophetic narrative of the church's adverse experiences: assailed first by non-believing Jews; second by the pagan Romans; third by heretics within the church after the Roman Empire became Christian; and fourth by "hypocrites," people who pretended to be good Christians but were not.[35] His complete vision of two parallel sets of seven seals in the times of the Old Testament and New Testament, however, offered an unprecedented kind of specificity. Joachim carefully noted that the final two persecutions, the sixth and seventh, should be taken as one overarching struggle for the church, symbolized by the "two gomors" of manna that the Jews collected in the desert on the sixth day before the Sabbath (Exod 16:22).[36] Doubling up the final persecution under the sixth seal left the seventh seal free from oppression or struggle, that is, it left the seventh seal open for some sort of respite or peace. Earlier in the *Genealogy*, Joachim suggested that after the final sixty years of history had passed, there might be a space of "forty-five days" (Dan 12:11) for the faithful to recover from trials of the end-times. The days in question, he qualified, could represent months, years, or some other amount of time. Here, we catch a tentative glimpse of the

[35] In addition to Wannenmacher, *Hermeneutik der Heilsgeschichte*, 37–58, see Wilhelm Kamlah, *Apokalypse und Geschichtstheologie: Die mittelalterliche Auslegung der Apokalypse vor Joachim von Fiore* (Berlin, 1935; repr., Vaduz: Krause, 1965).

[36] Potestà, "Die Genealogia," 94–95 (esp. lines 78–79). The *Table of Concords* featured in BNF, Lat. 11864, fol. 151v, just like other versions of the table (e.g. Tondelli, Reeves, and Hirsch-Reich, *Il libro delle figure*, plate X), does not designate a double persecution during the sixth seal of the New Testament; rather, it assigns a "grave persecution" to the opening of the seventh seal. Technically, as Joachim explained elsewhere, the seventh persecution pertained to the seventh seal, even if it would in fact occur and end during the sixth preceding seal.

abbot's take on some sort of future Sabbath age before history's conclusion.[37]

On the Seven Seals revisits and highlights Joachim's commemoration of history based on a series of corresponding persecutions, against the Jews in the Old Testament and against the church in the New Testament.[38] This tract, from a later stage in the abbot's writing around the late 1180s, was clearly intended to condense his ideas about the Book of Revelation.[39] Summarized briefly, the seals feature as follows:

First seal, Old Testament Abraham, Isaac, and Jacob Persecution of Israel by the Pharaoh Giving of the Law	**First seal, New Testament** Zachary, John the Baptist, and Christ Separation of the faithful from synagogue Preaching of the Gospels
Second seal, Old Testament Battles between Israel and Canaanites	**Second seal, New Testament** Battles between pagans and holy martyrs
Third seal, Old Testament Battles between Israel and Syrians, Philistines, etc. Schism between the ten tribes of Israel and Judah	**Third seal, New Testament** Battles between Catholics and Arians Schism between Latins and Greeks
Fourth seal, Old Testament Emergence of Elijah, Elisha, and other prophets Assyrians conquer the ten tribes of Israel	**Fourth seal, New Testament** Flourishing of virgins and hermits Conquests of Saracens (Muslims)
Fifth seal, Old Testament Kingdom of Judah upheld Prophets Isaiah, Jeremiah, etc. warn of coming evils Kings of Egypt and Babylon persecute Judah	**Fifth seal, New Testament** Latin church (New Jerusalem) upheld Spiritual men preach "word of the Spirit" Princes, especially Germans, afflict church

[37] Potestà, "Die Genealogia," 992–93 (lines 38–44). See Lerner, "Refreshment of the Saints," who stresses the importance of Dan 12:11 as a source of inspiration for twelfth-century ideas about a possible "Sabbath age" at the end of time, preceding and independent of Joachim's vision of the third *status*.

[38] Wannenmacher, *Hermeneutik der Heilsgeschichte*, 336–55.

[39] Formatted almost like a table itself, *De septem sigillis* typically appears in the manuscript tradition alongside the *Book of Figures*. See Marjorie Reeves, "The Seven Seals in the Writing of Joachim of Fiore with Special Reference to the Tract *De septem sigillis*," *Recherches de théologie ancienne et médiévale* 21 (1954): 211–47.

Old Testament	New Testament
Sixth seal, Old Testament Transmigration of Jerusalem Double affliction (Judith and Esther) Rebuilding of the Temple and Jerusalem's walls	**Sixth seal, New Testament** Transmigration of spiritual Jerusalem Double affliction (Holofernes and Aman) Rebuilding of holy city (church of the elect)
Seventh seal, Old Testament History and prophecy ceases Sabbath for the People of God Final persecution under Antiochus Birth of Christ	**Seventh seal, New Testament** Opening of seals ceases Sabbath for the People of God Final persecution under Gog Christ's return in the Final Judgment

In addition to marking persecutions of God's people, the seven seals revealed other crucial developments in the past with implications for the present-day conditions of the Christian church: the emergence of different religious orders, including prophets, virgins, hermits, and monastic spiritual men; the schism between Latin and Greek churches, paralleling the division between the ten tribes of Israel and Judah; and the chosen lot of the Roman church, preserved from the devastating Saracen conquests.[40] *On the Seven Seals* also directs the reader's attention to the sixth seal's double persecution, recorded in the Old Testament by the Books of Judith and Esther. The opening of the sixth seal in the New Testament would likewise feature a double persecution under the new Holofernes and Aman, Antichrist and his servants. And yet, even in the midst of these trials, the holy city of the church would be restored, just like Jerusalem in the waning days of the Babylonian Captivity, leaving the seventh seal as one of peace, a Sabbath for the people of God.[41]

That opening of the sixth seal lay just around the corner. One can clearly sense apocalyptic imminence in Joachim's *Letter to All the Faithful.* In this address, the abbot struck a remarkably different tone from the measured exegesis of the *Genealogy* and *On the Seven Seals.*

40 On the split between the Latin and Greek churches, and the preservation of the Latin church from the Islamic conquests, see Brett Whalen, "Joachim of Fiore and the Division of Christendom," *Viator* 98 (2003): 89–108; and Felicitas Schmieder, "Two Unequal Brothers Split and Reunited: The Greeks in Latin Eschatological Perceptions of Politics and History before and after 1204," in *Quarta Crociata: Venezia—Bisanzio—Impero Latino*, ed. G. Ortalli, G. Ravegnati, and P. Schreiner (Venice: Istituto Veneto di Scienze Lettere, 2006), 633–51.

41 For other examples of Joachim's presentation on the seven seals, see *Expositio in Apocalypsim*, fols. 6r–11r; Selge, "Eine Einführung Joachims von Fiore in die Johannesapokalypse," 102–15; and Daniel, "Abbot Joachim of Fiore: The *De ultimis tribulationibus*," 175–77.

Here, he speaks in the mode of an Old Testament prophet, warning the people of God that the end is near. Indeed, the abbot explicitly compared himself to the "watchman" from the Book of Ezekiel, tasked by the Lord with sounding the alarm to alert the people that the sword is coming against their land. If the watchman performed his duty and the people did not listen, the blood lay on their hands, but if the watchman was delinquent, God would hold him responsible.[42] Joachim would not be delinquent. Other "religious men" had encouraged him to write, as the signs of the end-times foretold by the apostle Paul (2 Tim 3:1–5) came to pass in what Joachim called "our times." The abbot put Christians everywhere on notice. "Death cries from the east, and destruction from the west," he warned. "The multitude of the Greeks have become Sodom, and the Latins Gomorrah. Among the former, the sign of Egypt is openly announced; among the latter, the confusion of Babylon. All conspire as one against God and all—as the prophet says—have forsaken God, blasphemed Israel, turned their backs, transgressed the Law, subverted justice, and broken the eternal covenant."[43]

Joachim's self-fashioning as the watchman, charged with sounding the alarm as the apocalypse approached, represented more than just a throwaway line or convenient analogy. It communicated an essential point about why the Calabrian abbot felt compelled to share his realizations about Scripture and the legibility of history. After all, God would spare just a few from the final tribulations, the righteous remnant like Lot in Sodom and Noah during the flood, past judgments that foreshadowed the approaching onslaught. Now was the time to "come out of Babylon" (Rev 18:4) through confession and penance, choosing to ascend the "mountain of contemplation" or to remain in an "active life of humility." Make no mistake, the abbot insisted, these things would come to pass "in your days, few and evil, not in those of your grandchildren or your children's old age."[44] At the end of his letter he briefly mentioned that God would afterwards console the remnant of faithful, an oblique reference to the Sabbath age. The *Letter to All the Faithful*, however, was not intended to reassure its readers about future blessings. On the contrary. It was supposed to invoke a salutary terror.

* * * *

[42] Bignami-Odier, "Notes sur deux manuscrits," 220–21.

[43] Ibid., 222–23.

[44] Ibid., 223. For a similar declaration by the abbot about his role as the watchman, sounding the alarm to battle so that his listeners could prepare their weapons or flee to safer ground, see the preface to *Concordia novi ac veteris testament*, 2:7–8.

The apocalyptic positioning of the contemporary Roman church at the close of history's long narrative arc forms a central message of Joachim's entire body of works, not just the ones examined above. The principle of concordance and sequence of the seven seals unambiguously placed the church of Rome in the waning of the fifth seal, the new Babylonian Captivity and "days of lamentation" predicted by the prophet Jeremiah. To grasp the significance of that position, one had to pay particular attention to the historical experiences of the papacy, elaborated by the abbot with greatest detail in the *Book of Concordance*. As we have seen, the succession of popes after the birth of Christ provided the organizational markers for the generational descent of the New Testament, rounded into increments of thirty years. Rome represented the new Judah, enjoying the "royal priesthood" (1 Pet 2:9), since Pope Sylvester had baptized Constantine, inaugurating the era of Christian empire before Constantine transferred the imperial capital to Constantinople. Under the third seal, both the western and eastern churches experienced invasions by Arian barbarians. The Roman church suffered but remained free from Arianism, while the Greeks fell into the heresy, although a remnant of them remained orthodox, providing a source of spiritual inspiration for the Latin monastic tradition.[45]

Under the fourth seal, punishing the Greeks for their sins, the Saracens overran most of the churches in the east, absorbing them and separating them from the faith of Christ. Under Pope Zachary, at the opening of the fifth seal, God transferred the power of empire from the Greeks to the Franks, starting with Charles Martel, who acted as the defender of the Roman church. In terms of concordance, Zachary aligned with pious, dying King Hezekiah of Judah, granted an additional fifteen years of life by the Lord. Among other things, this "great miracle"—revealed as the lines turned backwards on the sundial of Achaz, Hezekiah's father—designated the additional fifteen generations of peace granted by God to the Latin church, sparing Latin Christians the full brunt of the Saracen conquests, just as the Lord spared Judah when the Assyrians conquered the ten tribes of Israel. Just as importantly, like the king of Babylon who treated Hezekiah with friendship, the new

[45] Books 3.1.3, 4.1.3, *Concordia novi ac veteris testament*, 2:314–21, 345–68. Joachim labeled the twelve generations from Christ to Sylvester the *prima distinctio*, followed by the twelve generations of Sylvester's successors, the *secunda distinctio* (book 4.1.4, *Concordia novi ac veteris testament*, 2:368–75).

Frankish emperors treated the popes of Rome with proper deference and respect.[46]

Following the principle of concordance, these generations of peace could not last, as the Roman church began to experience the bondage of the new Babylonian Captivity, oppressed by the New Chaldeans, the rulers of the Germans and other peoples. By Joachim's calculations, thirty-six generations after Christ, Pope Leo IX aligned with Josiah, the king of Judah who tried to reform the worship of God as Judah slid into corruption and idolatry.[47] Just as Josiah miscalculated and suffered defeat in battle against the Egyptians, Leo led an army against the Normans, suffering a disastrous defeat. Like King Joachaz, pressured by the Babylonians and carried off by the Egyptian pharaoh, thirty-seven generations after Christ, Pope Gregory VII struggled against the German ruler, Henry IV, and fled into exile with the Normans. Like King Joachim, made into a servant by King Nebuchadnezzar of Babylon, thirty-eight generations after Christ, Pope Paschal II was seized by Emperor Henry V, who extorted the right of investiture from him. Under Kings Jeconiah and Zedekiah, Judah experienced a schism, as some people went into exile with Jeconiah in Babylon, while others remained in Jerusalem under Zedekiah, installed on the throne by Nebuchadnezzar. Likewise, thirty-nine generations after Christ, the Latin church experienced a schism between Pope Alexander III and the anti-pope Octavian, installed on the papal throne by Emperor Frederick I. Confusion reigned, as some Christians supported the rightful pope while others favored the emperor. A nominal peace between the papacy and the German Empire had been restored in the following, fortieth generation, although in recent memory, under Popes Urban III and Lucius III, the Germans had begun again to infringe on the church's liberty.[48]

Joachim's close reading of the papacy's recent struggles with the German emperors reveals his "reformist" sensibilities, a key

[46] Books 3.2.4–5, 4.1.27, *Concordia novi ac veteris testament*, 2:322–32, 419–32. Zachary marks the begin of the *tertia distinctio*. The miraculous "sundial of Achaz," which allowed Joachim to square his double lines of generational concordance through the "judges" and "fathers" (see above, n. 32), while allowing him to align the waning days of Judah with the Roman church of his own day, represents a fascinating and under-studied aspect of his apocalyptic exegesis. Briefly, see Potestà, *Il tempo dell'apocalisse*, 142–43, 194–95.

[47] Josiah is thirty-sixth in the line of the judges, twenty-eighth in the line of fathers. In this section of the concordance, Joachim deliberately follows the line of judges.

[48] Book 4.1.30–37, *Concordia novi ac veteris testament*, 2:446–52.

characteristic of the twelfth century's apocalyptic revival. His concordance between the final kings of Judah and the last several generations of popes attributed a providential significance to the political landscape of the past few generations, including violence on the Italian peninsula, the Investiture Controversy, and schisms in the papal office. For the abbot, who lived through Emperor Henry VI's attempt to conquer southern Italy and claim the Italo-Norman kingdom for the Hohenstaufen dynasty, the perils of the fifth seal were evident right in his backyard.[49] Oppression by the Germans, however, did not account alone for the new Babylonian Captivity. Rather, one witnessed its bondage in the internal failings of the church, its pride and misplaced forms of resistance to worldly powers. "It is better to stand in servile humility than prideful liberty," as Joachim observed in *An Understanding of the Fig-Baskets*. "I say, better to be humble rather than proud, prostrate before powerful rather than exalted."[50] Pointing to Leo IX's defeat by the Normans, and to a similar outcome when Pope Innocent II took the field against them in 1139, the abbot emphasized the need to prepare "spiritual arms" rather than "material" ones for battle. The true struggle for the church's liberty was a moral, not temporal one.[51]

Looking beyond the apocalyptic present, Joachim offered signposts for what lay ahead. The faithful faced the two imminent persecutions of the sixth seal: one in the forty-first generation since Christ, the other in the forty-second generation.[52] Although the details changed between his various works, the main outlines remained the same. One of those persecutions would come from without, waged by pagan peoples, most likely Saracens, who would invade the western empire. Joachim, who lived through—and according to some accounts, prophesied—the recapture of crusader Jerusalem by Saladin in 1187, sensed a resurgence of infidel power, even if the armies of the First Crusade had struck what seemed to be a fatal blow against the followers of the false prophet,

[49] On Joachim's engagement with the relationship between "church" and "empire" in this context, see H. Grundmann, "Kirchenfreiheit und Kaisermacht um 1190 in der Sicht Joachims von Fiore," *Deutsches Archiv für Erforschung des Mittlealters* 19 (1963): 353–96.

[50] *Intelligentia super calathis*, 139.

[51] Ibid., 140–44. Leo IX's defeat also features on the *Table of Concords* (Tondelli, Reeves, and Hirsch-Reich, *Il libro delle figure*, plate X, left-hand margin by the year 1050). Joachim offered a similar message about the need to prepare the "spiritual arms" for the trials of the end-times in *De prophetia ignota*, 220.

[52] Books 3.2.6, 4.1.40–45, *Concordia novi ac veteris testament*, 2:332–35, 461–75.

Muhammad.[53] He typically associated such external sources of persecution with the ten barbarian kings symbolized by the ten "little horns" on the beast in the Book of Daniel, who would assault the Roman Empire.[54] Then there would come the persecution of *the* great Antichrist, the "son of Perdition," the "eleventh horn" emerging from the midst of the ten others. At points, Joachim followed conventional apocalyptic wisdom, identifying the great Antichrist with the Jews; at others, he linked Antichrist with the Saracens. But the abbot also seemed to suggest that Antichrist would come from within, being born from among the Christian people.[55]

Yet all hope was not lost for the beleaguered church. The persecution aligned with the forty-second generation in theory would actually end in the forty-first generation, leaving the final generation as an era "without war, without scandal, without worry or terror," blessed by the Lord.[56] Like the Temple in Jerusalem after the Babylonian Captivity, even as the ten kings of Antichrist reigned, the Roman church would be rebuilt "in the narrowness of time."[57] A "new leader" (*dux novus*) would emerge for God's people, as a new order of "spiritual men" (*viri spirituales*) spread the gospel, redeemed the fallen, and achieved lives of exceptional spiritual perfection, leading the schismatic Greeks and finally the Jews to join the sheepfold of the faithful.[58] In his principal works, Joachim identified this era with the *status* of the Holy Spirit. Whether he presented that future time as the third *status*, the final generation of history, or the seventh seal, the abbot anticipated conditions of peace and betterment on earth, the source of his lasting legacy in the Western millennialist tradition. Even after that Sabbath age, nonetheless, the church would still face one final persecution before the Final

[53] See E. R. Daniel, "Apocalyptic Conversion: The Joachite Alternative to Crusade," *Traditio* 25 (1969): 127–54, who downplays Joachim's support for the crusades. For some contrary views, Rubenstein, *Nebuchadnezzar's Dream*, 181–209.

[54] In his exegesis of the "world empires" based on the statue from Dan 2, book 5.6.4, §4, *Concordia novi et veteris testament*, 3:967–73, Joachim associates the Saracens, rather than the Roman Empire, with the statue's "iron" legs, anticipating the final kingdom of Antichrist (the feet mixed from iron and clay).

[55] As discussed by R. Lerner, "Antichrists and Antichrist in Joachim of Fiore," *Speculum* 60 (1985): 553–70.

[56] Books 3.2.7, 4.1.45, *Concordia novi ac veteris testament*, 2:336–37, 471–73.

[57] This proclamation (*Hic iterum restaurabitur romana ecclesia in angustia temporum, regnantibus .X. regibus qui romanum imperium percussuri*) features prominently on the *Table of Concords* (Tondelli, Reeves, and Hirsch-Reich, *Il libro delle figure*, plate X, left-hand margin, opposite the years 1200 and 1230).

[58] On this new leader (*novus dux*), see book 4.1.45, *Concordia novi ac veteris testament*, 2:471. See also Whalen, *Dominion of God*, 100–24.

Judgment, the tail of the dragon, symbolizing the peoples of Gog and Magog. History, it seems, could not help but remain a place of travail.[59]

* * * *

Looking back at the patterns of the past with certainty and anticipating the future with confidence, Joachim nevertheless refused to be completely precise about the timetable for things to come. He was a good enough Augustinian to appreciate the dangers of predicting the end-times in absolute terms, setting oneself up for failure and disillusionment if one got the numbers wrong. Yes, Joachim declared that forty generations had passed, leaving just two more of thirty years each. On the *Table of Concords*, those last two generations are numbered from MCC to MCCXXX and from MCCXXX to MCCLX—the apocalyptic year 1260. Reading the abbot's works carefully, however, one finds ample qualifiers about the need for caution when calculating the end-times. He made this point in the *Genealogy* and repeated it frequently. In the *Book of Concordance*, the abbot compared the generational computations of the past to the navigation of safe shores; heading into the final generations, one entered uncharted waters. He seemed especially sensitive to the possibility that annals and chronicles, his sources for history after the Bible, might conflict or introduce inconsistences into his calculations, throwing off readers or encouraging skeptics. Ultimately, as was made clear by scriptural and patristic authorities, only God knew the exact hour of the end, reserving the right to make the final generations of history longer or shorter.[60]

By his own admission, Joachim of Fiore's apocalyptic memory had its blind spots and lapses. As the apocalyptic revival of the twelfth century gave way to the widespread and fervid apocalypticism of the thirteenth century, the abbot's successors would show less caution. Informed and inspired by Joachim's ideas, Christians ranging from popes to dissident friars tried to discern the providential meaning of events unfolding in their times: the Fourth Crusade's sack of Constantinople; the emergence of the mendicant orders; ongoing but generally disastrous crusades; and the next round of epic battles between the Roman papacy and the Hohenstaufen dynasty. When Joachim's works did not

59 As featured, among numerous other places, in the figure of the red, seven-headed dragon from Rev 12 (Tondelli, Reeves, and Hirsch-Reich, *Il libro delle figure*, plate XIV, designating the tail: *Gog. iste est ultimus antichristus*). See also Lerner, "Antichrists and Antichrist."

60 Book 4.1.38, *Concordia novi ac veteris testament*, 2:453–55.

give them enough material to work with, they crafted their own apocalyptic memories, mixing them with prophecies attributed to Merlin and the pagan Sibyls, even though Joachim himself deliberately eschewed such suspect materials.[61] One especially zealous Franciscan, Gerard of Borgo San Donnino, insisted that Joachim's major works formed nothing less than a new, eternal gospel, portending the end of the present-day church. He was condemned and imprisoned.[62]

Undeterred, other Joachites awaited 1260 as the approaching year of millennialist transformation promised by the abbot of Fiore. Of course, they waited in vain. While some of Joachim's admirers experienced a profound sense of disillusionment when the year 1260 passed, others adjusted, recalculated, and fixed the end of the world to a later date. New generations of apocalyptic exegetes in the late thirteenth century and the fourteenth century, figures such as Peter John Olivi and John of Rupescissa, updated, adapted, and revitalized the Joachite reading of Scripture. Generations later, Christopher Columbus, who viewed his voyages of discovery as part of God's plan for the end-times, invoked Joachim of Fiore. So too did Reformation-era Protestant radicals, as Europe's new printing-houses began to publish and disseminate the abbot's works, genuine and spurious, to new readerships. In such ways, the twelfth century's apocalyptic revival left a far-reaching and long-lasting legacy.[63]

Selected Further Reading

Lerner, Robert. "Antichrists and Antichrist in Joachim of Fiore." *Speculum* 60 (1985): 553–70.

McGinn, Bernard. *The Calabrian Abbot: Joachim of Fiore in the History of Western Thought*. New York: Macmillan, 1985.

[61] See the preface to the *Concordia novi ac veteris testament*, 2:7–15, where the abbot highlights his reliance on scripture and rejects "frivolous apocryphal books" with prophecies about the end-times. On the prophetic climate at the thirteenth-century papal curia, see C. Jostmann, *Sibilla Erithea Babilonica: Papsttum und Prophetie im 13. Jahrhundert*, MGH 54 (Hanover: Hahn, 2006).

[62] On the "Scandal of the Eternal Evangel," see Reeves, *The Influence of Prophecy*, 59–70.

[63] In addition to Reeves, *The Influence of Prophecy*, see P. M. Watts, "Prophecy and Discovery: On the Spiritual Origins of Christopher Columbus's 'Enterprise of the Indies,'" *American Historical Review* 90 (1985): 73–102. For an even longer-term look at Joachim's influence (genuine and imagined), see Marjorie Reeves and Warwick Gould, *Joachim of Fiore and the Myth of the Eternal Evangel in the Nineteenth Century* (Oxford: Clarendon, 1987).

Reeves, Marjorie. *The Influence of Prophecy in the Later Middle Ages*. Oxford: Oxford University Press, 1969; repr., Notre Dame, IN: University of Notre Dame Press, 1994.

Reeves, Marjorie, and Warwick Gould. *Joachim of Fiore and the Myth of the Eternal Evangel in the Nineteenth Century*. Oxford: Clarendon, 1987.

Reeves, Marjorie, and Beatrice Hirsch-Reich. *The Figurae of Joachim of Fiore*. Oxford: Clarendon, 1972.

Reidl, Matthias, ed. *A Companion to Joachim of Fiore*. Leiden: Brill, 2018.

Rubenstein, Jay. *Nebuchadnezzar's Dream: The Crusades, Apocalyptic Prophecy, and the End of History*. New York: Oxford University Press, 2019.

Tondelli, Leone, Marjorie Reeves, and Beatrice Hirsch-Reich, eds. *Il libro delle figure dell'abate Gioachino da Fiore*, 2 vols. Turin: Società Editrice Internazionale, 1953.

Wessley, Stephen E. *Joachim of Fiore and Monastic Reform*. New York: Peter Lang, 1990.

Whalen, Brett. *Dominion of God: Christendom and Apocalypse in the Middle Ages*. Cambridge, MA: Harvard University Press, 2009.

12 Apocalyptic Sensibility in Renaissance Europe

IAN BOXALL

SEEING THE WORLD APOCALYPTICALLY

The visitor who cares to linger in front of an apparently straightforward fifteenth-century painting of the Nativity in London's National Gallery will soon discover that this work has secrets to reveal. Painted by the Florentine Renaissance artist Alessandro (Sandro) Botticelli in 1500, *The Mystic Nativity* is in fact a vivid apocalyptic commentary on the contemporary city of Florence, through a complex exegetical interweaving of Luke's birth narrative (Luke 2:1–20) with passages from the Book of Revelation.[1]

Apart from the predictable Holy Family in a stable-like structure, the newborn Christ being adored by angels, there are little demons lurking in the crevices, some of them apparently speared on their own forks. At the front, three pairs of angels and humans embrace as if about to dance in celebration of the nativity they are witnessing, while twelve angels hover in a circle over the stable. Other angels wave olive branches, symbols of peace, as they whisper in the ears of the attendant shepherds. Most surprising, however, is the inscription Botticelli has provided at the top of the painting, written not in the conventional Latin but in Greek, the language newly learned by so many figures of the Italian Renaissance:

> I, Alexandros, was painting this picture at the end of the year 1500 in the [troubles] of Italy in the half time after the time according to the eleventh [chapter] of St John in the second woe of the Book of Revelation in the loosing of the devil for three and a half

[1] On Botticelli's *Mystic Nativity*, see, e.g., Rab Hatfield, "Botticelli's *Mystic Nativity*, Savonarola and the Millennium," *Journal of the Warburg and Courtauld Institutes* 58 (1995): 88–114; Natasha O'Hear, *Contrasting Images from the Book of Revelation in Late Medieval and Early Modern Art* (Oxford: Oxford University Press, 2011), 105–34.

years. Then he will be chained in the twelfth [chapter] and we shall see him [about to be buried/trodden down] as in this picture.[2]

For Botticelli, both the Gospel and the Apocalypse have become inspired lenses through which to interpret the troubling times Italy was experiencing in the apocalyptically significant year 1500 ("the half time after the time"). His joyful scene, which includes the trampling of demons, is a promise of a new age, about to be born out of the struggles of the present, albeit dependent upon the piety of the Florentine people. Trials give way to an age of peace. Apocalypse is the key to contemporary history.

Botticelli's *Mystic Nativity* is a potent visual symbol of much that the Renaissance prized: renewal of Greek learning; humanity's solidarity with the angelic world; hope in the classical idea of a "golden age." Moreover, its symbolic subject-matter is a *renaissance*, a "rebirth," or what the Italian humanist Petrarch (1304–74), often considered a pioneer of the Renaissance, called a *renascita*. For Botticelli, the rebirth is a new nativity, about to take place in the city of Florence, making it a kind of "new Jerusalem" (Rev 21). Yet there are also elements of Botticelli's painting which hint at his growing unease with aspects of the Italian Renaissance: a return to a more medieval style of painting; the somewhat agitated and elongated figure of St. Joseph; the inscription itself, with its reference to apocalyptic woes preceding the new birth. For many interpreters of Botticelli, the influence of the fiery Dominican prophet-preacher Girolamo Savonarola (1452–98) is palpable in this canvas. Before his death, Savonarola announced that the Virgin Mary now wanted to give birth again, this time to "the Florentine people, a spiritual people, a good people," despite the impending tribulations of the dragon-Antichrist.[3] Now that he has been martyred, Savonarola's conviction apparently lives on in Botticelli's canvas. Indeed, the Greek inscription's allusion to Rev 11 may well suggest that, for Botticelli, the Apocalypse's "two witnesses" are Savonarola and his collaborator Fra Domenico da Pescia, who "prophesied" in Florence for about three and a half years (see Rev 11:3).[4]

[2] Trans. in O'Hear, *Contrasting Images*, 125.

[3] Quoted in Hatfield, "Botticelli's *Mystic Nativity*," 97.

[4] Ibid., 98–99. On Savonarola, see, e.g., Roberto Ridolfi, *The Life of Girolamo Savonarola*, trans. Cecil Grayson (London: Routledge & Kegan Paul, 1959); Bernard McGinn, trans., *Apocalyptic Spirituality*, Classics of Western Spirituality (New York: Paulist, 1979), 183–91; James Hankins, "From the New Athens to the New Jerusalem: Florence between Lorenzo de' Medici and Savonarola," in *Botticelli's Witness:*

For the Renaissance in general, the "rebirth" was much broader, encapsulating the rediscovery of classical texts, renewed focus on aspects of classical education largely sidelined in the medieval universities, such as grammar and rhetoric, and developments in the visual arts.[5] But despite the frequent assertion that the Renaissance represented a shift from a theocentric to an anthropocentric universe, "apocalyptic sensibilities"—outlooks shaped by apocalyptic traditions and texts, not least the Book of Revelation—were a significant dimension of this cultural, political, and artistic "rebirth." What follows is an attempt to describe the main strands in this Renaissance apocalypticism.

Of course, to make such claims about "the Renaissance" is controversial, given that its definition and parameters remain contested questions: whether, for example, there are multiple Renaissances, tied to different geographical locations, or to different movements (e.g., in art or politics) that need to be disentangled.[6] This essay will utilize the term broadly to incorporate various movements in that transitional period between the late Middle Ages and the so-called early modern period (i.e., from the fourteenth century to the sixteenth), beginning in Italy but spreading into northern Europe, and eventually beyond that continent, insofar as they engage with Jewish and Christian apocalyptic thought and writings, notably the biblical books of Daniel and Revelation.

Two aspects of the Renaissance most directly pertain to the interpretation of apocalyptic texts. First is the emergence of humanism, a "refocusing of old learning"[7] through a return to the sources and a revival of the study of Greek, which received a significant boost by Johannes Gutenberg's invention of the movable-type printing press.

Changing Style in a Changing Florence, eds. Laurence B. Kanter, Hilliard T. Goldfarb, and James Hankins (Boston: Trustees of the Isabella Stewart Gardner Museum, 1997), 13–20; Lauro Martines, *Scourge and Fire: Savonarola and Renaissance Florence* (London: Jonathan Cape, 2006).

5 See, e.g., Paul Oskar Kristeller, *Renaissance Thought and Its Sources*, ed. Michael Mooney (New York: Columbia University Press, 1979); Jerry Brotton, *The Renaissance: A Very Short Introduction* (Oxford: Oxford University Press, 2006); Kim W. Woods, ed., *Making Renaissance Art* (New Haven, CT: Yale University Press in association with the Open University, 2007); Michael Wyatt, ed., *The Cambridge Companion to the Italian Renaissance* (Cambridge: Cambridge University Press, 2014).

6 Michael Wyatt, "Renaissances," in *The Cambridge Companion to the Italian Renaissance*, ed. Wyatt, 1–16.

7 Diarmaid MacCulloch, *Reformation: Europe's House Divided* (London: Penguin, 2003), 76–87.

Second, the Renaissance saw significant developments in visual art, both in Italy (arguably going back as far as Giotto) and in the Low Countries (exemplified, e.g., by Hans Memling and Jan van Eyck).[8] As Botticelli's *Mystic Nativity* illustrates, visual artists in this period continue to explore apocalyptic themes, including the visualization of the Apocalypse of John, not least to address pressing contemporary concerns.

CONTINUITY AND CHANGE

For all that was new in Renaissance thought, engagement with apocalyptic ideas and texts during this period was not a radical break with a medieval past. As Marjorie Reeves noted some years ago,

> "It is now generally recognized that, whilst Renaissance scholars were rediscovering the glories of the classical inheritance, their perspective was still in large measure governed by the Christian concept of end-time, with all the traditions of Last Things built up in the Middle Ages."[9]

On the contrary, the late medieval challenge posed by Joachim of Fiore to the Tyconian-Augustinian reading of Revelation as a vision of the church in every age continued to make its presence felt in movements such as the Beguins, Fraticelli, Lollards, Hussites, and Taborites.[10] Nor was this restricted to marginal groups. More mainstream Renaissance figures could hold to a belief in a coming millennial age, the expectation of an angelic pope, and hope for church and political renewal, perhaps after a period of onslaught from Antichrist.[11]

Social and political events heightened such apocalyptic sensibilities. The trauma of the Black Death, although not as transformative for apocalyptic ideas as might be expected, provoked apocalyptic texts

8 Donatello's pendentive roundel of St. John on Patmos in the Old Sacristy of San Lorenzo, Florence (1428–43), for example, reflects the interests of Renaissance artists in perspective. Both Memling and van Eyck produced dramatic visual interpretations of the Apocalypse: Memling in his *St. John Altarpiece* (ca. 1479) and van Eyck in his *Ghent Altarpiece* (1432).

9 Marjorie Reeves, "The Development of Apocalyptic Thought: Medieval Attitudes," in *The Apocalypse in English Renaissance Thought and Literature*, eds. C. A. Patrides and Joseph Wittreich (Ithaca, NY: Cornell University Press, 1984), 61–62.

10 Ibid., 60–61.

11 Sharon Leftley, "The Millennium in Renaissance Italy: A Persecuted Belief?," *Renaissance Studies* 13, no. 2 (1999): 117–29.

such as the *Book of Secret Events* by the Franciscan John of Rupescissa.[12] With the Ottoman ascendancy in the mid-fifteenth century, the Turks came to play an increasingly central role in millennial expectations. In a 1529 sermon (*Heerpredigt wider die Türken*), Martin Luther identified the Turks with the "little horn" on the fourth beast of Daniel 7 (Dan 7:8, 21), developing that well-established tradition of interpreting Daniel's four beasts as a succession of oppressive empires. Though the "little horn" would do battle with "the holy ones," it would ultimately be defeated, because of the judgment of the Ancient of Days.[13]

Other Reformers would follow Luther's Turkish identification (e.g., Philipp Melanchthon), or identify Daniel's "little horn" with Antichrist, manifested militarily by the Ottoman Turks and spiritually by the papacy (e.g., Johannes Oecolampadius).[14] Nor was this development restricted to the West. The Turkish threat gave the Apocalypse of John new importance in the Orthodox world after centuries of relative neglect due to canonical disputes and consequent absence from the liturgical lectionary.[15]

The Renaissance return *ad fontes* gave renewed focus to those elements in late medieval apocalypticism that hoped for the renewal of the church. The sixteenth century witnessed the Capuchin reform of the Franciscans by Matteo da Bascio (1495–1552) and the founding of the Society of Jesus by Ignatius Loyola (1491–1556), as well as the emergence of Protestantism.[16] Moreover, renewed attention to non-Christian classical sources meant that apocalyptic hopes for a millennial age after the time of Antichrist were often merged with the classical idea of a golden age. Revelation's vision of the New Jerusalem, as a

[12] Bernard McGinn, "Apocalypticism and Church Reform: 1100–1500," in *Encyclopedia of Apocalypticism*, vol. 2, *Apocalypticism in Western History and Culture*, ed. Bernard McGinn (New York: Continuum, 2000), 97.

[13] Nathan Rein, "The Bible in Political Thought and Political Debates, ca. 1500–1750," in *The New Cambridge History of the Bible*, vol. 3, *From 1450 to 1750*, ed. Euan Cameron (Cambridge: Cambridge University Press, 2016), 599–600.

[14] Euan Cameron, "The Bible and the Early Modern Sense of History," in *The New Cambridge History of the Bible*, 3:671–72.

[15] Later manifestations of this renewed interest are the unpublished Greek commentaries on Revelation from the sixteenth and seventeenth centuries, including those by Maximos the Peloponnesian (1565/70–1621/31) and Georgios Koressios (1566–1654), the latter decidedly anti-Ottoman. Athanasios Despotis, "Orthodox Biblical Exegesis in the Early Modern World (1450–1750)," in *The New Cambridge History of the Bible*, 3:525–26.

[16] Adriano Prosperi, "Religion," in *The Cambridge Companion to the Italian Renaissance*, ed. Wyatt, 282–83.

perfect city which was also paradise restored (Rev 22:1–2), encouraged such assimilation. Savonarola was not unique in his prophecy that Florence was about to be reborn as a manifestation of the New Jerusalem. Similar claims would be made for Strasbourg by Melchior Hoffman and for Münster by Anabaptists, while some of the Marian exiles would see in Elizabeth I's restoration of Protestantism to England an anticipation of the holy city's descent.[17] Papal Rome, by contrast, wavered between being regarded as New Jerusalem and the present manifestation of Babylon.

The influence of Savonarola's combination of apocalyptic optimism and foreboding on Botticelli's *Mystic Nativity* has been mentioned already. But that influence may already be present in Botticelli's *St. John on the Island of Patmos* (ca. 1490; Galleria degli Uffizi, Florence), a predella panel to his *Coronation of the Virgin* altarpiece, painted for the Dominican Church of San Marco in Florence. This unusual panel depicts John sitting on a deserted Patmos, his back to a pile of book-shaped rocks, scribbling furiously his new revelation in an open book. The precise significance of the "petrified library" is unclear. It could represent the Old Covenant, now supplanted by John's own prophetic inspiration, which brings his predecessors such as Ezekiel and Daniel to completion. Alternatively, it could be an early indication of Savonarola's influence, a rejection of the ancient classical texts so central to the so-called new learning, even before the "bonfire of the vanities."[18]

The latter is a plausible explanation, given that Savonarola began preaching a series of sermons on the Apocalypse in San Marco in August 1490, around the time Botticelli was finishing his altarpiece for that church. As Savonarola would later record, his message in these sermons focused on that dual message of hope and foreboding, of a renewal of the church preceded by a great scourge against Italy.[19] Equally apocalyptic was his "Renovation Sermon," preached on January 13, 1494/95, which interpreted each of the four horsemen in Rev 6:1–8 as symbolizing a different period in church history: the white horse the apostolic age, the red the time of the martyrs, the black the time of heretics. Savonarola

[17] Judith Kovacs and Christopher Rowland, *Revelation: The Apocalypse of Jesus Christ*, Blackwell Bible Commentaries (Malden, MA: Blackwell, 2004), 19; Florence Sandler, "*The Faerie Queene*: An Elizabethan Apocalypse," in *The Apocalypse in English Renaissance Thought and Literature*, eds. C. A. Patrides and Joseph Wittreich (Ithaca, NY: Cornell University Press, 1984), 159–60.

[18] Ian Boxall, "In Search of John's Island: Patmos in Botticelli and Burgkmair," *Relegere: Studies in Religion and Reception* 3, no. 1 (2013): 29–34.

[19] Ibid., 32.

saw his own age as that symbolized by the pale horse, "the time of the lukewarm": "Therefore, I told you that the renewal of the Church had to be undertaken, and soon. Otherwise, God will give His vineyard, that is, Rome and the Church, to others to cultivate, because in Rome there remains no charity at all, but only the devil."[20] This would be followed, as he makes clear in an Advent sermon from 1494, by a fifth period, a time of conversion and renewal, in which Florence would play a key role, if only it reformed itself.[21] We are well on the way here to the sentiments of Botticelli's 1500 *Mystic Nativity*.[22]

HUMANISM AND THE BOOK OF REVELATION

Rather more sober than the fiery apocalypticism of Savonarola was the scholarly enterprise of the humanists, with their interests in philology, the study of ancient biblical languages, textual criticism, and the recovering of original meaning.[23] Migration of Greek scholars to the West following the collapse of the Byzantine Empire reinvigorated the study of Greek, as well as making accessible valuable New Testament manuscripts. Translations of the New Testament from the Greek were made by such humanist scholars as Giannozzo Manetti (1396–1459), while his associate Lorenzo Valla (ca. 1407–57) composed influential exegetical notes based on the Greek text. Fresh translations of the Greek fathers into Latin also facilitated the renewal of patristic scholarship.

Desiderius Erasmus of Rotterdam (ca. 1466–1536), perhaps the best-known of humanist biblical scholars, is significant for the study of the Book of Revelation for at least two reasons: a famous error in his textual-critical work, and his reopening of the question of canonicity.

20 *Selected Writings of Girolamo Savonarola: Religion and Politics, 1490–1498*, trans. and ed. Anne Borelli and Maria Pastore Passaro (New Haven, CT: Yale University Press, 2006), 66.

21 Ibid., 154.

22 A similar message of troubles followed by renewal of the church based on the Apocalypse was preached by the Augustinian General Egidio Antonini of Viterbo, who saw the opening of the Fifth Lateran Council in 1512 as the beginning of that renewal: Nelson H. Minnich, "Prophecy and the Fifth Lateran Council (1512–1517)," in *Prophetic Rome in the High Renaissance Period*, ed. Marjorie Reeves, Oxford-Warburg Studies (Oxford: Clarendon, 1992), 67.

23 See, e.g., Alastair Hamilton, "Humanists and the Bible," in *The Cambridge Companion to Renaissance Humanism*, ed. Jill Kraye (Cambridge: Cambridge University Press, 1996), 100–17; Jerry H. Bentley, *Humanists and Holy Writ: New Testament Scholarship in the Renaissance* (Princeton, NJ: Princeton University Press, 1983).

The first is a consequence of Erasmus working with a single Greek manuscript of the Apocalypse for his 1516 edition of the Greek New Testament: Codex Reuchlini, a manuscript of Andreas of Caesarea's sixth-century commentary on Revelation, in which the biblical text was embedded in, and indistinguishable from, the commentary proper.[24] Moreover, this manuscript lacked the last six verses of the book, causing him to translate them back into Greek from the Latin Vulgate. This produced a glaring error in Rev 22:19: "from the book of life" rather than "from the tree of life." The error in the Vulgate is understandable because of a scribal miscopying *ligno* ("from the tree") as *libro* ("from the book") in a two-verse passage in which the word "book" occurs no fewer than four times.[25] However, it is a reading found in no actual Greek manuscript. The error was perpetuated by Robert Estienne's Textus Receptus of 1552, and thence in English translation by the Geneva Bible and the King James Version.[26] It was corrected in Erasmus's fourth edition (1527), on the more substantial textual evidence of the Complutensian Polyglot, instigated by Cardinal Ximénez, archbishop of Toledo.[27]

Erasmus's interest in patristic discussions also reopened the question of Revelation's canonicity for sixteenth-century authors, particularly among the Reformers. Questions about Revelation's authorship and canonical status had emerged already in third-century Alexandria, when Bishop Dionysius concluded on stylistic and grammatical grounds that the Apocalypse and Fourth Gospel had different authors.[28] Although Dionysius did not dispute Revelation's authority, debates about its place in the canon would continue in the East for centuries. Erasmus raised similar doubts about apostolic authorship and (at least implicitly) canonicity on the basis of the patristic sources, in his annotation on Rev 22:12, which would provoke a fierce backlash from Frans Titelmans, a Franciscan scholar of Louvain, as well as the Protestant Reformer Theodore Beza.[29]

[24] David C. Parker, *An Introduction to the New Testament Manuscripts and Their Texts* (Cambridge: Cambridge University Press, 2008), 228.

[25] Bruce M. Metzger, *A Textual Commentary on the Greek New Testament*, 2nd ed. (Stuttgart: Deutsche Bibelgesellschaft, 1994), 690.

[26] The reading "book" is, of course, also present at Rev 22:19 in versions made directly from the Vulgate, such as Douai-Rheims.

[27] Bentley, *Humanists and Holy Writ*, 134.

[28] Eusebius, *Historia Ecclesiastica* 7.25.

[29] Irena Backus, "The Church Fathers and the Canonicity of the Apocalypse in the Sixteenth Century: Erasmus, Frans Titelmans, and Theodore Beza," *Sixteenth Century Journal* 29, no. 3 (1998): 651–65.

Erasmus noted Jerome's admission of Greek doubts about its canonical status, together with the purported view of "very many very learned men" that "it says nothing that would seem worthy of apostolic grandeur."[30] He also noted that the Greek manuscripts of the Apocalypse he had previously consulted attributed the text not to "John the Evangelist" but to "John the theologian." Yet he drew back from dismissing Revelation's canonical status and apostolic authorship, treating the ecclesial consensus as binding. Moreover, he maintained the book's usefulness, despite the patristic debates, as an allegory of the early history of the church. Nonetheless, the damage was done, and this further increased in his 1522 edition, which included additional patristic sources questioning Revelation's canonical status. The importance of this issue for him is clear from the length of his discussion, almost a page and a half in the 1535 edition of his *Annotationes* out of a total of only seven covering the whole of Revelation.[31]

Erasmus's discussion is a vivid example of how humanist scholarship laid many of the foundations of later biblical criticism. Many critical commentaries on Revelation would discuss both authorship and the book's checkered canonical history with reference to the same patristic sources. Influential too are some of the arguments of Erasmus's detractors. Beza's response, namely that the stylistic differences between John's Gospel and Revelation are genre-related (he proposed that the Apocalypse was written in the unpolished style of the Hebrew prophets),[32] is occasionally taken up by modern defenders of common authorship.

Erasmus's general biblical method also exemplifies humanism's break from the medieval fourfold sense, focusing instead on the literal sense and "a generally spiritual or moral sense."[33] His specific approach to Revelation was to treat it as a book of figures or allegories, thereby distancing it from the chiliastic readings that had provoked the original patristic debates. However, his moral, exhortatory approach to Scripture was taken up by the Zurich Reformer Leo Jud (or Judah), who resolved Erasmus's omission of Revelation from his *New Testament Paraphrase*. At the end of his German translation of Erasmus, published in 1542, Jud

30 Annotations on Rev 22:12 in ibid., 653.

31 By contrast, his Annotation on the much shorter 1 Peter extends to over twelve pages: Anne Reeve and M. A. Screech, introduction to *Erasmus' Annotations on the New Testament: Galatians to the Apocalypse*, ed. Anne Reeve, Studies in the History of Christian Thought 52 (Leiden: Brill, 1993).

32 Backus, "The Church Fathers," 664.

33 Hamilton, "Humanists and the Bible," 112.

provided his own paraphrase on the Apocalypse.[34] His comments on Rev 1:1–3, for example, emphasize the doctrinal dimension of what John heard and saw, and its usefulness for the practice of Christian living in this world: "Whiche doctrine shall be very profytable unto every one that shall reade & understand this prophecye, so far as he shall endeuer himself to lyve thereafter, preparinge & appointynge himself thorowe a true faith and a christen conuersacion to please the lorde in this lyfe, whiche is shorte and transitorye, and the ende thereof, uncerten."[35] In contrast to Erasmus, however, Jud's *Paraphrase* strongly supported canonicity, and even added a "liturgical" argument: its canonical status is proved by its use in the church's liturgy.

REFORMATION ANXIETIES AND CATHOLIC RESPONSES

Erasmus's musings about Revelation's status are paralleled in the treatment of this book by the magisterial Reformers.[36] Neither John Calvin nor Huldrych Zwingli wrote commentaries on the book, in Calvin's case only one of three New Testament books on which he failed to comment (the others being the Second and Third Letters of John). However, Calvin did utilize Revelation elsewhere, not least in his *Institutes*.[37] But his humanist scholarship, albeit combined with elements of anti-papal polemic, is best evident in his commentary on Daniel, which is strongly philological and interprets Daniel's visions historically, describing the period between Daniel and the coming of Christ, in contrast to the actualizing tendencies of other Reformers.[38]

Martin Luther's attitude to the Apocalypse developed significantly. In his initial *Preface to Revelation* in his September 1522 Testament, Luther dismissed it out of hand. First of all, he objected that the apostles "do not deal with visions, but prophesy in clear and plain words,"

[34] Irena Backus, *Reformation Readings of the Apocalypse: Geneva, Zurich, and Wittenberg* (Oxford: Oxford University Press, 2000), 29–30.

[35] Leo Jud, *The seconde tome or volume of the Paraphrase of Erasmus upon the newe testament: conteynying the Epistles of S. Paul, and other the Apostles. Whereunto is added a Paraphrase upon the Reuelation of S. John* (London: Edwarde Whitchurche, 1549), on Rev 1:3.

[36] See, e.g., Jaroslav Pelikan, "Some Uses of Apocalypse in the Magisterial Reformers," in *The Apocalypse in English Renaissance Thought and Literature*, eds. C. A. Patrides and Joseph Wittreich (Ithaca, NY: Cornell University Press, 1984), 74–92; Backus, *Reformation Readings*.

[37] I am indebted to Matthew Gore for this insight.

[38] John J. Collins, *A Commentary on the Book of Daniel*, Hermeneia (Minneapolis, MN: Fortress, 1993), 120–21.

following Christ's example in the Gospels. Revelation, on the other hand, is much closer to Fourth Ezra in its stress on visions and images. Second, the author commends his writing too highly for Luther's liking, even to the extent of warnings against adding to or subtracting from it. Third, he notes, in terms which echo Erasmus, how "[m]any of the fathers also rejected this book long ago." His final objection is more personal: "My spirit cannot accommodate itself to this book. For me this is reason enough not to think highly of it: Christ is neither taught nor known in it. But to teach Christ, this is the thing which an apostle is bound above all else to do."[39] His consequent reordering of the canon meant that Hebrews, James, Jude, and Revelation were grouped together at the end and, unlike the other New Testament books, unnumbered, as not clearly written by apostles.[40]

Yet this was not Luther's final word on the subject. Subsequent events (and, one suspects, the success of Lucas Cranach the Elder's woodcuts to his September 1522 edition, with their anti-papal depiction of Babylon) seem to have drawn him to late medieval historical-prophetic interpretations of Revelation and Daniel, such as those found in the Franciscan Nicholas of Lyra (1270–1349) and more radical Franciscan and Wycliffite texts, reshaped in light of the papacy's ongoing opposition, the Peasants' War, and the Turkish threat.[41] He wrote a positive preface in 1528 to the Lollard *Commentarius in Apocalypsin ante centum annos aeditus*, which he also edited. Moreover, his 1530 Preface was also more positive:

> Since it is intended as a revelation of things that are to happen in the future, and especially of tribulations and disasters that were to come upon Christendom, we consider that the first and surest step toward finding its interpretation is to take from history the events and disasters that have come upon Christendom till now, and hold them up alongside these images, and so compare them very carefully.[42]

39 "Preface to the Revelation of St. John," September Testament of 1522, trans. in *Luther's Works*, vol. 35, *Word and Sacrament 1*, ed. Theodore Bachmann (Philadelphia: Fortress, 1960), 398–99.

40 Euan Cameron, "The Luther Bible," in *The New Cambridge History of the Bible*, 3:227.

41 Philip D. W. Krey, "Luther and the Apocalypse: Between Christ and History," in *The Last Things: Biblical and Theological Perspectives on Eschatology*, eds. Carl E. Braaten and Robert W. Jenson (Grand Rapids, MI: Eerdmans, 2002), 140.

42 "Preface to Revelation" (1530), in *Luther's Works*, 35:401.

Luther's new apocalyptic interest focused particularly on Antichrist as manifested in the contemporary papacy, a theme which he found not only in Revelation, but also in Dan 8 and 11:36–12:12. The emergence of Michael in Dan 12 was a specific prophecy of the papacy's downfall.[43]

If the Book of Revelation, and apocalyptic sensibilities generally, were marginal to at least some of the magisterial Reformers, such was not the case with their successors. A significant stream of commentaries on the Apocalypse emerged in the sixteenth century, notably those by François Lambert, Sebastian Meyer, Leo Jud, Heinrich Bullinger, and David Chytraeus.[44] Genevan Calvinists tended to replicate traditional patterns of interpretation, with some anti-papal polemic. In Zurich, the emphasis (e.g., in Jud) was more practical. Some of the Lutheran commentators (e.g., Chytraeus) saw the book as being fulfilled in a particular way through the Reformation, while certain of his followers identified Luther himself as the angel with "the eternal gospel" of Rev 14:6.[45]

Some of the reserve regarding matters apocalyptic among the magisterial Reformers may have been a response to the more prominent apocalyptic imagination of the radical Reformation. One such example is Thomas Müntzer (ca. 1485–1525), whose political activism seems to have been crucially shaped by the Book of Daniel. In a dramatic example of apocalyptic actualization, Müntzer's "Sermon before the Princes" draws heavily on Dan 2 in order to urge the German political leadership to act on behalf of the peasants, the contemporary "saints of the Most High" (Dan 7:27). Müntzer saw himself in the guise of Daniel interpreting Nebuchadnezzar's dream, equipped "to commune with God and have that inner knowledge which God offers through the divine Spirit," while the sixteenth-century divines were the counterparts to Nebuchadnezzar's soothsayers.[46]

The anti-papal polemic of much Protestant interpretation of Revelation understandably provoked reactions from the Catholic side, particularly among Jesuit exegetes. Sixteenth-century anti-Roman readings of the Apocalypse could be categorized in two ways, either as claims

[43] Collins, *A Commentary on the Book of Daniel*, 119.

[44] See, e.g., Backus, *Reformation Readings*.

[45] Ibid., 135–38; Pelikan, "Some Uses of Apocalypse in the Magisterial Reformers," 74–75.

[46] Christopher Rowland, "The Book of Daniel and the Radical Critique of Empire: An Essay in Apocalyptic Hermeneutics," in *The Book of Daniel: Composition and Reception*, eds. John J. Collins and Peter W. Flint, Supplements to Vetus Testamentum 93 (Leiden: Brill, 2001), 2:450.

that John's first-century prophecy directly predicted the Protestant Reformation and the corruption of ecclesiastical Rome, or as vivid actualizations in which interpreters saw a clear analogy between John's situation and their own. The commentary by the English ex-Carmelite and Henrician exile John Bale, *The Image of Both Churches* (ca. 1545), veers in the latter direction. Bale draws a direct parallel between his own exile status and that of the seer of Patmos, exploiting the fact that they share the same name: "At the writing of this prophecie felt Johan of their cruelte beinge exiled into Pathmos an Ile of Licia for the faithfull testimonie of Jesu. And so did I poore creature with my poore wife and children at the gathering of this present commentarie, fleinge into Germanye for the same."[47] The Catholic response against such historical-prophetic and actualizing approaches was twofold. Either the visions of the Apocalypse had largely been fulfilled in the time of imperial Rome, and therefore had nothing to say about the Christian Rome of the popes, or their focus was primarily futurist. The former, preterist approach was advocated by Luís de Alcázar (1554–1613), building on the ideas of John Hentennius. It was also adopted by Francisco Suárez (1548–1617) after his initial espousal of a futurist position. The second alternative is particularly associated with Francisco de Ribeira (1537–91), whose view was shaped by his interpretation of the Old Testament prophets: although the first five seals (Rev 6:1–11) described the period of the early church up to the reign of Trajan, the bulk of John's visions concerned the end of history, not the intervening history of the church.[48]

APOCALYPTIC OPTIMISM AND THE NEW WORLD

Despite the redirection of Apocalypse exegesis by Alcázar, Suárez, and Ribeira, the Jesuits were not immune from treating it as a window onto contemporary events. Jesuit missionaries could see themselves as key instruments in the final stages of history.[49] One sixteenth-century

[47] *The Image of Both Churches*, q7v–q8r, quoted in Gretchen E. Minton, "'Suffer me not to be separated | And let my cry come unto thee': John Bale's Apocalypse and the Exilic Imagination," *Reformation* 15 (2010): 86.

[48] Arthur W. Wainwright, *Mysterious Apocalypse: Interpreting the Book of Revelation* (Nashville, TN: Abingdon, 1993), 61–66; Jean-Robert Armogathe, "Interpretations of the Revelation of John: 1500–1800," in *Encyclopedia of Apocalypticism*, vol. 2, ed. McGinn, 186–93.

[49] Robin Barnes, "Images and Hope and Despair: Western Apocalypticism: ca. 1500–1800," in *Encyclopedia of Apocalypticism*, vol. 2, ed. McGinn, 159.

Pseudo-Joachite treatise even made the bold claim that the Society of Jesus was Joachim's prophesied spiritual order, which would evangelize the New World as the decaying second *status* gave way to the third age of the Spirit.[50] But such apocalyptic optimism relating to missionary activity did not begin with the Counter-Reformation. The age of exploration at the end of the fifteenth century already witnessed the coming together of medieval millennial hopes (such as the emergence of a last emperor and angelic pope) with Renaissance interest in the classical golden age.[51] Franciscan missionaries in the New World had already exploited the potential in their own apocalyptic traditions.[52] Moreover, explorers such as Christopher Columbus and Amerigo Vespucci were strongly influenced by apocalyptic texts and the conviction that biblical prophecy was being fulfilled.

On Columbus's third voyage in 1498, he wrote that the islands and Cuban coastland he encountered were "the new skies and the new land mentioned by Our Lord through St. John's Apocalypse, after having been revealed by the words of Isaiah."[53] Two years later, he began to compile a *Book of Prophecies*, assisted by the Carthusian monk Gaspar Gorricio, consisting of biblical, classical, and patristic texts and fragments of Joachim of Fiore, concerning the conversion of the nations, the liberation of Jerusalem, and the dawn of a millennial age.[54] To the likes of Columbus and Gorricio, the conversion to Christianity of peoples living in far-flung parts of the earth seemed to herald the fulfillment of prophetic texts such as Isa 60. In his own additions to the book, Gorricio even discusses contemporary debates as to whether, as traditionally thought, the apostles had completed the universal mission to "make disciples of all the nations" (Matt 28:19), or whether a new evangelization was to be expected in the last days.[55] Like Columbus, Amerigo Vespucci could

[50] For the ongoing influence of Joachite and Franciscan apocalyptic thought on the Americas in the seventeenth century, see Jaime Lara, "Francis Alive and Aloft: Franciscan Apocalypticism in the Colonial Andes," *The Americas* 70, no. 2 (2013): 139–63.

[51] Alain Milhou, "Apocalypticism in Central and South American Colonialism," in *Encyclopedia of Apocalypticism*, vol. 3, *Apocalypticism in the Modern Period and the Contemporary Age*, ed. Stephen J. Stein (New York: Continuum, 1998), 1–35.

[52] Adriano Prosperi, "New Heaven and New Earth: Prophecy and Propaganda at the Time of the Discovery and Conquest of the Americas," in *Prophetic Rome in the High Renaissance Period*, ed. Reeves, 290–95.

[53] "Letter to the Wet Nurse of Prince Don Juan," in Milhou, "Apocalypticism," 7.

[54] *The Book of Prophecies Edited by Christopher Columbus*, ed. Roberto Rusconi, trans. Blair Sullivan, Repertorium Columbianum 3 (Berkeley: University of California Press, 1997).

[55] Ibid., 29.

also appeal directly to John's Apocalypse in commenting on his own journeys. As he wrote in a letter to Lorenzo di Pierfrancesco de' Medici, "We found such a multitude of people in those regions that no one could count their number (as one reads in the book of the Apocalypse)."[56] Nor is this apocalyptic optimism absent from visual art of the period. Hans Burgkmair the Elder's famous *St. John the Evangelist in Patmos* (1508–18; Alte Pinakothek, Munich), the central panel of a triptych altarpiece, depicts John's island as a lush tropical island, paradise restored, with exotic foliage and colorful birds, including a South American macaw.[57] Compositionally, it closely models Burgkmair's woodcut of Adam and Eve in the Garden of Eden. Appropriately, the island of Patmos from which John sees the Edenic New Jerusalem descend has now become that earthly paradise. Pictorially, Burgkmair vividly conveys the apocalyptic optimism of the age, for whom the discovery of new islands on the edge of the known world heralded the arrival of "a new heaven and a new earth" (Rev 21:1).

ENOCH AND THE QUEST FOR HIGHER WISDOM

The end-time focus of many of the figures and movements discussed in this chapter reflects the eschatological emphasis of the two biblical apocalypses, Daniel and Revelation. Yet, although often tied in the popular imagination to eschatology or the Last Things, apocalyptic *per se* is concerned primarily with the unveiling of heavenly mysteries.[58] Its origins in Israel may be as much related to mantic wisdom as to biblical prophecy, reflected in the interest of early apocalyptic traditions in revelation concerning cosmology, angelology, and astronomy as well as the end-times. This is particularly the case with that rich body of traditions associated with the mysterious character of Enoch, who according to the Bible "walked with God; then he was no more, because God took him" (Gen 5:24).

One intriguing dimension of the Renaissance interest in apocalyptic traditions is precisely this fascination with Enoch, long before the rediscovery of 1 (or Ethiopic) Enoch by the Scottish explorer J. Bruce in 1773, and its surprising connection with magic and occult practices. Magical

[56] *Letters from a New World: Amerigo Vespucci's Discovery of America*, ed. Luciano Formisano (New York: Marsilio, 1992), 48 (quoting Rev 7:9).

[57] See Boxall, "In Search of John's Island," 34–36.

[58] Christopher Rowland, *The Open Heaven: A Study of Apocalyptic in Judaism and Early Christianity* (London: SPCK, 1982), 7–189.

concerns might appear to conflict with new interest in scientific advances. Yet magic had a robust intellectual underpinning for Renaissance thinkers: the quest for *exaltatio*, the deification of humans, which some at least saw as rooted in the Bible. Genesis revealed the dignity of Adam (therefore of humanity) prior to the Fall, including his ability to speak with God and his commission to name other animals, both reflecting Adam's extraordinary linguistic abilities.[59] According to the Swiss philosopher Paracelsus (1493–1541), Adam's descendant Enoch was the last human to speak the Adamic language, i.e., the language of the angels, considered by Renaissance philosophers as the key to perfect knowledge.[60] Moreover, Enoch's own literal *exaltatio*, as he was believed to have been "taken" from earth to heaven, made him the ideal role model in the quest for humanity's deification.

One of the most famous Enochic "questers" was the English Renaissance scholar John Dee (1527–1608), Fellow of Trinity College, Cambridge, mathematician, astronomer, natural philosopher, and advisor to Queen Elizabeth I.[61] Dee's learning meant that he was a major channel of European thought into England. He accumulated a vast library of nearly 4,000 volumes at his house in Mortlake, including classical texts, theological works, and books on mathematics, science, mysticism, and magic. In the words of one scholar of Dee's work: "The whole Renaissance is in this library."[62] Unsurprisingly, his interest in magic meant that Dee was held in suspicion by many of his contemporaries. The Protestant martyrologist John Foxe famously described him as "Doctor Dee the great Conjurer."

Intellectual influences on Dee include a string of Florentine Neoplatonists, such as Marsilio Ficino (1433–99) and Giovanni Pico della Mirandola (1463–94), the latter a follower of Savonarola, as well as the German Benedictine Johannes Trithemius (1462–1516), known for his study of angelology. Particularly influential on Dee's thinking was the Florentine Renaissance magus Agrippa (1486–1535), whose *De occulta*

[59] György E. Szőnyi, *John Dee's Occultism: Magical Exaltation through Powerful Signs*, SUNY Series in Western Esoteric Traditions 14 (Albany: State University of New York Press, 2004), 20.

[60] Ibid., 136.

[61] See Peter French, *John Dee: The World of an Elizabethan Magus* (London: Ark, 1987); Deborah E. Harkness, *John Dee's Conversations with Angels: Cabala, Alchemy, and the End of Nature* (Cambridge: Cambridge University Press, 1999); Szőnyi, *John Dee's Occultism*. On the broader, non-magical, aspects of Dee's scholarship, see William H. Sherman, *John Dee: The Politics of Reading and Writing in the English Renaissance* (Amherst: University of Massachusetts Press, 1995).

[62] Frances Yates, *Theatre of the World* (London: Routledge & Kegan Paul, 1969), 12.

philosophia divided the world into the elementary (the focus of the natural sciences), celestial, and intellectual or spirit world. Through *exaltatio*, enabled by certain preparatory techniques, the human was capable of communing directly with that higher world.[63] For Dee, this meant access to that higher wisdom and knowledge that would allow him to read "the corrupted Book of Nature" more perfectly.[64]

Dee claimed this ability to commune with angels, notably with the assistance of his associate Edward Kelley, through the practice of "scrying," in which Dee functioned as magus, offering the preparatory incantations, and Kelley as scryer, gazing at a crystal "shew-stone" (believed by Renaissance magi to have been used by high priests in Israel) and providing the voice for the apparitions. In these sessions, Dee believed that he communicated through Kelley with a succession of angels, including the archangels Michael, Gabriel, Uriel, and Raphael.[65]

The contents of the angelic revelation purportedly made to Kelley and Dee, of which the latter made copious notes, was a complex system that came to be known as Enochian magic.[66] It included the communication of the angelic or Enochian language, the language whereby Enoch had communicated with the angels,[67] prayers to specific angels, and other revelations. Dee's persistent belief was that this engagement with the mystical dimensions of Enochic apocalypticism brought him close to the goal of his scientific quest for "the ultimate truths of nature."[68]

CONCLUSION

The diversity of responses to apocalyptic traditions during the Renaissance should not surprise, given the complexity of the period in question and the diverse movements described under this umbrella term. The Renaissance witnessed apocalyptic optimism related to exploration and consequent renewal of missionary activity, controversial debates over the interpretation of Revelation during the sixteenth-century

[63] Agrippa, *De occulta philosophia* 1.1. See Szőnyi, *John Dee's Occultism*, 34–37.

[64] Harkness, *John Dee's Conversations with Angels*, 3–4.

[65] *John Dee: Essential Writings*, ed. Gerald Suster, Western Esoteric Masters Series (Berkeley, CA: North Atlantic Books, 2003), 68–69; Harkness, *John Dee's Conversations with Angels*, 46–51.

[66] *The Enochian Magick of Dr John Dee*, ed. and trans. Geoffrey James (St. Paul, MN: Llewellyn, 1994).

[67] Donald C. Laycock, *The Complete Enochian Dictionary: A Dictionary of the Angelic Language as Revealed to Dr. John Dee and Edward Kelley* (York Beach, ME: Weiser, 1994).

[68] Szőnyi, *John Dee's Occultism*, 182.

Reformation, and the more "sober" dimensions of humanist scholarship, as well as that intriguing focus on apocalyptic traditions associated with Enoch, seeing in this biblical patriarch a precursor of "the Renaissance man." The fact that there are strong elements of continuity with late medieval apocalypticism, notably its tension between fear of Antichrist and hopes for the future, echoes criticisms from elsewhere of making too harsh a distinction between the Renaissance and the preceding "Middle Ages."

Yet, in an important way, Renaissance, especially humanist, engagement with apocalyptic texts was also laying down patterns for the future. Modern critical scholarship on texts such as Daniel and the Apocalypse is richly indebted to many of its concerns: debates about authorship and, in the case of Revelation, canonicity; the centrality of original languages (whether Hebrew, Aramaic, or Greek) for translation and commentary; the contribution of textual criticism. There is also a very clear trajectory linking sixteenth-century Jesuit exegesis of Revelation to contemporary interpretations of the book, both scholarly (Alcázar's preterism) and popular (Ribeira's futurism). Identifying such connections should not, of course, gloss over the differences. Sixteenth-century preterism differs from the concerns of modern historical critics in that it treats the book's visions as predictive prophecy, albeit prophecies primarily fulfilled in the early centuries, rather than as historical indicators of the world which John inhabited. Nonetheless, the former undoubtedly made possible the latter.

Finally, the more esoteric interests of Renaissance scholars like John Dee are not unrelated to contemporary scholarly discussions of the nature of the apocalyptic tradition. However alien to modern sensibilities, Dee's quest for angelic communication is a potent reminder that apocalyptic thought and literary apocalypses are concerned with far more than revelation of the end of history. They claim to communicate heavenly mysteries, providing mortals access to a higher wisdom, a deeper knowledge of the structure of the universe. In the words of Daniel to King Nebuchadnezzar: "there is a God in heaven who reveals mysteries" (Dan 2:28).

Selected Further Reading

Backus, Irena. *Reformation Readings of the Apocalypse: Geneva, Zurich, and Wittenberg*. Oxford: Oxford University Press, 2000.

Bentley, Jerry H. *Humanists and Holy Writ: New Testament Scholarship in the Renaissance*. Princeton, NJ: Princeton University Press, 1983.

Hatfield, Rab. "Botticelli's *Mystic Nativity*, Savonarola and the Millennium." *Journal of the Warburg and Courtauld Institutes* 58 (1995): 88–114.
Leftley, Sharon. "The Millennium in Renaissance Italy: A Persecuted Belief?" *Renaissance Studies* 13, no. 2 (1999): 117–29.
Minton, Gretchen E. "'Suffer me not to be separated | And let my cry come unto thee': John Bale's Apocalypse and the Exilic Imagination." *Reformation* 15 (2010): 83–97.
O'Hear, Natasha. *Contrasting Images from the Book of Revelation in Late Medieval and Early Modern Art.* Oxford: Oxford University Press, 2001.
Szőnyi, György E. *John Dee's Occultism: Magical Exaltation through Powerful Signs*. SUNY Series in Western Esoteric Traditions. Albany: State University of New York Press, 2004.
Vespucci, Amerigo. *Letters from a New World: Amerigo Vespucci's Discovery of America.* Edited by Luciano Formisano. New York: Marsilio, 1992.
Wyatt, Michael, ed. *The Cambridge Companion to the Italian Renaissance.* Cambridge: Cambridge University Press, 2014.

13 "Pride & Vanity of the Imagination, That Disdains to Follow This World's Fashion": Apocalypticism in the Age of Reason

CHRISTOPHER ROWLAND

Apocalyptic ideas formed a significant, but too often neglected, part of early modern theology. In the seventeenth century, interpretation of the Book of Revelation had some distinguished advocates, particularly Joseph Mede, whose *Clavis Apocalyptica* was so important for the prophetic studies of Isaac Newton.[1] In addition to the more conventional wisdom of Mede, however, there was also an undercurrent of esotericism typified by John Dee (1527–1608), for whom Enoch was a paragon of the kind of communion with the angels that he actualized.[2] Enoch, briefly mentioned in Gen 5:22–24, was a channel of revelations and offered a model of access to heavenly wisdom. A century later, Jane Lead (1624–1704), part of a group responsible for introducing the ideas of the apocalyptic seer Jacob Boehme into English theology, was attracted to the figure of Enoch, as her work *The Enochian Walks with God Found Out by a Spiritual-Traveller Whose Face towards Mount-Sion Above Was Set* indicates.[3]

The sixteenth and seventeenth centuries saw the emergence of a pattern of interpretation of the Book of Revelation in which the visionary variety of its apocalyptic images was transformed either by relating the visions exclusively to the situation in which John of Patmos was writing, thereby reducing its contemporary significance (e.g., Hugo

[1] Christopher Burdon, The *Apocalypse in England: Revelation Unravelling, 1700–1834* (London: Macmillan, 1997); Judith Kovacs and Christopher Rowland, *Revelation: The Apocalypse of Jesus Christ* (Malden, MA: Blackwell, 2004), 7–10.

[2] Glyn Parry, *The Arch-Conjuror of England: John Dee* (New Haven, CT: Yale University Press, 2011); G. Szőnyi, *John Dee's Occultism: Magical Exaltation Through Powerful Signs* (Albany: State University of New York Press, 2004).

[3] Christopher Rowland, "Blake, Enoch, and Emerging Biblical Criticism," in *Sibyls, Scriptures, and Scrolls: John Collins at Seventy*, ed. Joel Baden (Leiden and Boston: Brill, 2016), 1145–65; A. Hessayon and S. Apetrei, eds., *An Introduction to Jacob Boehme: Four Centuries of Thought and Reception* (New York: Routledge, 2014); A. Hessayon, *Jane Lead and Her Transnational Legacy* (London: Palgrave Macmillan, 2016).

Grotius), or by using reason to render a systematic outline of salvation history. With regard to the latter, the English commentator Joseph Mede's *Clavis Apocalyptica* in particular was influential, and was taken up with alacrity by other learned commentators, not least Isaac Newton, who paid due regard to the influence of his distinguished Cambridge predecessor. The effect of the commentaries of Mede and Newton was to reduce the Book of Revelation by decoding its images and rendering them in the form of a theology of history with its repetitions and overlaps duly explained. The detail of this is less important than the effect it had in curbing enthusiasm of those who found in the Apocalypse a license for their own visions and the challenge which they offered to respectable religion.

Throughout the history of the exegesis of biblical apocalyptic texts there have been very different kinds of interpretation. On the one hand there has been the relating of the images to specific persons and events as the picturesque apocalyptic images are "decoded." Usually, the true meaning of the text is then elucidated, whether that is in respect to the beast or the whore being linked to a particular person or institution, or a moment in the Apocalypse—such as the opening of a seal, the blast of the trumpet, or the pouring forth of a bowl—is to be understood as a particular historical moment. Once the apocalyptic code is cracked, then the apocalyptic sequence can be rendered as a narrative of the Last Things.

On the other hand there are interpretations that apply the text to a variety of situations as the apocalyptic imagery is juxtaposed with the interpreter's own circumstances, to inform understanding and action. Part of this pattern of interpretation includes the ways in which later visionaries are prompted by the apocalyptic images to have their own visions or to see again things similar to what had appeared to John.

A feature of this period is that there was much "enthusiasm": more of "immediate revelation" as a mode of understanding and engaging with the divine, which subordinates the position of institutions, Scripture, and convention. It may occasionally involve disregard of, or disobedience to, the law, but need not and indeed arguably even in the most extreme cases includes some of the main ethical themes of the law. As such, while its primary concern is with strands of theology from the early modern and modern periods, it concerns an issue that goes all the way back to the New Testament and indeed is a feature one may find much more widely in the study of religion. Not prioritizing rules and regulations, indifference to law and custom, even appearing to be sexually immoral or blasphemous, and offending against convention are often symptomatic of prioritizing another source of authority, which is experiential and indeed apocalyptic. It is an individual's claim to knowledge based on divine inspiration. The conviction that God has spoken by dream or revelation, and indeed is revealed independently of established patterns of discerning the divine will, is evident in different parts of the New Testament itself, as in the passages from the later Christian tradition which I will consider. As a result, inspiration then is given priority over obedience to convention. As we shall see when we consider William Blake's writing, that should not lead us to think that he naïvely supposed that appeal to "Memory" wasn't crucial to him. No one used his intellectual ancestors' work to better effect, in reaction and as an inspiration, than Blake.[4] Milton, Swedenborg—not to mention the Bible—both influenced Blake, stimulated his imagination, and concentrated his mind to articulate his resistance to them.

This chapter outlines a dominant understanding of the inadequacy of the visions unless they are attended by careful rational explanation in line with Christian tradition. The contrast is then offered, with reference to the trial of Anne Hutchinson and the writings of her contemporary Gerrard Winstanley, followed by a particular consideration of the apocalypticism of William Blake. The chapter concludes with a consideration of the indebtedness of these apocalyptic themes to the New Testament, followed by some hermeneutical reflections.

"THE SOUL OF THE VISION IS THE DOCTRINE ITSELF, FROM WHENCE FAITH IS BORN"

No words better encapsulate the triumph of reason over apocalypse than those of John Calvin in his commentary on Exod 33:19: "the soul of the vision is the doctrine itself, from whence faith is born." No more clear-cut statement of this can be found than in Calvin's sermon on Exodus and his writings on Ezekiel's visions. In the following extract from his commentary on Exod 33:19, Calvin lucidly explains why visions are so much less satisfactory and indeed less important for Christianity than the explanatory power of words:

[4] Indeed, he mentions as much, e.g., *The Marriage of Heaven and Hell*, 5, 21–22; *The Complete Poetry and Prose of William Blake*, ed. David V. Erdman (Berkeley: University of California Press, 1982), 35, 42 (all references to Erdman are to this edition). See Harold Bloom, *The Anxiety of Influence: A Theory of Poetry*, 2nd ed. (New York: Oxford University Press, 1997).

> Let it be observed that although a vision was exhibited to his eyes, the main point was in the voice because true knowledge of God is received more by the ears than by the eyes. A promise indeed is given that he shall behold God, but the latter blessing is more excellent: that is, that God will proclaim his name so that Moses may know him more by his voice than by his face. For speechless visions would be cold and altogether evanescent if they do not borrow efficacy from speech (*ex sermone*). Therefore just as the logicians compare a syllogism to the body and the reasoning which it includes to the soul, so—properly speaking—the soul of a vision is the doctrine (*doctrina*) itself, from whence faith is born.[5]

Calvin wrote no commentary on the Book of Revelation, although his contemporary Martin Luther—in his earlier preface to his translation of the New Testament in 1520—called the book "neither apostolic nor prophetic" because "Christ is not taught or known in it." This likely aligns with Calvin's view as well. Luther's major criticism of Revelation in both the first and second versions of his preface—and what makes it "neither apostolic nor prophetic"—is that its visionary character means that it does not "prophesy in clear, plain words," as do Christ and the apostles. In the later "Preface to Revelation," Luther took up a similar theme and pointed to three types of prophecy in the Bible: one without imagery, which is in every way preferable to teaching prophetically the way of God; the second in images but with interpretation; and the third without either words or interpretation, but in images and figures, of which Revelation is an example. As long as this kind of prophecy remains without interpretation, Luther describes it as "a concealed and mute prophecy" which is of little benefit to Christendom.[6]

So what we have here is a declaration of the superiority of the transparency of God's communication. Apocalypse is about doctrine, not the vague ambiguities of visions and dreams. Calvin's view of Ezekiel, for example, is not the details of the visions so much as that to which the vision is directed and with what intention. The role of the responsible interpreter is to discern the vision's aim and particularly the

[5] Trans. in E. de Boer, *John Calvin on the Visions of Ezekiel: Historical and Hermeneutical Studies in John Calvin's "sermons inédits,"* Kerkhistorische Bijdragen 21 (Leiden: Brill, 2004), 107–08; see also A. Mein, "Seeing Ezekiel's Visions in Early Modern England," paper presented at the annual meeting of the European Association of Biblical Studies, Amsterdam, July 23, 2012.

[6] Kovacs and Rowland, *Revelation: The Apocalypse of Jesus Christ*, 44–45.

teaching to which it points. The problem with apocalyptic texts is their ambiguity when contrasted with the transparency of the gospel, a view which is echoed by Luther in his various comments on the Book of Revelation. This view indicates not only a reaction to the visual culture of the medieval period, but also a suspicion of enthusiasm and prophecy which was a live issue, given the prophetic claims made by those on the radical wing of the Reformation.[7]

This attitude could not be more different from that of William Blake, who championed "that which is not too explicit as the fittest for instruction," with the Bible as a book that appealed primarily to the imagination:

> The wisest of the Ancients considerd what is not too Explicit as the fittest for Instruction, because it rouzes the faculties to act. I name Moses, Solomon, Esop, Homer, Plato …
>
> … Why is the Bible more Entertaining & Instructive than any other book? Is it not because they are addressed to the Imagination, which is Spiritual Sensation, & but mediately to the Understanding or Reason?[8]

The problem with apocalypticism was that the language of vision and appeal to an authority which transcended social status, conventional wisdom, and the established institutions was deemed to be threatening to social order. Two aspects of the theological background are important for understanding the suspicion towards apocalypticism in the age of reason. The emergence of an historical approach to the Book of Revelation and the subordination of apocalyptic images to the relative clarity of words are two features of the early modern period that characterize the ways in which apocalypse was managed.

"AN IMMEDIATE REVELATION": ANNE HUTCHINSON AND GERRARD WINSTANLEY

An event in 1637 encapsulates the theme of this chapter and the situation of apocalypticism in an age of reason. At the climax of the trial of Anne Hutchinson in New England there is a crucial exchange in which, after a prudent and careful testimony, Hutchinson confesses "speaking what in my conscience I know to be truth." She compares the inner

7 P. Matheson, *The Imaginative World of the Reformation* (Edinburgh: T&T Clark, 2000).

8 Blake, letter to Trusler, 1799; Erdman, 702–03.

intimations of the divine will, which supersede the written command, by comparing her situation with that of Abraham, where the inner intimations of the divine will supersede the written command. She is then further interrogated by the Deputy Governor, John Winthrop:

Mrs. H.	How did Abraham know that it was God that bid him offer his son, being a breach of the sixth commandment?
Dep. Gov.	By an immediate voice.
Mrs. H.	So to me by an immediate revelation.
Dep. Gov.	How! an immediate revelation.
Mrs. H.	By the voice of his own spirit to my soul.

The governor's reaction typifies the fear of those in authority—and indeed the intellectual elite more generally—towards "enthusiasm," which apocalyptic visions and their subversive potential epitomize. Hutchinson's public appeal to the authority of "immediate revelation," based on her conviction of communing with the divine, subordinated the position of institutions like law, religion, and tradition to an inferior status. That proved to be intolerable and opened the door to antinomianism, the tyranny by the "sort of men who follow Anabaptism, Familism, Antinomianism, and other fanatic dreams."[9] John Winthrop thanked divine providence for making Hutchinson "lay open her self and the ground of all these disturbances to be by revelation."[10] She demonstrated what Governor Winthrop considered "bottomlesse, revelations, as came without any word [of Scripture] or without the sense of the word."[11]

The 1630s Antinomian Controversy in New England was the tip of the iceberg of a network of beliefs that reverberated around Old England in the following decades, in which primary place was given to the apocalyptic, viewed in its epistemological—rather than eschatological—sense. For example, the importance of "immediate revelations" was confirmed and justified by Anne Hutchinson's English contemporary Gerrard Winstanley (1609–76), who wrote that "if you say that visions and

[9] Milton, "On Divorce," 14; see also "Antinomianism," in *Encyclopedia of the Bible and Its Reception*, vol. 2 (Berlin: de Gruyter, 2009), 244.

[10] D. Hall, *The Antinomian Controversy, 1636–1638: A Documentary History* (Middletown, CT: Wesleyan University Press, 1968), 337, 341; M. G. Ditmore, "A Prophetess in Her Own Country: An Exegesis of Anne Hutchinson's 'Immediate Revelation,'" *The William and Mary Quarterly* 57 (2000): 349–92.

[11] Michael Winship, *The Times and Trials of Anne Hutchinson: Puritans Divided* (Lawrence: University of Kansas Press, 2005), 111–12.

revelations are ceased ... then you erre mightily."[12] Galatians 1 is alluded to in Anne Hutchinson's similar confession, "after he was pleased to reveal himself to me" (Gal 1:15; see also Isa 49:1).[13] Gerrard Winstanley described his conversion to another kind of Christian profession using language from Gal 1 and Revelation. He wrote of the way in which he was previously a devout Christian "but since God was pleased to reveal his son in me [Gal 1:16] and caused me to speak what I know from an inward light and power within."[14] Thus like Paul he entered on a new phase of life. Paul the apostle had used words from Jeremiah and Isaiah to describe what had happened to him (see Gal 1:15; where Paul alludes to Isa 49:1 and Jer 1:5). Paul's words offered Winstanley a way of articulating his own experience.

Primary among the revelations given to him and determinative for him and his companions embarking on the project for which they are remembered, Winstanley was prompted by divine revelation: "That the earth shall be made a common Treasury of livelihood to whole mankind, without respect of persons." That revelation included also a commission to act, as it had done for the prophets of old (Ezek 2:1–3; Isa 6:5–9; Jer 1:6–10). Winstanley too was impelled by the immediate revelation to "declare it all abroad, which I did obey."[15]

Winstanley begins his treatise *The Saints Paradice* with a quotation from Jer 31:34, "And they shall teach no more every man his neighbour, and every man his brother, saying, Know the Lord: for they shall know me, from the least of them unto the greatest of them, saith the Lord." It is not the verse that mentions the law written on the heart (Jer 31:33). The quotation is put to use as part of Winstanley's challenge to acceptance of "the tradition from the mouths & pen of others." Indeed, the whole treatise is a challenge to those "professors" who may know the Bible and its history well, but "who worshipped a God, but neither knew who he was, nor where he was." What is required is "a teacher within yourselves (which is Spirit)" who "will teach you all things, and bring all things to your remembrance,[16] so that you shall not need to run after

[12] Gerrard Winstanley, "Truth Lifting His Head," in *The Complete Works of Gerrard Winstanley*, eds. T. Corns, A. Hughes, and D. Loewenstein, 2 vols. (Oxford: Oxford University Press, 2009), 1:410.

[13] Ditmore, "A Prophetess in Her Own Country," 383.

[14] Winstanley, "New Law," in *Complete Works*, 1:567.

[15] Winstanley, "A Watch-Word to the City of London," in *Complete Works*, 2:80, noted by Ditmore, "A Prophetess in Her Own Country," 352 n. 5, from the earlier "New Law of Righteousnesse," in *Complete Works*, 2:513.

[16] Echoes here of John 14:26 and 1 Cor 2:14–15, in addition to Jeremiah.

men for instruction." Winstanley denies the authenticity of even "the most glorious Preacher, or professor of literal gospel" who may end up as "the subtilest hypocrites, if they do not know the power of God." It is not the words of the letter of the Bible, for example, adherence to what is "called the ten Commandments," for "it is the manifestations of God in all, or any one of his attributes, shining forth upon, and in his creature."[17]

John Milton believed that "On the introduction of the gospel, or new covenant through faith in Christ, the whole of the preceding covenant, in other words the entire Mosaic law, was abolished. Jer. xxxi.31–33,"[18] and that "we ought to believe what in our conscience we apprehend the Scripture to say, though the visible church with all her doctors gainsay."[19] Among Winstanley's more radical contemporaries were Laurence Clarkson (1615–67) and Abiezer Coppe (1619–72). Coppe was one of the most colorful and controversial figures of his day, and his *A Fiery Flying Roll*—which provoked parliament's censure and later the Blasphemy Act of 1650—suggests that he was more interested in challenging the conventional hierarchy of values as a result of his overwhelming experience of being indwelt by God. Coppe in *A Fiery Flying Roll* writes, "Why should I turn away mine eyes from mine own flesh? Why should I not break bread to the hungry, whoever they be?"[20]

Particularly evident in mid-seventeenth-century radical English nonconformist theology is the assumption that God is present in all, so there is no need to attend to another source of authority. Richard Coppin, a writer who may have influenced Coppe, wrote: "God is all in one; and so in everyone; the same all which is in me, is in thee; the same God which dwels in me dwels in another; and in the same fullness as he is in me, he is in everyone."[21] This is echoed in a reminiscence of Blake by Henry Crabb Robinson. When asked about the divinity of Christ, Blake responded, "he is the only God," but then he added, "And so am

[17] *Complete Works*, 1:313.

[18] *De doctrina Christiana*, 27, in *Complete Prose Works of John Milton*, ed. Don Wolfe (New Haven, CT: Yale University Press, 1953), 6:525–32.

[19] *Treatise of Civil Power*, see C. Hill, *Milton and the English Revolution* (London: Faber, 1977), 314.

[20] *A Fiery Flying Roll*, ii.18. Cf. Coppe's words, "we as lief be dead drunk every day of the weeke, and lye with whores i'the market place, account these as good actions as taking the poore abused, enslaved ploughmans money from him." "Antinomianism," 246.

[21] *Divine Teachings*, quoted in A. L. Morton, *The Everlasting Gospel: A Study in the Sources of William Blake* (London: Lawrence & Wishart, 1958), 58.

I and so are you."[22] It parallels "The worship of God is. Honouring his gifts in other men each according to his genius."[23] Such statements reflect the conviction of the innate character of the individual human person as being indwelt by God.

"JESUS WAS ALL VIRTUE, ACTED FROM IMPULSE, NOT FROM RULES": WILLIAM BLAKE AND THE PRIORITY GIVEN TO "INSPIRATION" OVER "MEMORY"

Blake never used the word "apocalypse" or "apocalyptic" in his writings, but his contemporary S. T. Coleridge, fascinated as he was by what he read of Blake's work, wrote: "A man of Genius ... a mystic emphatically. You perhaps smile at my calling another Poet, a Mystic, but verily I am in the very mire of commonplace common-sense compared with Mr. Blake, apo-, or rather ana-, calyptic Poet, and Painter!"[24] Coleridge's assessment captures not only Blake's indebtedness to the Apocalypse, the Book of Revelation, but the apocalyptic character of his texts and images, whose intent was (to use Blake's words) to cleanse the doors of perception, to lift the veil on the everyday world and see it in the light of eternity. This was the heart of Blake's prophetic vocation.

William Blake was not alone in seeing himself as a prophet. His prophetic contemporaries Richard Brothers (1757–1824) and Joanna Southcott (1750–1814) offer contrasting pictures of apocalypticism at the end of the eighteenth century and the beginning of the nineteenth.[25] Brothers believed that he was the prophet who would be revealed to the Jews as the one to lead them to the land of Israel, and that their government under God would be committed to him as the agent of the everlasting Covenant with David. He expected this event to take place in 1794 or 1798. Later in life Brothers expressed his exasperation that this did not take place as he had expected, and in so doing he manifested a theologically rather conventional acceptance of divine

[22] G. E. Bentley, ed., *Blake Records: Documents (1714–1841) Concerning the Life of William Blake (1757–1827) and His Family*, 2nd ed. (New Haven, CT: Yale University Press, 2004), 696.

[23] *The Marriage of Heaven and Hell*, 22; Erdman, 43; repeated in *Jerusalem*, 91:7; Erdman, 25.

[24] Quoted in Christopher Rowland, *Blake and the Bible* (New Haven, CT: Yale University Press, 2010), 241.

[25] S. Juster, *Doomsayers: Anglo-American Prophecy in the Age of Revolution* (Philadelphia: University of Pennsylvania Press, 2003), 4; C. Garrett, *Respectable Folly: Millenarians in the French Revolution in France and England* (Baltimore: Johns Hopkins University Press, 1973).

inscrutability in respect of the unfulfilled prophetic promises.[26] Brothers's reading of the Scriptures, inspired by revealed knowledge, opened up their true meaning. He it was who expounded the "strange" and "difficult" allusions made by John of the Apocalypse, whose true meaning had been sealed until "the full time" when the appointed person (Brothers) would make known the message. Brothers, like Southcott, turned to Rev 12 and the vision of the "Woman Clothed with the Sun." He saw himself as the man-child, identified with Shiloh, who was to come, identified in the King James Version marginal notes and indeed Jewish interpretation as the Messiah. So whereas Southcott throughout her prophetic activity linked herself with Rev 12 and the "Woman Clothed with the Sun" and finally identified herself with the woman who would give birth to the Messiah, Brothers thought that he was the messianic agent and the *nasi*, the prince, mentioned in the prophecy of Ezekiel (37, 44, 45). His prophecy made quite an impact and was widely distributed, and his followers included figures like the orientalist and Member of Parliament Nathaniel Brassey Halhed (1751–1830). Not surprisingly, his activities attracted the attention of those in power. While he was in an asylum, his prophetic understanding moved from the urgent and violent rhetoric of millennial doom to a more optimistic, utopian vision. The self consciously marginal and displaced prophet of the earlier writings became God's agent; the appointed ruler in a new "Hebrew Constitution" for the Jewish people, a key actor in his own apocalyptic drama; and so one who had a significant part in the fulfillment of the scriptural promises. Some of Brothers's followers later became followers of Southcott.[27]

Joanna Southcott was born in Devon. In 1792 she claimed to have heard the Spirit of God warning her that the coming of Christ was imminent. From the start of her prophetic ministry until her death she claimed to be the "Woman Clothed with the Sun" of Rev 12:1 and the Bride of Christ (Rev 19:7). Indeed, Southcott believed she was called to be the one whose seed was "to bruise the serpent" (Gen 3:15). Southcott's theology was based on her interpretation of the Fall. God's

[26] *Wisdom and Duty* (1805), 35–36; D. Madden, *The Paddington Prophet: Richard Brothers's Journey to Jerusalem* (Manchester: Manchester University Press, 2010).

[27] Jon Mee, *Dangerous Enthusiasm: William Blake and the Culture of Radicalism in the 1790s* (Oxford: Clarendon, 1992); Madden, *The Paddington Prophet*; Philip Lockley, *Visionary Religion and Radicalism in Early Industrial England: From Southcott to Socialism* (Oxford: Oxford University Press, 2013); M. Niblett, *Prophecy and the Politics of Salvation in Late Georgian England: The Theology and Apocalyptic Vision of Joanna Southcott* (London: Tauris, 2015).

purposes in redemption were to be fulfilled in the advent of a second Eve who would fulfill the salvation begun by Christ. Like Richard Brothers, Southcott saw herself as the authentic interpreter of the Scriptures. While she affirmed that all truth was contained in Scripture, she believed that its meaning had not been made clear, and its correct interpretation awaited the right moment in salvation history when its import could be revealed. In this she based herself on biblical precedents like Dan 12:9: "for the words are to remain secret and sealed until the time of the end." While she always considered the Bible to have a unique authority, the relationship between her inspired insights and the Bible itself was often ambiguous. It is nowhere better illuminated than in a remarkable communication received by Southcott in April 1806. It followed a dream, in which she dreamt of binding her personal Bible tight with cord before boiling it, only for it to rise up out of the water. As she came to open the boiled Bible it began to disintegrate, such that she required a *second* Bible in order to read the passages in the Psalms where the first had been opened. The meaning of the dream, revealed by the Spirit, was that the binding of the first Bible referred to the way in which its meaning was hidden—"perfect so is the mystery of my Bible [that] it is a Book bound up from the wisdom of all men." The opening of the boiled Bible at the second Psalm referred to the contemporary visitation of the Spirit to Southcott. The second Bible was none other than "thy Prophecies, which all men will find is the Word of God, like the Bible that is bound up and sealed up." Not only was this new activity of the Spirit necessary "to throw open all mysteries and make every truth clear, before the Bible can be discerned to what its perfect meaning is," but also Southcott's prophecies achieved a status on a par with authoritative Scripture.[28]

Initially, Southcott's activity initiated a John the Baptist–like preparatory movement summoning people to be sealed in imitation of Rev 6–7 in preparation for the imminent judgment of God.[29] In the last year of her life, however, she believed that she was called to actualize her vocation as the "Woman Clothed with the Sun" and literally to give birth to the Messiah. She believed that she was pregnant with the male child whom she identified with the enigmatic Shiloh mentioned in Gen

[28] "Communication Given to Joanna Southcott, April 3rd 1806, on Boiling the Bible," Panacea Society (now known as The Panacea Charitable Trust, Bedford, UK), MSS 114, 212–20.

[29] J. K. Hopkins, *A Woman to Deliver Her People: Joanna Southcott and English Millenarianism in an Era of Revolution* (Austin: University of Texas Press, 1982), 20, 33; Juster, *Doomsayers*, 246–58.

49:10. That conviction had a remarkable effect on her followers. She died supposedly giving birth to her messianic child. Her followers rapidly believed that, as the text of Revelation says, the messianic child was caught up to heaven. After her death there emerged a series of prophetic movements that spanned three continents and persist in different forms to the present day. That set in train a series of interpretations of the child's future coming.

A younger contemporary of Brothers, Southcott, and Blake was John Ward, alias "Zion" Ward (1781–1837). "Zion" was a follower of Joanna Southcott who later believed himself to be her successor. In 1828 he claimed that Joanna had visited him and given instructions to pass on to her surviving followers that they should accept Ward as their leader. Among his several claims, he asserted that God was present in himself, as he identified with the messianic child born to Southcott in 1814. Ward mixed radical politics with millenarianism and theological assertiveness, as Philip Lockley has shown.[30] He spoke at the time of agitations connected with the Reform Bill in 1831, attracting large audiences to the Blackfriars Rotunda theater in London. Ward asserted that the Bible was not history but allegory and a prediction of the coming Messiah, namely himself. His message was universalist and directed to those who "knew no peace," needing to deny "priestcraft" and accept a message that God is love. He rejected heaven as a discrete place, hell and eternal damnation, the virgin birth, and the existence of the historical Jesus. Perhaps not surprisingly, he was imprisoned for blasphemy in 1832.

All these figures offer contrasting, though overlapping, examples of the way in which biblical images and figures could be interpreted and applied to themselves in the context of what they deemed to be a critical moment in history. Ward's claims seem the most extreme, in effect challenging the orthodox Christian understanding of a decisive fulfillment of prophecy in Christ 1800 years before. But all of them take the Bible and apply it in particular ways to themselves. Its contents are seen to have especial significance for the interpretation of their persons.

Several commentators over the years regarded Blake as a paradigmatic apocalyptic enthusiast.[31] In his amusing, satirical work *The Marriage of Heaven and Hell*, we find a challenge to dualism and intriguing echoes of the views of the gnostic Carpocrates of Alexandria according

[30] Lockley, *Visionary Religion and Radicalism in Early Industrial England*.

[31] E.g., Morton, *The Everlasting Gospel*; E. P. Thompson, *Witness against the Beast* (Cambridge: Cambridge University Press, 1993).

to the church father Irenaeus: "they maintain that things are evil or good, simply in virtue of human opinion."[32] Compare "From these contraries spring what the religious call Good & Evil. Good is the passive that obeys Reason[.] Evil is the active springing from Energy. Good is Heaven. Evil is Hell."[33] Here Blake offers his most explicit and succinct statement about Jesus as the pioneer of radical religion who acted "from impulse not from rules":

> The Devil answer'd: ... did he not mock at the sabbath, and so mock the sabbath's God? murder those who were murder'd because of him? turn away the law from the woman taken in adultery? steal the labour of others to support him ? bear false witness when he omitted making a defence before Pilate ? covet when he pray'd for his disciples, and when he bid them shake off the dust off their feet against such as refused to lodge them? I tell you, no virtue can exist without breaking these ten commandments. Jesus was all virtue, acted from impulse, not from rules.[34]

It is the critical moment in a debate that persuades the angel to come over to the side of the devils, given that the Jesus who the angel thought was on his side, as a supporter of the religion of commandments, was in fact an exponent of all that he had been opposing. It is easy to be put off by William Blake's hyperbole here and as a result fail to see that he has put his finger on something very important in the Jesus tradition, even if one cannot go along with the details of his exegesis.

William Blake's view of Jesus as one who "acted from impulse, not from rules" exhibits the same kind of prioritization of the subjective experience as compared with the subservience to authoritative texts or tradition. Though Blake does not use the word "impulse" very frequently, he probably meant "divine impulse." The priority of "intimate impulses" from God is an issue wrestled with by Milton in *Samson Agonistes*: "That what I motion'd was of God; I knew From intimate impulse."[35] It was part of the language of the activity of the Spirit used by the prominent seventeenth-century puritan divine John Owen, who

[32] *Adversus Haereses* 1.25.4.

[33] Blake, *The Marriage of Heaven and Hell*, 3; Erdman, 34.

[34] *The Marriage of Heaven and Hell*, 24; Erdman, 43.

[35] *Samson Agonistes*, 222–23. Cf. "didst plead | Divine impulsion prompting how [he] might'st | Find some occasion to infest [Israel's] foes," ibid., 421–23; cf. 300–20 and R. Grey, *The Complicity of Imagination: The American Renaissance, Contests of Authority, and Seventeenth-Century English Culture* (Cambridge: Cambridge University Press, 1997), 217.

in fact brings together the words used by both Hutchinson and Blake in his phrase "an immediate revelation or divine impulse and impression."[36]

Elsewhere in the Blake corpus the incomplete verses of "The Everlasting Gospel" (ca. 1820) show Blake contrasting "Inspiration" with "Memory," a regular feature of his writing.[37] Jesus lived by the inspiration of the Spirit and exhibited the kind of religious enthusiasm that was despised by the wise of the world:

> Like dr. Priestly & [Sir Isaac del.] Bacon & Newton—
> Poor Spiritual Knowledge is not worth a button! ...
> For thus the Gospel Sir Isaac confutes:
> 'God can only be known by his Attributes;
> And as for the Indwelling of the Holy Ghost
> Or of Christ & his Father, it's all a boast
> And Pride & Vanity of the imagination,
> That disdains to follow this World's Fashion...'[38]

Francis Bacon, John Locke, and Isaac Newton—pioneers of empirical philosophy and modern science—are a trinity of names that are referred to throughout Blake's work as representing that occluded vision which Blake criticizes and demands should be extended by imaginative engagement with the world. In an 1802 letter to his friend Thomas Butts, Blake wrote of "Newton's sleep instead proposing the need for fourfold vision which contrasts with the single vision of the empiricists":

> Now I fourfold vision see
> And a fourfold vision is given to me
> Tis fourfold in my supreme delight
> And threefold in soft Beulah sight
> And twofold Always. May God us keep
> From Single vision & Newtons sleep
> (E722)

The charge often made against enthusiasts is that "they placed exclusive emphasis on the infusion of grace as an emotional experience,

[36] John Owen, *Pneumatologia* (1674), 184; cf. "If by some revelation or impulse of the Spirit" (Sermon 14, "The testimony of the church is not the only nor the chief reason of our believing the scripture to be the word of God").

[37] E.g., in the preface found in some versions of *Milton: A Poem*; Erdman, 95.

[38] "Everlasting Gospel," Erdman, 519; Rowland, *Blake and the Bible*, 192.

so that once they possessed that emotional conviction, no other principle of ethics could be consulted to question it, as they discarded the notions of reason and of ecclesiastic tradition."[39] This is probably an appropriate assessment of the position taken by Anne Hutchinson. On the other hand, Blake argues that there was a balance between reason and Spirit. Thus Blake writes of the inspiration of the "comforter or Desire that Reason may have Ideas to build on."[40] In writing of the Bible he advocates an immediate appeal to the imagination, though reason has its part to play.[41]

Notwithstanding the rhetoric of the simple contrast between "Inspiration" and "Memory," we should not neglect the complexity of Blake's work. It should not surprise us, given that for him "Contraries" are the very stuff of existence ("Without Contraries is no progression").[42] As already mentioned, engagement with his intellectual ancestors' work, by way of critical response and as a stimulus to his own creativity, is central to Blake's genius. That is how the dialectic of "Contraries" works for him.[43] The dialectic between constraint and freedom, Memory and Inspiration, is crucial.

We misunderstand Blake's apocalyptic thought unless we appreciate the importance of the dialectic between desire and reason, Inspiration and Memory, the prolific and the devourer. It is not about Inspiration negating Memory, for it is the very dialectic between the two that allows the motor of inspiration to function. How else can we understand the way in which Blake engages with the Bible, with Milton and many of his predecessors, unless we see someone who allowed "Vision," Inspiration, and Apocalypse the prime place to initiate the process which is then worked and thought about and indeed painted and printed? Blake's revealing words in his *Descriptive Catalogue* show us an artist who accepted the importance of the constraints alongside inspiration: "The great and golden rule of art, as well as of life, is this: That the more distinct, sharp, and wirey the bounding line, the more perfect the work of art ... Leave out this l[i]ne and you leave out life itself; all is chaos again, and the line of the almighty must be drawn out

[39] Gertrude Huehns, quoted in J. Moskal, *Blake, Ethics and Forgiveness* (Tuscaloosa: University of Alabama Press, 1994), 14.

[40] *The Marriage of Heaven and Hell*, 6; Erdman, 35.

[41] Letter to Trusler, 1799; Erdman, 703, quoted above, p. 235 note 8.

[42] *The Marriage of Heaven and Hell*, 3; Erdman, 34.

[43] He mentions as much, e.g., *The Marriage of Heaven and Hell*, 5, 21–22; Erdman, 35, 42; See Bloom,*The Anxiety of Influence*.

upon it before man or beast can exist."[44] There is a constant need to "transcend the closed circle," to borrow the words of John Bowker,[45] so that the "Poetic or Prophetic Character" can break the vise-like grip of "the same dull round."[46]

Jon Mee has rightly pointed out in Blake's later works that there is an emphasis on the need for "the constant casting off of 'Selfhood'… too great a concern for the continuity of the self could only limit the opportunity of enthusiasm to harvest new forms of knowledge and identity."[47] Whereas in 1769 Sir Joshua Reynolds warned aspiring painters that "mere enthusiasm will carry you but a little way," Blake in his annotations to Reynolds's lectures wrote: "Meer Enthusiasm is the All in All!"[48] "What may seem 'meer possibilities,'" as Blake puts it in *Jerusalem*, "to those who enter into them they seem the only substances."[49] Piously regulated "enthusiasm" was acceptable to someone like Coleridge—though he warned against any tendency to subversiveness—whereas for Blake, enthusiasm acted as "a Source of Immortal Joy even in this world" (E705).[50] Blake held a positive view of Teresa of Avila,[51] whereas Coleridge wrote disparagingly of her enthusiasm that "she was a Woman" who was prone to such dangerous ecstasies. What he preferred was a philosophy that never allowed its adherents to forget the world in which they lived.[52]

ECHOING THE NEW TESTAMENT

Such ideas have roots in the Bible, particularly the New Testament.[53] As the messianic agent whose vocation was endorsed by a heavenly vision, Paul therein subordinated all human tradition to that apocalyptic moment (Gal 1:1). Thinking of oneself as a prophet, rather than

44 *Descriptive Catalogue*, 64; Erdman, 550.

45 John Bowker, *Why Religions Matter* (Cambridge: Cambridge University Press, 2015), 162.

46 *There Is No Natural Religion*, Conclusion; Erdman, 3, 2.

47 Mee, *Romanticism, Enthusiasm, and Regulation*, 258–59.

48 Erdman, 645.

49 *Jerusalem*, 13:64–65; Erdman, 158.

50 Mee, *Romanticism, Enthusiasm, and Regulation*, 263.

51 *Jerusalem*, 72:50; Erdman, 227.

52 *The Notebooks of Samuel Taylor Coleridge*, ed. Kathleen Coburn (New York: Pantheon Books; Princeton: Princeton University Press, 1957–2002), 3:3911, 3935; Mee, *Romanticism, Enthusiasm, and Regulation*, 291.

53 Christopher Rowland, *Radical Prophet: The Mystics, Subversives and Visionaries Who Strove for Heaven on Earth* (London: Tauris, 2017).

merely interpreting authoritative prophetic texts, characterizes many aspects of the New Testament. Here, the prophetic is bound up with the messianic and the eschatological, which pervades the New Testament as a whole. It is explicitly found in one of the programmatic biblical texts used by Jesus according to the Gospel of Luke. In Luke 4:18–21, Jesus reportedly applied to himself Isa 61, where the prophet asserts that he himself is anointed to bring good news to the poor and to bind up the broken-hearted. In different ways, Richard Brothers and Joanna Southcott thought of themselves both as authoritative interpreters of biblical prophecy and as having a prophetic vocation, and indeed as agents in the eschatological drama set out in the biblical writings which they saw being fulfilled in their own lives and times. Blake too saw his words as being in continuity with what John saw on Patmos.[54] In one of his early works, *The Marriage of Heaven and Hell*, over the words "As a new heaven is begun, and it is now thirty-three years since its advent,"[55] Blake has written "1790" immediately above the words "new heaven," which probably draws attention to the year 1757, the year of Blake's birth. For Blake, it is the moment when there is opened up "the return of Adam into Paradise"[56] and the eschatological age is initiated. For Jesus, after his call and testing, according to Mark 1:15: "the time (*kairos*) is fulfilled and the kingdom of God has come near" (see also John 13:1; 7:6). Such prophetic actualization is found elsewhere in the pages of the New Testament. Jesus is the apocalyptic Son of Man, John the Baptist is Elijah who is to come (e.g., Matt 11:14; 17:13). Paul believes himself to be the Messiah's agent of salvation to the nations in the last days, and John on Patmos saw in his day the heavens opened just as Ezekiel had seen by the rivers of Babylon. As Paul wrote to the Corinthians, they were the ones on whom the ends of the ages had come (1 Cor 10:11).

One of the most striking passages of all is 1 Cor 2. It is a chapter full of apocalyptic terminology. For example, the language in verse 1 about "mystery" echoes apocalyptic elements such as we find in Dan 2:28 (and elsewhere in the New Testament, e.g., Mark 4:11; Rom 16:25; Eph 1:9; 3:3; Col 1:26; 1 Tim 3:16). In 1 Cor 2:7 we have the sharing of secrets. Paul saw himself and his companions as mediators of divine mysteries (see also 1 Cor 4:1). It is reminiscent of the kind of apocalyptic mediation claimed for the Teacher of Righteousness in the Habakkuk

[54] *Four Zoas Night*, 8–115[111]: 4; Erdman, 385.

[55] *The Marriage of Heaven and Hell*, 3; Erdman, 34, in Copy F (1794), New York, Pierpont Morgan Library.

[56] Ibid.

Commentary from the Dead Sea Scrolls (1QpHab 7) "to whom God made known all the mysteries of the words of his servants the prophets."[57] Receipt of the Spirit enables "immediate revelation," as 1 Cor 2:10–16 shows (see also 1 Cor 3:16; 6:19).

It is the Gospel of John that prioritizes "immediate revelation." The Johannine Jesus is one who seems willing to flout the law, impelled by some higher call. This appeal to a higher authority becomes the criterion for his action, not the Law of Moses. As with Isaiah, who "saw his glory and spoke about him" (John 12:41; see also Isa 6:1, 5), what Jesus has seen and heard about—and from—the Father is the basis of his authority. So John Ashton can write, "these claims are, in the strong sense, apocalyptic."[58] In the Gospel of John, Jesus is depicted as a visionary prophet who sees God and reports what he has seen and heard, and is sent by the Father. In ancient Jewish and early Christian tradition, Isaiah was remembered as faithful to his vision and as showing hidden things before they happened.[59]

The Johannine Jesus is impelled by "divine impulse," a higher authority than the Torah, which is the basis of his actions. Jesus claims to offer revelation of God (in his person) and also revelation about God in his words from what he has seen and heard in heaven (John 12:49–50).[60] Like Jeremiah, Jesus found himself on the brink of death for speaking what he believed to be given to him by God, a message that contrasted starkly with what the prophets and priests of his day asserted (Jer 28 and 29; John 7). The basic issue arises from his claim to a higher authority than the Law of Moses. The Gospel of John is among other things a story about the conflict over different sources of authority. It is a narrative of the power struggle over "immediate revelation" as the basis for Jesus's claim to be God's agent in contrast with those who saw themselves as disciples of Moses (John 9:28).

HERMENEUTICAL REFLECTIONS

We have seen various examples of attempts to negotiate a course between two extremes, one giving greater explicit weight to external

[57] See Matt 11:25–27; 13:35; 1 Cor 14:2; 15:51; Col 1:26, cf. Rom 8:30; 16:25; Eph 1:4; 3:1–13; 1 Pet 1:20; Rev 13:8.

[58] John Ashton, *The Gospel of John and Christian Origins* (Minneapolis, MN: Fortress, 2014), 116, 201–05.

[59] Wisdom of Jesus ben Sirach 48:22, 25; Ascension/Martyrdom of Isaiah 2–3.

[60] See further Ernst Käsemann, *On Being a Disciple of the Crucified Nazarene* (Grand Rapids, MI: Eerdmans, 2010), 138–39.

authorities, and the other to the divinely inspired self, as a source of wisdom as applied to a particular time and place. Blake differed from much Christian mainstream hermeneutics in his conviction that the Spirit is not some privileged property of Christians but that which all humans possess by virtue of their humanity. What one finds in his interpretation is a realistically positive view of humanity. The pouring-out of the Spirit on all flesh is the normative experience of humanity; the problem is raising awareness about the perspective that the Spirit gives, which Blake saw as his vocation to fulfill. One might summarize the heart of his position in the light of First Corinthians as one form of the exploration of the discernment of the mind of Christ, which is not already known in advance by resort to any external authority, the Law written on the heart included. Already in First Corinthians we find Paul asserting the need to follow his example since he had the mind of Christ (1 Cor 2:16; 11:1). There may well have been a development in Paul's understanding of this, from simply the person being "taught by God" (1 Thess 4:9) and 1 Cor 2:10–16 on the one hand, to the more considered and law-friendly Rom 8, where pre-existing rules—albeit written on the heart—are acknowledged, not to mention the appeal to wider practice and custom (1 Cor 14:33).[61]

* * * * * *

Selected Further Reading

Blake, William. *The Complete Poetry and Prose of William Blake*. Edited by David V. Erdman. Berkeley: University of California Press, 1982.

Burdon, Christopher. *The Apocalypse in England: Revelation Unravelling, 1700–1834*. London: Macmillan, 1997.

Kovacs, Judith, and Christopher Rowland. *Revelation: The Apocalypse of Jesus Christ*. Malden, MA: Blackwell, 2004.

Lockley, Philip. *Visionary Religion and Radicalism in Early Industrial England: From Southcott to Socialism*. Oxford: Oxford University Press, 2013.

Mack, Phyllis. *Visionary Women: Ecstatic Prophecy in Seventeenth Century England*. Berkeley: University of California Press, 1992.

Mee, Jon. *Dangerous Enthusiasm: William Blake and the Culture of Radicalism in the 1790s*. Oxford: Clarendon, 1992.

Rowland, Christopher. *Blake and the Bible*. New Haven, CT: Yale University Press, 2010.

Rowland, Christopher. *Christian Origins: The Setting and Character of the Most Important Messianic Sect of Judaism*. Rev. ed. London: SPCK, 2002.

[61] Rowland, *Blake and the Bible*, 201–07.

Rowland, Christopher. *Radical Prophet: The Mystics, Subversives and Visionaries Who Strove for Heaven on Earth.* London: Tauris, 2017.
Winship, Michael P. *The Times and Trials of Anne Hutchinson: Puritans Divided.* Lawrence: University of Kansas Press, 2005.
Winstanley, Gerrard. *The Complete Works of Gerrard Winstanley.* Edited by Thomas N. Corns, Ann Hughes, and David Loewenstein. 2 vols. Oxford: Oxford University Press, 2009.

14 The Formation of Antichrist in Medieval Western Christian Thought

KEVIN L. HUGHES

The figure of Antichrist is one of the most significant (and distinctively Christian) elements of apocalyptic thought, but it seems to have fallen on hard times in modernity, becoming more subject to attention in cheap horror films than in serious religious discourse. Like much of the Christian apocalyptic tradition, Antichrist can seem to be something of an embarrassment among the theologically educated. In our own age, for the most part, Christian theological reflection has abandoned Antichrist to the slings and arrows of outrageous fundamentalisms. Even the Catholic lectionary, which aims to proceed systematically in the course of a year through much of the Old and New Testaments, seems determined to omit key verses referring to the "man of sin, the son of perdition" (2 Thess 2:3–12) or the "beast rising out of the sea" (Rev 13:1–10). Embracing this willful amnesia, however, Christian theologians have turned away from a sophisticated tradition of symbolic theology and a powerful tool for reflection on the "signs of the times," where faith meets history. In our own age of polarization, the rehabilitation of the Antichrist figure may seem like a terrible idea, giving credence to the worst stereotypes of a violent and divisive religion. And yet, retrieved in its proper context, this tradition may help to discern the lines of our divisions with greater wisdom. This essay may be a small step towards that retrieval, but it is one we may see already taken up in some surprising places.

In order to retrieve, one must first remember. Much of this essay will be a sort of *aide-mémoire*, a recovery of the shape and scope of what, for lack of a better term, we may call the "Antichrist tradition," a tradition that begins in fragments. As many will know, Antichrist—with a capital "A"—is not found as such in the Scriptures. Instead, we have in First John "antichrists," named simply as (any of) those who oppose Christ. In early Christian exegesis, this term "antichrist" was borrowed from First John and woven together with other hints and glimpses of apocalyptic enemies in Rev 13, Daniel, the "little apocalypse" of the Synoptic Gospels (Mark 13, Matt 24, Luke 21), and, above all, the second chapter of Second Thessalonians. As I have argued elsewhere at length, it is around the skeletal frame of 2 Thess 2 that the Antichrist tradition takes shape, and its basic outlines remained constant from the early church fathers to the tenth-century "antihagiography" of Adso of Montier-en-Der, to Joachim of Fiore's prophetic resistance, to the *Play of Antichrist* in the fourteenth century and the mutual accusations of Luther and the papacy in the sixteenth century as "Antichrist." But this tradition is not simply a case of univocal repetition; instead, 2 Thess 2 established a narrative frame within which theological, historical, and literary invention could work and play. "Invention" here is meant in its classical sense, for *invenire* more often means "to discover" than "to create." The rich literary and theological tradition of Antichrist can be seen as a series of discoveries of interpretive possibilities, of creative fidelities both to text and history, as Christian thinkers sought to discern the "signs of the times." In our own age, after something of a hiatus, we find thinkers as diverse as Ivan Illich, René Girard, and Giorgio Agamben once again taking up this task of creative fidelity.

THE SKELETON OF ANTICHRIST

The skeletal framing elements of the Antichrist narrative are derived from 2 Thess 2, which I offer here in my own translation of the Latin Vulgate,[1] since the Latin translation of the letter bears the authority over most of the centuries and regions I am describing:

Second Thessalonians 2:1–12

1. And so we implore you, brothers, as to the coming of our Lord Jesus Christ and of our gathering into him,
2. that you be not easily moved from your senses nor be frightened, either by spirit or by word or letter as if from us, as if the Day of the Lord approaches.
3. Let no one persuade you in any way, since unless the desertion [*discessio*] will have come first and the man of sin, the son of perdition will have been revealed,

[1] All translations from the Latin sources are my own unless otherwise indicated.

4. the one who is opposed to and exalted above everything which is called God or which is worshiped, so that he may sit in the temple of God, displaying himself as if he were God.
5. Do you not remember that I was telling you these things while I was still there with you?
6. So now you know what holds him, that he may be revealed in his own time.
7. For now the mystery of iniquity is already at work, such that the one who holds now may hold until he be taken from the midst.[2]
8. Then that iniquitous one will be revealed, whom the Lord Jesus will kill with the breath of his mouth. With the brilliance of his coming, he will destroy
9. him whose coming is by the work of Satan, in all power and with lying signs and prodigies,
10. and with every seduction of iniquity for those who are perishing because they have not accepted the love of truth that they may be saved.
11. so God sent them a work of error that they may believe in the lie
12. such that all those who have not believed in the truth but have consented to iniquity may be judged.

In its context, we can see what Paul seeks to do with this letter. The Thessalonians had grown concerned by Paul's verses in First Thessalonians that had seemed to claim that the end of days will come before those he addresses, who are still alive "until the coming of the Lord" (1 Thess 4:15), have died, and that the end will come "like a thief in the night" (1 Thess 5:2). Paul's task in Second Thessalonians is to reassure his Thessalonian friends that the imminence of the end is not quite so imminent. He lays out a sequence of events that he says he has already taught them, so that they may be better equipped to read the signs and wait in joyful hope.

The sequence of events that Paul describes in 2 Thess 2 may be seen as a kind of distillation of several strands of Hellenistic Jewish apocalyptic thought, from Daniel and elsewhere, and, in its basic narrative shape, it bears remarkable similarities to the synoptic "little apocalypse." But Second Thessalonians bears a distinctively Pauline

[2] The 1969 Stuttgart Edition of the Vulgate reads, "*tantum ut qui tenet nunc donec de medio fiat*," or "such that until the one who now holds is taken from the midst." I have chosen to translate the verse as it appears in D (see below) and in six Vulgate manuscripts: "*tantum ut qui nunc tenet teneat donec de medio fiat.*" This is the version found in most of the commentaries on Second Thessalonians.

theological stamp, and it is this distinctiveness that makes this text so central for the theological tradition that follows from it. Glen Holland's study of Second Thessalonians notes a threefold symbolic progression from the general to the specific.[3]

In its reception, however, this brief summary reminder of the sequence of eschatological events becomes the rough blueprint out of which richer narratives develop. The vagueness of the text's referents creates a wide exegetical space for later interpreters to speculate and so to fill in details. The key inflection points center on certain basic exegetical questions: What is the "desertion" (*discessio*)? Is the "man of sin" truly a single human? A demon? The devil? And how will he work with "power" and with "lying signs"—that is, will he be primarily a false teacher/wonder-worker? Or will he be a political tyrant? What is meant by "the temple of God"? Literally, the Temple in Jerusalem, perhaps rebuilt? Or figuratively, the church? What is it, exactly, that "holds back" the arrival of the "man of sin"? Can we discern the "mystery of iniquity" already at work here and now? These questions each admit of a variety of possible answers.

Indeed, if we were to imagine the range of interpretive possibilities that are generated around these texts, we could almost "map" them along three different axes, three different polarities. Bernard McGinn has put two of these forward,[4] and my own study suggests a third. The first polarity is between deception and dread. Will Antichrist be primarily a deceiver, a "false Christ" who fools people into abandoning Christ and the church and turning to him instead? Or will he be a tyrant, a persecutor of the faith who openly attacks the church and martyrs the faithful? The second polarity is related to the first, internal vs. external. Will Antichrist rise up from within, as perhaps a false teacher or heretic, or false pope? Or will he threaten from without, a foreign enemy or rival religion? Lastly, the third polarity is one of focus: immanent or imminent? Present or to come? Are we now living in the "last days"? Or is the end still at some remove from us? To be more precise, this polarity reflects a sense of where the primary focus of our "apocalyptic concern" should be. For someone like Gregory the Great, the actual end of the ages may be ahead in some unknown time, but we should not let

[3] Glen Holland, *The Tradition that You Received from Us: 2 Thessalonians in the Pauline Tradition*, Hermeneutische Untersuchungen zur Theologie (Tübingen: Mohr Siebeck, 1988), 112.

[4] Bernard McGinn, *Antichrist: Two Thousand Years of the Human Fascination with Evil* (New York: HarperSanFrancisco, 1994), 1–6.

speculation about the coming Antichrist prevent us from seeing the presence of his body already, corporately, socially, embedded among us. Indeed, as Augustine said, "There are many Antichrists, and everyone must ask himself whether he be such."[5] While contemporary interpreters as diverse as D. H. Lawrence and McGinn tend to reduce the theological weight of Antichrist into this question of immanent evil, I contend that an important facet of Antichrist's symbolic power is this "sense of an ending," the sense that present choices, present failures, are connected intimately, corporally, to an uncertain future. If Antichrist symbolically embodies human evil, it is always an evil that is in process, in motion in time and history.

So, taken all together, what we see in the Antichrist tradition is a kind of three-dimensional ellipsoid field of possibilities, of various combinations of emphases. In the early patristic sources, these would seem to be just one-off possibilities. But the achievement of the exegetical traditions that really constitute the Antichrist tradition in the Western churches is that these three axes are brought into living relation with each other: it becomes very difficult to make a particular claim about Antichrist without bringing into relation the other interpretive possibilities. These various polarities, in other words, are in tension, and the tension is mutually corrective. What we see in the case of this tradition of thinking about Antichrist is a rich and sophisticated symbolic matrix through which one can ponder the nature of human evil and of human destiny in time. Paul Ricoeur wrote a whole book premised on the idea that "the symbol gives rise to thought."[6] What we see in this Antichrist tradition is a kind of *symbolic rationality*, articulated in and through, not over against, the apocalyptic texts of Scripture. It is in this way an inquiry into the nature of human evil, the signs of the times, and a discerning of the "powers of this present age" (Eph 1:21). In practice, as exegetes sought to fill the gaps in the narrative, their answers began to constellate into two distinct but not entirely separate theological traditions of interpretation.

The first, which I have earlier called "apocalyptic realism," tends to be future-oriented and to center upon the historical character of the events of the end. In early Christian exegesis, the major figures in the development of this apocalyptic realist tradition are Ambrosiaster,[7]

[5] Augustine, *Homilies on 1 John*, 3:4, PL 34, 2000.

[6] Paul Ricoeur, *The Symbolism of Evil*, trans. Emerson Buchanan (Boston: Beacon, 1969).

[7] For an introduction to Ambrosiaster and a discussion of the *status quaestionis* of the author's identity, method, and theologial interest, see Theodore S. de Bruyne, Stephen A. Cooper, and David G. Hunter, Introduction to *Ambrosiaster's Commentary on the*

Theodore of Mopsuestia, Pelagius, and Jerome. Ambrosiaster's and Theodore's commentaries were received in the later tradition under the authoritative name of "Ambrose," and Jerome and Pelagius are both received as "Jerome," and so all are treated as significant authorities.[8] The exegetical energy in these commentaries grapples with, for example, whether the Roman Empire is the "restraining force" that holds back the eschatological end, or whether perhaps it is the church, or, even more generally, the decree of divine providence itself. Similarly, this tradition is concerned to distinguish this apparently miraculous "man of sin" from the fully human, fully divine Son, the incarnate Christ. Here, it is christologically important that the "man of sin" is just a man, because the devil is not capable of any kind of "incarnation." Antichrist cannot in any real sense be "equal and opposite" to Christ, but always a lesser "cheap imitation." As I have said elsewhere, "the distinctive feature of the apocalyptic realist strain is the vision of Antichrist as the 'one who is coming', an individual person who will perform specific sorts of actions in the future, to the detriment of the Church."[9] Antichrist may be prefigured in historical characters such as Simon Magus in the Book of Acts or the Emperor Nero, but these are just shadows of a future historical person who will be the Final Enemy.

The second exegetical tradition I have called the "Latin spiritual interpretation." It finds its roots in the outcast Donatist exegete Tyconius, and it is taken up and developed primarily by Augustine and Gregory the Great. None of these thinkers denied the historicity of that future coming individual, Antichrist, nor did they dispute the rough sequence of events laid out in 2 Thess 2. Indeed, both Tyconius and Gregory the Great seemed quite convinced that the eschatological end was near. Augustine, while remarkably reticent to speculate on eschatology, never disputes the eschatological history sketched in 2 Thess 2. What makes the tradition they generated distinct is not, then, what they deny, but where they expand the interpretation. None of these figures devotes much—if any—exegetical attention to the kinds of questions in the apocalyptic realist tradition. Instead, Tyconius's *Book of Rules* sees 2 Thess 2 as the interpretive key, not only to the future eschatological events, but also to the entire history of the church.

Pauline Epistles: Romans, trans. Theodore S. de Bruyne, Writings from the Greco-Roman World 41 (Atlanta: Society of Biblical Literature, 2017).

[8] See Kevin L. Hughes, *Constructing Antichrist: Paul, Biblical Commentary, and the Development of Doctrine in the Early Middle Ages* (Washington, DC: Catholic University of America Press, 2005), chap. 2, for deeper discussion of each source.

[9] Ibid., 81.

Tyconius used 2 Thess 2 as a lens through which, in the history of the church, a corporate, social "body of Antichrist" is revealed to dwell within and alongside the Body of Christ that is the church itself. The history of the church, the *mysterium salutis*, the mystery of salvation in the world, is, at one and the same time, the history of the *mysterium iniquitatis*, the "mystery of iniquity already at work" (2 Thess 2:7). The "desertion" (*discessio*) (2 Thess 2:3) is a hinge-point in history, when the bodies of Christ and Antichrist will be separated out, paving the way for the culminating eschatological conflict. Tyconius's exegesis of Second Thessalonians lies at the root of Augustine's ecclesiology of the *corpus permixtum*, the mixed body of saved and reprobate that are to be found in the church this side of the end. When First John says, "There are many antichrists," Augustine adds, "Everyone must ask whether he be such."[10] Gregory the Great then picks up this legacy with his characteristic rhetorical flair, inviting his congregation to aim to discern the limbs and bowels of the body of Antichrist in their own midst, and, indeed, in their own hearts.[11] The Latin spiritual tradition found in these three voices extends the reach of Antichrist back from the eschatological end into the present and past, and thus makes the figure of Antichrist a profound pastoral and spiritual tool for discerning and diagnosing the "signs of the times" as partial participations in the final coming eschatological crisis. McGinn has distinguished between an apocalyptic "predictive imminence"—the sense that we see the signs of the actual end unfolding before us and set a date (the year 1000, for instance) for its arrival—and a "psychological imminence," the lived sense, even (perhaps especially) in the absence of a concrete date and timeline, that our present actions participate in an apocalyptic crisis, a decision for or against Christ, anticipating an end that can come at any time "like a thief in the night."[12] The Latin spiritual interpretive tradition becomes the vessel and expression of this vivid psychological imminence, a looming presence of Antichrist in the lived experience of the present church and of every believer. All the faithful could feel themselves living in the (perhaps long) shadow of the End—an apocalyptic sensibility that persists in medieval culture precisely because it is not tied to any particular prediction of its coming.

[10] Augustine, *Homilies on 1 John*, 3:4, PL 34, 2000.

[11] Gregory, *Moralia in Iob* 34.4.8, CCSL 143B (Turnhout: Brepols, 1985).

[12] Bernard McGinn, "The End of the World and the Beginning of Christendom," in *Apocalypse Theory and the Ends of the World*, ed. Malcolm Bull (Oxford: Blackwell, 1995), 63.

ANTICHRIST AND HIS BODY IN THE MIDDLE AGES

Beginning in the Carolingian era (ca. 800 CE), medieval Christian thinkers came to understand themselves as living in a different age from the church fathers who preceded them. Figures such as Charlemagne's court scholar Alcuin of York considered it their task to retrieve, preserve, and integrate the teachings of the fathers into a program of Christian education. The parallel traditions of interpretation of Antichrist were carried into this project, and scholars such as Rabanus Maurus and Haimo of Auxerre sought to integrate these traditions into one. The resulting synthesis remained fascinated with the particulars of the literal and historical traditions of interpretation, wondering when Antichrist would arrive and how they would know if and when he did. Indeed, some have argued that the intensity of apocalyptic concern was heightened in the Carolingian epoch by the speculation that Charlemagne himself might be the apocalyptic "Last World Emperor" whose reign would precede the arrival of Antichrist and the End. If reckoned by the older *anno mundi* calendar, dating from the supposed date of creation, the crowning of Charlemagne on Christmas Day, 800, was on the first day of the year AM 6000, anticipating the approaching sabbath of the "world-week." None of the scholarly Carolingian discussions of Antichrist care to speculate in specific terms about the date of his coming, but they do remain fascinated with the possible permutations of that event. On the whole, their reflection on the events of the apocalyptic end remain somewhat detached and analytical, a sifting of the patristic sources for the best theological reading of the Adversary and his arrival. But into the midst of this apocalyptic realist interpretation, most Carolingian exegetes fold significant elements of the Latin spiritual interpretation, bringing them together in a new kind of synthesis, reflecting both Antichrist and his body.

For Rabanus Maurus (780–856)[13], for example, the Antichrist to come will be a tyrannical attacker from without—a rival king who will break with the (now restored?) empire and persecute the church. But more than this Rabanus does not really say. For Rabanus, Antichrist's arrival is restrained by nothing other than the decree of divine providence that he come at the proper time. The Irish monk Sedulius Scotus (ca. 800–74),[14] on the other hand, is quite confident that "what

[13] Rabanus Maurus, *Expositio in epistolam secundam ad thessalonicenses*. PL 112, 565–80.

[14] Sedulius Scotus, *Collectanea in epistulam secundam ad Thessalonicenses*, PL 103, 221–24.

restrains" the coming of Antichrist is the "king of the Romans" (*rex Romanorum*), Charlemagne, and his heirs. For Sedulius, Antichrist's primary work will be an attempt to rebuild the temple in Jerusalem and to reestablish the ceremonial Jewish law. But both scholars agree that Antichrist's path to the persecution and/or deception of the church will be eased by the internal, ecclesial presence of the body of Antichrist as members of the church slide into heresy and apostasy in the great "falling away" (*discessio*).

Haimo of Auxerre (ca. 790–865), a contemporary of Rabanus and Sedulius, appears to be an exception to the fusion of realist and spiritual traditions. Haimo, truly one of the most extraordinary and understudied scholars of the Carolingian age, devotes his commentary on Second Thessalonians to a fascinating interpretation of the apocalyptic realist tradition with seemingly no attention to the body of Antichrist.[15] This commentary will serve, as we will see below, as an important source for the popular letter "On the Origin and Time of Antichrist," written by Adso of Montier-en-Der to the Saxon queen Gerberga as the year 1000 loomed dangerously close. But, among the ninth-century exegetes, Haimo offers a distinctive and illuminating realist interpretation of the apocalyptic events of the end. His "biography" of Antichrist reads like an epitome of the realist tradition that precedes him: Antichrist will be the "man of sin" because, although only a man, he will be the "font of all sinners."[16] He is called the "son of perdition" because he is the devil's son "by imitation but not by nature."[17] His deepest sin, in imitation of Lucifer, will be to "exalt himself over all other divine powers, whether pagan or Christian, elevating himself above the Trinity itself." The apex of his blasphemy is his session in the "temple of God," and here Haimo allows both possibilities: either he will be a Jew born of the tribe of Dan, come to Jerusalem claiming to be the Messiah, and rebuild the Temple, or he will take his place in the church, as if he himself were God.

[15] Haimo's commentary is attributed in the PL to Haimo of Halberstadt, but twentieth- and twenty-first-century scholarship has challenged this attribution consistently. Haimo of Auxerre [Haimo of Halberstadt], *Expositio in epistolam secundam ad Thessalonicenses*, PL 117, 765–84. For a longer discussion of Haimo, see Hughes, *Constructing Antichrist*, chap. 4, and Dominique Iogna-Prat, Colette Jeudy, and Guy Lobrichon, *L'École carolingienne d'Auxerre: de Muretach à Remi 830–908* (Paris: Beauchesne, 1991).

[16] PL 117, 779D.

[17] Ibid.

As for "what restrains," Haimo repeats the traditional understanding that it is the Roman Empire. However, Haimo does not believe, like nearly all of his contemporaries, that the Roman *imperium* has been translated to the Carolingian dynasty; instead, he says, ". . . the Lord will not come in judgment before the defection of the human kingdoms, *which we already see fulfilled*, and the appearance in the world of Antichrist, who will kill the witnesses of Christ."[18] In Haimo's view, the defection of the nations from the Roman Empire has already occurred, and this leaves him with an apocalyptic problem: Why has Antichrist not yet come? He resolves the problem this way: "Indeed, when the apostle says, 'then that perverse one will be revealed after the Roman Empire will have been destroyed, he should not be understood to have said that [Antichrist] will come immediately, but rather that first the empire will be destroyed and then Antichrist will come, at a time chosen by God."[19] Haimo here envisions himself and the church living in the "time in between." The "restraining force" of the Roman Empire is gone, but Antichrist has not yet come. For Haimo, then, what we call the "Middle Ages" is indeed in the middle, suspended between two apocalyptic signs. One has long passed, and the second is still coming. This entire "middle age" is for Haimo an eschatological age, an age in which we watch and wait. His discussion of the "career" of Antichrist is thus a way of equipping the church to be attentive for his arrival, so that the faithful may not be deceived by his "lying signs and prodigies" (2 Thess 2:9). There seems to be no room in Haimo's interpretation of Second Thessalonians for the Tyconian body of Antichrist; instead, his eyes seem fixed looking outward to the horizon for the first glimpse of the man of sin.

And yet this impression may deceive. Haimo of Auxerre also composed an influential commentary on the Apocalypse of John, and his entire reading of this work is through the Latin spiritual lens of Tyconius, Augustine, and Gregory. In this text, Haimo usually refers to "Antichrist and his members" as one reality, to include the "heretics and sons of pride within the church."[20] For Haimo, the Apocalypse is the book of the church, the book best read allegorically for the dynamics of self-deception and failure. The Apocalypse is therefore the natural complement and supplement to Paul's apocalyptic sketch in 2 Thess 2. By separating out the elements of the apocalyptic tradition according to

[18] Ibid., 780C, italics mine.
[19] Ibid., 781C.
[20] Haimo, *Expositio in Apocalypsim*, PL 117, 1092D.

the biblical book, Haimo has given more, rather than less, impetus to the fusion of the realist and spiritual readings, or, at least, to their complementarity. Paul's historical schema equips the faithful to look to the horizon for the approach of the apocalyptic Adversary. In the meantime, the reading of the Apocalypse nourishes the self-reflection of the church on its own conduct and failures in an apocalyptic key. The Apocalypse and the apostle Paul both become essential to the identification of Antichrist and his body.

Both of Haimo's commentaries were quite popular in the years that follow, largely because of their disciplined focus and relentless detail. They were often copied and so survive in numerous manuscripts. Haimo's depiction of Antichrist in Second Thessalonians became a major source for Peter Lombard's own commentary, and exerted significant influence well into the scholastic era in the twelfth and thirteenth centuries. One instance of its influence merits particular attention: as mentioned above, Haimo's interpretation was taken up as the key source for Adso of Montier-en-Der's "anti-hagiography" of Antichrist, which we usually call "On the Origin and Time of Antichrist," written sometime around 950.[21] Daniel Verhelst has identified some 170 surviving manuscripts of the text in various redactions around Europe, suggesting that it was an immensely popular text.[22] Adso's text is written as a letter of consolation to the Ottonian queen Gerberga of Saxony, assuaging her fears of Antichrist with the assurance that his coming is forestalled as long as the Ottonian dynasty lasts. Adso adopts elements of the genre of hagiography in his text, stood on their head to identify the "man of sin" and not the saint, but he relies heavily on Haimo's summary of the "facts" of Antichrist's life. But Adso clearly departs from Haimo's belief that the Roman Empire had already fallen. Instead, he asserts (to the Ottonian queen!) that the Ottonian dynasty carries forward the dignity and authority of Rome, and thus Antichrist is kept at bay. He also emphasizes the claim he finds in Haimo that Antichrist will be born "a Jew of the tribe of Dan" in Babylon, and thus not in Europe, perhaps to remove the suspicion that more local rivals to Ottonian rule might themselves be the apocalyptic Adversary himself.

21 *Adso Dervensis, De ortu et tempore Antichristi*, ed. Daniel Verhelst, CCCM 45 (Turnhout: Brepols, 1976). English translation in Bernard McGinn, *Apocalyptic Spirituality*, Classics of Western Spirituality (Mahwah, NJ: Paulist, 1979), 89–96.

22 Daniel Verhelst, "Adso of Montier-en-Der and the Fear of the Apocalyptic Year 1000," in *The Apocalyptic Year 1000: Religious Expectation and Social Change, 950–1050*, eds. Richard Landes, Andrew Gow, and David C. Van Meter (New York: Oxford University Press, 2003), 81–92.

What makes this text of Adso so interesting, then, is that his purpose is clearly conservative: he aims to tamp down apocalyptic anxieties about Antichrist's arrival by placing him at somewhat a safe distance, both chronologically and geographically. But, while aiming to be conservative, Adso cannot help but tie the apocalyptic events of Antichrist to the somewhat fragile future of the Ottonian Franks. No effort here seems to be made to "spiritualize" Antichrist in a way that would draw attention away from the apocalyptic crisis, nor even to exploit Haimo's own indefinite deferral of Antichrist's arrival into some future moment known to providence alone. Indeed, the Latin spiritual Antichrist tradition makes no appearance at all. Why this is so, one can only speculate. Perhaps, as the year 1000 approached, the "imaginary"—the pre-reflective assumptions of a culture about how the world fits together and what is possible within it[23]—did not permit a broader, less clearly pinned-down mode of speculation that marked the works of a century before.

But of course, the year 1000 arrived and passed without the arrival of Antichrist. In the eleventh and twelfth centuries, the tactful and thorough exegesis of the Carolingians was taken up by early scholastic authors and adapted to a form suited to instruction in the nascent universities and *studia* throughout Europe. The Carolingians' fusion of the realist and spiritual traditions thus became the standard account of Antichrist in the scholastic period, even while the scholastic disposition seemed less inclined to focus upon Antichrist and the world-historical end as a major theological locus. Theological attention to "Last Things" began to focus more on personal eschatology—on death, judgment, heaven, and hell—and so the Adversary seemed to recede from scholarly attention.[24]

Until, that is, the writings of the eccentric apocalyptic prophet Joachim of Fiore (ca. 1135–1202) were taken up in a bitter argument within the new and growing Franciscan order about the nature of their vocation. In a wide array of writings, Joachim had envisioned an apocalyptic theology of history in which the complex, repeating, and interlocking patterns of scriptural history foretold of the church's own historical growth and eschatological destiny. For Joachim, history had a Trinitarian structure, with three overlapping "ages" or *status* within history's movement. The *status* of the Father

[23] Charles Taylor, *Modern Social Imaginaries* (Durham, NC: Duke University Press, 2003), chap. 2.

[24] Hughes, *Constructing Antichrist*, chap. 5.

> ... was begun from Adam, bore fruit from Abraham, and was consummated in Christ. The second [*status*, the age of the Son] was begun from Ozias, bore fruit from Zachary, the father of John the Baptist, and will have consummation in these times. The third [*status*, of the Holy Spirit] had its beginning from Saint Benedict, began to bear its fruit in the twenty-second generation from that saint, and will be consummated in the consummation of the world.[25]

Joachim had envisioned that the third *status* would be ushered in and brought to fruition by two orders of "spiritual men," possessed of special gifts of *intellectus spiritualis*, of spiritual understanding of the Scriptures. Many members of the young Franciscan movement came to believe that they were one of the orders prophesied by Joachim, making their evangelical preaching and form of life of apocalyptic significance. Joachim's writings thus became increasingly controversial as the thirteenth century progressed. Those who would later be known as "spiritual Franciscans" found in Joachim both promise and a blueprint for a revolutionary spiritual life of the church as, they believed, the apocalyptic clock ticked closer to the end.[26] Those who opposed the Franciscans, in turn, speculated whether the arrival of these radicals was itself a sign of Antichrist in the last days.[27]

Joachim of Fiore does not point explicitly to Augustine or Tyconius or Gregory, but he includes his own variation on the "body of Antichrist" within the history of the church. In his dramatic illustrated figure of the dragon of the Apocalypse, Joachim explained:

> John and John's Master [Christ] say many Antichrists will come. Paul, on the other hand, foretells that there will be one. Just as many holy kings, priests and prophets went before Christ who was king, priest, and prophet, so likewise many unholy kings, false prophets, and antichrists will go before the one Antichrist who will pretend that he is a king, a priest, and a prophet.[28]

25 Joachim of Fiore, *Liber de Concordia Noui ac Veteris Testamenti* 4.2.1, ed. and trans. E. Randolph Daniel, Transactions of the American Philosophical Society 73, part 8 (Philadelphia: American Philosophical Society, 1973). Quoted in Bernard McGinn, *The Calabrian Abbot: Joachim of Fiore in the History of Western Christian Thought* (New York: Macmillan, 1985), 187.

26 David Burr, *The Spiritual Franciscans: From Protest to Persecution in the Century after Saint Francis* (University Park: Pennsylvania State University Press, 2001).

27 Penn R. Szittya, *The Antifraternal Tradition in Medieval Literature* (Princeton, NJ: Princeton University Press, 2014).

28 Leone Tondelli, Marjorie Reeves, and Beatrice Hirsch-Reich, eds., *Il libro delle figure dell'abate Gioachino da Fiore*, 2 vols. (Turin: Società Editrice Internazionale, 1953), Tavola 14. Translation from McGinn, *Apocalyptic Spirituality*, 139.

The dragon figure is shown with seven heads, each labeled for one of the "many antichrists" in salvation history: Herod, Nero, Constantius, Muhammad, Mesemoth, Saladin, and "the seventh king, who is properly called Antichrist, although there will be another like him, no less evil, symbolized by the tail."[29] Joachim called this "tail" the "greatest Antichrist," *maximus Antichristus*, and he seems to have believed that he had been born and was alive in the world.

It would take too long to detail all the ways in which this vibrant Joachimist apocalyptic thought was taken up by the Franciscans. I will offer just one example, and a moderate one: that of St. Bonaventure of Bagnoregio, the so-called second founder of the Franciscan order. Bonaventure became the leader, the Minister General, of his community in 1257. In part, he was elected because of his even-handed moderation. Bonaventure was no radical. And yet we can see him wrestling with the influence of Joachim, aiming to bring it into harmony with the exegetical tradition that preceded any Joachimist controversy.

Bonaventure's election took place in the wake of scandal. The Franciscan Gerard of Borgo San Donnino had written and published a tract in 1254 called the *Introduction to the Eternal Evangel*, which argued that, in the coming *status* of the Spirit, the writings of Joachim would be elevated to the status of Scripture, and the spiritual men of the Franciscan movement were destined to be the leaders in a new era of the church. This work was quickly condemned, and all copies of the book were ordered to be burned. The Minister General at the time was John of Parma, whose sympathies lay with the Joachimist movement, if not fully with Gerard. But his association with Gerard made it impossible for him to serve his order, so he resigned, recommending Bonaventure of Bagnoregio as his replacement. Bonaventure was an ideal candidate, because he shared John's passion for the Franciscan charism, but he was also intelligent and even-handed in his judgment. He was an incepted member of the theology faculty at the University of Paris, so he had mastered the dialectical skills of the theologian, but he was also passionately devoted to Francis and his vision of evangelical poverty. He served as Minister General for sixteen years.

Bonaventure's final and incomplete theological work was a series of lectures delivered to the Franciscan students and masters studying in Paris in 1273. Using the six days of creation from Gen 1 as his frame, Bonaventure delivered a synthetic vision of human understanding,

[29] McGinn, *Apocalyptic Spirituality*, 136.

beginning with "natural understanding" and ascending through the understanding with the light of faith, the light of Scripture, contemplation, prophecy, rapture, and glory. He was forced to break off his lectures abruptly after the fourth vision, of contemplation, since he had been made Cardinal Archbishop of Albano and summoned to Lyons to organize the Second Council called there for 1274. Bonaventure died in Lyons in 1274, and so the *Collations on the Hexaemeron* remained unfinished. But the twenty-three conferences he gave remain a fascinating critical and integrative vision of Franciscan scholastic and spiritual insight, including treatment of Antichrist and the apocalyptic end. In them we can see Bonaventure working to moderate, but still appreciate, the insights of Joachim and his Franciscan interpreters, bringing them into harmony with the longer exegetical tradition we have already studied.[30]

Bonaventure's apocalyptic thought first appears in the third vision, that of "understanding instructed by the Scriptures." He divides scriptural understanding into three separate categories. First, the traditional four senses of Scripture—literal, allegorical, moral, and anagogical—provide a basic understanding of the text. Building on that foundation, the second dimension of scriptural understanding explores the twelve mysteries of salvation that chart the development of salvation history from Genesis to Revelation. They fall into four groups of three. In the "time of nature" (A), the three mysteries are the creation (A1—Gen 1 and 2), the purgation of crimes (A2—Noah and the flood), and the call of the patriarchs (A3—Abraham). In the "time of the law" (B), the three mysteries are the promulgation of the law (B1—in Exodus, Leviticus, Deuteronomy, and Numbers), the conquering of enemies (B2—Joshua), and the advancement of judges (B3—Judges and Ruth). In the time of prophecy (C), the three mysteries are the anointing of kings (C1—1 and 2 Samuel), the revelations of the prophets (C2—Psalms and prophets), and the restoration of princes and priests (C3—Ezra, Nehemiah, Maccabees). Lastly, the three mysteries in the "time of grace" (D) are the redemption of humanity (D1—the Gospels), the diffusion of spiritual gifts (D2—Acts and epistles), and the unsealing of the Scriptures (D3—Apocalypse).

[30] Bonaventure, *Collationes in Hexaemeron*, in *Opera omnia*, vol. 5 (Quarrachi: Ex typographia Collegii S. Bonaventurae, 1887), 328–455. I have used the new translation: Bonaventure, *Collations on the Hexaemeron*, trans. Jay M. Hammond (St. Bonaventure, NY: Franciscan Institute Publications, 2018).

Within each of these mysteries, Bonaventure finds four sacramental figures of Christ. For example, in the promulgation of the law (B1), sacramental figures of Christ are the staff of Moses, the Ark of the Covenant, the adornment of the High Priest, and the rite of sacrifice. Each of these dimensions of the story prefigures Christ's redemptive action. Clearly, to lay out the four figures of Christ for each of the twelve mysteries would be overwhelming to the reader, so hopefully this will suffice. For our purposes, what is most important is that, within each of the twelve mysteries in the Scriptures, there is found a figure of Antichrist as well, a kind of "anti-sacramental" figure. Only one figure of Antichrist is offered per mystery, not four as there are for Christ. To follow the same example, in the mystery of the promulgation of the law (B1), Antichrist is figured by the flawed prophet Balaam, "who gave the worst advice, was an idolater, and, although he would say many good things, nevertheless he built altars and sought divinations." The intricacy of Bonaventure's layered patterns can be overwhelming, but the point is clear: Bonaventure aims to root reflection on Antichrist within the scriptural witness, from the beginning of salvation history. He sets aside, as a distinct form of scriptural understanding, this typological understanding of the figures of Antichrist present throughout salvation history, from creation to the end. To recognize Antichrist in these figures is to come to know that he will be (A1) most unclean, (A2) most proud, (A3) most deceitful, (B1) the worst idolater, (B2) most greedy, (B3) most cruel, (C1) magnificent on the outside and blasphemous against the people of God, (C2) intellectually astute, (C3) a destroyer of gospel law and killer of martyrs, (D1) most malicious, (D2) the greatest liar, and (D3) consummate in all evil. For Bonaventure, then, it is not just a matter of seeing Antichrist present in his body in the history of salvation. Even more, it is a matter of learning to recognize his traits through the study of the Scriptures. In this way, Bonaventure integrates the Latin spiritual tradition of Tyconius, Augustine, and Gregory with the "heads of Antichrist" in Joachim, drawing the latter into the bounds of Scripture and bringing both the Tyconian and the Joachimist traditions into the service of educating the faithful.

Bonaventure's *Collations* bear witness to the ongoing power of the dynamic relationship between the Latin spiritual and the realist traditions, but also to their subtle transformation to fit the needs of a new age. For Bonaventure, the scriptural figures of Antichrist sharpen the awareness of the faithful to the mystery of iniquity at work in their midst, teaching them what to guard against whenever Antichrist may arise. If the very structure of Scripture gives abundant testimony to the mystery of salvation achieved in Christ, it also bears within it the glimpses of that other, iniquitous mystery, always already at work to resist Christ.

CODA AND CONCLUSION: ANTICHRIST AND HIS BODY IN CONTEMPORARY REFLECTION

Thus far we have traced the emergence of a tradition of interpretation of the figure of Antichrist. Paul's Second Letter to the Thessalonians provided the skeletal frame for reflection, and around this frame, images of Antichrist took shape along three thematic axes: deception/dread, internal/external, and immanent/imminent. Early exegetes plotting their interpretations around these three axes tended to constellate into two clusters or families of interpretations, which I have referred to as the apocalyptic realist and Latin spiritual traditions. The achievement of early medieval exegesis was to interweave these traditions in creative and adaptive ways, keeping the full range of interpretive possibilities open for thought. Antichrist worked both internally and externally. Antichrist was both present (in his members) and to come. As we see in Bonaventure, that tradition proved adaptive enough to absorb and refine the revolutionary ideas of Joachim of Fiore. This portrait of Antichrist, against the backdrop of salvation history and its eschatological end, provided a fruitful lens through which to consider the hidden movement of human history and the full range of human evil. This tradition survived into the Reformation era; while Antichrist occasionally seemed to be little more than a rhetorical brickbat lobbed across the divide between Protestant and Catholic, one can also see in the Reformed critique of Catholicism the enduring marks of the medieval Antichrist tradition. For Luther, the Catholic Church itself had been the locus of the "desertion" (*discessio*), and the Pope the Antichrist: "For who is the man of sin and the son of perdition, but he who with his doctrines and his laws increases the sin and perdition of souls in the church; while sitting in the church as if he were God? All this the papal tyranny has fulfilled, and more than fulfilled, these many centuries."[31] And yet the Reformation marks the beginning of a decline in the symbolic power of Antichrist. As McGinn suggests, conflict in the Reformation led to the univocal identification of Antichrist as the external opponent, the "them" to our "us," and this was true of

[31] Martin Luther, "The Babylonian Captivity of the Church," in *Three Treatises*, trans. Charles M. Jacobs (Philadelphia: Fortress, 1970), 3.31.

Catholic invocations of Antichrist as much as Protestant ones. This "symbolic flattening of Antichrist"[32] into polarized scapegoating essentially sapped this pluripotent theological symbol of its power, because it upset the balance between internal and external that has always lain at its heart.

How interesting it is, then, to see in recent years, at and after the turn of the millennium, a subtle return to the Antichrist tradition. Antichrist's return has appeared at the margins of theological inquiry, among those often considered idiosyncratic or outsiders. For example, Antichrist and the *mysterium iniquitatis* lie at the center of historian and theologian Ivan Illich's assessment of modernity itself as the "corruption of Christianity."[33] Similarly, one can find a fundamental turn to the apocalyptic in the later works of René Girard, especially his last, *Battling to the End*.[34]

A fascinating and recent intervention by Giorgio Agamben is the first explicitly to call to mind the Tyconian tradition in his reflection on the relationship between spiritual and temporal power.[35] Agamben's ongoing reflection on the legitimacy of institutional power over many books lies in the background, but his short reflection was provoked by Pope Benedict XVI's decision to abdicate and step away from the power of the papacy, much to the surprise of all. Agamben sees in Benedict echoes of Tyconius, where the *discessio* of Second Thessalonians represents the departure of the faithful church from the "dark church" that is a perversion or distortion of the spiritual power of the gospel. In forgetting the eschatological tension of the "corpus permixtum," the Body of Christ living intimately alongside the body of Antichrist, the church makes itself the instrument or pawn of temporal political power: "By renouncing every eschatological experience of its own historical action, the church ... has itself created the specter of the *mysterium iniquitatis*. If it wants to free itself of this specter, it is necessary for it to find again the eschatological experience of its historical action—as a drama

32 McGinn, *Antichrist*, 248.

33 David Cayley, *The Rivers North of the Future: The Testament of Ivan Illich as Told to David Cayley* (Toronto: House of Anansi, 2005). See also Charles Taylor, *A Secular Age* (Cambridge, MA: Harvard University Press, 2007), 737–44.

34 René Girard, *Battling to the End: Conversations with Benoît Chantre*, trans. Mary Baker (East Lansing: Michigan State University Press, 2010). On Illich and Girard as apocalyptic thinkers, see Kevin L. Hughes, "The Providential Failure of Christianity: René Girard, Ivan Illich, and the Renewal of Apocalyptic Theology," *Pro Ecclesia* 28, no. 4 (2019), 432–45.

35 Giorgio Agamben, *The Mystery of Evil: Benedict XVI and the End of Days*, trans. Adam Kotsko (Stanford, CA: Stanford University Press, 2017).

in which the decisive conflict is always underway."[36] For Agamben, the church is constituted, at its very heart, by the invitation to say "yes" or "no" to Christ, and so by the tension between the two bodies, of Christ and Antichrist. "[The] 'great *discessio*' ... is not only a future event that, as such, must be separated from the present and isolated in the end of days: it is, rather, something that must orient *here and now* the conduct of every Christian ..."[37] With Illich and Girard, Giorgio Agamben is calling from the margins of the Christian tradition for the renewal and recovery of the symbol of Antichrist, in all its rich complexity. May it flourish.

Selected Further Reading

Agamben, Giorgio. *The Mystery of Evil: Benedict XVI and the End of Days.* Translated by Adam Kotsko. Stanford, CA: Stanford University Press, 2017.

Bull, Malcolm, ed. *Apocalypse Theory and the Ends of the World.* Oxford: Blackwell, 1995.

Burr, David. *The Spiritual Franciscans: From Protest to Persecution in the Century after Saint Francis.* University Park: Pennsylvania State University Press, 2001.

Cayley, David. *The Rivers North of the Future: The Testament of Ivan Illich as Told to David Cayley.* Toronto: House of Anansi, 2005.

Girard, René. *Battling to the End: Conversations with Benoît Chantre.* Translated by Mary Baker. East Lansing: Michigan State University Press, 2010.

Hughes, Kevin L. *Constructing Antichrist: Paul, Biblical Commentary, and the Development of Doctrine in the Early Middle Ages.* Washington, DC: Catholic University of America Press, 2005.

Hughes, Kevin L. "The Providential Failure of Christianity: René Girard, Ivan Illich, and the Renewal of Apocalyptic Theology." *Pro Ecclesia* 28, no. 4 (2019), 432–45.

Landes, Richard, David Van Meter, and Andrew Gow, eds. *The Apocalyptic Year 1000: Religious Expectation and Social Change, 950–1050.* New York: Oxford University Press, 2003.

McGinn, Bernard. *Antichrist: Two Thousand Years of the Human Fascination with Evil.* New York: HarperSanFrancsisco, 1994.

McGinn, Bernard. *Apocalyptic Spirituality.* Classics of Western Spirituality. Mahwah, NJ: Paulist, 1979.

McGinn, Bernard. *The Calabrian Abbot: Joachim of Fiore in the History of Western Christian Thought.* New York: Macmillan, 1985.

Tondelli, Leone, Marjorie Reeves, and Beatrice Hirsch-Reich, eds. *Il libro delle figure dell'abate Gioachino da Fiore*, 2 vols. Turin: Società Editrice Internazionale, 1953.

36 Ibid., 37.

37 Ibid., 15.

15 From Dabiq to Jerusalem: Trajectories of Contemporary Salafi-jihadi Apocalypticism

DAVID COOK

Salafi-jihadism has not always been known for apocalyptic tendencies. From its inception in the 1950s through its growth in the 1970s and 1980s towards its global prominence during recent decades,[1] Salafi-jihadism has shied away from specific predictions of the future. However, with the rise of the Islamic State (IS) in 2013–14, this trend changed quite radically, as this latter group embraced apocalyptic fighting traditions—usually those centered geographically in Syria and Iraq—and adopted the mythology of an end-times battle, similar to Armageddon, to occur in the valleys of northern Syria. This chapter will trace the thought behind this change and speculate about its importance for contemporary Muslim apocalyptic as a whole.

At the very beginning of the earliest Muslim apocalyptic book that has come down to us—that of Nu`aym b. Hammad al-Marwazi († 844)—there is the following tradition ascribed to the Prophet Muhammad:

> God lifted the world up to me so that I could look at it and to what will happen in it until the Day of Resurrection just as I am looking at my palm now. This was a revelation (*jillyan*) from God to His Prophet, just as he revealed it to those prophets prior to him.[2]

This opening indicates that for segments of the early Muslim population the future was a known quantity. Although the Qur'an details comparatively few elements of the events due to happen before the end of the world, this lack was rectified by the development of a large

[1] Salafi-jihadism is a combination of the theological trend of Salafism, with its strong opposition to Sufism and its demand to establish an Islamic state, joined together with the method of jihad or sacral fighting (one should remember that not all Salafis are jihadis, nor are all jihadis Salafis).

[2] Nu`aym b. Hammad al-Marwazi, *Kitab al-fitan* (Beirut: Dar al-Fikr, 1993), 13; and see my translation in *"The Book of Tribulations": The Syrian Muslim Apocalyptic Tradition* (Edinburgh: Edinburgh University Press, 2017), 1. Translations of all sources herein are mine.

body of tradition concerning the subject. Since this apocalyptic tradition was largely developed in Syria, which was the scene of large-scale battles between the Muslims and the Byzantines during the seventh and eighth centuries—including two major failed attempts to take Constantinople—it is not surprising that wars with the Byzantines are a major theme.

For the Muslims the Byzantine Empire was the primary foe. After the fall of Sasanian Persia in the middle of the seventh century, Byzantium was the only centralized state bordering on Muslim territory that supported a high culture as well as being a center for Christianity and having historical ties to the large Christian communities scattered throughout the Muslim empire. Byzantium also had an army as well as a navy that was capable of inflicting defeats upon the Muslims.

The inability of the Muslims to conquer the Byzantine Empire, and most especially its capital of Constantinople, was a tremendous frustration for them. This was redoubled because of the sense that the Muslim conquests during the seventh and eighth centuries were a visible demonstration of God's support for Islam. Since according to the Muslim analysis there were good theological reasons why God should have judged the Byzantines and would cause them to suffer final defeat (see below), Muslims had to ask why this defeat was deferred. In general the answers can be found in the apocalyptic literature which was produced during that time period.

THE IMPORTANCE OF CONSTANTINOPLE TO THE EARLY MUSLIMS

That the Muslims would attack the Byzantine Empire with such ferocity was by no means a given. After all, the Prophet Muhammad in the Qur'an (30:1–2) had supported the Byzantines during their lengthy war with Sasanian Persia (602–29), even when an outside observer might have concluded that the former were finished. Qur'anic teachings about Christianity contain strong polemics against the doctrine of the Trinity and the crucifixion of Jesus, but are often either neutral or positive towards Christians as a group. The Prophet, however, during the final years of his life, sent three expeditions against the Arab (usually Christian) tribes inhabiting the marginal regions of Syria—Palestine, and during the decade after his death in 632 the Muslims quickly conquered the entire region from the Byzantines.

In general, the front between the Muslims in Syria and the Byzantines in Anatolia was quiet for some forty years following the conquests.

The Muslims had the initiative in other directions—most critically for the Byzantines, in Egypt and North Africa—and during part of this time they were engaged in civil wars requiring truces with the Byzantines. However, after the fall of Spain to the Muslims during the first decade of the eighth century, it was clear that a major campaign had to be mounted against Constantinople. This was in order to complete the Muslim domination of the Mediterranean basin. As noted above, the early Muslims viewed themselves as the avengers of God, and Constantinople, according to their descriptions, was the major city that needed to be punished:

> I [Ka`b al-Ahbar] have heard that [the destruction of] Constantinople is in return for the destruction of Jerusalem, since she [Constantinople] became proud and tyrannical, and so is called "the haughty." She [the city] said: "The throne of my Lord is built upon the waters, and I [the city] am built upon the waters." God promised punishment [for it] on the Day of Resurrection, and said: "I will tear away your decoration, and your silk, and your veil, and I will leave you when there is [not even] a rooster crowing in you, and I will make you uninhabited except for foxes, and unplanted except for mallows, and the thorny carob, and I will cause to rain down upon you three [types] of fire: fire of pitch, fire of sulfur, and fire of naphtha, and I will leave you bald and bare, with nothing between you and the heavens. Your voice and your smoke will reach Me in the heavens, because you have for such a long time associated [other deities] with God, and worshipped other than Him."
>
> Girls who will have never seen the sun because of their beauty will be deflowered, and none of you who arrive will be able to walk to the palace (*balat*) of their king [because of the amount of loot]—you will find in it the treasure of twelve kings of theirs, each of them more and none less than it [the one before], in the form of statues of cows or horses of bronze, with water flowing on their heads—dividing up their treasures, weighing them in shields and cutting them with axes. This will be because of the fire promised by God which makes you hurry, and you will carry what of their treasures you can so you can divide them up in al-Qarqaduna [Chalcedon].[3]

[3] Nu`aym, *Fitan*, 284; trans. in Cook, "*The Book of Tribulations*," 280–82.

In this tradition we can see that the sins of Constantinople are numerous. First of all, Constantinople is responsible for everything that the Roman Empire did, most especially the destruction of the Second Temple in 70 CE at the hand of the future emperor Titus, whose name is frequently mentioned in the Muslim literature. However, it is not clear from this apocalyptic tradition whether the Muslims really believed that the Romans and the Byzantines were identical or whether they understood that Constantinople had not been the capital of the Roman Empire when the Temple was destroyed. Among the city's other sins arrogance is singled out. Again, this theme is taken from the Qur'an, although in the above tradition there are strong biblical influences as well as leveling anti-urban feelings.

Constantinople is also clearly seen as the focus for Trinitarian Christianity, which at the time it clearly was. From the above tradition there is a blurring of the lines between paganism and Christianity, and it seems that there was not much effort to differentiate between the two. A direct connection between paganism and Christianity, emphasizing the unacceptability of the Trinity for Muslims, was very effective propaganda, and no doubt had resonance with certain Christian groups as well. It is clear that Constantinople is also being judged because of its excessive luxury, from which the Muslims are predicted to loot at the fall of the city.

But the dominant theme of this tradition is that God is behind the fall of Constantinople, and that in taking and destroying the city, the Muslims are accomplishing His will. It is God who is offended by the false worship practiced by the city and angered by the city's arrogance. It is from God that the different types of fire will fall which will consume the city, and it is His promise that will render the city ultimately uninhabited forever. Although the Muslims will benefit from the spoil of the city, and from its political demise, ultimately the question here is a religious one. The apocalyptic scenario helps paint the larger picture of what the stakes truly are as the Muslims fight for Constantinople, and demonstrates the rightness of their ultimate victory.

APOCALYPTIC WARS AND SCENARIOS ASSOCIATED WITH THE A'MAQ

It is ironic, therefore, that in most apocalyptic scenarios, the wars with the Byzantines that will ultimately conquer Constantinople start out with a mixing of Muslims and Christians in a number of joint ventures against various enemies. The apocalyptic separation described in the previous tradition is not the full story. In fact, it usually starts with an alliance:

> There will be a truce (*hudna*) and a peace (agreement?) between the Muslims and the Byzantines, such that they will fight together against an enemy of theirs, and will divide between the two of them the spoils [of the enemy]. Then the Byzantines will fight together with the Muslims against Persia, and will kill their fighters and take their children captive. The Byzantines will say: "Divide with us the spoils just as we divided with you [previously]," and so they [the Muslims] will divide with them the infidel property and children. But then the Byzantines will say: "Divide with us those of your children you have captured." They [the Muslims] will say: "We will never divide with you the children of the Muslims, ever."[4]

This is an extraordinarily interesting sequence, if only because it portrays a picture of the relations between the Byzantines and the Muslims that is so radically different from the one given in the historical sources. We see here five groups: the Byzantines and the Syrian Muslims form an axis, who make a truce and a peace. I am hesitant to take the word *sulh* much further than to say that it usually means a peace, but if it is placed together with the word *hudna*, a truce or a cease-fire, one might speculate that there is some type of an agreement that is being implied here. That far more than a simple "truce" is being described here is clear from the fact that these two previously warring allies immediately join together to attack an enemy of the Byzantines, a third group mentioned in the apocalypse.

Speculating as to the identity of this enemy is difficult. It cannot have been the Armenians because, although they were enemies of both the Muslims and the Byzantines, they played off both sides, and attacking them would have exacerbated the differences between Byzantines and Muslims, rather than minimizing them. This enemy would seem to have been one that worried the Byzantines, which probably eliminates those nomads to the north of the Black Sea. This only leaves some type of enemy beyond Constantinople, or even further to the west, perhaps Sicily or Italy.

Whoever they were, the Muslims and Byzantines demonstrated an extraordinarily high level of trust to accomplish this task. The Muslims

[4] Nuʿaym, *Fitan*, 259; trans. in Cook, *"The Book of Tribulations,"* 245.

would have had to deputize an army—at a time when manpower was desperately thin—and the Byzantines would have had to trust the Muslim army to go through Constantinople, something like the Crusaders were to do going in the opposite direction approximately 400 years later. If the enemy against whom they were fighting was in either Sicily or Italy there would have been a need for the Muslim troops to be transported by Byzantine ships, again requiring some amount of trust on both sides.

The last two groups that form an axis are the Muslims of Persia and their infidel allies. It is quite interesting that the apocalypse makes clear that there *were* non-Muslims fighting together with the Muslims of Iraq. All-in-all, Muslims on both sides of the Syrian–Iraqi divide are morally compromised by fighting against each other instead of together and preferring alliances with non-Muslims. However, there are some limits that still remain: the Syrian Muslims are unwilling to allow the Byzantines to take Iraqi Muslims captive, and on this note the two allies divide. In other versions the split between the Byzantines and the Muslims is portrayed as a religious one:

> The Byzantines will say: "You have only prevailed over them [the Iraqi Muslims] through the cross," and Muslims will say: "Nay, by Allah and His Messenger we have prevailed over them." The issue will go back and forth between them, and the Byzantines will be enraged. A man of the Muslims will rise up and break their cross, and the two [armies] will separate; the Byzantines taking cover so that a river will divide between the two forces. Thus the Byzantines will break the peace (*sulh*), and they will kill the Muslims in Constantinople.[5]

Although this scenario is a plausible one, it strikes the reader as a bit contrived in such a situation. Does it seem likely that the religious differences between the Byzantines and the Muslims would have gone unnoticed until this point? Would the commanders on both sides, who presumably would realize the importance of the alliance, have allowed their soldiers to drive this disagreement forward without any attempt to intervene? However, from the point of view of the Muslim apocalyptic writer, this ending serves to bring what must have been an unnatural alliance to a close on a suitably religious issue.

[5] Nu`aym, *Fitan*, 273; trans. in Cook, "*The Book of Tribulations*," 261.

The apocalypse continues:

> They will say: "You have betrayed us," and the Byzantines will return to their master in Constantinople, and say to him: "The Arabs betrayed us. Since we are greater than them in number, have better equipment and are stronger than them, allow us to go and fight them." He will say: "I would not want to betray them, since they have had the better of us for a while," and then they will come to the master of Rome and inform him of this, and he will send 80 flags on the sea, under each flag 12,000 [against the Muslims?]. Their master will say to them: "When you anchor on the coastlands of Syria, burn your boats so that you have to fight for your lives" and they will do just that. They will take all of the land of Syria, its land and sea, other than the city of Damascus and Mt. Mu`tiq and will lay waste to Jerusalem.[6]

The Byzantines here view the lack of reciprocity as constituting a betrayal on the part of the Muslims, and are willing to take things a step further. It is interesting that in a *Muslim* apocalypse, apparently dating from the late seventh or early eighth century, the Muslims would view the Byzantines as stronger than they are, as portrayed by the "war-hawk" party's presentation of the strategic situation. The emperor, however, views things a little differently: he sees the larger picture, and does not want to commence hostilities because of the miserable Byzantine military track-record. So the war-hawk party then goes to Rome, where presumably the "master" of the city is the Pope, and convinces him to deputize a massive force of what would be 960,000 soldiers—a force that even the Roman Empire in its heyday would have had difficulty mustering—and conquer Syria.

THE CONQUEST OF CONSTANTINOPLE

The actual conquest of Constantinople is often placed within a separate framework that, although it has some common elements to the above, also has a number of problems. A standard version of this sequence reads:

> You will raid Constantinople three times: during the first, disaster will strike. The second will be a peace between you and them, such that you will build a mosque in their city, and you together with them will raid one of their enemies beyond Constantinople. Then

[6] Nu`aym, *Fitan*, 259; trans. in Cook, "*The Book of Tribulations*," 245–46.

> you will return [to Syria] and raid it a third time, and Allah will conquer it for you.[7]

If it were possible to identify the first raid in this neat presentation of the apocalyptic wars with the Byzantines, perhaps it would be possible to date the tradition. Unfortunately, there were two "raids" on Constantinople during this time period: the one of Mu`awiya in 676–80 and the one of Sulayman in 715–17. The first one would be the more logical choice, in which case we could say that this apocalyptic tradition was composed just before the initiation of the second attempt in 715. This identification would then help us place the apocalypse into the category of "spin" for the invasion: since it acknowledges the failure of the first invasion, and the morally dubious alliance with the Byzantines (to which we shall return below), it essentially says: Third time is the charm! It also could be a fit because as an apocalypse this identification would place it just before the Muslim year 100, about which there are many datable apocalyptic traditions. And the caliph Sulayman clearly saw himself as a candidate for being the Mahdi, the Muslim messianic figure, although he was unable to foresee his own death from gluttony just before the year 100/717. However, this identification is difficult because of the fact that Mu`awiya's invasion left little historical trace in the Muslim records. We would have to assume that in the collective conscious of the Syrian Muslims it left more of an impression in order to accept this identification.

Certainly there is a great deal more historical material on the failed 715–17 attack on Constantinople, which definitely fits into the category of a catastrophe for the Muslims. For years after this disaster, which heralded the end of easy conquests lasting almost a full century, the Syrian Muslims avoided any aggressive moves against the Byzantines. After the loss of this army, the Umayyad dynasty suffered from a severe lack of man power, which ultimately aided in the downfall of the dynasty in 747. Identification of the "first raid" on Constantinople, therefore, with the invasion of 715–17 would be preferable, except that it leaves the question of the "second raid," which is also a problem for the earlier identification as well. Just as with the tradition cited earlier, it seems to point to an alliance between the Muslims of Syria and the Byzantines during the course of which not only does the attack on the as-yet unidentified enemy of the Byzantines "behind them" occur, but a mosque is built in Constantinople. Although there is evidence from a

[7] Nu`aym, *Fitan*, 268; trans. in Cook, *"The Book of Tribulations,"* 254.

later period of mosques being built in Constantinople for Muslim merchants and travelers, this mosque would probably have to date from either the late seventh or early eighth century, and is unattested by other sources.

Whichever date one is inclined to accept, it seems clear that the apocalypse's purpose is to stir up the expectation that Constantinople would be conquered in the very near future. A great many other traditions tell us what the Muslims expected to find when they did conquer the city. There are reports of crossing the Bosphorus on dry land like the Israelites did (Exod 14), and attacking from the land-side of Constantinople. Most probably this is as a result of the collective recollection of the failed sea attack in 715–17. The Muslims will shout *Allahu akbar* seven times, just as Joshua did at Jericho (Josh 6), and the walls will fall down. Fantastic tales of booty and spoil are told of this conquest, and it is clear that for the Muslims of Syria Constantinople represented something of an El Dorado, a place of unimaginable wealth that was waiting for the right time to be seized.

Unfortunately for the Syrian Muslims that time did not happen immediately or even within the next centuries, but had to wait until 1453 when Constantinople was a mere shadow of its earlier self, having already been pillaged by the Crusaders in 1204. The conquest of Constantinople is one of the prerequisites for the messianic peace to be achieved. There are no clear references to what the role of Constantinople would be in the messianic kingdom; in some versions of its fall, as cited above, God will destroy it utterly for its sins, while in others it will be turned into a Muslim city.

However, it is certain that the conquest of Constantinople was one of the most important signs that needed to happen before the end of the world. For Muslims of the seventh and eighth centuries it represented the supreme disconfirmation of their hopes, since the city should have been conquered during the initial conquests. Strategically the fact that it remained unconquered represented the inability of the Muslims to complete their conquest of the Mediterranean Basin, and it was a continual threat to the Syrian Muslims because of both the land power of the Byzantines and their sea power.

When one looks at this material today, having the perspective of the Byzantine material as well, one is struck by the exaggerated assessment of Byzantine strength that is revealed by the Muslim apocalyptic literature. Conquering Constantinople was not just a religious and a strategic necessity, but also represented a supreme challenge: to finish off a powerful empire. Byzantinists would be amazed that during the same time when the empire was at its weakest—during the seventh and eighth centuries—the Muslims were in awe of its strength and actively worried that it might destroy their center in Syria.

IS AND APOCALYPSE

Although these apocalyptic fragments are merely several of a whole heritage, they give us a very good idea of the apocalyptic hopes and fears of the Syrian Muslims during this time. Whether they indeed have a historical kernel to them is another question. Transitioning to the contemporary period, we can continue to see the relevance of the traditions concerning the Byzantines. During the recent past debate has raged among scholars as to whether the group-state known as the Islamic State (also the Islamic State of Iraq and Syria, ISIS, or the Islamic State of Iraq and the Levant) is an ideological or opportunistic group. Although IS has now fairly deep roots in contemporary Salafi-jihadism, being placed within the following of the Jordanian Abu Muhammad al-Maqdisi (although he now disavows it) and founded by Abu Musa`b al-Zarqawi (d.2006), and having gone through numerous name changes, there is no consensus on the matter.

One cannot say that this lack of consensus exists because of a lack of materials. On the contrary, IS is probably one of the most prolific Salafi-jihadi groups of all time, existing in printed documents (many of them collected and studied by Aymenn Jawad al-Tamimi),[8] online magazines such as *Dabiq*, which will be discussed below, public proclamations, twitter accounts, videos, and interviews with both present and past members of the group as well as its victims (those who have survived), in addition to the hard facts on the ground, including its trail of destruction. Trying to make sense of this mass of material is daunting.

But one place to start is apocalypse. There are very good reasons to start there. First of all, the group's flagship publication *Dabiq* takes its name from the apocalyptic tradition:

> The Hour will not arise until the Byzantines descend upon the A`maq (valleys) or in Dabiq, so an army from Medina will emerge against them, who are the best of the earth's people at that time. When they will line up for battle, the Byzantines will say: "Give

[8] Aymenn Jawad al-Tamimi, www.aymennjawad.org/ (accessed October 15, 2019).

> way between us and those who were made captive from among us, so we can fight them," but the Muslims will say: "We will never make way between you and our brothers," so they will fight them. One third will retreat, who God will never accept their repentance, one third will be killed, who are the best martyrs (*shuhada'*) in God's eyes, and one third will conquer, who will never be tempted (*yuftanuna*), then they will conquer Constantinople. While they are dividing the spoils, having hung up their swords on olive trees, Satan will shout among them: "The [false] Messiah is behind you, among your families!"[9]

Historically, this tradition dates from the middle Umayyad period (or perhaps later Umayyad period), and reflects the battles that raged during the eighth century between the Muslims and the Byzantines in the area to the north of Antioch and Aleppo. In the apocalyptic literature, especially the early text of Nu`aym b. Hammad, which was collected in Syria-Palestine, the "valleys" of north Syria were to be the location of a number of cataclysmic battles between these opposing sides.

Within the context of mainstream Sunni Muslim tradition, however, the Dabiq tradition is alone. Other traditions allude to apocalyptic battles, and certainly the Byzantines are mentioned by name a good deal, but only this tradition is the equivalent of an "Armageddon"-style geographically placed tradition. It is a sign of IS's revolutionary interpretation of Islamic tradition that it has chosen to tie itself so closely to this tradition. No doubt this was abetted by the fact of the Syrian civil war, and the fact that Dabiq fell early into the hands of IS, but nonetheless it is surprising.

With the loss of Dabiq by IS, as one might predict, the group merely began to emphasize the more global aspects of apocalyptic battle by renaming its publication *Rumiyya*. Essentially, while Dabiq would be the equivalent of "Armageddon" in the Muslim context, Rumiyya would be the equivalent of "world Christianity." Even in retreat, IS still chooses to emphasize the ideal that it is fighting a much larger enemy or group of enemies than merely being a major participant in the Syrian civil war.

Less surprising than the appearance of Dabiq is the use of the black banners and their association with the revival of the caliphate. Here the prominent traditions are associated with the revolutionary movement of the `Abbasid dynasty (742–49), which employed black banners and

[9] Muslim, *Sahih* (Beirut: Dar al-Jil, n.d.), viii, 175–76.

clothing as their sign: "then the black banners will rise from the east, and they will kill a number of you the like of which has never been seen previously ... when you see him [coming] swear allegiance to him, even if you have to crawl on the snow, for he is the caliph of God, the Mahdi."[10]

All the way back to the rise of the Islamic republic in Iran, then to the rise of the Taliban in Afghanistan in 1994–96 and to al-Qaeda in the early 2000s, the use of the black banners has been a constant. However, IS has added the brilliant stroke of placing the *shahada*, "There is no god but Allah ..." etc., on the black banners in early Islamic script, to emphasize the revival of the earliest Muslim forms of government.

The catch is that here the tradition implies that this form of government will be messianic, that of the Mahdi, who is a God-empowered figure, sent at the end of time, "to fill the world with justice and righteousness, just as it had been filled with injustice and unrighteousness."[11] IS's revolutionary interpretation of this is to revive the caliphate, a Sunni office dormant since 1924. There should be no doubt about the significance of this revival, as one of the mainstream traditions states, "whoever dies without swearing allegiance to the caliph of their time dies the death of the *jahiliyya*" (or as a non-Muslim). For this reason we find so often those carrying out "lone wolf" attacks in the west making sure that they pledge allegiance—one of the signs that no matter how secular and non-Islamic their lifestyles have been until that time, they want to die as Muslims.

Is IS, however, proclaiming itself to be a messianic state? The figure of the Mahdi, strong and messiah-like in Shi`ism, is far less defined in Sunnism. It is not easy, within the Sunni apocalyptic literature, to define how precisely the Mahdi differs from an idealized or ideal caliph. Does he, for instance, have to be a descendent of the Prophet Muhammad? Must he fulfill all of the prophecies concerning him, which include appearing at Mecca and Medina during the hajj and receiving the oath of allegiance from large numbers of Muslims? It is significant that while IS has revived the caliphate, it has not claimed the title of Mahdi for its caliph, Abu Bakr al-Baghdadi, who took the regnal title, Ibrahim or Abraham.

Indeed, the caliph Ibrahim, by the title he took, is fairly obviously claiming to be the upholder, and perhaps even the reviver, of monotheism. There is no doubt that IS sees itself as being the last in a long string

10 Ibn Maja, *Sunan* (Beirut: Dar al-Fikr, 1988), ii, 1366 (no. 4082).
11 Abū Dā'ūd, *Sunan* (Beirut: Dār al-Jīl, 1988), iv, 105 (no. 2485).

of groups separate from the larger Muslim community, which has upheld the true Islam. "A group of my [= Muhammad's] community will continue fighting for the truth, victorious over those who oppose them, with none able to oppose them, until the edict of God comes to fruition."[12] As implied by this tradition, at the time of the end the numbers of Muslims will be limited, and (perhaps the majority) will have apostacized. This is a difficult message to proclaim to world Islam, and it is not surprising that IS has been attacked as non-Islamic, or by scholars as merely a political movement.

IS IS AN APOCALYPTIC MOVEMENT?

One of the problems with apocalypse is the process of making classical prophecies relevant to the contemporary world. This difficulty can be easily understood with reference to the Dabiq tradition cited above. There, the relevant question is, who or what are the Rum (Byzantines)? There are two basic lines of interpretation: one is conceptual, and the other is topographical. The conceptual one would follow the line that the Byzantines were Christians, Christians are the most prominent (although by no means the only) opponents of Islam during the present time, and therefore the Rum are world Christians.

The problem with this identification is that it lacks a sense of reality. World Christianity might in general be opposed to Islam (although there are more than a few ecumenical or interfaith endeavors that apocalyptic interpreters ignore), but it is not organized in terms of a state or even states that could field a plausible army, let alone one of the magnitude demanded by the tradition above. Therefore, a more common interpretation would be to gloss Christians by "the west" or some other entity, such as the United States. With the latter, one comes to a type of equivalence: the Byzantine Empire was the dominant Christian entity of its time and the most strenuous opponent of the Muslim empire (as witnessed by the apocalyptic traditions), and if one takes a paranoid and malevolent view of the contemporary role of the United States then one has an equivalent. The major difficulty with this interpretation is simply the fact that the United States, hitherto, has not played an important or even semi-important role in the Syrian civil war, and there is little indication that it would massively attack,

12 Ibn Maja, *Sunan*, ii, 1304 (no. 3952).

or if it did, that the direction of its attack would be from the region of Turkey.

This brings us to the second line of interpretation, the topographical one. The former Byzantine Empire of the eighth century is for the most part (at least in Anatolia) the present-day country of Turkey. In addition, the Ottoman rulers of Turkey traditionally viewed themselves as the heirs of the Byzantine Empire. However, Turks are Muslims, so that fact makes it difficult to understand the nature of the tradition: why would two groups of Muslims fight at Dabiq in an Armageddon-style battle?

But the relationship between Salafi-jihadis and Turks has always been a rocky one, with Turkish Islam frequently being perceived as more liberal or even western-influenced than Middle Eastern Arabic-language Islam. In spite of the fact that the Turks conquered Constantinople in 1453, while the Arabs did not, there exist a number of traditions that indicate that the Antichrist will appear seven years after the conquest of the city. Since this did not in fact happen in 1460, it raises the possibility that the "true" conquest of Constantinople (Istanbul) is yet in the apocalyptic future. If that were to be taken as fact, then one could speculate about whether the Turks are in fact Muslims at all, a line of thinking that was prominent in Arabic-language apocalyptic books during the early 1990s. Indeed, IS has not shied away from the idea that Turkey needs to be conquered—"purified"—from an incorrect form of Islam, in order for the region to be admitted into the future messianic Islamic state. It may be that the increasingly prominent IS terror attacks in Turkey are representative of this trend.

In IS's publications there are elements of both of these interpretive lines, both of which are useful to the group in different ways. The first serves to highlight the future cataclysmic battle, and IS's projected heroic role as the vanguard of the Muslim community in it, while the second serves to delegitimize a form of political Islam—the unusually successful Turkish model associated with the AK party—that from IS's point of view distracts from the attractiveness of its caliphate. Thus apocalyptic ambiguity serves the group rather well.

But does it give us a sense of the apocalyptic framework of IS? How can we be certain that apocalypse is not just a cover for other more fundamental political calculations? For one thing, we can note the fact that even though Turkey has consistently (albeit passively) aided IS since 2013, IS has not demonstrated a reciprocal desire to refrain from carrying out suicide attacks within its boundaries. However, are there further criteria that could be used to judge the ideological depth of IS's apocalyptic mindset?

TESTING THE CASES

There is a paranoia at the core of Salafi-jihadism that really believes the entire world is out to get it. This type of Manichaean worldview is based upon the so-called hadith of Thawban, one of the most commonly cited traditions:

> The Messenger of God said: The nations are about to flock against you [the Muslims] from every horizon, just as hungry people flock to a kettle. We said: O Messenger of God, will we be few on that day? He said: No, you will be many as far as your number goes, but you will be scum, like the scum of the flash-flood, since fear will be removed from the hearts of your enemies, and weakness (*wahn*) will be placed in your hearts. We said: O Messenger of God, what does the word *wahn* mean? He said: Love of this world and fear of death.[13]

Like the tradition about the group fighting until the end of the world cited previously, this tradition separates out the saved Muslims from the vast majority who have gone astray. Moreover, it gives us the criterion by which one can find out whether one is saved or not: Is one's Islam a self-sacrificial Islam? According to the tradition of Thawban, that is the primary criterion by which one will be judged.

Testing IS's apocalyptic tendencies is not easy. But there should be several criteria:

1. Events or policies that demonstrate a sharp and bridge-burning break with the larger Muslim community, and beyond them the non-Muslim world. With regard to IS the two that stand out are the extremely literal and brutal punishments that the group metes out for all infractions of the *shari`a*, and the revival of sexual slavery (starting in 2014), especially of Christian and Yezidi women.[14]

   Sunni Muslims have continually discussed since the rise of political Islam in the 1940s and 1950s what practically speaking the imposition of *shari`a* would mean in the contemporary world. Even those Muslim countries or regions (Saudi Arabia, Sudan, Iran, Pakistan, Aeh in northern Indonesia, the twelve northern Muslim states of Nigeria for example) that do apply *shari`a* usually are open to critique on the basis of their compromises. Salafis repeatedly through the 1980s and 1990s critiqued the most prominent of all,

[13] Abū Dā'ūd, *Sunan*, iv, 108 (no. 4297).

[14] CNN, www.cnn.com/2014/10/12/world/meast/isis-justification-slavery/index.html (accessed October 15, 2019).

Saudi Arabia, as hypocritical in its practice. So it is not surprising that IS stands for full imposition of *shari`a*. Even its most implacable Salafi critics have not been able to find loopholes in its application of *shari`a*, only taking issue with the complete absence of compassion.

More surprising is the revival of slavery.[15] Although the abolition of slavery during the nineteenth and early twentieth centuries by the Muslim world was not one that ever received religious justification, and it is possible within the context of ethnically ot religiously based wars to find slavery (such as in the Sudan during the period 1990–2005), there was no push within the broader Muslim world to revive the practice. IS's doing so should be seen as part of its desire to fundamentally flout global Muslim and non-Muslim norms, as well as to cater to its core constituency of single young males seeking rewards for being fighters.

2. Choice of targets or enemies. IS has deliberately attacked all of its neighboring states and publicly proclaimed that it is at war with the entire world. There are no examples of countries recognizing IS, unlike the Taliban (which maintained relations with Saudi Arabia, the United Arab Emirates and Pakistan). It is clear that IS views itself not just as an Islamic state, but as *the* Islamic State, and as the only legitimate state in the world. Strategically any belligerent country may feel free to attack its neighbors; however, even very belligerent countries usually do not attack all of their neighbors as a strategy.
3. IS has not tied itself to a specific datable timeline. To the best of my knowledge there is no published research on the part of its scholars as to when the end of the world (even approximately) will occur. Such a dating, even if it was general (hypothetically, "we are the last generation before the end ..." for example) would represent the ultimate in bridge-burning, since it is quite difficult to reinterpret such exactitude after it has been proven false.

Testing the apocalyptic or ideological tendencies of any group is difficult. Groups speak with a multiplicity of voices—what is known and believed in one section of a given group may be unknown or doubted in another—and individuals are made up of complex motivations that are not always easily expressible with reference to ideological reference-points. Even so, there will be actions, such as

[15] Clarion Project, clarionproject.org/docs/islamic-state-isis-magazine-Issue-4-the-failed-crusade.pdf (accessed October 15, 2019).

attacking Turkey, or proclamations, such as the revival of slavery, that help us to see that this is not merely another political group, but an actual apocalyptic group.

CONCLUSIONS

According to the evidence IS is an opportunistic apocalyptic Salafi-jihadi movement that holds itself to be the continuation of the classical Syrian-Muslim tradition hoping for a conquest of the Byzantine state. One should note the high level of supercessionism and the idea that it sees itself as an agent of divine retribution: its overall goals and methodologies are apocalyptic and cataclysmic by nature. Its most probable scenario is a duality: messianic with regard to the Muslim world in the sense that it seeks to found a pan-Islamic messianic caliphal state, and Manichaean with regard to the rest of the non-Muslim world. In other words, IS takes the al-Qaeda use of the "crusade" of after September 11, 2001 to a new level, and hopes by causing repeated attacks in the non-Muslim, mainly western, world to bring about an Armageddon-style dichotomy conflict.

During the course of this conflict, IS expects that the entire Muslim world, if it has not done so already, will line up to support its caliph, who will be victorious over the non-Muslims, and then be able to establish the messianic, idealized state. One has to say that this timeline does not have a completely coherent basis in the mainstream apocalyptic traditions, but by using parts of it, while ignoring others, it is possible to support it textually.

As a result of IS's recent losses, it is possible that soon we will have the opportunity to watch the level of the group's association with the apocalypse symbolized by the adoption of Dabiq as its symbol and the expropriation of the narratives concerning the Byzantine–Muslim conflicts. As Dabiq is now lost, we should look for a new symbol. Most likely that symbol will be Jerusalem, as the recovery of Jerusalem would be something a broad spectrum of Muslims could support. IS will by its own nature be required to justify the loss of Dabiq as part of the apocalyptic scenario, and will presumably use the loss to generate energy on the part of the believers to recover it, or perhaps abandon its association with apocalypse.

Selected Further Reading

Cook, David. *Contemporary Muslim Apocalyptic Literature*. Syracuse, NY: Syracuse University Press, 2005.

Cook, David. *Studies in Muslim Apocalyptic*. Princeton, NJ: Darwin, 2002.
Cook, David, ed. and trans. *"The Book of Tribulations": The Syrian Muslim Apocalyptic Tradition*. Edinburgh: Edinburgh University Press, 2017.
Filiu, Jean-Pierre. *Apocalypse in Islam*. Translated by M. B. Debevoise. Berkeley: University of California Press, 2011.
McCants, William. *ISIS: The Apocalypse; The History, Strategy and Doomsday Vision of the Islamic State*. New York: Palgrave Macmillan, 2015.

16 American Evangelicals and the Apocalypse

DANIEL G. HUMMEL

In the twenty-first century, evangelical visions of the apocalyptic pervade American culture, from popular novels to films, merchandise, and music. But this cultural footprint is only the most visible sign of their influence. The apocalypse, and the deep preoccupation with its details, have also shaped American religion and politics and fueled evangelical political activism, helping millions of Americans to interpret the news and plan for the future. Underlying both the cultural and political relevance of the American evangelical understanding of the apocalypse is a story of how the theology of "dispensational premillennialism," which has decisively informed evangelical apocalypticism more than anything else, came to dominate American evangelical theology.[1] This development, dating to the mid-nineteenth century, is especially important in order for us to chart the depth of apocalyptic thinking in modern American evangelicalism and its expansion into American popular culture.

By linking these three levels of the apocalypse in American evangelicalism—theology, culture, and politics—this essay emphasizes the broader questions of belief that have so often animated American evangelicals. Though frequently obscured by bizarre predictions or gruesome details, the apocalypse has loomed as a penetrating and existential issue in American evangelicalism. It has acted as an engine for theological debate, cultural production, and political activism, and continues to shape evangelical attitudes in the twenty-first century.

DEFINITIONS

American evangelicals—and Christians more generally—have developed specialized language to talk about the apocalypse, often in order to

[1] On the history of dispensationalism and evangelicalism see George Marsden, *Fundamentalism and American Culture*, 2nd ed. (New York: Oxford University Press, 2006), 44–48, 118–23; Paul Boyer, *When Time Shall Be No More: Prophecy Belief in Modern American Culture* (Cambridge, MA: Belknap, 1994), 86–90.

distinguish opposing views. Acknowledging some of these key terms helps us to appreciate the significance of the apocalypse to evangelical theology, American culture, and United States politics.

Although modern evangelicals have become the poster children for American apocalyptic teachings, this was not always the case. Before the mid-nineteenth century evangelicals tended towards a variety of teachings on "eschatology," a technical term designating "Last Things" including the end of the world. For much of their history, American evangelicals and other Protestants were predominantly *postmillennial* in their belief that the Second Coming and the apocalypse would occur *after* a millennial period when Christ "will reign . . . a thousand years" as foretold in Rev 20:1–8. The apocalypse—the cataclysmic battle between Jesus and the forces of Satan—would happen in the far distant future after Christianity vanquished rival religions and converted the world.[2]

The beliefs of postmillennialism dated back to the church fathers and were obviously far older than American evangelicalism. But it was the New England Calvinists, including Jonathan Edwards, who made this view central to Americans. Edwards, for example, interpreted revivals such as the First Great Awakening as God's chosen method to usher in the millennial age. For many North American colonists, the creation of an American republic was a sign of postmillennial progress. As one clergyman observed in 1859, postmillennialism became "the commonly received doctrine" of American Protestantism through the mid-nineteenth century.[3]

The predominance of postmillennialism, however, did not last. A rival view foresaw Christ's return as a sudden and violent event, a radical undermining of the current order to establish the millennium and wipe away evil. The basic *premillennial* belief that Christ would return *before* the millennium also predated American evangelicalism, but as a philosophy that rejected inevitable progress and the human capacity to usher in God's kingdom it emerged with force in the nineteenth century.[4]

[2] On the rival views of millennialism, see Stanley Grenz, *The Millennial Maze* (Downers Grove, IL: InterVarsity Press, 1992).

[3] James Moorhead, "Between Progress and Apocalypse: A Reassessment of Millennialism in American Religious Thought, 1800–1880," *Journal of American History* 71, no. 3 (December 1984): 525; E. Brooks Holifield, *Theology in America: Christian Thought from the Age of the Puritans to the Civil War* (New Haven, CT: Yale University Press, 2005).

[4] James Moorhead, "The Erosion of Postmillennialism in American Religious Thought, 1865–1925," *Church History* 53, no. 1 (1984): 61–77.

In the decades after the American Civil War (1861–65), much of American Protestantism could be found in one of the two camps. Postmillennialism dominated the teachings of established denominations such as the Presbyterians, Methodists, and Episcopalians. Premillennialism grew popular among the Anglo-American laity and flourished on the margins, among sects in Britain and America such as the Millerites (Seventh-Day Adventists), Irvingites (the Catholic Apostolic Church), and Plymouth Brethren. While today postmillennialism is associated with progressive Christianity and premillennialism with conservative evangelicalism, in the nineteenth century these divisions would have made little sense to Americans.

A second distinction relates to the rapture, the event in which elected Christians are to rise into the air to meet Jesus. For most Christians, including Catholics, Eastern Orthodox, and most Protestants, the rapture will be a single event at the very end of the last days that signals "a new heaven and a new earth" of Rev 21. For premillennialists, however—and especially, as we will see, those who became *dispensational* premillennialists—the rapture will be an event that will involve only living Christians, who will meet Jesus in the air. This rapture could happen at any moment, and so it is often called the imminent rapture. Thus there is an important distinction between *pre-tribulational* and *post-tribulational* raptures—that is, the timing of the rapture before the tribulation (involving just living Christians) or after (implying that current Christians will live through the tribulation and be joined by all living and dead Christians).

These distinctions, about which hundreds of books have been written over the centuries, deserve scrutiny as a pivotal area of evangelical Christian thought even though outsiders might scratch their head on the modest changes the differences seem to entail. Of course, eschatology must be understood as merely one dimension of evangelical theology. Rarely has it been the preeminent field of research, but just as rarely has its influence in other areas of evangelical theology been absent. The place of eschatology in evangelical theology has changed over time, often in response to political and cultural forces. Its importance as a signifier of American evangelical identity is deeply intertwined with the story of American Protestantism, especially its transition from a society dominated by an exceptionally broad evangelical consensus in the nineteenth century (what historian Martin Marty has termed the "Evangelical Empire") to a fractured

Protestantism and a far more pluralistic religious landscape in the twentieth century.[5]

THE RISE OF EVANGELICAL APOCALYPTICISM

The point in time when we begin to see the rise of a distinctly American apocalypticism, dominated by the teachings of dispensational premillennialism, also coincides with major ruptures in American society. To many Americans, the cataclysmic Civil War sent disturbing signals about the moral achievements of the country after its first century of nationhood. Most religious Americans had been at least nominally supportive of the postmillennial vision of God's kingdom advancing through the American republic. Even the war, Northern supporters argued, had occasioned unprecedented bloodletting, but the blight of slavery had finally been expunged. Julia Ward Howe's popular wartime hymn, "The Battle Hymn of the Republic," proclaimed the postmillennial cry, "Mine eyes have seen the glory of the coming of the Lord | He is trampling out the vintage where the grapes of wrath are stored."

This postmillennial sentiment not only was optimistic about the future, but represented a theological middle ground in a society rapidly absorbing new scientific knowledge. Postmillennialism, teaching that God would bring his kingdom to earth through the work of his followers, acknowledged the broad outlines of new scientific and evolutionary findings but retained a commitment to God's ultimate sovereignty over creation. In the Social Gospel movement of the early twentieth century, the emphasis on human agency increased. The millennial kingdom became an ethical dominion dependent not on Christ's personal intervention or prophetic fulfillment, but on concerted moral and structural reform through human governance and natural processes. This transformation of postmillennialism after the Civil War extended its life among some clergy and laity, but it was increasingly abandoned by most of American Protestantism.[6]

The Civil War, however, had multiple and sometimes contradicting legacies. In contrast to postmillennialism, a new brand of premillennialism gained a broad hearing among American Protestants in the war's

[5] William R. Hutchison, *Religious Pluralism in America: The Contentious History of a Founding Ideal* (New Haven, CT: Yale University Press, 2003); Martin E. Marty, *Righteous Empire: The Protestant Experience in America* (New York: Dial, 1970).

[6] Gary Dorrien, *The Making of American Liberal Theology: Idealism, Realism, and Modernity, 1900–1950* (Louisville, KY: Westminster John Knox, 2003).

aftermath, as well. It might be better described as a *re*-gaining of credibility after the discrediting of apocalypticism in an earlier era. In the decades before the Civil War, premillennial movements had withered, mostly in the shadow of the Millerites. William Miller, a Baptist minister in eastern New York, spent the early 1830s studying the apocalyptic Book of Daniel before going public with his conclusion that Jesus would return soon. Miller was confident he could pinpoint the date. Taking the prophecy of Dan 8:14 ("And he answered him, 'For two thousand three hundred evenings and mornings; then the sanctuary shall be restored to its rightful state'") and converting "evenings and mornings" into years, he argued that the cleansing of the earth would take place in March 1843. By 1837, with the help of the publicist Joshua V. Himes promoting his teachings in all corners of the country, hundreds of thousands of Americans prepared for the end. But March 1843 passed without event, as did later recalculations. After the final date, October 22, 1844, came and went, the movement disbanded amid disappointment, denominational crackdowns (Miller was defrocked), and charges of profiteering. Miller would go on to found the Adventist movement, which remains active, but the Millerite episode was soon coined the "Great Disappointment." It sullied the reputation of apocalyptic speculation for more than a generation.[7]

After the Civil War, however, premillennialism reemerged as a popular teaching—and the causes for its increasing popularity were as plentiful as those for postmillennialism's decline. Two deserve special attention. The first is the theological influence of John Nelson Darby (1800–82), an Irish Anglican whose system of biblical interpretation and doctrines became known to later Christians as dispensational premillennialism. Darby, a leader of the anticlerical Plymouth Brethren movement in Great Britain, toured the United States in the 1860s and 1870s, spreading his teachings to those attracted to his prophetic insights. Darby promoted his beliefs through his followers in the interdenominational Niagara Bible Conference, an Anglo-American progenitor of the fundamentalist movement.[8]

Darby's teachings had lasting effects on American Protestantism and the apocalypse in American culture. He divided all biblical history

[7] Sydney E. Ahlstrom, *A Religious History of the American People*, 2nd ed. (New Haven, CT: Yale University Press, 2004), 478–81.

[8] Mark S. Sweetnam and Crawford Gribben, "J. N. Darby and the Irish Origins of Dispensationalism," *Journal of the Evangelical Theological Society* 52, no. 3 (2009): 569–77.

into "dispensations," each marking a period of God's relationship to humanity. The first dispensation ended with the expulsion of Adam and Eve from the Garden of Eden, the second with the Great Flood, and so on. The death and resurrection of Jesus inaugurated the fifth dispensation, but this period was irregular. In previous dispensations, God had worked through his covenanted people, the nation of Israel. With the Jewish rejection of Jesus and his crucifixion, God's plans with Israel were put on hold. The church, a new covenanted community, was brought into being and given its own dispensation, which continues today. The church is to evangelize to "all tribes and peoples and languages" (Rev 7:9). The church, however, is a "parenthesis" in God's work through Israel. In the future, when the church has fulfilled its role, it will be suddenly raptured from the earth and God will complete his original plan to redeem the world through Israel.[9]

Darby and his followers were not all equally fervent in their apocalyptic speculations about the near future, but all of them believed in an imminent (any moment) rapture: a sudden transportation of all elect Christians into God's presence.[10] Darby's copious writings touched on the apocalyptic details of the seven-year tribulation, which his followers would apply to current events in each subsequent generation: the rise of an Antichrist figure to helm a one-world government; a seven-year period of tribulation with rampant persecution of the new "saints" (people who turned to God after the rapture) and plagues; religious leaders and movements establishing a heretical false religion; diplomatic machinations in the Middle East leading to the creation of a Jewish state, a deceptive peace deal, and a foretold "abomination of desolation" to occur in a rebuilt Holy Temple; and a climactic Battle of Armageddon between the Antichrist and the forces of God, which Jesus will personally win to usher in the millennial kingdom.[11]

Darby relied on passages in the two apocalyptic books of the Bible, Daniel and Revelation, to describe many of these events, but he and his followers engaged with much more in the Scriptures to construct

[9] Darrell L. Bock and Craig A. Blaising, *Progressive Dispensationalism* (Wheaton, IL: BridgePoint, 1993), 9–56.

[10] Alan Terlep, "Inventing the Rapture: The Formation of American Dispensationalism, 1850–1875" (PhD diss., University of Chicago, 2010); Timothy P. Weber, *Living in the Shadow of the Second Coming: American Premillennialism, 1875–1925* (New York: Oxford University Press, 1983).

[11] Ernest R. Sandeen, *The Roots of Fundamentalism: British and American Millenarianism, 1800–1930* (Chicago: University of Chicago Press, 1970).

their theology. Dispensationalists were like many Americans of the nineteenth and early twentieth centuries who idealized technological methods of quantification and classification and applied scientific methods to the Bible. For dispensationalists the entire Bible was a set of propositional statements revealing truths about God in both the past and future. Thus each verse—sometimes each word—deserved scrutiny and was to be interpreted "plainly" or "literally." In the popular dispensationalist refrain, when the biblical text mentioned "Israel" it always meant the same thing: the physical descendants of Abraham. Other Christians privileged allegorical, metaphorical, or analogical interpretations that interpreted "Israel" as the chosen people of God, at one point in the Old Testament the nation of Israel but in the New Testament (and today) the church. This difference, which filtered into every aspect of prophecy interpretation, pitted dispensationalists against other Protestants as "literalists" against "spiritualists" in the common theological parlance of the early twentieth century.

Dispensational doctrines also relied on less obvious passages. The doctrine of the rapture, for example, relied mostly from a single passage in Paul's First Letter to the Thessalonians:

> For the Lord himself, with a cry of command, with the archangel's call and with the sound of God's trumpet, will descend from heaven, and the dead in Christ will rise first. Then we who are alive, who are left, will be caught up in the clouds together with them to meet the Lord in the air; and so we will be with the Lord forever. (1 Thess 4:16–17)

To develop other teachings, passages from the prophetic books—Jeremiah, Ezekiel, and Isaiah—were merged with those in Daniel, Amos, or the prophecies of Jesus.

In addition to the influence of Darby and his followers, premillennialism grew in the late nineteenth century because it offered theological explanations to pressing intellectual and social challenges of the era. Like postmillennialism, dispensational premillennialism was a compromise between new scientific knowledge and the Bible. While postmillennialists incorporated scientific understandings of historical processes to make sense of their millennial expectations, premillennialists applied scientific methods to the biblical text itself in order to protect, in their view, the teaching of God's supernatural intervention into history. The historian Brendan Pietsch goes so far as to categorize dispensationalism as a type of modernism, fixated on systematization of the Bible's theology, taxonomy, and classification, and promoting an aesthetic of order and uniformity.[12]

Propounded in Bible institutes, speaking circuits, and pulpits, dispensational ideas spread rapidly in this period. The aforementioned Niagara Bible Conference, an annual Bible study that met from 1876 to 1897, introduced hundreds of evangelical leaders to dispensational premillennialism. Organized by James H. Brookes, the Niagara meetings (named for their location at Niagara-on-the-Lake, Ontario) featured pastors and evangelists, many with large followings in metropolitan centers such as Chicago, Detroit, St. Louis, and Boston. Although Brookes studiously downplayed Darby's singular influence on dispensationalism, Darby's signature teachings, including the imminent rapture and the continuing importance of the Jewish people, made their way into the center of Brookes's teachings, too. The generation's most influential evangelist, Dwight Moody (1837–99), fused dispensationalism with his evangelistic revival teachings, famously proclaiming the apocalyptic message, "I look upon this world as a wrecked vessel. God has given me a lifeboat and said, 'Moody, save all you can.'"[13]

THE SPREAD OF DISPENSATIONALISM

Although it achieved stunning success within the fundamentalist movement, dispensationalism never had a monopoly on premillennialist thought. This fact is important for an understanding of three later developments: the drive by dispensationalists to systematize their theology and defend it from theological attacks; the increasing popular, as opposed to scholarly, influence that dispensationalism attained; and the eventual decline of dispensationalist theology in evangelical seminaries later in the twentieth century.

Historic premillennialists (named to claim a deep connection to church history) rejected dispensational doctrines including the pretribulational rapture. Although the differences between dispensationalists and historic premillennialists were minor to outsiders, in fact the two diverged on basic understandings of God's plans for humanity and the identity of God's chosen people. To take one example, by rejecting an imminent rapture, historic premillennialists committed Christians to suffer through the events of the tribulation, a fate that

[12] Brendan M. Pietsch, *Dispensational Modernism* (New York: Oxford University Press, 2015).

[13] Quoted in Marsden, *Fundamentalism and American Culture*, 38.

dispensationalists found anathema to God's promises. More significantly, historic premillennialists emphasized the church as the culmination of God's plans and looked forward to a millennium wherein the church, not Israel, would be rewarded for its faith.[14]

Historic premillennialists claimed the second-century church father Irenaeus as their own, but, like dispensationalists, also based their pedigree on more recent theologians. Never comprising an active network like the dispensational Niagara Bible Conference, historic premillennial theologians—Robert Cameron, William J. Eerdman, and Nathaniel West (who converted from an imminent rapture position in the early 1880s)—often worked against the tide of rising dispensationalist popularity. The monuments to their influence are theological tomes, many over 1,000 pages long, that made the theological case for their brand of premillennialism.[15]

In the short term, the world seemed to validate dispensational apocalypticism. The First World War helped to legitimize their view of the future. "Dispensationalists did not change their views to fit the events of World War I," writes the historian Timothy Weber; "the war seemed to follow an already existing and well-formulated premillennial script for the last days." Dispensationalist theologians cited verses in Daniel and Revelation to predict a massive redrawing of the boundaries in Europe to create a revived Roman Empire, the final of four empires prophesied in Dan 7. The collapse of the German, Austro-Hungarian, Russian, and Ottoman Empires seemed to play into this scenario. Further signs of fulfilled prophecy—including the British capture of Jerusalem, the Balfour Declaration, and the collapse of the Ottoman caliphate—bolstered dispensationalist confidence. Here was empirical proof that millennia-old prophecies continued to have relevance, and that the Bible, more than scientific or academic prognosticators, could predict the future.[16]

By the 1920s, when Protestants separated into modernist and fundamentalist camps with accompanying institutions, world events appeared to validate dispensationalism's ascendance as the most

[14] Timothy Weber, "Dispensational and Historic Premillennialism as Popular Millennialist Movements," in *A Case for Historic Premillennialism: An Alternative to "Left Behind" Eschatology*, eds. Craig Bloomberg and Sing Wook Chung (Grand Rapids, MI: Eerdmans, 2009), 1–22; Grenz, *The Millennial Maze*, 127–48.

[15] See, for example, Nathaniel West, *The Thousand Year Reign of Christ* (Grand Rapids, MI: Kregel, 1899).

[16] Weber, *Living in the Shadow of the Second Coming*, 106.

popular form of premillennialism. Dispensationalism emerged as the closest thing to an official eschatology for the fundamentalist movement, sidelining historic premillennialists for decades. Popular writers including Arno Gaebelein and Lewis Sperry Chafer, and evangelists including Billy Sunday, Harry Ironside, and Reuben A. Torrey, preached dispensationalism to the masses.[17]

The decisive advantage dispensationalism enjoyed at the crucial birth of the fundamentalist movement was the culmination of its spread beyond elite theological circles. Most significant was the publication of the *Scofield Reference Bible*, the first systematized and comprehensive presentation of dispensationalism, written as annotations to the biblical text. Its principal author, Cyrus I. Scofield, was an ex-Confederate soldier and, like Darby, a lawyer by training. By the 1880s Scofield was a regular at the Niagara Bible Conference. He first published his reference Bible in 1909. By 1929 the *Scofield Reference Bible* had sold one million copies for Oxford University Press. By the end of the Second World War the number had increased to two million.[18]

The success of the *Scofield Reference Bible* was an indication of how dispensationalism took hold in the sprawling network of Bible institutes and seminaries created or led by fundamentalists in the 1920s and 1930s. Moody Bible Institute in Chicago became an important trainer of dispensational pastors and missionaries. So, too, did the Bible Institute of Los Angeles, founded in 1908 and funded by the oil magnate Lyman Stewart. Some of the largest conservative Protestant mission agencies, including China Inland Mission and the Christian and Missionary Alliance, become hotbeds of dispensationalism. In 1924 Lewis Sperry Chafer opened Evangelical Theological Seminary (later Dallas Theological Seminary), which would become the center of dispensational theology for the rest of the century.[19]

The highpoint of dispensational theology—as judged through theological production, institutional support, and church adoption—came because of these advances. From 1940 to 1965, there was a type of scholastic golden age for dispensationalism. Dozens of dense theological works

[17] Matthew Avery Sutton, *American Apocalypse: A History of Modern Evangelicalism* (Cambridge, MA: Belknap, 2014), 114–47.

[18] Timothy Gloege, *Guaranteed Pure: The Moody Bible Institute, Business, and the Making of Modern Evangelicalism* (Chapel Hill: University of North Carolina Press, 2015).

[19] Brendan Pietsch, "Lyman Stewart and Early Fundamentalism," *Church History* 82, no. 3 (2013): 617–46; John D. Hannah, *An Uncommon Union: Dallas Theological Seminary and American Evangelicalism* (Grand Rapids, MI: Zondervan, 2009).

were published, creating a scholarly community of discourse. Dallas Theological Seminary featured such writers as John F. Walvoord, Charles Ryrie, and J. Dwight Pentecost. Ryrie's 1965 book *Dispensationalism Today* crystallized the theology's doctrines, which were held by millions of American Christians. Alva McClain, a one-time teacher at the Bible Institute of Los Angeles, founded Grace Theological Seminary in 1937. Talbot Theological Seminary, a West Coast version of Dallas Theological Seminary, was founded in 1952 by an alumnus, Charles Feinberg.[20]

These dispensationalist institutions and theologians were also integral to the reemergence of American evangelicalism after the Second World War. Walvoord and McClain were founding members of the Evangelical Theological Society, for example, with many less well-known dispensationalists as members. Dispensationalism appeared to have become not only the semi-official theology of fundamentalism, but an important contributor to a revived postwar evangelicalism. Billy Graham intoned dispensationalist themes in his sermons; half of the founding faculty of the new Fuller Theological Seminary in 1947 were dispensationalists.[21]

The creeping divisions between dispensationalist and historic premillennialism reemerged, however, in postwar evangelicalism. Dispensationalism's close association with fundamentalism bubbled up in these same decades that dispensationalists enjoyed widespread success. Fuller Theological Seminary was a case in point. While half of its original faculty was dispensationalist, the other half was not, with the century's most influential historic premillennialist, George Eldon Ladd, joining the faculty in 1950. Ladd's criticisms of dispensationalist theology, his rejection of the literalist hermeneutic, and his refutation of the church as a "parenthesis" in the story of Israel gave dispensationalists a challenge within the ranks of the evangelical movement. From *Crucial Questions about the Kingdom of God* (1952) to *A Theology of the New Testament* (1974), Ladd led the way in detaching conservative evangelical theology from dispensationalism.[22] His overriding goal, as

20 See Charles Ryrie, *Dispensationalism Today* (Chicago: Moody Press, 1965); J. Dwight Pentecost, *Things to Come: A Study in Biblical Eschatology* (Findlay, OH: Dunham, 1958); Alva J. McClain, *The Greatness of the Kingdom: An Inductive Study of the Kingdom of God as Set Forth in the Scriptures* (Grand Rapids, MI: Zondervan, 1959).

21 George Marsden, *Reforming Fundamentalism: Fuller Seminary and the New Evangelicalism* (Grand Rapids, MI: Eerdmans, 1987).

22 George Eldon Ladd, *Crucial Questions about the Kingdom of God* (Grand Rapids, MI: Eerdmans, 1952); George Eldon Ladd, *A Theology of the New Testament* (Grand Rapids, MI: Eerdmans, 1974).

his biographer John D'Elia writes, was to wrest evangelical theology out of fundamentalism's (including dispensationalism's) grip and win "a place at the table" of the broader Protestant theological conversation. In toppling dispensationalism's mantle in evangelical theology, Ladd was largely successful. By 1984, when the historian Mark Noll took a poll of the same Evangelical Theological Society that dispensationalists had a hand in founding, Ladd's *A Theology of the New Testament* was tied for the most influential text. Other major evangelical theologians of the era, including Carl F. H. Henry, Merrill Tenney, and Harold Lindsell, advanced Ladd's assault on dispensationalism as well (all three were also historic premillennialists).[23]

Yet at the same moment of dispensationalism's intellectual decline, it was enjoying an explosion of cultural and lay interest. The spark for this brushfire again consisted of geopolitical events, including the creation of a European Common Market in 1957 and the Arab–Israeli War in June 1967, both stirring apocalyptic interest and conforming to dispensationalist predictions. Just as important was the skillful popularization of dispensationalism by Hal Lindsey, a Dallas Theological Seminary graduate. With the help of a ghostwriter, Carol Carlson, Lindsey wrote the bestselling nonfiction book of the 1970s, *The Late Great Planet Earth* (1970).[24]

Lindsey's book translated the eschatology of dispensationalism into a stylish and more experiential idiom. He described the rapture as "the ultimate trip"—a play on the youth drug culture of the same historical moment. He honed his years of experience as a campus evangelist and offered a grand narrative of the near future for students who had become disillusioned with the drift of American society, describing how the Antichrist will subjugate most of the world's population and eventually betray Israel. Divine plagues and disasters will then ravage humanity. Jesus will return to defeat the Antichrist and establish his new kingdom in Jerusalem. Although these events were disclosed only in prophetic Scripture, Lindsey assured his readers that the preparatory steps and

[23] John A. D'Elia, *A Place at the Table: George Eldon Ladd and the Rehabilitation of Evangelical Scholarship in America* (New York: Oxford University Press, 2008); R. Todd Mangum, *The Dispensational–Covenantal Rift: The Fissuring of American Evangelical Theology from 1936 to 1944* (Eugene, OR: Wipf & Stock, 2007); Mark A. Noll, *Between Faith and Criticism: Evangelicals, Scholarship, and the Bible in America*, 2nd ed. (Vancouver: Regent College Publishing, 2004), 226.

[24] Mark S. Sweetnam, "Hal Lindsay and the Great Dispensational Mutation," *Journal of Religion and Popular Culture* 23, no. 2 (2011): 217–35.

portents were discernible—in the Middle East and the cultural revolutions of the 1960s.[25]

The popularity that Lindsey garnered did not, however, translate into a revival of dispensational theology. From its highpoint in the 1940s and 1950s, dispensationalism became an increasingly populist theology with declining scholarly engagement. While Dallas Theological Seminary continued to thrive, other centers of evangelical training, including Fuller Theological Seminary, Gordon-Conwell Theological Seminary, and Southern Baptist Theological Seminary, were decidedly not dispensationalist. By the twenty-first century, once stalwart dispensationalist citadels such as Moody Bible Institute and Talbot Theological Seminary were less dogmatic, as well.

These schools remained squarely within evangelicalism, but promoted a mix of historic premillennialism, amillennialism (the rejection of a thousand-year millennial kingdom in any form), and a general anti-apocalypticism. Ladd, who died in 1982, had helped resurrect historic premillennialism within the evangelical scholarly ranks. Apocalyptic fervor continued in popular evangelical culture, in print media, and on the internet, but it was taught less and less in evangelical seminaries. This decades-long trend—dispensationalism's cultural popularity amid its marginal academic standing—helps explain why its popularizers have been masters at marketing and media outreach while often lacking academic and institutional credentials.

CONSUMING THE APOCALYPSE

What dispensationalism lacked in academic respectability it made up for in its adaptability, marketability, and countenance of cultural anxieties in modern America. In each major medium of communication in the twentieth century—print, radio, and film—dispensationalism became the defining vision of American apocalypticism. For its promoters, dispensational apocalypticism was wildly profitable and applicable to virtually every crisis. For its increasing base of consumers, apocalypticism offered up-to-date commentary on global events, a tangible sense of the Bible's relevance, and, not to be underestimated, a potent source of entertainment.[26]

[25] Melani McAlister, *Epic Encounters: Culture, Media, and U.S. Interests in the Middle East since 1945*, 2nd ed. (Berkeley: University of California Press, 2005), 165–78.

[26] Amy Frykholm, *Rapture Culture: Left Behind in Evangelical America* (New York: Oxford University Press, 2004).

The popular cultural success of dispensational apocalypticism predated the twentieth century. In 1878 the evangelist and missionary William E. Blackstone published *Jesus Is Coming*, a popularization of the still-unsystematized teachings of Darby that emphasized real world events, especially in Palestine, that aligned with biblical prophecy. By Blackstone's death in 1935, *Jesus Is Coming* had been translated into more than forty languages and had sold more than one million copies.[27] Blackstone's *Jesus Is Coming*, like Hal Lindsey's *Late Great Planet Earth* almost a century later, simply assumed the validity of dispensational ideas. The literalist approach to passages of prophecy connected to current events helped solidify dispensationalism as the dominant theology through which Americans consumed the apocalypse. Although other genres of apocalyptic writing flourished in American culture, including scientific and later environmental apocalypticism (seeing humanity's extinction in technological mismanagement or the destruction of the environment), biblical prophecy interpretation was quickly dominated by dispensationalists.[28]

The genre interpreted prophecy texts "literally" with headline events. The First World War, the Balfour Declaration, the Bolshevik Revolution, and the rise of Stalin, Mussolini, and Hitler were each analyzed as signs of prophecy fulfillment. When the prophet Zechariah foresaw the horror—"Their flesh shall rot while they are still on their feet; their eyes shall rot in their sockets, and their tongues shall rot in their mouths" (Zech 14:12)—dispensationalists wondered whether this was a description of nuclear warfare. While dispensationalist theologians eschewed hard date setting, self-described prophecy experts often had fewer inhibitions. The desire for precision motivated more detailed analysis. In a century of increasing scientific authority, dispensationalists, while skeptical of Darwinism and geological dating, committed themselves to the values of precision, systematization, and prediction in their writings.[29]

Dispensational voices were amplified by the widespread adoption of radio in the 1920s, propounding a particularly populist version of apocalypticism. Charles Fuller, Carl McIntire, William Ward Ayer, Martin De Haan, and Billy Graham each gained a national religious

27 Jonathan David Moorhead, "Jesus Is Coming: The Life and Work of William E. Blackstone (1841–1935)" (PhD diss., Dallas Theological Seminary, 2008).

28 Lisa Vox, *Existential Threats: American Apocalyptic Beliefs in the Technological Era* (Philadelphia: University of Pennsylvania Press, 2017).

29 Hal Lindsey with C. C. Carlson, *The Late Great Planet Earth* (Grand Rapids, MI: Zondervan, 1970), 163–64.

following from the airwaves. Two of the leading apocalyptic voices in the early age of radio were Paul Rader and Aimee Semple McPherson. Based in Chicago and pastor of Moody Memorial Church from 1915 to 1921, Rader carried forth the legacy of Dwight Moody and helped establish dispensationalism as the semi-official theology of fundamentalism. Rader was no ideologue, but his premillennial assumptions pervaded his radio sermons and colored his concern for changing social norms and gender roles in the 1920s. McPherson, a rare female public voice in prophecy interpretation, made the apocalypse a cornerstone of her Pentecostal ministry, based in Los Angeles and over the airwaves of KFSG, which McPherson's new denomination, the Foursquare Gospel Church, purchased in 1924. McPherson preached on the signs of the "last days," writes her biographer Matthew Sutton; time was short, and "the pentecostal revival signified the imminence of the apocalypse." McPherson took a special interest in Palestine, traveling there in 1926 and 1930. Institutionalizing her millenarian beliefs, she made the fourth tenet of her "foursquare gospel" the "soul-enrapturing visions of the coming King."[30]

After the Second World War, apocalypticism reached Americans by way of radio and television, and by writers who could reach a mass audience through paperbacks. Operating outside the strictures of denominations and often heading their own parachurch organizations, these promoters reached millions of Americans with a dispensational-inspired message of the apocalypse. Unlike those of theologians and church leaders, their motives were less in systematizing Darby's teachings or establishing theological doctrines than in evangelizing and building a popular audience. The increasingly decentralized and consumer-oriented market for apocalyptic prophecy interpretation shaped the content of apocalyptic analysis itself. Less tethered to a systematized dispensationalism and less beholden to church or seminary authorities, the promoters reflected the demands and fears of consumers as much as they did traditional teachings.[31]

In the burgeoning postwar world of parachurch organizations, television empires, and personality-driven ministries, apocalyptic

[30] Sutton, *American Apocalypse*, 142; Matthew Avery Sutton, *Aimee Semple McPherson and the Resurrection of Christian America* (Cambridge, MA: Harvard University Press, 2007), 41; Tona J. Hangen, *Redeeming the Dial: Radio, Religion, and Popular Culture in America* (Chapel Hill: University of North Carolina Press, 2002).

[31] Crawford Gribben, *Writing the Rapture: Prophecy Fiction in Evangelical America* (New York: Oxford University Press, 2009).

preaching and speculation were ubiquitous, especially in radio and television. Early pioneers in the 1950s included Billy Graham and the Pentecostal healing ministers Rex Humbard and Oral Roberts. In the 1970s and 1980s the televangelism boom included Pat Robertson, Jerry Falwell, Jack Van Impe, Jim and Tammy Bakker, and Jimmy Swaggart. All of these media-savvy personalities were at least nominally dispensationalist in their outlook. They often combined an intense interest in evidences of the Holy Spirit, supernatural healing, and intercessory prayer—distinctly Pentecostal concerns—with warnings of an imminent rapture.[32]

For all the success and influence of radio and television, print still ruled the apocalypse market in the 1970s. Lindsey's *Late Great Planet Earth*, selling more than ten million copies in the decade (35 million copies by 2017), was a high-water mark. Lindsey would go on to write dozens of books in the same genre, including the bestsellers *There's a New World Coming* (1973) and *The 1980s: Countdown to Armageddon* (1980). But Lindsey was only the most successful in a lucrative and expanding nonfiction genre. America's most famous evangelist, Billy Graham, consistently published apocalyptic tracts. Inspired by dispensational teachings, including the rapture, Antichrist, and the prophetic future of Israel, Graham published titles such as *World Aflame* (1965), *Approaching Hoofbeats* (1983), and *Storm Warning* (1992), each predicting a looming apocalypse. The independent church pastor Tim LaHaye, who would go on to cowrite the *Left Behind* series, first made his mark on the apocalypse with *The Beginning of the End* (1972) and *No Fear of the Storm* (1977). Pat Robertson, founder of the Christian Broadcast Network and host of *The 700 Club*, put forth his idiosyncratic view of the end in *The New World Order* (1991).

Even Robertson, whose apocalyptic tract was labeled anti-Semitic by American Jewish groups for its preoccupation with well-worn conspiracy theories, operated within what could feasibly be described as the "mainstream" of dispensational apocalypticism. Other apocalyptic writers strayed from the norms of the genre and developed followings for even more outlandish, and precise, speculation. Reviving the spirit of William Miller, the retired NASA engineer Edgar C. Whisenant claimed in his bestseller *88 Reasons Why the Rapture Will Be in 1988*

[32] John Wigger, *PTL: The Rise and Fall of Jim and Tammy Faye Bakker's Evangelical Empire* (New York: Oxford University Press, 2017); Jeffrey K. Hadden, *Prime Time Preachers: The Rising Power of Televangelism* (Reading, MA: Addison-Wesley, 1981).

(1988) that the rapture would occur between September 11 and 13, 1988. The book was mailed to hundreds of thousands of pastors and sold more than four million copies. When the dates came and went, Whisenant revised his predictions to 1993, and again to 1997. He died in 2001. A similar prognosticator, the radio evangelist Harold Camping, first announced on his Family Radio stations that the Second Coming would take place between September 15 and 27, 1994. When the dates passed, Camping revised his argument in a 2005 book, *Time Has an End*, to claim that Jesus had in fact come back in secret in 1994 and that the rapture would occur on May 21, 2011. Camping again reinterpreted events after they failed to occur and insisted that October 21, 2011 was the end of the world. He died in 2013, still attempting to decode the biblical timeline.[33]

Whisenant and Camping, though unsuccessful in their interpretations of biblical prophecy, impacted the popular image of the American apocalypse as much as Lindsey and Robertson. The American interest in hidden knowledge, numerology, and ancient secrets embedded in sacred texts, especially as a detailed roadmap of the future, has grown exponentially since the 1980s. Popular radio shows like *Coast to Coast AM*, which regularly features segments on biblical prophecy, UFOs, and conspiracies—and television programs like the History Channel's exposés of the sixteenth-century French seer Nostradamus and *Decoding the Bible's Secrets*—share in the basic dispensational-inspired eschatology of popular American apocalypticism. These cultural productions operate in a general premillennialist expectation of an imminent cataclysm on the horizon, with special insights marketed at a premium.[34]

Even as the worlds of Robertson, Lindsey, Whisenant, and Camping are distant from the scholastic and theological debates that preoccupied theologians and church leaders from an earlier era, there have been some scholarly dispensational attempts to capitalize on popular apocalyptic energy. Following the Arab–Israeli War of October 1973 and the Arab oil boycott, the Dallas Theological Seminary president John

[33] Matthew Avery Sutton, "Preparing for Doomsday," in *Faith in the New Millennium: The Future of Religion and American Politics*, eds. Matthew Avery Sutton and Darren Dochuck (New York: Oxford University Press, 2016), 234–49; Amy Frykholm, "Apocalypticism in Contemporary Christianity," in *The Oxford Handbook of Apocalyptic Literature*, ed. John J. Collins (New York: Oxford University Press, 2014), 441–56.

[34] Richard G. Kyle, *Apocalyptic Fever: End-Time Prophecies in Modern America* (Eugene, OR: Cascade, 2012).

Walvoord wrote *Armageddon, Oil and the Middle East Crisis* (1974), which argued that the centrality of oil in the global economy indicated the rise of the Middle East in global politics and the approaching time for the rapture. The book was revised and reissued in 1990 in anticipation of the Gulf War (and again in 2007) and has sold more than two million copies. Walvoord's Dallas Theological Seminary colleague Charles Dyer made similar inroads into the popular market with his 1990 study of Saddam Hussein, *The Rise of Babylon* (1990). Convinced that Hussein was rebuilding the ancient city of Babylon in accordance with prophecy, Dyer portrayed an American–Iraqi confrontation as a cosmic, biblical struggle. The book was revised and reissued in January 2003, just weeks before the start of the Iraq War.

These dispensational theologians, like the most popular writers in the genre, have resisted precise date setting, recognizing both the limit of certainty in the biblical text and a self-interest in avoiding embarrassing failed predictions. The remarkable lasting power of prophecy interpretation in light of major world events, including the fall of the Soviet Union and the rise of the Internet, is due to this adaptability to new geopolitical situations. While individual prophecy experts have lost credibility after a date-setting scandal, the genre as a whole operates on a perpetual imminency paradigm that fits the apocalyptic message to each new historical moment. In recent years prophecy writers have speculated about the identity of the Antichrist as Barack Obama, Vladimir Putin, or Bashar Al-Asad, and the cosmological significance of the Arab Spring and Syrian Civil War, and the Arab–Israeli conflict. The commercialized logic of the genre, as one of mass cultural production, rewards writers who carve out novel and unique interpretations. The peculiar demands of biblical prophecy—requiring any interpretation to be tethered to the text of the Bible—constitute practically the only inhibitor to new speculations.

The same flexibility and market logic is a major part of the success of prophecy fiction. While the *Left Behind* series (1995–2007), with sixteen core novels, has sold upwards of 65 million copies, it is just the most recent (and most commercially successful) in the genre of prophecy fiction. The first innovators included Joshua Hill Foster, author of *The Judgement Day* (1910), and British writer Sidney Watson, who wrote a trilogy of prophecy novels in the 1910s. Even at this early stage, dispensationalism quickly became the operating cosmology. Although these novels did not explicitly adopt a dispensationalist framework, the critic Crawford Gribben observes, they operated under the expectation that most readers assumed dispensationalism was true.

Like nonfiction prophecy books, the novels reflected the geopolitical, social, cultural, and religious settings in which they were written. In *Be Thou Prepared for Jesus Is Coming* (1937), Forrest Loman Oilar critiqued the market capitalism that he blamed for the Great Depression; Dayton Manker's *They That Remain* (1941) raised the specter of communism as the beast of Revelation and was the first novel, according to Gribben, to imagine Christians suddenly raptured from automobiles, trains, and cockpits—now a trope of American apocalyptic culture. Manker and Ernest Angley, who wrote *Raptured* (1950), were also some of the first apocalypticists to contemplate the threat of secularism to American society.[35]

A shared dispensationalist backdrop did not eliminate disagreements on the details. Authors differed on the timing of the rapture, the identity of the Antichrist, the nature of the mark of the beast, and many other facets. The aim of the genre was unified, however: winning converts to Christianity, instructing and comforting fellow Christians, and increasing sales. Novels such as Salem Kirban's *666* (1970) sold half a million copies in three years, while other contributions, such as Morris Cerullo's *The Omega Code* (1981) and Pat Robertson's *The End of the Age* (1995), fit neatly into broader personality-based empires.

Prophecy fiction also advanced onto the big screen, first finding success with *A Thief in the Night* (1972), a low-budget rapture movie that its producers estimated was eventually shown to over 100 million viewers. The film's director, Donald Thompson, would also direct *Prodigal Planet* (1983), the final of four installments in the *Thief in the Night* series. The surprising crossover success of *The Omega Code* (1999), written by the televangelist Paul Crouch, capitalized on the Bible Code phenomenon. *Left Behind*'s first movie adaptation was released directly to video in 2000 and sold more than three million copies in its first year. After two more films and a 2014 reboot starring Nicolas Cage, the Left Behind brand appears to have waned. However, other rapture films including *The Mark* (2012) and *Final: The Rapture* (2013) point to the continuing interest in producing and marketing dispensational apocalypticism.

Each of these films is notable not only because it evidences the continuing popular interest in dispensational apocalypticism, but because it fuses religious teachings with contemporary popular culture trends. *A Thief in the Night* situates the oppressive one-world

[35] Gribben, *Writing the Rapture*, 11–12.

government in the United Nations, playing into evangelical concerns about internationalism; *The Omega Code* imagines how the power of computers, then overtaking all aspects of American life in the 1990s, could unlock hitherto unknowable biblical secrets; *Final: The Rapture* adapts the same narrative framework as the award-winning *Babel* (2006), following four discrete storylines but in this case as they respond to a rapture scenario. Other films, including the comedies *This Is the End* (2013) and *Rapture-Palooza* (2013), merely use the trope of a rapture as a narrative device.[36]

Judged by sales, by the year 2000 prophecy fiction had replaced prophecy nonfiction as the primary cultural shaper of evangelical beliefs about the apocalypse. The change in genre revealed the evolving role of prophecy belief in American evangelicalism. Fiction allowed more room for speculation and imagination on the part of prophecy writers and more fully embodied the commercialization and consumer appeal of the apocalypse. Even less relevant for fiction than for nonfiction, authorial credentials, theological orthodoxy, and institutional affiliations were eclipsed by writing and marketing skills—in short, entertainment value. While some writers still seek to advance theological and moral arguments in prophecy fiction, many others pay homage to the genre by expanding the marketing appeal of the apocalypse and assuming, without reflection, its dispensational underpinnings.[37]

THE POLITICS OF APOCALYPSE

Tracking alongside the theological story of dispensationalism and its commercialization are the political consequences of apocalypticism in American society. Though only one of many motivations for evangelicals to enter the political fray, dispensational apocalypticism has shaped major political debates in three areas in particular: the Cold War, United States domestic politics, and the United States' support for the state of Israel.[38]

[36] Boyer, *When Time Shall Be No More*, 267–69. See also John Walliss and James Aston, "Doomsday America: The Pessimistic Turn of Post-9/11 Apocalyptic Cinema," *Journal of Religion and Popular Culture* 23, no. 1 (April 2011): 53–64; and John Walliss and Lee Quinby, eds., *Reel Revelations: Apocalypse and Film* (Sheffield: Sheffield Phoenix, 2010).

[37] On the centrality of prophecy fiction to modern evangelicalism, see Crawford Gribben and Mark S. Sweetnam, eds., *Left Behind and the Evangelical Imagination* (Sheffield: Sheffield Phoenix, 2011).

[38] See especially Sutton, *American Apocalypse*; Angela M. Lahr, *Millennial Dreams and Apocalyptic Nightmares: The Cold War Origins of Political Evangelicalism* (New York: Oxford University Press, 2007); Melani McAlister, "Prophecy, Politics,

In the wake of the Second World War, apocalyptic anxieties wracked the American public. Looming mushroom clouds and fears of another world war fed the rising influence of dispensational apocalypticism. The "Age of Anxiety," as the poet W. H. Auden labeled the immediate postwar period, also shaped the politics of the early Cold War and fueled anticommunist activism both at home and abroad. For many dispensationalists, the Cold War itself was part of the prologue to the end-times—as much a cosmic confrontation between Christianity and communism as an ideological battle between the United States and the Soviet Union.[39]

In dispensational prophecy interpretations, the evil prince of Ezek 38:1, "Gog, of the land of Magog," was identified with the ancestral kingdoms of Russia. This and other passages, including Gog's resurfacing in Rev 20:8, supplied evangelicals with prophetic sanction to oppose the Soviet Union. In the most prominent dispensational reading, Gog, identified as the "Prince of Rosh, Meshech, and Tubal" (the first two names stipulated to be eerily similar to "Russia" and "Moscow"), will be allied with Satan and lead an alliance of countries against Israel. God will supernaturally protect the Jewish state and set in motion the tribulation; the timing of the rapture in relation to Gog's invasion is up for debate among dispensationalists, though most insist the rapture could happen at any moment.[40]

Looking for prophecy fulfillments in daily headlines conditioned evangelicals to view communism as a monolithic ideology; divisions between and among communist movements were subsumed under a conviction that Moscow and the writings of Marx were the keys to understanding communism wherever it appeared. Likewise, many evangelicals viewed communism as a rival religion battling for souls in the last days. "You see, every communist is a convert-maker," explained the popular preacher George Sweeting in 1961. "For communism he gives up amusements, social life and even takes an inferior job in order to bring his message into a new place ... Communists have taken over

and the Popular: The 'Left Behind' Series and Christian Fundamentalism's New World Order," *South Atlantic Quarterly* 102, no. 4 (2003): 773–98.

39 W. H. Auden, *The Age of Anxiety: A Baroque Eclogue*, ed. Alan Jacobs (1947; Princeton, NJ: Princeton University Press, 2011). See Andrew Preston, *Sword of the Spirit, Shield of Faith: Religion in American War and Diplomacy* (New York: Knopf, 2012), 465–95.

40 Timothy P. Weber, *On the Road to Armageddon: How Evangelicals Became Israel's Best Friend* (Grand Rapids, MI: Baker Academic, 2005), 70–72; Boyer, *When Time Shall Be No More*, 154–62.

the methods Christ used and meant His church to use." American evangelicals, with global missionary networks, were aware not just of locations where the Cold War turned hot—the Korean Peninsula, Vietnam, the Middle East—but of societies in which Christian missionary access and influence diminished: in Marxist redoubts of China, Cuba, and Eastern Europe.[41]

Apocalypticism was also a feature of the anticommunist right. The McCarthyist inquisitions in the 1950s of anyone connected to communism bolstered the prospects of fundamentalist and evangelical dispensationalists. Anticommunist organizations with dispensationalist leaders flourished: Fred Schwarz's Christian Anti-Communism Crusade, Edgar C. Bundy's Church League of America, Billy James Hargis's Christian Crusade. Not to be outdone, more moderate evangelicals also capitalized on American receptivity to apocalyptic anticommunism. Billy Graham "masterfully blended," writes the historian Matthew Sutton, "the apocalyptic urgency of interwar fundamentalism with the respectability of postwar evangelicalism," ushering dispensationalist categories into the center of American political culture. Graham's world travels and meetings with leaders convinced him that an apocalyptic dread pervaded global politics and, as a silver lining, drew more attention to the authority of the Bible.[42]

Even as American prophecy writers identified enemies of America with the forces of evil, they often resisted sacralizing the United States government. The conservative "anti-statist statism" that defined late twentieth-century evangelical politics was built in part on apocalyptic thinking. The absence of the United States in biblical prophecy made many evangelicals hesitant to equate the United States government with God's will. Moreover, and dating to the writings of Darby and Scofield, dispensationalists maintained a strict theological distinction between what it defined as the church and "the nations." As a gentile nation, the United States was not a covenantal agent of God's plans on par with Israel or the church. In the Bible, "the nations" of Egypt, Persia,

[41] George Sweeting, "Communism or Christ," *King's Business* (October 1961): 11. See Axel R. Schäfer, "Evangelical Global Engagement and the American State after World War II," *Journal of American Studies* 51, no. 4 (2017): 1069–94; and Sarah Ruble, *The Gospel of Freedom & Power: Protestant Missionaries in American Culture after World War II* (Chapel Hill: University of North Carolina Press, 2012), 35–90.

[42] Axel R. Schäfer, *Piety and Public Funding: Evangelicals and the State in Modern America*, Politics and Culture in Modern America (Philadelphia: University of Pennsylvania Press, 2012), 49; Sutton, *American Apocalypse*, 328.

and Assyria were mentioned only as they intersected with the story of Israel. Modern nations maintained a similar relationship. For dispensationalists the United States was an instrumental good—worthy of support when it contributed to the cause of world evangelization and protecting Israel (the other covenantal partner with the church)—but also deeply compromised by worldly interests. Hal Lindsey defined America's role in precisely these terms, explaining "why the U.S. has been preserved as a free country" as including: "that this country is made up of a large community of true believers in the Lord Jesus Christ ... has supported and provided for missionaries ... has stood behind Jews and the state of Israel in their times of need ... that God's people pray." Dispensationalists approached American politics through these categories. They endorsed limited government and laissez-faire economics *because* they were historically boons to American churches and the cause of missions.[43]

As American society and the United States government became secularized in the latter half of the twentieth century, dispensationalists detected a plot to undermine the health of the church and Israel. Their widespread support and activism on behalf of the New Right was premised on confronting "secular humanism" in government, education, and culture. An apocalyptic interpretation of the fading Christian America supplied a "politicized nostalgia" that appealed to mostly white Americans uncomfortable with rapid social change and increasing pluralization. The evangelical right's most influential leader, Jerry Falwell, was an independent Baptist dispensationalist. Other leaders, including Tim LaHaye, James Robison, and James Dobson, operated more or less explicitly under the assumptions of dispensationalism.[44]

While dispensationalists were the backbone of what became the "Christian Right," historic premillennialists joined them to win back Christian America from the grips of secular humanism. Perhaps the most electrifying Christian Right organizer of the late 1970s and early 1980s, Francis Schaeffer, came from conservative, historic premillennialist roots. This did not stop him from using apocalyptic imagery in

[43] Hal Lindsey, *The 1980's: The Countdown to Armageddon* (Opelousas, LA: Westgate, 1980), 156–57. See also Daniel G. Hummel, "The Limits of Evangelical Nationalism in the Cold War," in *North American Churches and the Cold War*, ed. Paul Mojzes (Grand Rapids, MI: Eerdmans, 2018), 414–17.

[44] Randall J. Stephens and Karl W. Giberson, *The Anointed: Evangelical Truth in a Secular Age* (Cambridge, MA: Belknap, 2011), 139–79; Daniel Williams, *God's Own Party: The Making of the Christian Right* (New York: Oxford University Press, 2010), 159–86.

his 1970 book *Pollution and the Death of Man* and in his oft-repeated jeremiads against abortion, euthanasia, and infanticide as constituting a looming "culture of death." But Schaeffer's historic premillennialism had a measurable impact on how he approached American culture. His rejection of the imminent rapture helped him develop a complicated cultural and philosophical critique of American culture—one that indicated his and his followers' readiness for a protracted culture war over the destiny of America. Later Christian Right leaders, claiming the same "worldview" approach to culture and politics, shared Schaeffer's eschatology. Leading figures in this mold included R. Albert Mohler, Jr., president of Southern Baptist Theological Seminary, Chuck Colson, and the author Eric Metaxes. These historic premillennialists sporadically leveraged apocalyptic language in their writings but rejected the theology that had originally made it popular.[45]

For dispensationalists, the role of Islam dominated prophecy writing and the politics attached to it since September 11, 2001, though this interest dated to the 1970s and the Arab oil embargo. In the 1990s, with the fall of the Soviet Union and the full turn of dispensational attention to the Middle East, such books as George Otis's *The Last of the Giants: Lifting the Veil on Islam and the End Times* (1991)— supported by the influx of works related to the Gulf War—shaped evangelical apocalyptic expectations that the Muslim world and especially the Islamic Republic of Iran were related to the prophetic villain Gog. In the wake of 9/11, a flood of prophecy speculation encouraged evangelicals to support the Global War on Terror and regard Islam as a violent religion. Hal Lindsey once again entered the fray with *The Everlasting Hatred: The Roots of Jihad* (2002), and Don Richardson, a one-time missionary, published *Secrets of the Koran* (2003). The apocalyptic dimension is part of what Richard Cimino termed the dispensational "polemic against Islam" after 9/11, seeing developments in the Muslim world as prophetically significant and interpreting an inevitable clash between Judeo-Christian and Islamic civilizations.[46]

Just as fervently as dispensationalists opposed Islamic extremism, they supported the state of Israel. Christian Zionism—the movement to politically and religiously support Israel on the basis of the Bible—was deeply entwined with dispensationalism. Early proponents of Jewish

[45] Barry Hankins, *Francis Schaeffer and the Shaping of Evangelical America* (Grand Rapids, MI: Eerdmans, 2008).

[46] Grayson R. Robertson, "The Influence of Dispensationalist Theology on Evangelical Perceptions of Muslims post-9/11" (PhD diss., Georgetown University, 2011).

settlement in Palestine such as William Blackstone were, as we have seen, instrumental to the success of dispensationalism and regarded any development in Jewish history, from pogroms to kibbutzim to the Holocaust, as prophetically significant. After the establishment of Israel in 1948, the first evangelical political activists on behalf of the state were dispensationalists. Apocalyptic fervor over Israel peaked when geopolitical developments appeared to align with dispensational expectations, such as those in 1948, 1967, and 1973—each an occasion of a major war in the Middle East.[47]

The close ties that Israel created with American evangelicals through tourism, fundraising, and organization building from the 1960s onwards marginalized, though hardly eradicated, apocalypticism from the leadership of the Christian Zionist movement. Through the 1980s and 1990s, the Israeli government courted Jerry Falwell, Pat Robertson, and other evangelicals who were either dispensationalists or deeply inspired by the theology to support Israel. But, unlike earlier dispensationalists, these late twentieth-century political leaders suppressed the gruesome details of their end-times predictions and curbed efforts to convert Jews.

American Christian Zionism's current leader, John Hagee, a Pentecostal pastor and founder of Christians United for Israel in 2006, embodies the uneasy balance that has been struck between apocalyptic and pragmatic politics. Hagee is both a political activist and a bestselling prophecy writer. He was raised as a dispensationalist who still remembers the night of May 14, 1948, when as an eight-year-old he listened to Israel's first prime minister David Ben-Gurion declare independence over the radio, and his entire ministry is shaped by an anticipation of Jesus's return. He became a bestselling author in the 1990s with a prophecy trilogy, *The Beginning of the End* (1996), *Final Dawn over Jerusalem* (1998), and *From Daniel to Doomsday* (1999). Like Pat Robertson and other prophecy writers, Hagee warns Americans that God will soon be passing his judgment on a secularizing America.[48]

In his prophecy writing Hagee mentioned Israel frequently, but bridging the gap from apocalypticism to activism required a venture into political theology. A Pentecostal minister and longtime preacher of

[47] Daniel G. Hummel, "A 'Practical Outlet' to Premillennial Faith: G. Douglas Young and the Evolution of Christian Zionist Activism in Israel," *Religion and American Culture* 25, no. 1 (2015): 37–81; Yaakov Ariel, *An Unusual Relationship: Evangelical Christians and Jews* (New York: New York University Press, 2013), 171–97.

[48] John Hagee, *In Defense of Israel*, rev. ed. (Lake Mary, FL: FrontLine, 2007).

the prosperity gospel—teaching that God desires to bless his followers with material wealth and physical health—Hagee turned to one of the key Christian Zionist verses in the Bible, Gen 12:3, to make the connection. Speaking to Abraham, God promises: "I will bless those who bless you, and the one who curses you I will curse; and in you all the families of the earth shall be blessed." Read through a dispensational interpretation, the verse promises Abraham's descendants, the nation of Israel, that they would be the mediators of God's blessings to the earth. Hagee had found the key to both individual and national renewal: bless Israel to receive God's blessings.[49] Linking this rationale for activism with his ongoing interest in the apocalypse (he published a new prophecy tract, *Four Blood Moons*, in 2013), Hagee became the most influential twenty-first-century Christian Zionist in America.[50]

Like many contemporary apocalyptic writers, Hagee adheres tenuously to dispensational teachings. As the subtitle of *Four Blood Moons*, "Something Is About to Change," indicates, his predictions are often vague, imprecise, and generalized. His brand of apocalypticism is perpetually imminent. Moreover, his prominent political role requires that many of his detailed views on prophecy remain opaque. What Hagee does pinpoint, however, is how apocalypticism has mixed with other theological and political concerns, adding energy and urgency to causes embraced for theological reasons by millions of American evangelicals.

CONCLUSION

The apocalypse in American evangelicalism has profoundly shaped and been profoundly shaped by evangelical theology, popular culture, and politics. Different understandings of the apocalypse and the precise details of its arrival have fostered disagreement and rival schools of interpretation. The rise of dispensational premillennialism from the late nineteenth century was significant, but it also never achieved academic respectability outside evangelicalism. By the 1960s dispensationalism's credibility as a theological system was on the decline, even as its cultural imprint grew.

49 Sean Durbin, "'I Will Bless Those Who Bless You': Christian Zionism, Fetishism, and Unleashing the Blessings of God," *Journal of Contemporary Religion* 28, no. 3 (2013): 507–21.

50 John Hagee, "Israel: God's Two-Minute Warning," May 1, 2016, www.youtube.com/watch?v=yLpMrKpIOAo (accessed October 16, 2019).

Although apocalyptic-themed popular culture predated the period after the Second World War, dispensational influence reached new heights in the 1970s. The bestselling book of the decade, Hal Lindsey's *Late Great Planet Earth*, popularized dispensationalist concepts including the rapture and the prophetic importance of the Cold War and the Middle East to millions of Americans. Indeed, the commercial logic of prophecy writing has shaped its popularity and even its content for decades. Expanding audiences and innovations in the genre have pushed apocalypticism into mainstream culture, both as distinctly evangelical productions (such as *Left Behind*) and as tropes used in the broader culture for diverse creative purposes.

Like its cultural footprint, apocalypticism's political influence has often played a role in American society. From the Cold War to support for Israel, the urgency that apocalypticism conveys is crucial to its allure. The adaptability of dispensationalism to political and social crises has made it an integral part of American evangelical politics. Even non-dispensationalist evangelicals, such as Francis Schaeffer, have leveraged latent apocalyptic language to frame their activism.

The life of dispensationalism is now largely separate from its religious history. When the author Tom Perrotta published his 2011 novel *The Leftovers* (also later adapted to an HBO series), he based its premise on the well-worn apocalyptic trope of a small percentage of the world's population suddenly vanishing into thin air. Perrotta was more interested in the survivors than in the causes of the "Sudden Departure," but his narrative reliance on the rapture is a testament to how widespread the teaching became to Americans of all religious persuasions. And unlike the authors of *Left Behind*, Perrotta had no evangelistic or Christian theological agenda. To judge by Perrotta's novel, the rapture has transcended its humble religious roots to become a quintessentially American concept dominated by commercial and market forces—a microcosm of dispensationalism's trajectory, as well.[51]

Selected Further Reading

Ariel, Yaakov. *An Unusual Relationship: Evangelical Christians and Jews*. New York: New York University Press, 2013.

Boyer, Paul. *When Time Shall Be No More: Prophecy Belief in Modern American Culture*. Cambridge, MA: Belknap, 1994.

[51] Andrew Crome, "Left Behind or Left Below? Parodies of Christian End-Times Fiction in American Popular Culture," *Journal of American Culture* 38, no. 4 (2015): 386–400.

Frykholm, Amy. *Rapture Culture: Left Behind in Evangelical America*. New York: Oxford University Press, 2004.

Gloege, Timothy. *Guaranteed Pure: The Moody Bible Institute, Business, and the Making of Modern Evangelicalism*. Chapel Hill: University of North Carolina Press, 2015.

Gribben, Crawford. *Writing the Rapture: Prophecy Fiction in Evangelical America*. New York: Oxford University Press, 2009.

Gribben, Crawford, and Mark S. Sweetnam, eds. *Left Behind and the Evangelical Imagination*. Sheffield: Sheffield Phoenix, 2011.

Hummel, Daniel G. *Covenant Brothers: Evangelicals, Jews, and U.S.–Israeli Relations*. Philadelphia: University of Pennsylvania Press, 2019.

Lahr, Angela M. *Millennial Dreams and Apocalyptic Nightmares: The Cold War Origins of Political Evangelicalism*. New York: Oxford University Press, 2007.

Marsden, George. *Fundamentalism and American Culture*. 2nd ed. New York: Oxford University Press, 2006.

17 Apocalypticism in the Contemporary World

LORENZO DITOMMASO

Apocalyptic thinking informs virtually every major aspect of life in the twenty-first century. Its themes and images have become a staple of popular culture. Its categories shape the tenor of social dissent. Its expectations frame views on the state of the economy and the environment. Its ideology animates fundamentalist strains in every major religion and propels nativist political movements across the globe.

The ubiquity of apocalyptic thought today is the result of a seismic shift in outlook that began in the late 1960s and 1970s. This chapter examines the causes of this *apocalyptic shift* and its propulsive acceleration since 2001. It focuses on three main expressions of the shift: (1) popular culture, (2) the resurgence of robust apocalypticism in religions both new and old, and (3) the "illiberal revolution" and the normalization of apocalyptic thinking today. Special attention is devoted to the ways in which traditional apocalyptic tropes have been redeployed in the modern vernacular, and how apocalyptic ideas have moved from the margins to the mainstream.

APOCALYPTIC AND APOCALYPTICISM

What is "apocalyptic"?[1] What makes anything "apocalyptic"? What is an apocalyptic idea or symbol? How do apocalyptic ideas of salvation differ from those of the biblical prophets or in Buddhism? What

[1] The ideas in this section are drawn from several essays, most recently Lorenzo DiTommaso, "Natura e necessità della comunicazione tra cielo e a terra nella letteratura apocalittica," *Rivista ricerche storico bibliche* 29 (2017): 171–92; *bibliche* 29 (2017): 171–92; "Apocalyptic Historiography," *Early Christianity* 10 (2019); and "Apocalyptic Literature in the Global Imagination," in *A Companion to World Literature. Volume 1*, ed. K. Seigneurie (New York: Wiley Blackwell, 2020): 215–26. They are expounded in full detail in Lorenzo DiTommaso, *The Architecture of Apocalypticism*, the first of a trilogy, forthcoming from Oxford University Press.

connects the eschatology of the ancient Apocalypse of John with that of the modern new religion Heaven's Gate? How can we appreciate "apocalyptic" as a global phenomenon, yet also account for the diversity of its expression in hundreds of different cultures over the past 2000 years? What, in short, is the "DNA" of apocalyptic? While the DNA analogy is imprecise, it gets to the heart of the problem and points to a common element that underpins all things "apocalyptic."

This element is the worldview, or "apocalypticism." The apocalyptic worldview is defined by its axiomatic propositions about the nature of space, time, and human existence. These axioms, considered together, anchor the claims of apocalyptic speculation and accord meaning to apocalyptic phenomena. Nothing is "apocalyptic" independent of the worldview. It is the apocalyptic worldview that gives things an apocalyptic valence, in the same way that the Buddhist worldview defines Buddhist texts and rituals, and Marxist ideology underwrites Marxist movements and manifestos.

- *The apocalyptic concept of space* presumes the existence of two discrete and separate realities. One reality is transcendent, the other is mundane. These realities are often called "heaven" and "earth," but in fact they are ontological categories, not physical or cosmological. In the apocalyptic mindset, Heaven is the genuine and perfect reality. Its most salient characteristic is its universal ultimacy. It is eternal, infrangible, and the sole source of accurate data. Earth, by contrast, is regarded as the opposite of Heaven in every respect. It was perfect, but is now flawed, having been irredeemably corrupted by evil. In the apocalyptic mindset, evil is a malignant, metaphysical force that is permanently in conflict with its opposite force, good. This conflict manifests itself in history in terms of radical binaries: truth versus lies, right versus wrong, light versus darkness, spirit versus flesh, life versus death. It also plays out on the group level, between the Elect, who are the intended audience of all apocalyptic speculation, and their opponents, the "Other."
- *Apocalyptic time* is wholly a property of the mundane or earthly reality. It is unidirectional, linear, and finite. In apocalyptic speculation, history has an ending, since it is the record of events in time. It is also predestined and revealed. As a result, apocalyptic history includes future events as well as those in the past and the present, since it purports to express the panoramic standpoint of the transcendent or heavenly reality. The Elect are always its focus, just as they are the center of the universe.

- The apocalyptic notions of space and time intersect in the conviction that the conflict between the forces of good and evil shall soon come to its predetermined end. In apocalyptic predictions in the "biblical" mode (see below), this expectation is phrased in terms of a divine plan whose culmination is the resurrection of the dead and the Final Judgment of individuals. In the secular mode, the plan and its culmination are articulated in different terms, but are functionally identical. No matter what its formulation, the message that the last days have come and the end is near constitutes *the existential dimension of the worldview.*

The primary operational function of apocalyptic speculation is to reveal the true nature of things to members of the group for which it is intended. Every other message depends on this function. This is a critical point if one recalls that apocalyptic speculation can and does extend to almost every subject. Whatever the object of its focus, apocalyptic prediction claims that its revelation originates from the one true reality, the sole source of wisdom. At its core, apocalyptic speculation is an information system. The revealed data are moderated by distinctive theories of knowing, history, justice, and salvation, each one a logical corollary of the underlying worldview. Salvation in the apocalyptic mindset, for example, is always imagined as salvation *out of* this world.

The primary social function of apocalyptic speculation is to maintain, reinforce, and validate group identity, typically in the face of threats, internal or external. Apocalyptic speculation is inherently reactionary, at least from the perspective of the group for which it is meant. It holds a special appeal for smaller groups that consider themselves oppressed, marginalized, or persecuted by the stakeholder elements in society.

And it is always about groups. A personal apocalypse is an oxymoron; apocalyptic predictions are not horoscopes. Even when the subject of the revelation stresses personal salvation or transformation, individuals are always considered as part of a group. Individuals are judged, but salvation comes through membership in a well-defined group. One is either part of the Elect or is not: infidel or heretic. One cannot "agree to disagree" when eternal life (or equivalent) is at stake.

To sum up, "apocalyptic" is encountered primarily at the experiential level: texts, music, art, symbols, communities, rhetoric, and so on. These phenomena manifest themselves in a variety of forms. Yet all acquire an apocalyptic valence by virtue of a notional framework that features claims regarding the nature of being, knowing, salvation, and justice. This *architecture of apocalypticism* rests on axiomatic propositions on the nature of space, time, and human destiny. The totality of these axioms and their claims describes a distinctive worldview. Investigating apocalyptic phenomena through the lens of the worldview thus allows us to distinguish the generic from the particular, and in so doing to identify things "apocalyptic" in their manifold cultural expressions across the centuries.

THE "APOCALYPTIC SHIFT"

The apocalyptic worldview emerged when a coalition of traditionalist Jews rebelled against their Seleucid Greek overlords during the Maccabean Revolt (167–164 BCE). The earliest apocalyptic writings date from these years, including the revelatory visions of the biblical Book of Daniel. Jesus of Nazareth, who lived two centuries later, was an apocalyptic preacher, and Christianity was an apocalyptic movement from its inception. An early product of this movement is the Apocalypse (or Revelation) of John, the final book of the New Testament. One of the most culturally influential books in history, its eschatological expectations set the pattern for much subsequent apocalyptic literature.

Apocalyptic speculation was central to medieval Christianity, Judaism, and Islam, the result of an earlier yet no less profound "apocalyptic shift" that occurred after the fall of the Roman Empire in the West. One result of this shift was the transmission of apocalyptic ideas across religious boundaries, to the extent that a common apocalyptic tradition can be detected in Christianity, Judaism, and Islam throughout the medieval millennium. Apocalyptic thinking shaped the Reformation that followed, during which time it also began to spread across the globe via European colonization. Lands conquered by Spain, France, and Portugal became heirs to the Catholic stream. Territories occupied by the Dutch and the British, notably the American colonies, became Protestant and the principle vector for the intromission of apocalypticism into the modern world. In every area, the worldview prompted the formation of millennial movements, often in hybridized forms (e.g., the 1850–64 Taiping Rebellion in China, the 1895–98 War of Canudos in Brazil).

The political, industrial, and scientific revolutions that have come to define the modern world also split apocalyptic speculation into two modes, biblical and secular. They essentially differ in their conception of the nature of the transcendent reality. Biblical (or traditional) apocalypticism is the mode of all Christian, Jewish, and Islamic apocalyptic speculation—pure or hybridized, robust or mild—from the ancient

Books of Daniel and Revelation to the present day. In this mode, the transcendent reality is Heaven/God (however defined). Secular apocalypticism is the mode of the worldview that grew out of Renaissance humanism and Enlightenment rationalism. It calibrates the propositions and claims of the apocalyptic worldview to historical situations and social settings within the aggregate of ideas that constitute what we call "modernity." In the secular mode, the transcendent reality might equate with a superhuman agency, a divinized form of humanity,[2] the "hidden hand" of history or the market, or even artificial intelligence. It also can be a placeholder reality against which the defective world is implicitly compared, as it is in much post-apocalyptic fiction (see the next section, below). In traditional apocalypticism, God is in; in secular apocalypticism, God is out.

The secularization of society in the West throughout the nineteenth and twentieth centuries gradually dampened robust apocalyptic speculation, especially among elites. Still, traditional forms of the apocalyptic worldview remained important in certain social milieus and among evangelicals. At the same time, secularized variants of the worldview emerged to fill the gap after the devastation of the First World War, notably in political formulations with millenarian overtones (e.g., Marxist-Leninism, National Socialism).

The late 1960s and the 1970s witnessed the start of a dramatic rise in the extent to which, and intensity with which, people in general came to regard their situations apocalyptically—that is, through the lens of the apocalyptic worldview. This "apocalyptic shift" has become a defining feature of the twenty-first century. While its causes have yet to be explained in detail, some preliminary observations may be tendered.

The apocalyptic shift has thus far undergone two phases. Its first phase began in the late 1960s and lasted until the end of the century. We cannot identify a coherent shift during that time, only diverse ecological, political, social, and religious movements. All were Western, with the United States the center of gravity and American culture the main locomotive force. These movements differed so greatly in their aims and audiences (what did the radical environmental group Earth First! have to do with Reagan-era neoconservatives?) that it was difficult to recognize that they were rooted in the same soil and were pointing in the same direction. They were protest movements. All were reactions

[2] John Gray, *Black Mass: Apocalyptic Religion and the Death of Utopia* (Toronto: Doubleday, 2007).

to the perceived impotency of traditional responses to the seismic changes that were underway.[3] They voiced the same kind of concerns and were using a common language to do so. That language was apocalyptic.

The second phase of the apocalyptic shift began with the twenty-first century. It was at this time that it acquired its coherent, global character. The earlier movements did not disappear, and many retain their identity today. However, as their root causes grew more acute and their social effects intensified, their audiences increased and acquired greater social volume and political leverage. The net result was a blurring of the boundaries among the movements and an overlapping of their perspectives. The 2016 vote for Brexit is a parade example of this confluence. This blurring of boundaries occurred not at the granular level—environmentalists still tend not to be political conservatives—but on the deeper strata of emotional response and social function. With no common agreement on the cause, there was a general sense that the world was getting worse in ways that seemed beyond human ability to fathom and beyond ordinary human means to retard or arrest.

The change in attitude was precipitated by four events:[4] the September 11, 2001 terrorist attacks and their knock-on effects, including the global refugee crisis; the Great Recession of 2008 and the acceleration of the hollowing-out of the traditional middle classes; the digital revolution; and the illiberal revolution.

The first two events nourished a growing sense among a significant proportion of the population worldwide that major systems—the global economy, liberal internationalism, standards of living, the social order, the food supply, electoral politics, the biosphere itself—were collapsing, in part because their limitations had been reached and in some cases exceeded. These concerns are neither academic nor altruistic. Rather, they are believed to pose a dire and immediate threat to daily life and existential wellbeing. At the same time, the conviction that such systemic problems can be solved though human industry, intellection, or ingenuity has steadily eroded. This sense of futility and helplessness has added a special dimension to the conviction that the world's systems are irrevocably broken and things are getting worse.

[3] J. Kaplan and H. Lööw, eds., *The Cultic Milieu: Oppositional Subcultures in an Age of Globalization* (Walnut Grove, CA: Altamira, 2002) is among the first studies to recognize this trend.

[4] None of these events occurred in a vacuum. The invention of intermodal transportation and the progressive weakening of international trade restrictions, for example, facilitated today's global trade.

This dimension is critical to the current apocalyptic shift and underscores how the apocalyptic worldview is literally a way of viewing the world. Consider, by way of contrast, the years from 1914 to 1945. This period witnessed two world wars, the Russian Revolution, the Great Depression, the 1918–20 influenza pandemic, the Holocaust, and the mass murder of millions of civilians. Yet a global apocalyptic shift did not emerge during these decades, despite acutely severe economic, political, and social crises. True, that era saw the rise of Russian Bolshevism and German National Socialism; each is a textbook illustration of a secular apocalyptic movement. But the mix of social pressures that enabled the proliferation of Marxism and fascism in Europe affected the rest of the world secondarily. Even in the West, and particularly in the United States and Britain, strong centrist counterforces dampened or deflected extremist impulses. These counterforces represented the stakeholder perspective in these and other nations. It quarantined the more radical, extremist, and fundamentalist voices on domestic and foreign policy, and allowed for the creation of the international liberal order after 1945.

The erosion of this centrist liberalism since 2001 is a key factor in the perfusion of the apocalyptic worldview in the social fabric across the planet. The digital revolution and the illiberal revolution have greatly facilitated this process.

The term "digital revolution" refers to the widespread implementation of new digital communications technologies and wireless social-media platforms. One result has been a democratization of information (with notable exceptions in nations with state censorship). Another has been the development of new types of multiform mass entertainment that have saturated everyday life to an extent unimaginable in the predigital age. The emergence of "superflat" apocalypticism, which is discussed in the next sections, reflects these social changes.[5]

The term "illiberal revolution" refers to the adoption, by a significant proportion of centrist and stakeholder elements in many democratic nations, of notions that once were considered extremist or fringe, particularly those that do not derive from liberal values. "Things fall apart; the centre cannot hold," as Yeats wrote in "The Second Coming." It is no coincidence that passages from this 1919 poem were quoted

[5] Here again this event did not occur in a vacuum. The ground for the present "superflat" mentality was long ago prepared by the incremental media substitution of form for content, as Neil Postman charted in *Amusing Ourselves to Death: Public Discourse in the Age of Show Business* (New York: Penguin, 1985).

more often in 2016, following the referendum decision for Brexit and the election of Donald J. Trump as president, than in any of the preceding thirty years.[6] Nor is it mere happenstance that civil liberties and political rights have been steadily eroding for the past thirteen years worldwide.[7] These and other data are symptomatic of a general global condition, the respiration and pulse of the current age.

THE "APOCALYPTIC SHIFT" AND CONTEMPORARY POPULAR CULTURE

A bellwether indicator of the contemporary apocalyptic shift is the striking increase in the incidence of apocalyptic fiction in popular culture. According to a recent study, approximately 80 percent of "apocalyptic" novels, films, and other popular media that have appeared since the late nineteenth century date from the period after 1970, and over 50 percent from after 1995.[8] Put another way, of the 1,000-plus specimens of pop-cultural apocalyptic media that have been composed, drawn, filmed, or otherwise generated since the 1895 publication of H. G. Wells's *The Time Machine*, over half are products of the past twenty-five years.[9]

Many of these items are set in a post-apocalyptic landscape, a characteristic trope of apocalyptic fiction. Strictly speaking, of course, nothing can be *post*-apocalyptic. The traditional apocalyptic narrative culminates with the final postmortem judgment of individuals, which represents the payoff for the Elect and the vanishing-point for all the apocalyptic perspectives on history, justice, and salvation.

[6] E. Ballard, "Terror, Brexit and U.S. Election Have Made 2016 the Year of Yeats," *The Wall Street Journal*, August 23, 2016.

[7] https://freedomhouse.org/report/freedom-world/freedom-world-2019 (accessed October 14, 2019). Freedom House is an independent watchdog organization dedicated to the expansion of freedom and democracy around the world.

[8] L. DiTommaso, "Apocalypticism and Popular Culture," in *The Oxford Handbook of Apocalyptic Literature*, ed. John J. Collins (New York: Oxford University Press, 2014), 473–509. Five years later, the percentage is even more inclined towards the present day.

[9] See E. K. Rosen, *Apocalyptic Transformation: Apocalypse and the Postmodern Imagination* (Lanham, MD: Lexington, 2008); P. Y. Paik, *From Utopia to Apocalypse: Science Fiction and the Politics of Catastrophe* (Minneapolis: University of Minnesota Press, 2010); and the essays in R. G. Howard, ed., *Network Apocalypse: Visions of the End in an Age of Internet Media* (Sheffield: Sheffield Phoenix, 2011) and L. A. Clark et al., eds., *The Last Midnight: Essays on Apocalyptic Narratives in Millennial Media* (Jefferson, NC: McFarland, 2016).

Yet even the ancient apocalypses such as Daniel and the Revelation of John assume an *end-time* or *eschaton*, a short span of time between the audience's present day and the Final Judgment, during which the predetermined events of the last days will unfold. The Middle Ages gave this eschatological age a fixed sequence of events and a focus on the figure of the Antichrist. Protestantism added the rapture and the tribulation. These events were expected to transpire during *the last days*, as the world hurtled towards its inevitable doom.

The stage was set for the transformation of the traditional "End of Days" into a secularized "post-apocalypse." The process began in the Enlightenment, accelerated during the Age of Progress, and attained its first full expression with the Atomic Age in 1945. The driving mechanism was the steadily increasing ability of humans to undertake actions that were once considered to be the province of the divine, including the ability to cause death and destruction on a planetary scale. After the end of the Cold War in 1989, the post-atomic setting was eclipsed in the pop-cultural imagination by a host of catastrophic scenarios that echoed current concerns, including economic collapse, scientific mishap, biological pandemic, political and social breakdown, and environmental degradation. These are the settings of contemporary pop-cultural apocalyptic and post-apocalyptic works (hereafter "post-/apocalyptic").

Most familiar to audiences are the novels, films, and television series. The following titles represent only a tiny sampling. Landmark novels include *A Canticle for Leibowitz* (1959, Walter Miller, Jr.), *The Handmaid's Tale* (1985, Margaret Atwood), the *Parable* books (1993 and 1998, Octavia Butler), *The Road* (2006, Cormac McCarthy), and *Station Eleven* (2014, Emily St. John Mandel).[10] Influential live-action films include *Dr. Strangelove* (1964, dir. Stanley Kubrick), *12 Monkeys* (1995, dir. Terry Gilliam), *The Matrix* (1999, dir. the Wachowskis), and *The Hunger Games* (2012, dir. Gary Ross).[11] Recent apocalyptic television series include *Jericho* (2006–08), *The 100* (2014–), and *The Rain* (2018–), as well as literary dramatizations such as *The Handmaid's Tale* (2017–).[12]

[10] D. J. Leigh, *Apocalyptic Patterns in Twentieth-Century Fiction* (Notre Dame, IN: University of Notre Dame Press, 2008).

[11] W. W. Davis, *Visions of the Apocalypse: Spectacles of Destruction in American Cinema* (London: Wallflower, 2003); K. Moana Thompson, *Apocalyptic Dread: American Film at the Turn of the Millennium* (Albany: State University of New York Press, 2007); and P. Szendy, *Apocalypse-Cinema: 2012 and Other Ends of the World* (French orig., 2012; New York: Fordham University Press, 2015).

[12] J. Aston and J. Walliss, eds., *Small Screen Revelation: Apocalypse in Contemporary Television* (Sheffield: Sheffield Phoenix, 2013).

All these are written or produced in English, the international lingua franca. But apocalyptic popular media are also prevalent in every other major language. Heading the list are the Japanese anime (animated films) and manga (graphic narratives).[13] Examples of apocalyptic anime include *Akira* (1984, dir. Ōtomo Katsuhiro), *Nausicäa of the Valley of the Wind* (1984, dir. Miyazaki Hayao), *Neon Genesis Evangelion* (1995, dir. Anno Hideaki), *Revolutionary Girl Utena* (1997, dir. Ikuhara Kunihiko), *Serial Experiments Lain* (1998, dir. Nakamura Ryūtarō), *Wolf's Rain* (2002, dir. Okamura Tensai), and *Ergo Proxy* (2006, dir. Murase Shūkō).[14]

Manga, however, are the real trend-setters in terms of their numbers and cultural impact. In fact many apocalyptic anime are adaptions of manga originals, e.g., *Akira* (1982–90) and *Nausicäa* (1982). Other milestone manga with an apocalyptic framework include *Tokyo Babylon* (1990–93, Clamp), *X* (1992–, Clamp) *Battle Angel Alita* (1990–95, Kishiro Yukito), *Blame!* (1998–2003, Nihei Tsutomu), *20th Century Boys* (1999–2006, Urasawa Naoki), *Otherworld Barbara* (2002–05, Hagio Moto), and *Biomega* (2004–09, Nihei Tsutomu). Again, these examples represent only a fraction of the total number.[15] Apocalyptic graphic narratives are commonplace also in the Francophonie (*Le Transperceneige* [1982–2015, Jacques Lob et al.]) and the United Kingdom (*V for Vendetta* [1982–89, Alan Moore and David Lloyd]). They have become hugely popular in the United States, including *Watchmen* (1986–87, Alan Moore et al.), *Wasteland* (2006–15, Antony Johnston et al.), and *The Massive* (2012–14, Brian Wood et al.). Of special note is *DMZ* (2005–12, Brian Wood et al.), which forecasts the polarization of American politics today with uncanny prescience.

How best to understand this tidal wave of apocalyptic popular culture? Is it merely cotton-candy entertainment, where post-apocalyptic wastelands substitute for the high-plains badlands of the old 1950s and 1960s westerns? Or is it sensitive in its own fashion to the tectonic changes that are currently underway, a barometer of existential

[13] Anime are produced as feature films, home video, and television series. The anime and manga are listed here by their English titles, which sometimes differ from the original Japanese titles. Personal names are listed with surname first, Japanese-style, as they are throughout this chapter.

[14] S. Napier, *Anime from* Akira *to Howl's Moving Castle: Experiencing Japanese Animation* (New York: Palgrave, 2005).

[15] An annual visitor to Japan since 2007, I have noticed a recent shift among Tokyo metro riders from reading manga in paperbacks to viewing manga (and anime) on their smartphones.

anxiety worldwide, reified in pop-cultural forms? While both views are valid, the second is more accurate.

On the one hand, apocalyptic popular culture is a facsimile analogue of the "superflat" nature of daily life in the Digital Age, existence on a data plane with an infinite horizon but no real depth or modulation.[16] Apocalyptic images and vocabulary bombard the audience, fabricating the contexts that substitute for content. From this perspective, "post-/apocalyptic" in series such as *The 100* and *DMZ* is merely a painted backdrop against which its soap-opera melodramas unfold each week or every issue, unmoored from existential relevance or social function. The cultural influence of these films, novels, and other "products" is minimal, and whatever traction they might have had in a previous age is lost in the micro-thin Teflon world of online social media. The prime function of apocalyptic popular culture is mass-market entertainment in the age of spectacle, the cultural equivalent of fast food.

On the other hand, if apocalyptic popular culture lacks conceptual depth, it is because the worldview itself is essentially an adolescent way of perceiving the world.[17] In the apocalyptic mindset, the world is divided into binary categories: good or evil, us or them. Personal choice is restricted by a dualistic cosmos and a pre-set timetable. Salvation is by means of a higher, paternalistic power that acts autonomously. Individuals may be more or less free to choose the path either to Heaven or to Hell, but there is no escaping the overall system. Even the Messiah is part of the eschatological drama, appearing onstage in the last act, as if on cue. The drama, moreover, features extended and vivid descriptions of punishment, torture, destruction, and death. These features underwrite the social function of apocalyptic speculation, but also seem to appeal to the puerile desire to see things smashed and to stomp what one does not like. It is little wonder that depictions of the end have been so popular in art, and now are equally popular on film.

The point is that while apocalyptic popular culture may be existentially shallow, so too is the vast bulk of apocalyptic writings *tout court*, including the biblical books of Daniel and the Revelation of John.[18] If

[16] R. Wagner, *Godwired: Religion, Ritual and Virtual Reality* (London: Routledge, 2012).

[17] Lorenzo DiTommaso, "The Apocalyptic Other," in *The Other in Second Temple Judaism: Essays in Honor of John J. Collins*, eds. Karina Martin Hogan, Matthew Goff, and Joel S. Kaminsky (Grand Rapids, MI: Eerdmans, 2011), 221–46.

[18] DiTommaso, "Apocalyptic Literature as World Literature." Only a tiny minority—Augustine's *City of God*, Dante's *Divine Comedy*, Milton's *Paradise Lost*, perhaps two dozen others—exhibit real existential depth, and only because they sublimate

anything, popular culture permits a degree of expressional latitude in apocalyptic media that was impossible in premodern examples.

Consider, for example, John Milton's portrayal of Lucifer in *Paradise Lost* (1667–74), which represents the greatest extent to which the figure may be stretched within the notional bounds of the worldview in its traditional biblical mode. Lucifer's powerful emotions and deep motivations make him a tragic quasi-hero. He revolts against the system, and is punished for his rebellion. Audiences identify with him as an anti-hero, and in this respect Milton's epic poem was groundbreaking. Yet for all that, Lucifer remains a two-dimensional figure, restricted by the conceptual strictures of the biblical story. The ending structures the whole narrative. Lucifer is fated to fail and to fall. The salvific hope for humanity is assured by his downfall and supported by the biblical texts on which the narrative is grounded. Although far more dynamic than the ice-locked Satan of Dante's *Inferno*, Milton's Lucifer remains a character in a cosmic drama whose part was written by God.

Contrast this with the figure of Lucifer Morningstar in the eponymous American comic-book series written by Mike Carey (2000–06). By the end of the story, Lucifer has abdicated his throne in Hell, recovered his angelic wings, defeated the heavenly host, and created his own universe as a way to show God what a terrible job he did the first time round. The series is notable also for its musings on the question of free will within a universe under divine rule. Although Carey's dialogue on the issue is theologically less subtle than that of patristic writers such as Jerome and Augustine, it is philosophically more satisfying, since it proceeds from the postmodern premise that all systems are merely constructs. Lucifer Morningstar is a protagonist, not an antagonist. Like the protagonists in a novel by Sōseki or Kawabata, he is bound by the choices that he makes within a society that has its rules, yet is not fated to make these choices by a predetermined narrative.

The same latitude of expression is witnessed in the manga *Blue Exorcist* (2009–, Katō Kazue), a Bildungsroman of sorts featuring Okamura Rin, the son of Satan and a high-school student. The premise is, of course, ludicrous, and Rin is more cartoonish than Carey's Lucifer (the series is pitched to teenaged boys). Yet the manga's ensemble cast still

their eschatological focus and *ex machina* dynamic within a grander superstructure that articulates human struggles in this corrupt and transitory world. The exception to this rule is Fourth Ezra (ca. 100 CE), which is the most theologically dense apocalypse ever composed. All these works speak to the human condition, living in the shadow of the apocalypse.

manages to articulate a wide range of thoughts and actions. The same is true for other traditional apocalyptic figures in contemporary dress, such as the minions of evil in the black comedy *El día de la Bestia* (1995, dir. Álex de la Iglesia) and the four horsemen of the apocalypse in the graphic series *East of West* (2013–, Jonathan Hickman and Nick Dragotta).

Obviously, most apocalyptic pop-cultural items do not achieve such levels, but these examples are not uncommon. The pop-cultural medium may obscure the message, but top-quality specimens such *Serial Experiments Lain* and *Otherworld Barbara* are as loaded with meaning as any premodern apocalyptic text.[19] "Fictional" is a meaningless distinction here. Fact and fiction are porous categories when applied to things apocalyptic, and all the more so in today's information-saturated world. Audiences today acquire much of their knowledge about the state of the world via pop-cultural channels, while major political leaders state unvarnished falsehoods or channel conspiratorial theories about the "deep state" and "enemies of the state" that not long ago would have been derided as nonsense (see "The Apocalyptic Shift and the Illiberal Revolution," below). All apocalyptic speculation is taken as factual by those for whom it has meaning.

"Meaning" is the key. Pop-cultural renditions of the worldview may be unmoored from traditional biblical theology, but they articulate present-day concerns that are no less meaningful. *Akira*, *The Matrix*, and their offspring reflect the same existential angst that underwrites apocalyptic speculation in general and motivates the current global apocalyptic shift in particular. The contemporary twist here is that group "identity" is often conceptualized in terms of larger groups, such as the species or even the biosphere.

The Massive, for example, is motivated by the prospect of imminent ecological collapse, as was *Nausicäa* before it.[20] *Le reste du monde* and *Le monde d'après* (2015, Jean-Christophe Chauzy) examine the social breakdown after a natural catastrophe. *The Matrix* reflects humanity's fears about artificial intelligence, as do many post-apocalyptic video

[19] It is perhaps significant here that both works deliberate the dimensions of space and existence rather than time and its end.

[20] Sometimes the collapse is avoidable. In the anime *Princess Mononoke* (1997, dir. Miyazaki Hayao), evil—here associated with industrialism and mechanized warfare—is turned aside and paradise restored through human agency. The idea of a restoration to an original balanced state also powers the juvenile-aimed animated television series *Avatar: The Last Airbender* (2005–08, created by Michael Dante DiMartino and Bryan Konietzko).

games.[21] The list goes on and contains examples from every culture worldwide, including indigenous ones,[22] as well as each of the landmark novels, films, series, anime, and manga that are mentioned in the lists above. Their cultural influence is staggering. *The Matrix* alone has had as much impact today on those born after 1990 as the Revelation of John once did. The same holds for Alan Moore's *V*, whose eponymous (and anonymous) protagonist conducts a campaign of terror and assassination against the ruling regime while concealing his identity behind a Guy Fawkes mask. This mask has since become a symbol of dissenters in the "hacktivist" movement "Anonymous" and of contemporary social protest around the world more generally.

The post-/apocalyptic imagination is also characterized by its amplification of human instrumentality within the binary apocalyptic framework. In 1973 Brian Aldiss noted how one type of the post-apocalyptic fiction of his day presented its readers and audiences with a "cozy catastrophe." While "everyone else is dying off," Aldiss observes, the [usually male] protagonist is "having a pretty good time (a girl, free suites at the Savoy, automobiles for the taking)."[23] The setting permits audience members to participate vicariously in a lifestyle that is well beyond the pale of their normal workaday lives, as in the film *Mad Max* (1979, dir. George Miller) and its hundreds of contemporary copy-cats.

But more is happening here than simple fantasy-fulfillment. The post-/apocalyptic dynamic is less "cozy" and more like the nihilistic *Mad Max*, where the protagonist finds himself/herself in a dire, post-apocalyptic situation and takes charge. If the contemporary apocalyptic shift mirrors the tenor of the global understanding that the world is becoming irredeemably worse, the protagonist's actions reflect those that *the audience members imagine that they themselves would take*.

These surrogate actions are a form of human instrumentality. End-time agency is God's prerogative in traditional apocalyptic speculation, but is transferred to non-divine agents in the secular expressions of the

[21] L. de Wildt et al., "'Things Greater than Thou': Post-Apocalyptic Religion in Games," *Religions* 9, no. 6 (2018): 169, DOI: http://10.3390/rel9060169.

[22] W. Rice, *Moon of the Crusted Snow* (Toronto: ECW, 2018), a post-apocalyptic novel that is set in a small Anishinaabe community in northern Ontario in Canada and oriented to indigenous identity and values.

[23] Brian W. Aldiss, *Billion Year Spree: The History of Science Fiction* (London: Weidenfeld & Nicholson, 1973), 293–94.

worldview. Yet even in the biblical apocalypses a measure of agency was vicariously enjoyed by their intended audiences. The intended audiences of Daniel and the Revelation of John, who were without the power to remedy their situation, nonetheless acquired it through the anticipated actions of God or a messianic figure at the end-time (punishing enemies, rewarding the righteous). The same social function is operative in the case of contemporary audiences and post-/apocalyptic media. The existential immediacy may differ, but the dynamic is equivalent. A textbook illustration is Lauren Oya Olamina, the female protagonist in Octavia Butler's *Parable of the Sower* (1993) and *Parable of the Talents* (1998), who staves off threats to the identity and integrity of her group, Earthseed.

The digital revolution not only amplified the degree of human agency in the end-time; it also added an active dimension. In video games such as *The Last of Us* (2013), *Fallout 4* (2015), and *Horizon Zero Dawn* (2017), player decisions constitute an extra measure of eschatological agency within the apocalyptic framework of the game.[24] Such games are twenty-first-century reifications of the basic apocalyptic schema, where human free will (the player) operates within a broadly deterministic universe (the creation of the game's designer instead of the divinity). In a further twist, games like *Bioshock Infinite* (2013) and *FarCry 5* (2018) call on players to postpone an apocalypse or avert the rise of an apocalyptic cult.

Two observations conclude this section. First, one should neither overstate nor underestimate the cultural significance of apocalyptic popular culture. The picture that I have drawn might suggest that apocalyptic anime, manga, and other forms of popular media exert a profound and sustained cultural impact today. They do, but this is a result of their sheer weight in numbers and variety of media, the impact of which occurs at the mass-cultural level. Whatever else apocalyptic popular culture might be, it is entertainment. The post-/ apocalyptic setting offers a venue where the adolescent mind can indulge its fantasies, either along the male-fantasy "cozy apocalyptic"

[24] I thank my graduate student Gisoo Kim for the idea of video-game instrumentality. See also R. Lizardi, "Repelling the Invasion of the 'Other': Post-Apocalyptic Alien Shooter Videogames Addressing Contemporary Cultural Attitudes," *Eludamos: Journal for Computer Game Culture* 3, no. 2 (2009): 295–308. On video-game instrumentality, see also R. Wagner, "X-Box Apocalypse: Video Games and Revelatory Literature," *SBL Forum* 7, no. 9 (2018), www.sbl-site.org/publications/article.aspx?ArticleId=848 (accessed October 14, 2019).

lines that Aldiss suggests or, with reference to the zombie-apocalypse phenomenon, with the current penchant for horror, sadism, violence, and gore.

That being said, the sheer numbers of media items, and in particular their global scope and progressive increase since 2001, must be explained. The simplest answer is that they reflect something profoundly significant about the society that spawned them and for which they have several levels of meaning. This explosion of apocalyptic popular culture is one of the prime symptoms of the apocalyptic shift.

The second observation is that, in addition to these secularized expressions, contemporary popular culture has also presented old-school Christian eschatology with a new voice.[25] The *Left Behind* series of books, by Tim LaHaye and Jerry B. Jenkins, is perhaps the best-known example. All told, the books have reportedly sold over 80 million copies. The instrumental dimension is equally present in this and other novels, whether in the vicarious form of the "Tribulation Force" of the *Left Behind* series (which battles the Antichrist and the forces of evil) or, more actively, Mark Andrew Olson's 2009 apocalyptic novel *The Warrior*, which, as the publisher's website blurb promises, will "enthrall, educate, and energize Christians into *participating in real-life strategic prayer*."[26]

Faith-based films, too, have gone mass-market. The *Left Behind* series was converted into film, and that is only the tip of the evangelical Christian iceberg. The vast bulk may be produced for a niche market, such as the four-film *Apocalypse* franchise (1998–2001, prod. Peter and Paul LaLonde), but many feature mainstream stars. The number of these films and novels has steadily risen over the past fifteen years, exactly paralleling the rise in apocalyptic popular culture more generally. Their influence, too, has increased correspondingly as religious fundamentalism has moved back to the mainstream, which is the topic to which we now turn.

[25] Another medium is music. Especially popular today is Christian "Apok-Rock" (the term is my own), which runs the gamut from folk music to hard rock and from punk rock to death metal, its doomsday warning on either the slow simmer or the high boil. See D. Janssen and E. Whitelock, *Apocalyptic Jukebox: The End of the World in American Popular Music* (Berkeley, CA: Soft Skull, 2009).

[26] http://bakerpublishinggroup.com/books/the-warriors/273913 (accessed October 14, 2019; italics mine). What exactly will be prayed for is not made clear.

THE "APOCALYPTIC SHIFT" AND THE FIFTH GREAT AWAKENING

Sociologists of religion in America identify four "Great Awakenings" or major periods of religious revival.[27] The first three were fundamentalist Protestant in all their salient features and display a common character. The Fourth Awakening began in the late 1960s. It shares only some features with the earlier revivals, and for this reason its existence is a matter of dispute.[28] Yet such differences are not so much deviations from a rigid pattern as a response to the changing nature of late twentieth-century society.

One hallmark of the Fourth Great Awakening was a massive surge in the formation of new religious movements (NRMs). Not all these movements were Christian in their outlook, and in fact some incorporated elements from diversity of religious and philosophical systems. But many NRMs of this period were fundamentally Christian and robustly apocalyptic in outlook (e.g., the Children of God, the Concerned Christians).[29]

A significant percentage of these apocalyptic NRMs engaged in violent behavior and/or were involved in violent situations.[30] The Peoples Temple (mass suicide 1978), the Branch Davidians (armed conflict with the FBI 1993), and Heaven's Gate (mass suicide 1997) are among the most notorious examples. The trend extended to other countries, as with the Order of the Solar Temple (France, Canada; mass suicides 1994–95), Aum Shinrikyō (Japan; mass murder 1995), and the Movement for the Restoration of the Ten Commandments of God (Uganda; mass murder 2000),[31] as well as to nativist anti-government

[27] The ideas in this section are drawn from several essays, most recently Lorenzo DiTommaso, "Class Consciousness, Group Affiliation, and Apocalyptic Speculation," in *The Struggle over Class: Socioeconomic Analysis of Ancient Jewish and Christian Texts*, eds. G. Anthony Keddie, Michael Flexsenhar III, and Steven J. Friesen, Writings from the Greco-Roman World (Atlanta, GA: Society of Biblical Literature, in press).

[28] R. W. Fogel, *The Fourth Great Awakening and the Future of Egalitarianism* (Chicago: University of Chicago Press, 2000).

[29] J. Kaplan, *Radical Religion in North America: Millenarian Movements from the Far Right to the Children of Noah* (Syracuse, NY: Syracuse University Press, 1997).

[30] J. Hall, ed., *Apocalypse Observed: Religious Movements, Social Order and Violence in North America, Europe, and Japan* (London: Routledge, 2000); C. Wessinger, ed., *Millennialism, Persecution, and Violence: Historical Cases* (Syracuse, NY: Syracuse University Press, 1997).

[31] For other examples, see J. R. Lewis, ed., *Violence and New Religious Movement* (Oxford: Oxford University Press, 2011).

groups such as Posse Comitatus (late 1960s) and the Justus (Montana) Freemen (1996), which are the progenitors of today's "alt-Right" movement in the United States. This kind of violence is *apocalyptic* violence: harmful actions and responses that are taken in consequence of the group's apocalyptic outlook, i.e., through the lens of the worldview, and thus, to its members, comprehensible and justifiable in view of its notional framework.

The same period also witnessed a grassroots resurgence of fundamentalism and robust apocalyptic speculation within traditional Protestant churches. Among its first-fruits was a stream of prophetic doomsday books by John T. Wolvoord, David Harold Chilton, and others. The marquee author here is Hal Lindsey, whose 1970 book *The Late Great Planet Earth* sold in the tens of millions of copies.

The influence of fundamentalist Christianity has risen steadily since the 1970s. Its members tend to be politically reactionary and socially conservative, and have a sharply binary perspective on the world and their place in it. By 1996 evangelicals constituted a quarter of the American population.[32] In 2000 the Christian Right helped elect an openly evangelical candidate, George W. Bush, to the White House (and it re-elected him four years later). In 2016 the same group—now far larger and more polarized in its outlook—did the same with Donald J. Trump. As Matthew Avery Sutton observes, "American evangelicalism is thriving in the twenty-first century."[33] The difference today is the way that it has largely lost its liberal, civil-rights dimension and gained an illiberal, nativist one, as discussed in "The Apocalyptic Shift and the Illiberal Revolution," below.

Although the fundamentalist Christian resurgence of the late twentieth century was relatively overlooked at the time,[34] it has proven to be more significant than the surge in apocalyptic NRMs, which in retrospect ought to be regarded as extremist manifestations of the same general trend.[35] This is clear now in the global transformation of the

[32] M. Durham, "Evangelical Protestantism and Foreign Policy in the United States after September 11," *Patterns of Prejudice* 38 (2004): 145–58.

[33] M. A. Sutton, *American Apocalypse: A History of Modern Evangelicalism* (Cambridge, MA: Belknap, 2014), 367.

[34] Although the first important books on the subject appeared in the 1990s (Garry Wills was among the earliest scholars to detect its true scope), the bulk of research is a product of the post-2001 world and was composed in light of its events.

[35] The fundamentalist resurgence, for example, has occurred in every other major religious tradition worldwide, but its significance in the post-2001 world was not recognized until recently.

character of religious expression that has occurred over the past twenty years. These changes are so pervasive in their scope and their effects are so profoundly felt that we may identify in them a new and unprecedented kind of religious revival—a Fifth Great Awakening.

The main characteristics of the Fifth Great Awakening are the unparalleled degree to which individuals are able to self-direct the channels of their religious expression and spirituality more generally; the seemingly paradoxical way in which such expressions can coexist in an otherwise highly secularized society; the expansion and migration of fundamentalist streams in every traditional religion from the margins to the mainstream; the global scope of these trends and the dissolution of many of the old boundaries not only among traditional religions but also in the varieties of religious expression; and the extent to which the digital revolution has facilitated all these changes and hyper-augmented their effects.

Some of these features are an intensification of trends that were already underway. Others are idiosyncratic to the post-2001 world or represent a change of kind rather than intensity. All these features, however, are common also to the apocalyptic shift in its second, post-2001 phase. In other words, the predominant feature of the current religious revival is its profoundly apocalyptic character, to the extent that the apocalyptic shift may be regarded as the background radiation of the Fifth Great Awakening.

All points of overlap between the two phenomena are mediated by the "superflat" nature of contemporary apocalypticism. The political dimensions of this overlap are explored below. The religious dimensions are exemplified by the "Mayan Apocalypse" of 2012. The story began in the 1970s and 1980s, when an ancient Mesoamerican calendar that was long known to specialists suddenly attracted the attention of some doomsday enthusiasts.[36] The objection that time in the Mayan calendar is cyclical (and not linear like apocalyptic time) proved to be no obstacle for those who were convinced that it predicted the end of the world. Over the next two decades the Mayan prophecy remained isolated among cranks and crackpots and under the public radar. It was one among hundreds of doomsday theories swimming in the sea of occult paperbacks or supermarket tabloids.

This changed after the turn of the century. In less than a dozen years, this relatively unknown and wholly undistinguished doomsday

[36] M. Restall and A. Solari, *2012 and the End of the World* (Lanham, MD: Rowman and Littlefield, 2011).

forecast evolved into a worldwide phenomenon that was centered on the terminal date of December 21, 2012. The medium of this remarkable transformation was the Internet. Its mechanism was the collective millions of individual decisions that were made via electronic platforms ranging from websites dedicated to the Mayan prophecy to casual Facebook chats among friends. Speculation ran rampant, attracting the attention of major news organizations and enhancing the prophecy's appeal. Some interpretations of the prophecy found traction and thrived; others did not, and died. Many people anticipated a traditional, biblical-style doomsday. Others saw a prediction of imminent political upheaval or social revolution, a quantum leap in human consciousness, the dawning of the Age of Aquarius, or the intromission of a new planet in our solar system. It was if the 2012 apocalyptic prophecy was the magnetic pole for the world's existential angst, and its resolution the solution to all its problems.

The 2012 "Mayan Apocalypse" was the first public apocalypse.[37] It embodies the twenty-first-century way of approaching religion and spirituality, one that is meaningfully democratic and fully international in its scope. The incessant speculation about the meaning of the prophecy that proliferated across a digitally interconnected planet underscores the integral role of the new communications technologies in the second phase of the apocalyptic shift. More importantly, this speculation had a generative effect insofar as it represents an amplification of human eschatological instrumentality in apocalyptic speculation. Whereas individual players of an apocalyptic video game make eschatological decisions within its designer software parameters (see above), here millions of people made decisions about an apocalyptic prophecy that *changed the parameters of the eschatology itself*.

This requires some unpacking. As noted, apocalyptic speculation is an information system. Its epistemology is inherently hierarchical, featuring a top-down system of knowledge-ordering and information-creation. These features shape the way in which revelation is generated, transmitted, and received in its social settings. Traditionally, apocalyptic predictions are the product of a single person, usually male. In group contexts, this person is typically its guiding light. His or her predictions are communicated along restricted channels and received by the group as divinely inspired. The system is resistant to external modification,

[37] It was also the first truly global apocalypse. It had a distant antecedent in the 1524 astrological doomsday predictions.

since information creation and communication tend to be intramural processes.

"Superflat" apocalypticism, by contrast, proceeds from an essentially heterarchical and nonlinear system of information-creation.[38] Open access to an electronic universe featuring instantaneous data retrieval, unlimited archival capability, and hypertext referencing connects any generative prophet to the full spectrum of apocalyptic predictions past and present. At the same time, user-generated content, multimedia interactivity, and virtual communities permit a real-time public dialogue of new apocalyptic prophecies. In theory, anyone can be a prophet and anyone can influence that shape of a prophecy. The back-and-forth dialogue between the creation and re-creation of apocalyptic prophecies occurs in a social-media forum that is dynamic, instantaneous, democratic, and outside the pale of old theological firewalls. Apocalypticists now bring an omnivorous intellectual appetite to a table where the menu has changed from *prix fixe* to *à la carte*, and the number of items available has increased a thousandfold. Syncretism is virtually inevitable.

The production of apocalyptic predictions in the digital era has become public, pervasive, and participatory. Gender, nationality, social status, and religious affiliation are less relevant in an era of avatars, aliases, and atomized populations. One self-selects to groups on the basis of habitual affiliation or personal inclination. The passport is Internet access. Where once apocalyptic revelation was transmitted from prophet or seer to prophetic community along restricted channels, now it can be broadcast across the entire social bandwidth. The prophet today has six billion faces, *and that prophet is us*.

THE APOCALYPTIC SHIFT AND THE ILLIBERAL REVOLUTION

The progressive and ongoing dissolution of the centrist/stakeholder faith in liberal values and democratic institutions *sensu lato* has paved the way for the march towards illiberal, populist politics and governments worldwide. Obviously states such as the People's Republic of China, Saudi Arabia, and North Korea have been authoritarian since their inception. Of greater relevance are those nations that have made an illiberal right turn in the three decades since the fall of the Soviet Union. As of 2019 the roster of countries that have made this turn

[38] Howard, *Network Apocalypse*.

includes global powers such as Russia, Brazil, India, and the Philippines, as well as former Warsaw Pact countries such as Hungary and Poland.

More important is the fact that illiberal politics have made tremendous headway in every democratic nation. This advance is occurring along a broad front. Many of these nations now feature successful new or revitalized hard-right political parties (Die Alternative für Deutschland in Germany; Il Movimento 5 Stelle in Italy; Le Rassemblement National in France) or established parties—normally but not always conservative—that either have adopted illiberal views or else nowadays feel empowered to ventilate them without voter backlash. Such views are always group-protective and identity-defensive. They include anti-immigration rhetoric, economic protectionism, the persecution and segregation of minority ethnic groups, and the promotion of conservative "values," along with proposals like Brexit and the United States–Mexico border wall.

Like all populist movements, the illiberal revolution exhibits regional variation among generic similarities. Central to all variations is the perception that the systemic problems in today's world are incomprehensible in their complexity and unsolvable by ordinary means. Climate change is a good example. Few persons are able to grasp (much less engage with) the full complexity of the scientific data. Yet the macro-effects of global warming are obvious: a rise in global temperatures and sea levels, and species extinction. The United Nations in its Sixth Global Environmental Outlook stated that climate change now imperils the "ecological foundations of society."[39] The issue has become part of the global consciousness, a threat to life on earth. This threat stands behind a general existential angst that, as we have seen, is partly responsible for the apocalyptic shift as expressed in popular media.

More relevant to populist movements, however, are the knock-on effects of climate change. Lakes dry, coastal areas flood, crops fail, social structures break down, internecine warfare erupts, and populations start to move. Domestic resources are strained. Existence becomes more difficult along all fronts, especially for stakeholders, who regard themselves as paradigmatic of their nation's identity. Males, especially among the working classes, have come to feel disassociated.[40] Real wages are falling, traditional jobs are vanishing, and conventional

[39] United Nations, Sixth Global Environmental Outlook (GEO-6), February 2019, www.unenvironment.org/resources/global-environment-outlook-6 (accessed October 14, 2019).

[40] See, among other studies, and with the usual caveats, W. Farrell and J. Gray, *The Boy Crisis: Why Our Boys Are Struggling and What We Can Do about It* (Dallas, TX: BenBella, 2018).

categories are dissolving. Simply put, a way of life that anchors one's ethnic, linguistic, cultural, and religious identity is disappearing.

This statement is too simplistic, of course. Although it is grounded on facts that bear a causal, real-world relationship to each other, the data are presented in cartoon fashion, stripped of nuance or context, and sequenced in a narrative that could have been lifted from a film or television series. Yet, as with climate change, *this is precisely the level at which these effects are understood and appreciated*—and exactly the point where the apocalyptic worldview enters the equation, especially in societies where sharp "class" differences already exist.[41]

Like all phenomena, international illiberalism is not in itself apocalyptic. Rather, the apocalyptic worldview provides core illiberal tenets with a notional framework that orients its perspectives and grounds its objectives. It functions like a polarizing filter by which certain details are brought into sharper focus, throwing the rest out of focus. In doing so, it streamlines a complex problem into one that (1) can be grasped in basic terms and (2) indicates a clear and unambiguous course of action.

Once again it all boils down to group identity. Threats to this identity are both the mortar that binds similarities and the chisel that chips away differences. Lines between groups become sharper, categories become radicalized. The colors of life wash out, leaving only shades of white or black. Existence whittles down to a choice between one way or the other, no middle path. From there it is only the smallest of steps to *either* us *or* them. No space is left in between.

It is no wonder that illiberal movements worldwide articulate their platforms in apocalyptic categories. The social function of the worldview finds its purpose here: its radical, "us" versus "them" dualism translates in the political idiom to ethnicity-based regionalism or nationalism in an attempt to strengthen group identity as the world around careens and collapses. The worse things seem to be, the more things spin out of control. "Things fall apart; the centre cannot hold."

The results are patent. The global illiberal revolution has been facilitated by the normalization of so much of what was once considered to be fringe or extreme. Unlike the period from 1914 to 1945, where the center held firmly enough to withstand the onslaught, today we are witnessing the gradual dissolution of the liberal-democratic center. The resulting polarization merely completes the feedback loop. Like hundreds of millions of individual metal filings between two magnets

[41] P. R. Pessar, *Brazilian Millenarianism and Popular Culture* (Durham, NC: Duke University Press, 2004).

that keep getting stronger, each filing moves irrevocably to one magnet or the other, to "us" or to "them."

The role of conspiracy theories here cannot be underestimated.[42] Like illiberalism, conspiracy theory is not apocalyptic; apocalyptic is apocalyptic. Both, though, are ultimately reductive in their reasoning and proceed from the conviction that the truth is "out there," even as the forces of the "other side" (or those who run it) seek to hinder its revelation and distort the message.

Conspiracy theories are as old as history: the Templars live on; the Jews control the world; the CIA killed Kennedy; Pearl Harbor and 9/11 were set-ups. Two characteristics, however, distinguish conspiracy theory in the post-2001 world as it is modulated by the "superflat" mentality and facilitated by the digital revolution. The first characteristic is the extent to which like-minded individuals are now able to communicate and coordinate, from political leaders across international boundaries to terrorists such as Brenton Tarrant, whose manifesto found after his 2019 massacre at New Zealand mosques referred to the 2017 Québec mosque killer Alexandre Bissonnette.

The second characteristic is the comparative lack of interest in the rational basis of the claim. Conspiracy has become the new normal.[43] It is simply enough to state the claim. Those in the choir nod. Those who object are met with the retort "Fake news!" Again, the increasing binarity of the world today allows for no middle ground. The threat of an ending to a way of life, and to the identities this encapsulates, prompts both sides to dig deeper trenches. This accounts for the rise and popularity of counter-illiberals such as Christopher Hitchens, Richard Dawkins, et al., and their own implicit insistence that now, more than ever, one has to pick a side.[44] Both sides in this battle have come to regard the stakes as *apocalyptic*.

And so we have arrived at our own contemporary apocalyptic shift, a place where there is no central truth, but rather two epistemologies—two ontologies, in fact—each with its own history and theories of justice and salvation. This is the apocalyptic conception of space. Each side cleaves to its own view, just as each side in the Protestant Reformation

[42] On conspiracy theories and modern millenarianism, see M. Barkun, *A Culture of Conspiracy: Apocalyptic Visions in Contemporary America* (Berkeley: University of California Press, 2003).

[43] R. Muirhead and N. L. Rosenblum, *A Lot of People Are Saying: The New Conspiracism and the Assault on Democracy* (Princeton, NJ: Princeton University Press, 2019).

[44] D. Soar, "Short Cuts," *London Review of Books*, March, 21 2019, 26.

painted the other in apocalyptic terms. For German Protestants, the Pope was the Antichrist; for Roman Catholics, the Antichrist was Martin Luther. The apocalyptic sense of time is propelled by the promise of a return to a pristine state, the second creation when the old will pass away. This is the hortatory dimension to apocalyptic speculation, part of its social function. Donald Trump's election slogan was "Make America Great Again"—and it still is, since the end-time has not yet come. Apocalyptic violence is a predictable outcome, particularly when sides are polarized and enemies are demonized. It is happening all over the world.[45]

The correspondence between illiberalism and the resurgent robust apocalypticism in mainline religions is similarly predictable. One might begin with the molecular bonding between evangelical fundamentals in America and the Republican Party, but the phenomenon predates Donald Trump and is worldwide.[46] Hindu hyper-nationalism is the foundation of Narendra Modi's India. Vladimir Putin has made common alliance with the traditional Russian Orthodox Church. In Poland, Jesus Christ was recently enthroned as king.[47]

The role of the apocalyptic worldview is revealed by categories that are deployed and the social functions that it enables. Threats to group identity within the dynamic are almost always a double-edged knife: threats internal and external—change from without and change from within. In the apocalyptic visions of Daniel, the threats were the Seleucid overlord Antiochus IV (external) and the Philo-Hellenistic Jews (internal). For the Revelation of John, they were the Romans (external) and the backsliding Christians (internal). In the seventh-century *Apocalypse of Pseudo-Methodios* they were the armies of Islam (external) and (again) the backsliding Christians (internal). For Luther, it was the Pope and the Turk (double-external) and the Jews (internal). The list goes on. Today, the illiberal revolution fractures along an aggregate of economic, social, racial, political, and linguistic lines. The moral and ethical dimension is typically freighted by the alliance with highly conservative, equally illiberal nativist religions.

[45] R. Moret, "Potential for Apocalypse: Violence and Eschatology in the Israel–Palestine Conflict," *Journal of Religion & Society* 10 (2008): 1–14, and S. Knowles, "Brexit, Babylon and Prophecy: Semiotics of the End Times," *Religions* 9 (2018): 396, DOI: http://10.3390/rel9120396.

[46] W. R. Mead, "God's Country?" *Foreign Affairs* 85, no. 5 (September–October 2006): 24–43.

[47] T. G. Ash, "Jesus Rex Poloniae," *New York Review of Books*, August 16, 2018.

CONCLUSION

The vocabulary of apocalyptic speculation was formulated long ago. It has come down to us primarily through the biblical apocalypses of Daniel and Revelation, with some calques from the patristic and medieval writings, and filtered largely through the vernacular of Protestant dispensationalism. The worldview is the language in which this apocalyptic vocabulary makes sense, and its notional architecture constitutes the syntax. Then as now, the power of the worldview resides in its ability to function as an international language. If language models reality, then the apocalyptic worldview offers a model of a new reality, one that extends beyond this space and time. This is no different in the twenty-first century than it was in the ancient world, and the issues that it addresses are the same. At its core, apocalyptic speculation deals with threats to group identity.

Over the past forty years, people around the world have increasingly come to regard themselves and their situations though the lens of the apocalyptic worldview. This "apocalyptic shift" is planetary in its scope. It has been accelerating in its extent and degree since 2001, on account of the digital revolution and the illiberal revolution. Three of its most important manifestations are contemporary popular culture, the surge in apocalyptic new religions and the resurgence of apocalyptic streams in mainline religions worldwide, and the international illiberal revolution.[48] For all three areas, the future is now, insofar as the critical changes have already transpired and their effects have set the course. The apocalyptic shift is like global warming: one might slow it down, but there seems to be no way to press a "reset" button and return to the way it was before.

Apocalyptic popular media likely will continue to be produced at a meaningfully high level, although the saturation point may have been reached. There is a limit to the number of apocalyptic novels, films, and manga that the market can take, especially since it is driven by commercial concerns. "Superflat" apocalypticism, however, is here to stay, as are its effects on popular culture in the twenty-first century.

The "superflat" mentality will also continue to play a central role in the formation of religious expression during what may very well be the Fifth Great Awakening. The creation of apocalyptic new religions will continue to flatline, at least over the short term. Much of their platform has been assumed by the fundamentalist streams in the mainline religions, with their robust, overt apocalypticism. It is difficult to envision

[48] The subject is explored in depth in the second book of my trilogy (see n. 1 above), entitled *Apocalypticism and the Modern World*.

an immediate or even long-term future in which this radicalizing movement subsides, much less reverses course. The margins have become the mainstream.

The same holds for the illiberal revolution, which, mortared with these resurgent fundamentalist religions, seems to be unstoppable, as is its chief effect, the unravelling of the international liberal order and all for which it stands. The systemic problems that drive the apocalyptic shift have not vanished, nor is there any foreseeable future in which they will do so. The ubiquity of apocalyptic today is neither a superficial veneer nor a passing phase. Its pop-cultural, religious, and political expressions are manifestations of tectonic changes that have been underway for decades. The apocalyptic shift is the symptom, not the cause. The apocalyptic worldview offers a means of identifying the problem, isolating its causes, and indicating a solution. That it does this so well today is the real sign of the times.

What is being lost is the middle voice, the place where the largest part of the West used to live, the end product of a long trajectory that began with Renaissance humanism and was shaped by the European Enlightenment. Eroding incomes, diminished opportunities, and a growing sense of disconnect and anomie have contributed to a loss of identity, exacerbated by the sense that the problems of the world have become too great for humanity to address, much less solve. This social terrain has always proven most fertile for the apocalyptic worldview.

Selected Further Reading

Collins, John J., ed. *The Oxford Handbook of Apocalyptic Literature*. New York: Oxford University Press, 2014.

DiTommaso, Lorenzo. *The Architecture of Apocalypticism*. New York: Oxford University Press, in press.

Jameson, Fredric. *Archaeologies of the Future: The Desire Called Utopia and Other Science Fiction*. London: Verso, 2005.

Lewis, James R. *The Oxford Handbook of New Religious Movements*. New York: Oxford University Press, 2008.

Lilla, Mark. *The Shipwrecked Mind: On Political Reaction*. New York: New York Review Books, 2016.

Stein, Stephen J., ed. *The Encyclopedia of Apocalypticism*. Vol. 3, Apocalypticism in the Modern Period and the Contemporary Age. New York: Continuum, 1998.

Strozier, Charles B., et al., eds. *The Fundamentalist Mindset*. New York: Oxford University Press, 2010.

Sutton, Matthew Avery. *American Apocalypse: A History of Modern Evangelicalism*. Cambridge, MA: Belknap, 2014.

Walls, Jerry L., ed. *The Oxford Handbook of Eschatology*. New York: Oxford University Press, 2008.

Appendix: Early Medieval Commentaries on the Apocalypse

COMPILED BY COLIN MCALLISTER

Year	Author or title of work	Sources	Edition / English translation (if any)
260	Victorinus of Petovium (Vc)		CCSL 5 (2017) / ACT (2011)
380	Tyconius (Tyc)		CCSL 107A (2011) / FC (2017)
398	Victorinus/Jerome (Vc/J)		CCSL 5 (2017)
426	Augustine of Hippo (Aug)[1]	Tyc	CCSL 47, 48 (1955) / *WSA* (2012)
508–18	Oecumenius (Oec)		TEG 8 (1999)[2] / FC (2006), ACT (2011)
510–37	Caesarius of Arles (Ce)	Vc, Tyc	G. Morin[3] / ACT (2011)
530–50	*Scholia in Apocalypsin*[4]	Didymus	P. Tzamalikos (2013)[5]
540	Primasius of Hadrumetum (Pr)	Vc/J, Tyc	CCSL 92 (1985)[6]
531–48	Apringius of Beja (Ap)	Vc/J	CCSL 107 (2003) / ACT (2011)
580	Cassiodorus (Cas)	Vc/J, Pr	CCSL 107 (2003)
550–600	*De Monogramma* (Dm)	Vc, Tyc, Pr	CCSL 107 (2003)

1 Not a commentary, but in *De civitate* 20:6–7, Augustine explicates his thought on Rev 20:1–6 (derived from Tyconius), as well as interpreting Gog and Magog (Rev 20:8) and the new heaven and earth (Rev 21:1). I include here because of the lasting influence it had on later exegetes.

2 Traditio Exegetica Graeca (Leuven: Peeters).

3 Ed. G. Morin (Maredsous, 1942).

4 Originally attributed to Origen by A. Harnack (1911); attributed to Cassian by P. Tzamalikos (2013).

5 P. Tzamalikos, ed., *An Ancient Commentary on the Book of Revelation: A Critical Edition of the Scholia in Apocalypsin* (Cambridge: Cambridge University Press, 2013).

6 No English translation has yet been made of this influential commentary.

(*cont.*)

Year	Author or title of work	Sources	Edition / English translation (if any)
550–600	Ps.-Cyril of Alexandria		Morgan MS. Copt. 591[7]
611	Andrew of Caesarea	Oec	MTS (1955)[8] / ACT (2011), FC (2011)
675–700	*Commemoratorium Pseudo-Jerome* (Co)	Vc, Tyc, Pr	CCSL 107 (2003) / MIP (2016)
675–730	lost hiberno-Latin commentary (HL)[9]	Tyc	
703	Bede the Venerable (Bd)	Vc/J, Tyc, Aug, Pr	CCSL 121A (2001) / ACT (2011), TTH (2013)
730	*De Enigmatibus/ Reference Bible* (En)	HL, Pr, Tyc	CCSL 107 (2003) / MIP (2016)
700–50	Cambridge Gloss Dd. X.16 (Cb)	HL, Vc, Tyc, Co	CCSL 108G (2013) / CCT (2020)
758–67	Ambrose Autpert (Am)	Vc/J, Pr	CCCM 27, 27A (1975)
776–86	Beatus of Liébana (Bt)	Vc/J, Tyc, Ap, Dm	CCSL 107B, 107C (2012) / O'Brien (2013–)[10]
800	Ps.-Alcuin	Bd, Am	PL 100: 1087–1156, CCS (2016)
810	Theodulf of Orleans (Td)	Vc/J, Co, HL	CCSL 107 (2003) / MIP (2019)
812	Smaragdus of St. Mihiel	Bd	PL 102: 48–55, 331–39, 475–77[11] / MIP (2019)
840	Haimo of Auxerre	Pr, Am, Bd	PL 117: 937–1220

7 *Encomium on Revelation 7–12*. There is no printed or critical edition of this Sahidic Coptic manuscript, although there are translations in Italian (by Tito Orlandi) and English (by Francesca Lecchi, with an introduction and notes by Francis X. Gumerlock, forthcoming).

8 Münchener Theologische Studien (Munich: Karl Zink Verlag).

9 Critical edition in progress by Francis X. Gumerlock.

10 English translation in progress by Maureen S. O'Brien, available on Amazon as a Kindle book.

11 These are three short sermons on Rev 1, 4, and 14.

Index

Other Titles in the Series (continued from page iii)

POSTMODERN THEOLOGY Edited by *Kevin J. Vanhoozer*

THE PROBLEM OF EVIL Edited by *Chad Meister* and *Paul K. Moser*

PURITANISM Edited by *John Coffey* and *Paul C. H. Lim*

THE QUR'AN Edited by *Jane Dammen McAuliffe*

QUAKERISM Edited by *Stephen W. Angell* and *Pink Dandelion*

KARL RAHNER Edited by *Declan Marmion* and *Mary E. Hines*

REFORMED THEOLOGY Edited by *Paul T. Nimmo* and *David A. S. Fergusson*

RELIGION AND TERRORISM Edited by *James R. Lewis*

RELIGIOUS STUDIES Edited by *Robert A. Orsi*

FRIEDRICH SCHLEIERMACHER Edited by *Jacqueline Mariña*

SCIENCE AND RELIGION Edited by *Peter Harrison*

ST. PAUL Edited by *James D. G. Dunn*

SUFISM Edited by *Lloyd Ridgeon*

SUMMA THEOLOGIAE Edited by *Philip McCosker* and *Denys Turner*

THE TALMUD AND RABBINIC LITERATURE Edited by *Charlotte E. Fonrobert* and *Martin S. Jaffee*

HANS URS VON BALTHASAR Edited by *Edward T. Oakes* and *David Moss*

JOHN WESLEY Edited by *Randy L. Maddox* and *Jason E. Vickers*